TRADE-RELATED INVESTMENT MEASURES

Theory and Applications

TRADE-RELATED
INVESTMENT
MEASURES

Theory and Applications

Chi-Chur Chao
Deakin University, Australia

Eden S. H. Yu
Chu Hai College of Higher Education, Hong Kong

Imperial College Press

ICP

Published by

Imperial College Press
57 Shelton Street
Covent Garden
London WC2H 9HE

Distributed by

World Scientific Publishing Co. Pte. Ltd.
5 Toh Tuck Link, Singapore 596224
USA office: 27 Warren Street, Suite 401-402, Hackensack, NJ 07601
UK office: 57 Shelton Street, Covent Garden, London WC2H 9HE

Library of Congress Cataloging-in-Publication Data
Chao, Chi-Chur.
  Trade-related investment measures : theory and applications / Chi-Chur Chao, Deakin University,
Australia, Eden S. H. Yu, Chu Hai College of Higher Education, Hong Kong.
    pages cm
  Includes bibliographical references and index.
  ISBN 978-1-78326-478-0 (hardcover : alk. paper)
  1. Investments, Foreign--China. 2. China--Commercial policy. 3. China--Foreign economic
relations. 4. International trade. I. Yu, Eden Siu-hung. II. Title.
  HG5782.C4312 2014
  332.67'30951--dc23

                                                                              2014019014

British Library Cataloguing-in-Publication Data
A catalogue record for this book is available from the British Library.

Typeset by Stallion Press
Email: enquiries@stallionpress.com

Printed in Singapore

Contents

Preface

This book is intended to make a contribution to the area of trade-related investment measures. The writing of this book has been largely inspired by the use of trade policies on foreign investment adopted in China and other nations in the last 30 years. Building upon the existing literature, the 20 chapters in the book use several versions of general equilibrium frameworks to examine the resource allocation and welfare effects of both trade-related investment measures and investment-related trade measures. Traditional and dual microeconomic techniques have been extensively utilized for analyzing various real-world trade and investment issues, especially those encountered in developing economies. Policy implications and optimal trade/investment policies arising from the analyses are also provided.

Acknowledgments

The intellectual capital stock enabling us to undertake this book project was not acquired in one day. We have benefited greatly over the years from the inspiring lectures and writings on trade theory and policies from distinguished scholars, such as Raveendra Batra, Ronald Jones, Ali Khan, Murray Kemp, Peter Neary, and the late Akira Takayama. For useful communication we are indebted to Hamid Beladi, Jim Brander, Eric Bond, Kenneth Chan, Jai-Young Choi, Kwan Choi, Win Lin Chou, Fumio Dei, Peter Egger, Wilfred Ethier, David Greenaway, Gene Grossman, Panos Hatzipanayotou, Kazuo Nishimura, Bharat Hazari, Hong Hwang, Charles Ingene, Jiandong Ju, Jean-Pierre Laffargue, Hiroshi Ohta, Pasquale Sgro, Makoto Yano, Xiaopeng Yin, Miaojie Yu, Wusheng Yu and Lex Zhao. We also thank Mi Lin and Wing Sum Ip for their able assistance. Last but not least, we wish to thank our own institutions and family members for their unfailing support and deep understanding throughout the long period of research and writing of this book.

The publisher and we wish to thank the following for permission to use copyrighted materials.

Elsevier Limited for the essays:

Chi-Chur Chao and Eden S. H. Yu, "Foreign capital inflows and welfare in an economy with imperfect competition," *Journal of Development Economics*, October 1994, pp. 141–154.

Chi-Chur Chao and Eden S. H. Yu, "Are wholly foreign-owned enterprises better than joint ventures?" *Journal of International Economics*, February 1996, pp. 225–237.

Chi-Chur Chao and Eden S. H. Yu, "Export-share requirements, trade balances and welfare: a two-period analysis," *Journal of Development Economics*, June 1998, pp. 217–228.

Chi-Chur Chao and Eden S. H. Yu, "Export-performance requirements, foreign investment quotas, and welfare in a small dynamic economy," *Journal of Development Economics*, October 2003, pp. 387–400.

Chi-Chur and Eden S. H. Yu, "Trade liberalization, foreign ownership, and the environment in a small open economy," *International Review of Economics & Finance*, 2007, pp. 471–477.

Chi-Chur Chao, W. L. Chou and Eden S. H. Yu, "Export duty rebates and export performance: theory and China's experience," *Journal of Comparative Economics*, June 2001, pp. 314–326.

Chi-Chur Chao, Eden S. H. Yu and Wusheng Yu, "China's import duty drawback and VAT rebate policies: A general equilibrium analysis," *China Economic Review*, 2006, pp. 432–448.

Charles A. Ingene, Eden S. H. Yu and Chi-Chur Chao, "The impact of export-share requirements under production uncertainty," *International Review of Economics & Finance*, 2004, pp. 201–215.

John Wiley and Sons for the essays:

Chi-Chur Chao and Eden S. H. Yu, "Content protection, urban unemployment and welfare," *The Canadian Journal of Economics*, May 1993, pp. 481–492.

Chi-Chur Chao and Eden S. H. Yu, "Should export-share requirements be implemented under quota protection?" *The Canadian Journal of Economics*, August 1994, pp. 568–579.

Chi-Chur Chao and Eden S. H. Yu, "Domestic equity controls of multinational enterprises," *The Manchester School*, December 2002, pp. 321–330.

Chi-Chur Chao and Eden S. H. Yu, "Profit-sharing and international capital mobility in developing countries," *Review of International Economics*, December 2002, pp. 744–752.

Chi-Chur Chao and Eden S. H. Yu, "TRIMs, environmental taxes, and foreign investment," *Canadian Journal of Economics*, January 2003, pp. 799–817.

Chi-Chur Chao, Win-Lin Chou and Eden S. H. Yu, "Domestic equity control, capital accumulation and welfare: theory and China's evidence," *The World Economy*, December 2002, pp. 1115–1127.

Eden S. H. Yu and Chi-Chur Chao, "On investment measures and trade," *The World Economy*, December 2002, pp. 549–561.

We wish to acknowledge that our research for the book was partially supported by various grants provided by the Research Grants Council of Hong Kong SAR Government, the Research Center for International Economics of City University of Hong Kong and Chu Hai College of Higher Education, Hong Kong.

Introduction

"不以規矩, 不成方圓"

"Without the compass and square, one cannot form squares and circles."
Mencius (372–289 BC)
Chinese philosopher

This book draws on our research in international trade theory and trade policies conducted over the past 20 years. It has four parts consisting of 20 chapters all on a central theme: trade-related investment measures (TRIMs) and foreign investment-related trade measures. The book examines the various impacts of these measures on a small open developing economy as well as on a big, open, emerging economy, such as China. To set the stage for subsequent analysis and discussions traditional and dual approaches to model an open economy with distortions in product and factor markets are sketched at the outset.

Part I: On Investment Measures, Trade, and the Environment

Chapter 1 provides an overall review of the studies on TRIMs, with focus on the resource allocation and welfare effect of TRIMs in the presence of other kinds of distortions in an economy. Specifically, measures regarding export shares, local content requirements and trade balancing can be used efficiently to correct for preexisting distortions, such as import tariffs and quotas. Further, the relationships between TRIMs and trade-related environmental measures (TREMs) are discussed. The microeconomic and mathematical tools of traditional and dual approaches, used in the book for studying the policy implications in general equilibrium open economy settings with distortions, are sketched in Chapter 2.

In Chapter 3, various second-best policy mixes of investment-related trade measures and environmental taxes for a polluted, small open economy with foreign capital and immovable trade restrictions are examined. The optimal policy mix depends on the types of trade restrictions. When tariffs are in place, strict policies of pollution taxes and export requirements are optimal for alleviating tariff-induced consumption and production distortions. When involuntary quotas are used in lieu of tariffs, however, the optimal policy mix is a zero export requirement and Pigouvian taxes on pollution. For the case of voluntary export restraints (VERs), however, the optimal policy demands export requirements and a less stringent pollution tax.

Part II: Export-Share Requirements

Following up on the issues related to TRIMs, Chapter 4 investigates the welfare impacts of export-share requirements (ESRs) in a general equilibrium framework with an import quota imposed in the home economy. We show that when foreign capital is located in specific economic activity zones identified with the importable sector, an increase in ESRs reduces welfare, owing to the price-induced higher payments to foreign capital.

Chapter 5 extends the analysis to a two-period, three-sector general equilibrium model for examining the effects of a temporary increase in ESRs upon foreign-owned firms on the trade balance and national welfare. The analysis suggests that the policy of a temporary rise in ESRs results in increases in the non-tradable prices for both periods as well as intertemporal welfare. The policy also leads to an improvement in the first-period trade balance.

In Chapter 6, the analysis on ESRs is further extended to a dynamic model with accumulations of domestic capital and foreign bonds. Assuming a preexisting tariff, the second-best policy for the host economy is a foreign-investment quota together with an ESR. Hence, completely eliminating the use of TRIMs, including ESRs, in the presence of tariffs, as agreed upon in the Uruguay Round of the General Agreement on Tariffs and Trade (GATT) in 1994, may be sub-optimal from the viewpoint of the host country.

Chapter 7 analyzes the welfare and resource allocation effects of an ESR policy imposed on foreign investors in a three-sector general equilibrium model of production under uncertainty. It is argued that the standard results obtained under certainty are a special case of our more general model. In particular, an ESR policy may reduce national welfare because the effect of uncertainty may cause an increase in production of a good that is already over-produced. Uncertainty also lowers the capital–labor ratio in both domestic industries, thereby raising the capital-rental rate while lowering the wage rate.

Part III: Content Protection, Equity Controls, and Foreign Investment

In this part, we examine from a historical perspective the two additional once-popular TRIMs, i.e., content protection and equity controls. Resource-limited economies, such as China, have relied on the use of foreign materials to achieve economic growth. However, to protect domestic producers, the policy of content protection had been implemented, which is inconsistent with the current competition policy of the WTO. Content protection means that a certain percentage of domestic intermediates is mandated to be used in the production of final products. Chapter 8 examines the effects of domestic content protection on resource allocation, urban unemployment and social welfare of the economy, while Chapter 9 extends the analysis to consider the trade balance effect of content protection in a two-period, general equilibrium framework.

Chapter 10 provides a general equilibrium model for examining the individual as well as the joint effects of export requirements and local equity controls of multinational firms. The results suggest that for a small open economy under tariff protection, the desirable policy is 100% foreign ownership of subsidiaries, coupled with an ESR.

Based on a dynamic framework, the welfare effect of domestic equity requirements on multinational firms in the presence of alternative types of trade instruments and varying degrees of the mobility of foreign capital is studied in Chapter 11. It turns out that, under quotas, raising equity requirements improves welfare in the short run but reduces welfare in the long run. In contrast, when tariffs are in place, the policy of domestic equity requirements lowers welfare in the short run but raises welfare in the long run.

Chapter 12 examines the effects of trade liberalization on firm ownership and the environment for a small open economy. It is found that trade liberalization via tariff reductions can result in a dramatic switch in firm ownership from domestic to foreign, coupled with a lower pollution tax.

In Chapter 13, we examine foreign capital and pollution tax policies on the host country's welfare when foreign investment tax credits are absent or present in the source country. In the absence of tax credits, the optimal policy is a pollution tax with a foreign investment tax or subsidy. The presence of tax credits may, however, result in a higher investment tax but lower pollution tax, leading to higher welfare but lower environmental quality in the host country. The source country's tax credits may cause a switch in the host country's capital subsidy to a tax, which may improve the environment.

Considering oligopolistic competition, Chapter 14 explores the resource allocation and welfare effects of exogenous inflows of foreign capital for the host economy with unemployment. Although the welfare impact for the short run is ambiguous and dependent upon the strength of excess profits and scale economies relative to unemployment in manufacturing, in the long run additional inflows of foreign capital always improve national welfare with capital mobility. Hence, attracting foreign capital remains a sound policy for economies characterized by imperfect competition, scale economies and regional unemployment.

By incorporating rural–urban migration, Chapter 15 analyzes and contrasts the short- and long-run effects of profit-sharing by workers. Specifically examined are the effects of profit-sharing on rural–urban migration, the degree of competition among urban firms, and international mobility of capital. It is found that although profit-sharing may raise urban employment in the short run, the scheme reduces urban employment and lowers the inflow of foreign capital in the long run.

In Chapter 16, we turn to the issue of privatization and foreign competition. Increased partial privatization or foreign competition can lead to wage inequality between skilled and unskilled labor. In addition, rising wage inequality can be triggered by inflows of unskilled labor or outflows of skilled labor and/or capital. Further, partial privatization or foreign competition reduces the urban output, thereby raising the goods price and unemployment ratio. These effects lower the social welfare of the economy.

Using a dynamic framework with capital accumulation, Chapter 17 considers the welfare effect of the domestic equity control on foreign-funded firms in a small open economy. An increase in domestic equity requirements directly raises the rental cost to foreign firms. This lowers welfare. On the other hand, the domestic equity policy may yield a beneficial effect through accumulation of domestic assets. If the gain in capital accumulation outweighs the loss from the higher rental cost, the policy of domestic equity requirements can be welfare enhancing. This result is supported by the empirical study on the impact of changes in domestic/foreign assets, on China's industrial outputs.

Part IV: Issues of Export Duty Rebates

Chapter 18 develops a general equilibrium model for an economy suffering from sector-specific unemployment to study the effect of export tax rebates on imported foreign intermediates. The tax rebate policy can expand its related down- and upstream industries, thereby boosting exports. This result is verified by using China's data; the export tax rebate, foreign income, and exchange rate volatility contribute significantly to China's exports in the long run, but only the export tax rebate promotes exports in the short run.

In Chapter 19, we study the effect of China's duty drawbacks and value-added tax rebate on exports. Simulations based on a computable general equilibrium (CGE) model, characterized by a dual production (domestic sales and export processing) and dual import structure (imports used in export processing and for other purposes), confirm our theoretical results on China's exports that (a) such policies are generally export promoting; (b) a small part of the export expansion comes at the expense of a slight decline of the domestic activity through factor reallocation and input substitution, whereas a larger portion of the expansion is attributed to cheaper access to foreign inputs; (c) export processors use more imported inputs and fewer domestic inputs; and (d) export-intensive sectors are positively affected by these policies, whereas traditional agriculture sector is impacted adversely. These policies generate welfare gains for China.

In Chapter 20 we provide a summary of the key findings presented in each of the preceding chapters and suggest possible topics in the area for future research. It should be mentioned that throughout the chapters in the book, we develop a variety of models involving relatively simple to quite complex structures and then utilize the models to derive the various results. Due to the limitation of the variety of mathematical notations that we can use to describe the research issues, some of the chapters share the same set of notations and symbols, while other chapters use different notations to suit the modeling needs of various settings and scenarios. Each chapter, though related to some of the other chapters, is largely self-contained with respect to a specific issue under study and thus can be read independently of the other chapters. However, it would be instructive to start by reading the first two chapters in Part I so as to facilitate reading of the materials contained in any of the subsequent chapters.

PART I

On Investment Measures, Trade, and the Environment

Chapter 1

On Investment Measures and Trade

1.1 Introduction

International trade and investment have played a key role in promoting economic growth, particularly for small open economies and developing countries. For the last three decades, two important developments have fundamentally influenced and reshaped national as well as global economic performance. First, nations in the world economy have become increasingly open and interdependent; and second, technological innovation has become an even more crucial contributor than resource endowments to sustain the growth of an economy.

In the literature, a majority of studies on trade policy have traditionally emphasized instruments and barriers that affect trade mainly in final goods and services, such as tariffs and non-tariff barriers. Rapid and innovative advances in communication and information, however, have resulted in attention switching to various issues of trade in factors and/or technology, which are the main sources of improving international competitiveness and enhancing national welfare.

While this study will touch upon the policy implications of trade in goods and services, its main focus is on resource allocation and welfare implication of policies regarding trade in factors. In particular, we examine policies on foreign direct investment (FDI) and the associated trade-related investment measures (TRIMs). In fact, member nations of the GATT (General Agreement on Tariffs and Trade) and its successor the WTO (World Trade Organization) have somehow recognized the trade-restricting and distorting effects of investment measures, and in the Uruguay Round agreements (1994) it was agreed that all TRIMs be eliminated within two, five and seven years, for developed, developing, and least-developed

3

contracting economies, respectively. Nevertheless, there is little consensus on how to define TRIMs broadly and what may be their effects on trade, investment and welfare (see Maskus and Eby, 1990). In this book, we aim to make a modest contribution toward the theoretical analysis of these issues. In particular, we illustrate the various effects of TRIMs from the perspectives of history, theory, and policymaking by way of presenting key results from mostly our own past research and published work on this topic.

In general, foreign firms invest in host countries for a variety of reasons, including the existence of investment incentives and/or bypassing protective trade barriers.[1] Usually, TRIMs are imposed on foreign firms as a precondition of their entry so as to protect domestic firms or achieve other social and political purposes. Therefore, TRIMs necessarily operate in a second-best environment, and thus the following two queries deserve consideration:

(i) Do TRIMs alone cause trade-restricting and distortionary effects? If yes, should TRIMs be used to correct preexisting distortions?

(ii) Are there any relationships between TRIMs and other types of investment measures, such as trade-related environmental measures (TREMs)?

The answer to the first query is that, in the presence of preexisting distortions, TRIMs may not cause welfare-reducing effects in view of the generalized second-best theory of distortion and welfare (cf. Bhagwati, 1971). Rather, TRIMs with given distortions can be used efficiently to correct the preexisting distortions.[2] We illustrate this point and delineate the optimal levels of TRIMs. In fact, TRIMs can generate double dividends in mitigating other existing distortions in the economy, for example, environmental pollution. In addition, we investigate the jointly optimal combinations of TRIMs and TREMs. However, we should mention that, in light of the existing agreements of the WTO and GATT to eliminate TRIMs over certain periods, the efforts are meaningful only if and when all initial distortions, e.g., tariff and quota, are eradicated. This has not yet been achieved. For example, in the case of China, the average tariff in 2010 for manufactured product was about 7.7% and for primary product around 11.2%. This dropped dramatically from about 40% in 1992. On the other hand, the countries that

---

[1] Other reasons for foreign investment involve export orientation of foreign firms, choice of mode for exporters, and global competition.

[2] Balasubramanyam (1991) shares the same view.

have given up the most as a result of eliminating TRIMs are developing nations rather than developed countries.

1.2 TRIMs, Resource Allocation, and Welfare

Although there is little consensus on the definition of TRIMs, there are eight types of TRIMs proposed in the literature:

   (i) local content requirements
  (ii) export performance requirements
 (iii) local manufacturing requirements
 (iv) trade-balancing requirements
  (v) production mandates
 (vi) foreign-exchange restrictions
(vii) mandatory technology transfers
(viii) limits on equity participation and on remittances.

However, only the first, fourth, and part of the sixth items on the list were covered in the agreement on TRIMs in the 1994 Uruguay Round GATT negotiation (see Graham and Sauve, 1998).[3] By 2008, the coverage had been extended to virtually all sorts of TRIMs. Similarly, the North American Free Trade Agreement (NAFTA) disallowed most of these requirements (the first six items on the list) on investment. Linking performance requirements to investment incentives is also prohibited.

In this section, we outline the effects of selected major TRIMs, such as export performance requirements, local content requirements, etc., on the entry of foreign-owned firms. As pointed out by Richardson (1993), it is customary for a host country to attract foreign firms by initially offering investment incentives and/or adopting import protection, i.e., tariffs and quotas. Subsequently, TRIMs are introduced to counter the monopoly power of foreign firms and/or reinforce the (partially mitigated) protection for domestic firms. Thus, TRIMs operate in a second-best environment. A general presumption is that TRIMs are trade restricting and distortionary and hence welfare reducing for the host country. It is worthwhile to examine whether this presumption is valid for all sorts of trade regimes. As can be seen in this and the subsequent chapters, the presumption does not hold in most instances.

---

[3]For a detailed list, see Greenaway (1992).

1.2.1 *Export performance requirements*

When protection for final importable goods is in place, foreign capital is attracted to the host country either by the potential for its product to penetrate into the domestic market or by its higher returns in the host country. The inflow of foreign capital to bypass tariffs or quotas leads to an expansion of the output of the protected sector. The welfare effect of capital inflows depends on changes in tariff revenue and payments to foreign-owned capital. As Brecher and Diaz Alejandro (1977) demonstrate, such capital inflows under tariff protection can be welfare reducing if the importables are capital-intensive. The reason for this immiserization of foreign investment is that the expansion of the protected sector in the host country lowers its imports and hence reduces its tariff revenue. Intuitively, the inflow of foreign capital exacerbates the existing distortion created by tariff protection, when the protected sector is relatively large to begin with. As pointed out by Greenaway (1992, p. 153), a policy designed to correct this distortion is welfare improving, if: (a) it reduces the supply of products which are over-produced; (b) it shifts production to domestically owned firms; and (c) it reduces payments to foreign-owned capital.

In a general equilibrium context, Rodrik (1987) proposes the policy of export requirements on foreign-owned firms, and such requirements meet the conditions for mitigating existing tariff distortions. First, the export requirements mandate foreign-owned firms to export a portion of their output produced in the host country. This export-promotion policy affects the over-produced importable industry through its impact of regulating both quantity and price. The quantity regulation simply reduces the supply of the importables and has the effect of generating more tariff revenue for the host country. The effect of price control works via the presence of tariffs, which render the domestic price of the importables higher than the world price. The policy of export requirements nevertheless lowers the effective importable price, a weighted average of the world price and the tariff-inclusive domestic price, to foreign-owned firms. This price effect leads to a shift in the production toward domestic-owned firms. As a result, the export requirements provide double dividends in: (a) mitigating the over-production of importables generated by the tariff protection; and (b) the fall in income to foreign capital due to the contraction of foreign production. In the presence of tariffs, which are immutable due to mostly political reasons, the policy of export requirements can be an efficient instrument for mitigating the production distortion aggravated by the inflow of foreign capital.

Nevertheless, the welfare-improving effect of export requirements does not prevail in the case of quota protection. As shown by Dei (1985a), the welfare impact of the inflow of foreign capital under quotas is dramatically different from that under tariffs (also see Buffie, 1985). Foreign capital inflows improve welfare via a reduction in the rate of return to foreign capital. Since export requirements discourage the inflow of foreign capital, we may logically conjecture that the requirements in the presence of quotas are welfare reducing. Chao and Yu (1994c) show that the conjecture is correct based upon the following observation: under quota protection, the volume of imports is fixed and hence the linkage between the domestic production of the importables and national welfare (pertinent to Greenaway's criteria [a] and [b] above) is cut off. The change in domestic welfare therefore depends only on the change of the rate of return on foreign capital (Greenaway's criterion [c]), which in turn depends on the domestic goods prices. An increase in export requirements lowers the domestic supply by foreign-owned firms, thereby pushing up the domestic price of the importables. This reduces national welfare via the higher price-induced payments to foreign capital if the importables are capital-intensive.

In summary, the welfare effects of TRIMs, e.g., export requirements, crucially depend on the types of the initial existing distortions. Subject to government analytical ability and administrative capacity, export requirements may be put to good use as a policy measure in the presence of tariff protection, which for some reasons cannot be abolished. (The best policy, of course, is the removal of tariffs, if removal is possible.) Nevertheless, export requirement policy may not be efficient when quotas are in place.

1.2.2   *Local content requirements*

Another once commonly used TRIM is local content requirement, which specifies that a certain proportion of intermediate inputs used by foreign firms be locally sourced. This input-based TRIM became popular among developing and semi-industrialized nations prior to the WTO agreement. Various aspects of domestic content protection have been explored by trade theorists. According to Greenaway (1992), the objective of this policy is either to achieve industry protection or production efficiency.

Resource-scarce economies have relied on the use of foreign materials to promote growth. Intermediate goods are imported for further processing and producing final products that can be exported. While increasing the use of imported materials helps to spur growth in the domestic final-product sector, the practice nevertheless generates an undesirable effect of lowering the domestic value added to the final product. The policy of domestic content requirement is thus implemented to protect domestic producers of intermediate goods. A seminal work in this area is Grossman (1981) — he examines the resource allocation effect of domestic content protection in a partial equilibrium setting. The analysis in such a framework is bound to be limited in its scope.

To better understand the efficiency issue of content protection, a general equilibrium framework is warranted. Richardson (1993) is the first study for utilizing a general equilibrium approach to examine the efficiency of content protection, which is used to mitigate the tariff-inflicted distortion. The focus of his study is on the welfare consequence of content protection in a full-employment economy. In addition to consumer welfare, two aspects of production efficiency deserve to be considered: microeconomic technical efficiency and macroeconomic allocative efficiency. The former pertains to the use of fewer inputs for producing the same level of output at the firm level, and the latter relates to the use of resources in the most productive and least costly manner at the national level.

From the policy perspective, it would be useful to study the allocative efficiency of content protection. A good policy should result in reduction in unemployment and/or reallocation of resources for use by relatively productive sectors. To illustrate this point, let us consider a dual economy consisting of urban and rural sectors. The urban sector produces a processed good, and the rural sector produces an agricultural commodity. The production of the urban processed good requires intermediate inputs, which can be imported or sourced locally. All three goods require labor inputs for production. Following Harris and Todaro (1970), a fixed minimum wage is institutionally set in the urban area, while a flexible wage prevails in the rural area. The fixed urban wage gives rise to urban unemployment. It can be easily shown that urban unemployment causes a gap between the marginal rate of transformation (MRT) of the two final goods and the relative goods price ratio. This gap implies an allocative inefficiency in production.

Assume that the domestic material sector is in an infant stage and its domestic price is higher than the world price. A protective policy, such as content requirement, may be implemented to ensure the industry survival. Consider first that the domestic material sector is located in the rural area (Chao and Yu, 1993). Content protection leads to an increase in the demand for the domestically produced materials, thereby expanding the rural sector and causing a reversed labor migration from urban to rural areas. Consequently, urban unemployment falls and the gap between the MRT and the relative goods price ratio shrinks. The use of domestic content requirements in this instance improves allocative efficiency. So, the policy of content protection can be put to good use for enhancing national welfare.

In contrast, if the domestic material sector is located in the urban area, a rise in domestic content requirements results in expansion in the urban sector at the expense of the rural sector, causing labor migration from the rural to the urban areas. This aggravates the problem of urban unemployment and thus widens the wedge between the MRT and the price ratio, signaling a larger allocative inefficiency. Content protection can then lower national welfare. Clearly, whether content protection is a sound policy or not depends on the location of the material-input sector in the economy.

1.3 TRIMs and Other Objectives

Aside from promoting the welfare of a nation, TRIMs were adopted by many developing countries for tackling their trade imbalance difficulties. The issue of trade balance implications of TRIMs, however, has received little attention in the trade and development literature.

An exception is perhaps the work of Chao and Yu (1998a). An intertemporal two-period setting is warranted to analyze the trade balance effect. The two periods are connected by the current account, in which deficits or surpluses can happen in the first period, but the current account must be balanced over the two periods. The following key question can be posed: Would a temporary rise in export requirements on foreign firms improve the first period's current account balance (i.e., trade balance minus repatriation of foreign capital return)? Here, the temporary policy of export requirements means an imposition of or an increase in the requirements in the first period only with the removal of the requirements in the second period.

To answer the question posed, let us assume that domestic and foreign firms operate in the home country in both periods. In the first period, domestic firms in the home country produce two types of goods, an exportable and a non-traded good. The importable good is not produced, perhaps due to the lack of requisite technology. Meanwhile, foreign-owned firms in the home country produce only the importable good, mainly to circumvent the tariff barrier. The home country thus implements export requirements on foreign firms but only in the first period. In the second period, all trade restrictions, including tariffs and export-share requirements (ESRs), will be completely removed.

The policy of export requirements has a direct impact of boosting exports, but an adverse effect on foreign-owned firms in the first period. Consequently, the foreign-owned firms lay off labor and part of the released labor is absorbed by the exportable sector. This resource allocation effect helps to improve the first-period trade balance. The improvement in the trade balance promotes national income, which in turn pushes up the non-tradable prices in both periods. The larger national income leads to increases in the demand for both the exportable and importable goods in the second period. This interperiod consumption-substitution effect reinforces the improvement in the first-period trade balance and offsets the deterioration in the second-period trade balance. So, the policy of export requirements works not only to mitigate the distortion created by initial tariffs but also to improve the overall current account balance.

1.4   Joint TRIMs

In view of the fact that TRIMs are used only in an environment with pre-existing distortions, such as investment incentives or trade barriers, which can influence the investment decision of foreign firms, questions may be posed regarding the optimal choice of instruments in two levels. First, what would be the optimal combinations of investment incentives/protection and TRIMs? Second, what would be the optimal mixes within and among TRIMs for a given set of investment incentives or protection? Some contributions have been made to the literature to address these issues.

1.4.1   *Investment taxes and export requirements*

To attract foreign investment, fiscal incentives, such as investment tax cuts or subsidies, have been offered to foreign investors in many countries. Kemp (1966), Jones (1967), and Neary (1988), among others, have examined the welfare effect of a tax/subsidy on foreign investment.

On the other hand, investment credits are frequently tied to performance and other requirements to counter the monopoly power of foreign firms as well as to protect local markets. Guisinger and Associates (1985) report that Mexico provides investment credits to petrochemical investors on the condition that a requirement of 25% of their output is exported for three years. Also, the joint-venture law of China specifies that joint ventures are encouraged to export products outside China and in turn foreign investors are provided with tax credits. A similar policy has been adopted by the UK toward foreign investment undertaken by the Japanese auto industry.

In spite of the relatively large literature now available on the individual effects of export requirements and a tax/subsidy on foreign capital, the linkages and interactions between these two sets of policies have received little attention with the exception of Chao and Yu (1996b). Their study examines the joint effects of foreign investment tax/subsidy and export requirements. It is shown that a rate-reducing investment tax coupled with an export requirement is a desirable policy. The analysis is extended to cover the case in which international investment tax credits are allowed by the country of residence of the (foreign) investors. When the tax credits are in place, an optimal inverse relationship exists between the investment taxes levied by the residence country and the ESRs on foreign firms by the source country. That is, the lower the investment tax on foreign-owned firms, the higher the desired level of export requirement. This result lends support to the empirical observation that the existence of an investment incentive is often a condition for deploying TRIMs on foreign-owned firms.

1.4.2 *Export requirements and equity controls*

Let us turn to the issue of optimal combinations among TRIMs for a given tariff. A nation can use TRIMs simultaneously. For example, Colombia required multinational firms involved in the petrochemical industry to export a minimum of 80% of their product in order to be granted 100% ownership (see Guisinger and Associates, 1985, p. 292, for a detailed discussion). Another example is the joint-venture law of China, which not only encourages foreign firms to sell their products outside China, but also promotes local participation of equity of global firms. Given that foreign firms attempt to penetrate the market of the host country, while the host country strives to protect the domestic producers, the interest of the foreign firms is apparently in conflict with the national interest of the host country. The solution to this conflict of interest seems to lie in the trade-off between releasing (gaining) equity control by foreign firms in exchange for permission to sell more (less) inside the host country.

Chao and Yu (1996a) suggest a straightforward policy choice regarding the optimal combinations of local equity and export requirements on foreign-owned firms. A key result that emerged from the analysis is that wholly foreign-owned enterprises, i.e., 100% foreign ownership by foreign firms, coupled with an export requirement, constitute the optimal policy for the host country. This analysis of the welfare impact of permitting wholly foreign-owned enterprises has an important bearing on policymaking by capital-importing developing nations. For example, China adopted open-door economic policies in 1978. The main method of foreign firms undertaking direct investment in China has been equity joint ventures (EJVs), which involve sharing of the capital investment between a foreign firm and a local partner. Recently, foreign firms have been allowed to make direct investment in China without any local participation. Both Hong Kong Bank and Citibank, as well as Merck Sharp & Dohme (marketers of pharmaceutical products), among other firms, have been allowed to establish wholly owned branches and operations inside China. Although the wholly foreign-owned firms are still limited in number, such firms and operations are nevertheless on the rise.

1.5   TRIMs and Other Investment Measures

While the welfare effects of several major TRIMs have been delineated above, other newly emerging issues pertinent to international investment have recently begun to receive some attention. A notable issue is the inter-linkages among trade, investment, and environment. In the face of growing concerns about deteriorating environmental conditions and stiffening environmental protection laws in many advanced countries, capital has moved out of these countries into countries with laxer regulations. This provides a major reason for the international relocation of capital, in addition to the tariff/quota-jumping purpose. As a result, foreign capital flows in. The job-creating effect encourages less environmentally conscious countries (mostly developing nations) to become "polluters' heaven." To mitigate the trend of environmental degradation, the WTO has suggested introducing environmental protection requirements, TREMs, on foreign investment (see Asakai, 1994). Maintaining the environment while liberalizing trade and investment will become a major issue in the next round of multinational trade negotiations.[4]

---

[4]There are objections to the TREMs proposal on the ground that environmental externalities apply to both domestic and foreign firms so that an optimal policy has to consider both types. The best policy of course will be some sort of environmental tax or price-based right to pollute.

This issue is examined by Chao and Yu (1997b) in a general equilibrium model incorporating export performance and environmental regulations. Foreign investment is assumed as induced by the motive to bypass trade protection. Two trade regimes are considered: tariffs and quotas. It is shown that under import tariffs, the inflow of foreign capital lowers the host country's welfare. Therefore, relatively strict policies of pollution tax (i.e., higher than its Pigouvian rate)[5] and full export requirements (i.e., 100%) can alleviate the tariff-induced distortions and the pollution-caused externality. In contrast, foreign investment improves welfare when imports are subject to quotas. The optimal investment policy then involves a zero export requirement coupled with a Pigouvian tax rate for internalizing the environmental externality.

Although there were no statutory export requirements in China, contractual export requirements for foreign investment were a common practice in the past. Export requirements were generally specified in the Sample Contract and Articles of Association for joint ventures. For example, it was stated in Article 20 of the Sample Contract that:

> The products of joint venture company will be sold both on Chinese market and on overseas market, the export part accounts for ____%, and ____% for domestic market.

An annual percentage and amount for outside and inside selling are written out according to practical conditions, and the amount for export shall at least meet the needs of foreign exchange expenses of the joint-venture company. Article 9 of the Sample Contract and Articles of Association is:

> The venture company may sell its products on the Chinese domestic market and on the international market, its selling proportion is as follows: ____ (year) ____ % for export; ____ % for the domestic market.

Thus, the export requirements were not unilaterally imposed by China in statute. The marketing method and obligations were stipulated according to real situations and were negotiated and agreed upon by the Chinese and foreign parties. The items of agreement were written into the contract documents.

As a policy, China prefers joint ventures with high export potential or of high technology. In the 1986 Provisions for the Encouragement of Foreign

---

[5]The Pigouvian tax is equal to the marginal social damage of pollution.

Investment, incentives are legally provided for two types of enterprises known as "export enterprises" and "technologically advanced enterprises." Export enterprises are those that export 50% or more of their products and generate foreign-exchange surplus. Special incentives provided to these two types of enterprise include tax reductions, workers' subsidies, and land-use fees. These enterprises also have priority in receiving loans and obtaining water, electricity, and transportation services. Export enterprises with an export share exceeding 70% in a year can enjoy further reductions in income tax for that year, subject to being certified on the basis of their contracts and the actual export performance. There are lists of such enterprises in cities like Beijing and Shanghai.

The following rare case study on China's export requirement practice draws from the results of a survey conducted by Wong (1992). The objective of the survey was to find out the export requirement policy, if any, and the actual export shares of joint-venture companies in China. A sample of joint ventures was drawn from the 1991 China Phone Book and Business Directory (July–December edition). Eight companies introduced by China Merchants Development Co. Ltd. were also contacted via mail. A total of 169 questionnaires were sent in January 1992 to the joint ventures in various coastal cities in China. Twenty-two questionnaires were returned, of which 16 usable returns were received.

The limited survey results are analyzed with respect to factor intensity. Overall, 56% of the joint ventures were subject to export requirements; 63% of these were required to export at least half of their output. Thus, the export requirements imposed were fairly extensive and high. Of the labor-intensive joint ventures, 75% were required to export at least half of their output, higher than the corresponding figures for the capital-intensive joint ventures. It was found that the companies in the Pearl River Delta, as compared with those in Shanghai, had more extensive and higher export requirements. However, the labor-intensive companies in Shanghai had higher actual export shares than their counterparts in the Pearl River Delta in 1991.

We can identify two additional characteristics of the export requirements in China from the survey results. Although the companies with contractual export requirements might not strictly abide by them, their actual export ratios were more often than not very close to their required ratios. This shows that the ESRs have some guiding effects on the actual export levels. On the other hand, of the five export-oriented companies (which exported at least half of their output), three did not have export requirements. This suggests that, for companies that would be predominantly export-oriented, there might not be a need to impose export requirements.

In retrospect, China's export-share policy appears not to aim at improving welfare as a direct objective. It is rather to protect the local industry, provide domestic employment, enhance the trade balance, transfer technology, and market internationally. In the 1970s, many developing countries set up "export-processing zones" (EPZs) or "free trade zones" (FTZs). These zones generally require the foreign-invested firms to export their products. Usually, either a certain proportion of the output is to be exported or the products for domestic sales have to be taxed for import duties.

Has China's export-share policy been successful? How well have the ESRs fulfilled the policy objectives? These questions can be answered by considering the export performance, domestic industry, domestic employment, foreign-exchange balance, technology transfer, and international market share in the years between the introduction of the open-door policy in December 1978 and by the time the policy ceased to work in the late 2000s. Further studies would be useful to shed light on these issues.

1.6   Concluding Remarks

In this chapter, we have argued that it is an overstatement to presume that TRIMs cause trade-restricting and distortionary effects. In the presence of investment incentives and/or protection, TRIMs may actually be used efficiently to mitigate the detrimental effect of the initial distortions. In addition, TRIMs may generate double dividends for the economy in terms of, for instance, a reduction in unemployment and an improvement in the current account balance. Simultaneous use of several TRIMs can also be desirable in real-world policy implementation. Furthermore, the relationships between TRIMs and other investment-related measures, e.g., TREMs, should be carefully taken into consideration in the design of policies. Policy coordination among trade, investment, and the environment has been and will continue to be an important issue in the discussions and deliberations among WTO member nations.

The results we obtained naturally follow from the set of assumptions adopted, in particular the existence of a distortion, e.g., tariffs, which is still in existence among developing nations despite the trade-liberalization trend in the past few decades. The case study on China presents a review of the extent of the use of export requirements in China in the early 1990s, similar to many other developing economies, with relatively high tariff and quota walls. The assumption of preexisting distortions is reasonable for developing countries but appears less realistic in the case of developed countries, for which it is less likely to come up with a welfare-improving TRIM. Thus, eliminating TRIMs altogether can mean a bigger sacrifice by developing nations than developed countries. However, it should also be recognized that TRIMs can be complex and administratively costly. It is, in practice, difficult for governments (which generally lack the analytical ability and administrative capacity) to efficiently operate a set of instruments to attain optimality, as prescribed by the theory.

Chapter 2

International Trade and Distortions: General Equilibrium Models

2.1 Introduction

Microeconomics provides analytical tools for studying the pure theory of international trade. This chapter summarizes relevant microeconomic tools that are used in this book, especially focusing on the dual relationships between production, cost, and revenue in general equilibrium settings. Samuelson (1953) pioneered the use of the cost function in the study of factor price equalization while Jones (1965) laid out its use in a general equilibrium framework for the trade models. Nonetheless, applications of the revenue, expenditure, and indirect utility functions to trade theory had not been popularized until Dixit and Norman (1980).[1] We will utilize the duality techniques to study a variety of issues on resource allocation and welfare for an open economy in the presence of tourism in this chapter, and trade-related investment measures (TRIMs) and strategies in the subsequent chapters.

2.2 Production Structures of the Economy

2.2.1 *Heckscher–Ohlin model*

The Heckscher–Ohlin production framework, the cornerstone of the trade theory, is based on a model of two countries, two commodities, and two

---

[1]The theory of duality can be found, for example, in Blackorby *et al.* (1978), Diewert (1978), and McFadden (1978), and its applications to international trade can be also found in Mussa (1979), Woodland (1982), Buffie (2001), Chao and Yu (2004), and Feestra (2004). Note that the standard treatment on duality between production and cost in Section 2.2 is drawn from Chao and Yu (2004).

factors, often regarded as a 2×2×2 model, to explain the patterns of trade. Let the two countries be Home and Foreign, the two goods be X and Y, and the two factors be labor (L) and capital (K). The production functions of goods X and Y can be expressed by:

$$X = X(L_X, K_X), \tag{2.1}$$

$$Y = Y(L_Y, K_Y), \tag{2.2}$$

where L_i and K_i are labor and capital employed in sector i, $i = X, Y$. It is assumed that the production functions exhibit constant returns to scale, i.e., homogenous of degree one, and each factor contributes positive marginal product but with diminishing marginal returns, i.e., $X_j > 0$, $Y_j > 0$ but $X_{jj} < 0$, $Y_{jj} < 0$, where $j = L_i$, K_i, and the subscript j denotes partial derivatives.

Letting good Y be the numeraire, the relative price of good X is denoted by p and the rates of return on labor and capital w and r, respectively. Under profit maximization by firms, factors are paid according to the values of their marginal productivities:

$$w = pX_L(L_X, K_X) = Y_L(L_Y, K_Y), \tag{2.3}$$

$$r = pX_K(L_X, K_X) = Y_K(L_Y, K_Y). \tag{2.4}$$

Assuming free mobility of labor and capital between sectors, factor prices are equalized in equilibrium as expressed by (2.3) and (2.4). Letting the endowments of labor and capital in the economy be L and K, the conditions of full employment require:

$$L_X + L_Y = L, \tag{2.5}$$

$$K_X + K_Y = K. \tag{2.6}$$

The production structure of the economy is depicted by (2.1)–(2.6), which consist of eight unknowns — X, Y, w, r, L_X, L_Y, K_X, and K_Y — with three parameters, p, L, and K.

It is notable that the Heckscher–Ohlin structure of the production can be neatly solved through its dual in the cost space. Define the total cost function of producing good X as: $C^X(w, r, X) = \min\{wL_X + rK_X : X = X(L_X, K_X)\}$ with respect to L_X and K_X. If the production function is homogeneous of degree one, then the total cost function becomes separable: $C^X(w, r, X) = \alpha(w, r)X$, where $\alpha(w, r)$ is its unit-cost function. Similarly, the unit-cost function of producing good Y, $\beta(w, r)$, is defined. Under perfect competition at the point of profit maximization, unit cost equals goods price, implying zero profit. Hence, the perfectly competitive equilibrium can be represented by equalizing unit cost and price, as follows:

$$\alpha(w, r) = p, \qquad (2.7)$$

$$\beta(w, r) = 1. \qquad (2.8)$$

Note that differentiating the unit-cost functions with respect to w or r respectively yields $\alpha_w(= \partial \alpha / \partial w = L_X/X)$, which denotes the labor requirement for producing a unit of good X, and $\alpha_r(= \partial \alpha / \partial r = K_X/X)$ the capital requirement for one unit of X (see Jones [1965] for details on the unit factor requirement). β_w and β_r can be similarly interpreted for a unit of good Y. This follows from Shephard's lemma, which states that the cost-minimizing factor demand is just given by the derivative of the cost function with respect to the corresponding factor price. Flexibility of the factor prices implies that the economy is fully employed, and the full employment condition in (2.5) and (2.6) can be written as:

$$\alpha_w(w, r)X + \beta_w(w, r)Y = L, \qquad (2.9)$$

$$\alpha_r(w, r)X + \beta_r(w, r)Y = K. \qquad (2.10)$$

Equations (2.7)–(2.10) represent the production structure of the economy in terms of its dual, consisting of four unknowns — w, r, X and Y — along with three parameters, p, L, and K. The structure is recursive so that (2.7) and (2.8) can be used for solving w and r as functions of p, and then (2.9) and (2.10) can be deployed to determine the impacts of changes in L and K on outputs X and Y.

Firstly, we examine the income distribution issue for the Heckscher–Ohlin model, which is known as the Stolper–Samuelson (1941) theorem. Differentiating (2.7) and (2.8), we can solve for the effects of a change in the goods price on the factor rewards for labor and capital:[2]

$$\frac{dw}{dp} = \frac{\beta_r}{D}, \qquad (2.11)$$

$$\frac{dr}{dp} = -\frac{\beta_w}{D}, \qquad (2.12)$$

where $D = \alpha_w \beta_w (\beta_r/\beta_w - \alpha_r/\alpha_w)$. Note that good X is said to be capital(labor)-intensive relative to good Y, if $K_X/L_X > (<) K_Y/L_Y$ or

---

[2]Since good Y is chosen as the numeraire, w and r are the real wage and rental rates in terms of good Y. See Bhagwati (1964) for discussion.

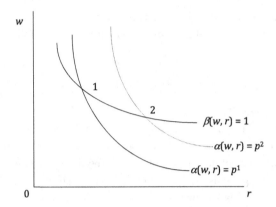

Figure 2.1   Stolper–Samuelson theorem.

equivalently $\alpha_r/\alpha_w > (<) \beta_r/\beta_w$.[3] Hence, a rise in the relative price of
good X lowers (raises) the wage of labor and raises (lowers) the rental on
capital provided that good X is relatively capital(labor)-intensive.

The isocost map depicted in the $w - r$ space in Figure 2.1 illustrates
the changes in income distribution resulting from a change in goods price
ratio, referred to as the Stolper–Samuelson effect. The isocost curves of
$\alpha(w,r) = p$ and $\beta(w,r) = 1$ plotted in the (w,r) space are the duals of
the isoquants of goods X and Y in the (K,L) space, not shown here. The
slopes of the isocost curves represent the capital–labor ratios. The shape
of the isocost curve is similar to that of the isoquant curves, both of which
are convex to the origin, as an increase in the wage–rental ratio leads to a
higher capital–labor ratio.[4] Consider the case in which good X is capital-
intensive relative to good Y. This implies that, ruling out factor intensity
reversal, the isocost curve of $\alpha(w,r)$ is steeper than that of $\beta(w,r)$ for any
given (w/r) ray from the origin.[5] At the point of competitive equilibrium,
the wages and rentals between the two sectors are equal. Thus, the initial
equilibrium is at point 1, where the two isocost curves intersect. A rise in the
relative price of good X from p^1 to p^2 shifts the $\alpha(w,r)$ curve to the right.

---

[3]Both cases are stable. See the studies on stability of the general equilibrium model
under constant and variable returns to scales by Jones (1968), Mayer (1974), and Neary
(1978a), among others.
[4]See Mussa (1979) for details.
[5]For example, the slope of the isocost curve, $\alpha(w,r) = p$, is: $dw/dr = -\alpha_r/\alpha_w = -K_X/L_X$.

This yields a new equilibrium at point 2, indicating a rise in the rental rate and a fall in the wage rate as predicted by the Stolper–Samuelson theorem.

Secondly, we examine the output effects of changes in factor endowments in the standard Heckscher–Ohlin model, and such effects are known as the Rybczynski theorem. Assuming constant commodity prices by (2.7) and (2.8), factor prices are constant too. Differentiating (2.9) and (2.10), the output effects of changes in the supplies of labor and capital can be obtained as:

$$dX = \frac{(\beta_r dL - \beta_w dK)}{D}, \qquad (2.13)$$

$$dY = \frac{(-\alpha_r dL + \alpha_w dK)}{D}, \qquad (2.14)$$

where recalling that $D[=\alpha_w\beta_w(\beta_r/\beta_w - \alpha_r/\alpha_w)] > (<) \, 0$ if good X is labor(capital)-intensive relative to good Y. The output result derived in (2.13) and (2.14) is stated as the Rybczynski theorem: At constant commodity prices, an increase in the supply of a factor will raise the output of the commodity that uses the factor intensively, and will lower the output of the good that uses the other factor intensively.

Consider again the case that good X is relatively capital-intensive. From (2.13) and (2.14), we have: $dX/dL < 0$, $dY/dL > 0$, $dX/dK > 0$ and $dY/dK < 0$. These results confirm the Rybczynski effect and can be illustrated in the commodity (X, Y) space of Figure 2.2, where the labor and capital constraints in (2.9) and (2.10) are represented by the linear LL and KK lines. Note that the slope of the LL/KK schedule is given by

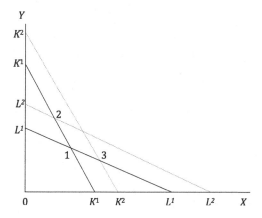

Figure 2.2 Rybczynski theorem.

the input/output ratios, α_w and β_w (α_r and β_r). At constant goods prices, the wage/rental is also given, implying constant capital–labor ratios, and hence constant input requirement ratios. Note further that the KK line is steeper than LL because good X is relatively capital-intensive. The initial equilibrium is located at point 1. An increase in the labor supply shifts the L^1L^1 line to L^2L^2, resulting in a rise in the equilibrium output of good Y and a fall in good X at point 2. Analogous analysis applies to the case of an increase in capital resulting in a new equilibrium at point 3.

It is notable that Samuelson (1953) and Takayama (1972) point out the reciprocity relationship between the Stolper–Samuelson and the Rybczynski effects, i.e., $dw/dp = dX/dL$ and $dr/dp = dX/dK$, etc.

The above production side of the economy can be summarized by the twice differentiable revenue function, defined as: $R(p_X, p_Y, L, K) = \max\{p_X X(L_X, K_X) + p_Y Y(L_Y, K_Y) : L_X + L_Y = L \text{ and } K_X + K_Y = K\}$. Note that $R(\cdot)$ is linearly homogenous and convex in prices p_X and p_Y, and concave in factor supplies L and K. Due to linear homogeneity and by choosing good Y as the numeraire (i.e., $p = p_X/p_Y$), the revenue function becomes $R(p, 1, L, K)$. Using the envelope theorem, we can derive the supply function of good X as $R_p(p, 1, L, K) = X$, where the subscripts in the revenue function denote partial derivatives. Since $R(\cdot)$ is convex in the prices, we have $R_{pp}(=\partial X/\partial p) > 0$ (i.e., the supply function is positively sloped). In addition, by the Rybczynski effect, $R_{pL} = \partial X/\partial L < (>) 0$ and $R_{pK} = \partial X/\partial K > (<) 0$ as good X is capital(labor)-intensive relative to good Y. Furthermore, because the revenue function is continuous, we have $R_{Lp} = R_{pL}$ and $R_{Kp} = R_{pK}$. The subscripts here denote the second-order (cross) partial derivatives.

Differentiating the revenue function with respect to the factor of production immediately provides the factor returns: $\partial R/\partial L = R_L(p, 1, L, K) = w$ and $\partial R/\partial K = R_K(p, 1, L, K) = r$. The second-order (cross) partial derivatives yield the Stolper–Samuelson effect that $R_{Lp} = \partial w/\partial p < (>) 0$ and $R_{Kp} = \partial r/\partial p > (<) 0$, if good X is capital(labor)-intensive relative to good Y. Note that due to the dichotomy property of the production structure, w and r are the function of p alone in (2.7) and (2.8). This yields that $R_{LL} = R_{KK} = R_{LK} = 0$; the factor rewards are independent of the factor endowments, a key feature in the Heckscher–Ohlin model.

2.2.2   *Specific-factor model*

Consider another commonly used trade model — the 2×2×3 model (a specific-factor model with two countries, two goods, and three factors).

This is also called the Ricardo–Viner–Samuelson model, discussed in Ricardo (1817), Viner (1931), and Samuelson (1971), and analyzed by Jones (1971), Mayer (1974), and Neary (1978), among others.

Let the two goods be X and Y, and their production functions:

$$X = X(L_X, K), \tag{2.15}$$

$$Y = Y(L_Y, T), \tag{2.16}$$

where L_i is labor employed in sector i, and K and T are capital and land used specifically by sectors X and Y, respectively. The production functions are subject to constant returns to scale technologies, and each factor contributes positively to production but with diminishing marginal returns. Under profit maximization, factors are paid according to the values of their marginal productivities:

$$w = pX_L(L_X, K) = Y_L(L_Y, T), \tag{2.17}$$

$$r = pX_K(L_X, K), \tag{2.18}$$

$$v = Y_T(L_Y, T), \tag{2.19}$$

where v denotes the rent to land in sector Y. Note that labor is the only intersectorally mobile factor. To close the production side of the model, it is assumed that the wage rate is perfectly flexible so that full employment of labor prevails:

$$L_X + L_Y = L. \tag{2.20}$$

Equations (2.17)–(2.20) contain seven endogenous variables — X, Y, w, r, v, L_X, and L_Y — and four parameters — p, L, K, and T — that can be used to solve for the factor price and output effects for a change in any of the parameters. For this specific-factor model (2.17), containing two equations, determines the allocation of labor between the two sectors. Equation (2.17) is illustrated in Figure 2.3, in which the horizontal distance measures the total fixed supply of labor in the economy and the vertical axis measures the value of marginal product of labor (VMPL). This allocation of labor also determines the rates of returns on capital, r, by (2.18) and on land, v, by (2.19).

Due to diminishing marginal returns of labor, the VMPL curve is downward sloping. The VMPL schedule for sector X is shown by the pX_L line, and for sector Y it is shown by the Y_L line. Note that the equilibrium in (2.17) is represented by the intersection of these two schedules at point 1, which indicates the initial allocation of labor between the two sectors.

Utilizing (2.17) and (2.20), and the homogeneity property of the production functions, the effects of changes in the goods price and factor supplies

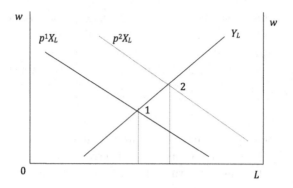

Figure 2.3   Labor allocation.

on factor prices can be obtained:[6]

$$\frac{dw}{dp} > 0, \quad \frac{dw}{dL} < 0, \quad \frac{dw}{dK} > 0, \quad \frac{dw}{dT} > 0, \qquad (2.21)$$

$$\frac{dr}{dp} > 0, \quad \frac{dr}{dL} > 0, \quad \frac{dr}{dK} < 0, \quad \frac{dr}{dT} < 0, \qquad (2.22)$$

$$\frac{dv}{dp} < 0, \quad \frac{dv}{dL} > 0, \quad \frac{dv}{dK} < 0, \quad \frac{dv}{dT} < 0. \qquad (2.23)$$

These results can be explained with the aid of Figure 2.3. A rise in p from p^1 to p^2 causes a rightward shift of the VMPL curve of sector X from $p^1 X_L$ to $p^2 X_L$, yielding an increased demand for labor in sector X. This pushes up the real wage rate in the economy. In addition, more labor employment in sector X (i.e., less labor employment in sector Y) causes the capital rental rate to rise in sector X but the land rent to fall in sector Y due to complementarities of labor and the other factor. Similar reasons apply for understanding the effects of changes in factor supplies on factor returns. For example, an increase in capital shifts up the VMPL curve of sector X, indicating a higher wage rate at the new equilibrium point 2 relative to the original equilibrium point 1. However, for the given goods price, the higher wage rate raises the cost of production, thereby dampening the rate of returns to the two specific factors, capital and land, in sectors X and Y, respectively.

---

[6]Using (2.17) and (2.19) we can obtain: $dw/dp = X_L Y_{LL}/D$, $dw/dL = pX_{LL}Y_{LL}/D$, $dw/dK = pX_{LK}Y_{LL}/D > 0$ and $dw/dT = pX_{LL}Y_{LT}/D > 0$, where $D = (pX_{LL} + Y_{LL}) < 0$. The others can be similarly derived.

Note that in contrast to the Heckscher–Ohlin mobile factor model, factor prices depend on factor supplies in addition to goods prices in the specific-factor model. As the number of factors is larger than the number of goods in the present model, the dichotomy of factor prices and factor supplies does not hold (Samuelson, 1971). The sectoral specificity of production factors may occur as a short-run phenomenon. In the longer run, factor specificity may be weakened and factors become mobile intersectorally.

Utilizing (2.15)–(2.17) and (2.20), we can solve for the effects of changes in the goods price and factor supplies on the outputs of goods X and Y:[7]

$$\frac{dX}{dp} > 0, \ \frac{dX}{dL} > 0, \ \frac{dX}{dK} > 0, \ \frac{dX}{dT} < 0,$$

$$\frac{dY}{dp} < 0, \ \frac{dY}{dL} > 0, \ \frac{dY}{dK} < 0, \ \frac{dY}{dT} > 0. \tag{2.24}$$

An increase in the goods price ratio of X raises the output of good X at the expense of good Y; the normal price-output response holds in the specific-factor model. Moreover, the production of both sectors expands as a result of an increase in the supply of the common factor, i.e., labor. However, an increased supply of capital promotes the production of good X at the expense of good Y. Analogy applies to the effects of an increased supply of land on the outputs of goods X and Y.

The above results on the specific-factor model can also be summarized by the revenue function, defined as: $R(p, 1, L, K, T) = \max\{pX(L_X, K) + Y(L_Y, T) : L_X + L_Y = L\}$ with respect to L_i, where $p(=p_X/p_Y)$ is the relative price of good X in terms of good Y. Note that $R(\cdot)$ is convex in prices and concave in factor supplies. The supply function of good X is $R_p(p, 1, L, K, T) = X$, and the various output effects can be deduced by $R_{pp}(=\partial X/\partial p) > 0$, $R_{pL}(=\partial X/\partial L) > 0$, $R_{pK}(=\partial X/\partial K) > 0$ and $R_{pT} = \partial X/\partial T < 0$.

As for the factor returns, we have: $R_L(p, 1, L, K, T) = w$, $R_K(p, 1, L, K, T) = r$ and $R_T(p, 1, L, K, T) = v$. The effects of changes in goods prices on factor prices are: $R_{Lp}(=\partial w/\partial p) > 0$, $R_{Kp}(=\partial r/\partial p) > 0$ and $R_{Tp}(=\partial r/\partial p) < 0$. As mentioned earlier, in the specific-factor structure, factor supplies in addition to goods prices affect factor prices, as follows: $R_{KL} > 0$, $R_{TL} > 0$, $R_{KT} < 0$, and $R_{jj} < 0$, where $j = L, K, T$.

---

[7]From (2.17) and (2.19), we have: $dX/dp = -X_L^2/D > 0, dX/dL = -pX_L X_{LK}/D > 0$, $dX/dK = X_L Y_{LL}/D > 0$ and $dX/dT = X_L Y_{LT}/D < 0$, where $D = (pX_{LL} + Y_{LL}) < 0$. Similarly, we can obtain the results for the changes in Y.

2.2.3 *A hybrid model*

Many real-world issues in international trade have been analyzed by using appropriate combinations of various components of the Heckscher–Ohlin and the specific-factor models in the literature. Consider the following hybrid model for a small open economy that consists of two domestic sectors and an export-processing zone: the former sectors produce an importable good X and a non-traded good N by using domestic labor and capital, while the latter produces an exportable good Y with domestic labor and foreign capital. The production functions are as follows:

$$X = X(L_X, K_X), \qquad (2.25)$$

$$N = N(L_N, K_N), \qquad (2.26)$$

$$Y = Y(L_Y, K_f). \qquad (2.27)$$

Note that foreign capital, K_f, is specific to the production of good Y. Full employment of domestic labor and capital is assumed:

$$L_X + L_N = L - L_Y, \qquad (2.28)$$

$$K_X + K_N = K, \qquad (2.29)$$

where L and K denote the endowments of domestic labor and capital. We choose good Y as the numeraire, and the prices of goods X and N are denoted by p and q, respectively. While the price of good X is equal to its world price $(p = p^*)$, the price of the non-traded good (q) is endogenously determined in the economy.[8]

The above production structure can be represented by its cost dual. Under perfect competition, unit cost equals unit price in equilibrium:

$$\alpha(w, r) = p, \qquad (2.30)$$

$$\gamma(w, r) = q, \qquad (2.31)$$

$$\beta(w, r_f) = 1, \qquad (2.32)$$

---

[8]See Komiya (1967) in a seminar article on non-traded goods, and Yano and Nugent (1999) for empirical evidence on the importance of the non-traded goods.

and the full employment conditions for labor, domestic and foreign capital are:

$$\alpha_w(w,r)X + \gamma_w(w,r)N = L - \beta_w(w,r_f)Y, \qquad (2.33)$$

$$\alpha_r(w,r)X + \gamma_r(w,r)N = K, \qquad (2.34)$$

$$\beta_r(w,r_f)Y = K_f, \qquad (2.35)$$

where w, r, and r_f denote the rates of return to labor, domestic capital, and foreign capital, and $\alpha(\cdot)$, $\gamma(\cdot)$, and $\beta(\cdot)$ are unit costs of producing goods X, N, and Y, respectively.

A standard assumption in the general equilibrium setting of international trade is perfect competition. Perfectly competitive firms are price takers. Thus, given the price q, the six unknowns — w, r, r_f, X, N, and Y — in the production side of the economy in (2.30)–(2.35) can be solved as functions of q and K_f. Note that the system is block recursive: (2.30) and (2.31) form a Heckscher–Ohlin subsystem, in which w and r can be obtained as functions of q alone. Furthermore, we obtain the Stolper–Samuelson effect, $\partial w/\partial q > 0$ and $\partial r/\partial q < 0$, if good X is capital-intensive relative to good N. We also obtain $\partial r_f/\partial q < 0$ from (2.32).

As far as the output effect of foreign capital is concerned, we have, from (2.35), $\partial Y/\partial K_f > 0$ for a given q, and hence the demand for labor rises in sector Y. This reduces the supply of labor available for sectors X and N, as indicated in (2.33), resulting in a Rybczynski effect, $\partial X/\partial K_f > 0$ and $\partial N/\partial K_f < 0$, if good X is relatively capital-intensive.

The above production structure of this hybrid model can be explained with the help of Figure 2.4. The Heckscher–Ohlin subsystem of (2.30) and (2.31) is depicted in quadrant I, while quadrant II plots the value of marginal product of labor (VMPL) in sector Y. For a given q, the employment of labor in sector Y is displayed by L_Y, yielding the allocation of labor for sectors X and Z by $L - L_Y$ in (2.33). This determines the output N, which yields the Rybczynski line as represented by the RR curve in quadrant III: the larger the $L - L_Y$, the more the output of good N, if it is labor intensive relative to good X. The supply of good N inversely affects its price q, which in turn gives rise to the Stolper–Samuelson effect as expressed by the SS curve in quadrant IV. For simplicity, we depict both $1/N$ and q by the same vertical axis between quadrants III and IV.

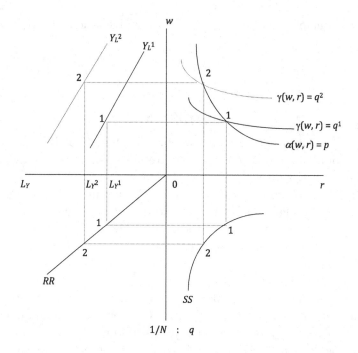

Figure 2.4   A hybrid production structure.

In Figure 2.4, suppose the initial equilibrium is at point 1. Because foreign capital is used exclusively for the production of good Y, the inflow of K_f shifts the VMPL curve for sector Y upward resulting in a new equilibrium at point 2 in quadrant II. Consequently, the amount of labor available for sectors X and N is reduced, thereby lowering the supply of good N in quadrant III. This can affect its price q and hence the capital rental and wage rates, as indicated in quadrants IV and I.

2.3   A General Equilibrium Trade Model with a Tourism Distortion

Tourism transforms the traditional non-traded goods and services into exportable goods and services. The models on non-traded goods have been utilized to study the welfare implications of tourism for the domestic economy (Hazari and Sgro, 2004; Tisdell, 2013). Tourism also generates a demand-side distortion arising from the terms-of-trade effect.[9]

---

[9]This section is adapted from Chao *et al.* (2009).

Suppose that the home country produces three goods — an agricultural good, X, a manufacturing good, Y, and a non-traded good, Z — in perfectly competitive markets. The production functions are: $X = X(L_X)$, $Y = Y(L_Y, S, K)$ and $Z = Z(L_Z, V)$. Unskilled labor (L_i) is a mobile factor used in all sectors, skilled labor (S) and capital (K) are specific factors to the manufacturing, and land (V) is a specific factor to the non-traded goods sector. The production functions display diminishing returns to factors. Letting L be the endowment of unskilled labor, full employment requires that $L_X + L_Y + L_Z = L$. Moreover, there are also inflows of foreign capital but its return is subject to investment taxes. To economize on notations, K denotes foreign capital. Foreign capital flows in until its return equals the world interest rate (r^*) plus the tax (τ) levied by the home country.

It is assumed that the home country exports good X and imports good Y. There are no impediments on exports but imports are subject to a specific tariff, t. Choosing the exportable good X as the numeraire, the domestic price of the importable good Y is $p(= p^* + t)$, where p^* is the given foreign price. The domestic relative price of the non-traded good Z, denoted by q, is endogenously determined in the home economy. Let w and s denote the wage rates of unskilled and skilled labor, and r and v be the rates of return on capital and land in the economy. Under perfect competition in the goods market, unit price equals its unit cost in equilibrium:

$$1 = c^X(w), \tag{2.36}$$

$$p = c^Y(w, s, r), \tag{2.37}$$

$$q = c^Z(w, v), \tag{2.38}$$

where $c^X(\cdot)$, $c^Y(\cdot)$, and $c^Z(\cdot)$ denote, respectively, the unit-cost functions of goods X, Y, and Z. By the envelope property, $c_w^X (= \partial c^X/\partial w)$ represents unit demand for unskilled labor in sector X, and so on. Under full employment, the employment conditions for unskilled labor, skilled labor, capital, and land are given in the following equations:

$$c_w^X(w)X + c_w^Y(w, s, r)Y + c_w^Z(w, v)Z = L, \tag{2.39}$$

$$c_s^Y(w, s, r)Y = S, \tag{2.40}$$

$$c_r^Y(w, s, r)Y = K, \tag{2.41}$$

$$c_v^Z(w, v)Z = V. \tag{2.42}$$

Equations (2.36)–(2.42) present the supply-side economy, which consists of seven endogenous variables — w, s, r, v, X, Y, and Z — for given prices p

and q and capital inflow of K. Note that at this stage the other exogenous variables are ignored. The above system is block recursive: w is fixed by (2.36), and then s, r, and Y are solved from (2.37), (2.40), and (2.41) as functions of p and K. From (2.38) and (2.42), v and Z are determined as functions of q alone. Finally, X is obtained from (2.39) as a function of p, q, and K.

The above supply-side information can be compactly represented by the revenue function: $R(p, q, K) = \max\{X(L_X) + pY(L_Y, S, K) + qZ(L_Z, V):$ $L_X + L_Y + L_Z = L\}$ with respect to L_i, $i = X, Y, Z$. Using subscripts in $R(\cdot)$ to denote partial derivatives, by the envelope property we have: $R_p = Y$, $R_q = Z$ and $R_K = r$. Further, we have $R_{qq} > 0$, showing that the positive supply of good Z is increasing in q, and $R_{qp} = R_{qK} = 0$ because Z depends only on its own price q. Note that due to the specific-factor model in (2.36)–(2.38), we have: $R_{pK} > 0$ and $R_{KK} < 0$. That is, a rise in capital raises the output of good Y but reduces the rate of return on capital.

Consider next the demand-side economy, which consists of domestic residents and foreign tourists. Domestic residents demand all three goods and their expenditure function is: $E(p, q, u) = \min\{C_X + pC_Y + qC_Z:$ $U(C_X, C_Y, C_Z) = u\}$, where C_i is demand for good i, $U(\cdot)$ is the utility function, and u is the utility level of domestic residents. Using the envelope property, we have $E_q = C_Z$ for the compensated demand for good Z by domestic residents, with $E_{qq} < 0$ for the downward-sloped compensated demand function. Note that $E_{qp} > (<) 0$ when goods Y and Z are substitutes (complements) in consumption. As far as tourists' demand is concerned, we follow the standard literature, we assume that they demand the non-traded good Z only and their demand function is: $D_Z(q, T)$, with $\partial D_Z/\partial q < 0$ and $\partial D_Z/\partial T > 0$, where T is a shift parameter that captures tourists' expenditure and other things, for example, taste.

Utilizing the above demand and supply information, the equilibrium conditions of the economy are characterized by:

$$E(p, q, u) = R(p, q, K) - r^*K + tM, \qquad (2.43)$$

$$M = E_p(p, q, u) - R_p(p, q, K), \qquad (2.44)$$

$$R_K(p, q, K) - \tau = r^*, \qquad (2.45)$$

$$E_q(p, q, u) + D_Z(q, T) = R_q(p, q, K), \qquad (2.46)$$

where M denotes the imports of good Y. Assuming that tariff revenue is returned to domestic residents, (2.43) expresses the budget constraint of the economy, in which domestic residents' expenditure equals net income from production plus revenue from tariff. Equation (2.44) denotes the imports of good Y as an excess demand function for good Y. Equation (2.45) describes the equilibrium condition that after-tax returns on capital between countries, while (2.46) shows the market-clearing condition for the non-traded good Z, in which total demand by domestic residents and foreign tourists equals supply from domestic production.

The tourist-receiving home economy described in (2.43)–(2.46) consists of four unknowns, u, M, K, and q, with an exogenous tariff t and investment tax τ. We will now examine the welfare effects of these two policies for a small open economy with inbound tourism.

2.3.1 Optimal tariff and investment tax

The general expression of the change in welfare of domestic residents can be obtained by totally differentiating (2.43):

$$E_u du = t dM + \tau dK + D_Z dq, \qquad (2.47)$$

where E_u is the inverse of the marginal utility of income. The first two terms on the right-hand side of (2.47) give the traditional volume-of-trade effects in imports and capital inflows. An increase (decrease) in them raises (lowers) domestic welfare, since tariffs and investment taxes restrict (don't restrict) imports of good Y and inflows of capital K. The last term in (2.47) captures the tourism terms-of-trade effect via the change in the relative price of the non-traded good Z, as tourism converts the formerly non-traded good to exports. A higher relative price of the non-tradable yields a gain from exporting to cater tourism, which contributes positively to domestic welfare.

The change in imports of good Y can be derived from (2.44) as follows:

$$dM = E_{pu} du + (E_{pp} - R_{pp}) dt + E_{pq} dq - R_{pK} dK, \qquad (2.48)$$

where $R_{pK} > 0$. The demand factors, such as real income (utility) and the prices of good Y and Z, all affect the change of imports in (2.48). In particular, when goods Y and Z are substitutes (complements) in consumption — i.e., $E_{pq} > (<) 0$ — a rise in the relative price of non-tradable q raises (lowers) demand for good Y according to the third term on the right-hand side of (2.48). As far as the supply factors are concerned, the change of capital affects production of good Y and hence the imports shown by the last term of (2.48). Note that the change in capital can be obtained by differentiating (2.45):

$$R_{KK}dK = -R_{pK}dt + d\tau, \qquad (2.49)$$

where $R_{KK} < 0$. Equation (2.49) indicates that the changes in tariffs and investment taxes affect inflows of foreign capital. It is important to note that increases in tariffs lead to the tariff-jumping inflow of foreign capital.[10]

By differentiating (2.46), we obtain the change in the relative price of the non-traded good:

$$\left(E_{qq} + \frac{\partial D_Z}{\partial q} - R_{qq}\right)dq = -E_{qu}du - E_{qp}dt, \qquad (2.50)$$

where $E_{qu}(=\partial C_Z/\partial u)$ expresses the income effect of demand for good Z by domestic residents. We assume that all goods are normal in consumption (i.e., $E_{pu} > 0$). Hence, both the income and substitution/complement effects as indicated in the first and the second term on the right-hand side of (2.50) affect the relative price of the domestic non-traded good Z.

We examine first the welfare effect of tariffs for a given and also for a zero investment tax. Solving (2.47)–(2.50), we obtain:

$$\frac{du}{dt} = -\frac{\left\{t\left[\left(E_{qq} + \frac{\partial D_Z}{\partial q} - R_{qq}\right)R_{pK}^2 + R_{KK}H\right] - \tau\left(E_{qq} + \frac{\partial D_Z}{\partial q} - R_{qq}\right)R_{pK}\right\}}{\Delta}$$

$$+ \frac{D_Z E_{pq} R_{KK}}{\Delta}, \qquad (2.51)$$

where $H = (E_{pp} - R_{pp})(E_{qq} + \partial D_Z/\partial q - R_{qq}) - E_{pq}^2 > 0$.[11] Also, by the stability condition, we have $\Delta = -R_{KK}[(E_u - tE_{pu})(E_{qq} + \partial D_Z/\partial q - R_{qq}) + E_{qu}(D_Z + tE_{pq})] < 0$.[12] In the absence of tourism (i.e., $D_Z = 0$) in (2.51), the conventional welfare result on tariffs for a small open economy is obtained. A rise in tariffs unambiguously reduces domestic welfare and hence free trade in goods is optimal when the investment tax is absent (i.e., $\tau = 0$). More importantly, the presence of tourism ($D_Z > 0$) in the

---

[10]See Brecher and Diaz Alejandro (1977) for a study on the welfare effect of capital inflows under tariffs. Also see Beladi and Parai (1993) for a related study.

[11]Because the expenditure function is concave in prices, we have: $E_{pp}E_{qq} - E_{pq}^2 > 0$. This gives $H > 0$.

[12]Following Dei (1985b), the adjustment for the price q of the non-traded good is: $\dot{q} = \rho A(q)$, where the dot over q is the time derivative, ρ is the speed of adjustments, and A denotes excess demand for good Z, i.e., $A = E_q(p, q, u) + D_Z(q, T) - R_q(p, q, K)$ in (2.40). A necessary and sufficient condition for stability of the economy is: $dA/dq < 0$. From (2.41) and (2.42), we obtain: $dq/dA = -E_u R_{KK}(1 - m_Y t/p)/\Delta$, where m_Y ($=pE_{pu}/E_u$) is the marginal propensity to consume good Y and is less than 1. Hence, stability requires $\Delta < 0$.

economy alters this free trade result. When the non-traded and importable goods are substitutes ($E_{pq} > 0$) (in the last term of [2.51]),[13] tariffs can actually improve the domestic welfare of a small open economy. Due to the substitution effect, the higher importable price of good Y by tariffs leads domestic residents to switch consumption to the non-traded good Z. This raises the relative price of the non-tradable, yielding a favorable tourism terms-of-trade or expenditure-shifting effect on foreign tourists. In this case, raising the price of the imports by tariffs can improve domestic welfare. Setting $du/dt = 0$ in (2.51), we can derive the optimum tariff, t^0, as:

$$t^0 = \frac{\left[D_Z E_{pq} R_{KK} + \tau \left(E_{qq} + \frac{\partial D_Z}{\partial q} - R_{qq} \right) R_{pK} \right]}{\left[\left(E_{qq} + \frac{\partial D_Z}{\partial q} - R_{qq} \right) R_{pK}^2 + R_{KK} H \right]}, \qquad (2.52)$$

which is positive for $D_Z > 0$ even in the absence of investment taxes (i.e., $\tau = 0$). This proves an important result: Free trade in goods is not optimal for the economy with inbound tourism.

Figure 2.5 provides a graphical illustration for the t^0 schedule in the policy space of (t, τ), in which the t^0 schedule is positively sloped and $t^0 > 0$ when $\tau = 0$. Note that domestic welfare is maximized at t^0 for a given τ. This can be seen by checking the curvature of the domestic welfare function. Following the technique used by Neary (1993), we substitute the expressions from (2.52) into (2.51) to obtain:[14]

$$\frac{du}{dt} = -\frac{\left[\left(E_{qq} + \frac{\partial D_Z}{\partial q} - R_{qq} \right) R_{pK}^2 + R_{KK} H \right] (t - t^0)}{\Delta}. \qquad (2.53)$$

Since $\Delta < 0$, we have: $du/dt > (<) \, 0$ when $t < (>) \, t^0$. This implies that u is a concave function of t. When t increases horizontally in Figure 2.5, domestic welfare increases initially, reaches a maximum at t^0, and then starts to decline. The horizontal arrows indicate these changes in domestic welfare. In view of this result, the conventional trade theory needs to be modified. In the presence of tourism with flexible prices for the non-traded

---

[13] The results below are reversed when they are complements ($E_{pq} < 0$).

[14] Due to the third-order partial derivatives involved in the functions of $E(\cdot)$ and $R(\cdot)$, it is impossible to check the second-order condition of welfare maximization for t^0 in (2.52) (i.e., $d^2 u/dt^2 < 0$). Therefore, a direct proof given in (2.53) is utilized to examine the curvature of the welfare function around point t^0.

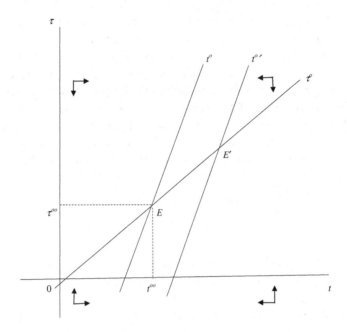

Figure 2.5   Optimal tariffs and investment taxes.

good, there exists an optimal tariff on traded goods that maximizes resident welfare.

We now examine the welfare effect of investment taxes for a given tariff. From (2.47)–(2.50), we obtain:

$$\frac{du}{d\tau} = -\frac{\left(E_{qq} + \frac{\partial D_Z}{\partial q} - R_{qq}\right)(\tau - tR_{pK})}{\Delta}. \tag{2.54}$$

A rise in investment taxes immediately reduces inflows of foreign capital by (2.49) and hence less domestic production of good Y. This leads to two forces that can conflict with each other on domestic welfare as shown in the first and the second term on the right-hand side of (2.54): The former reduces welfare via less tax revenue, whereas the latter raises welfare by more tariff revenue. By setting $du/d\tau = 0$, we can obtain the optimal investment taxes, τ^0, as follows:

$$\tau^0 = tR_{pK}. \tag{2.55}$$

Since $R_{pK} > 0$, the positive-sloped τ^0 schedule is depicted in Figure 2.5, in which $\tau^0 = 0$ when $t = 0$. Note that for a given t, domestic welfare is maximized at τ^0. This can be shown by substituting τ^0 in (2.55) into (2.54) to rewrite the change in domestic welfare as:

$$\frac{du}{d\tau} = -\frac{\left(E_{qq} + \frac{\partial D_Z}{\partial q} - R_{qq}\right)(\tau - \tau^0)}{\Delta}. \qquad (2.56)$$

Because of $\Delta < 0$, we have $du/d\tau > (<) \, 0$ when $\tau < (>) \, \tau^0$ in (2.56). That is, any vertical movements of the investment tax τ toward its optimal rate τ^0 are necessarily welfare improving.

We are now in a position to consider the jointly optimal tariffs and investment taxes, denoted by t^{00} and τ^{00}, for the domestic economy in the presence of tourism. Solving (2.52) and (2.55), we obtain:

$$t^{00} = \frac{D_Z E_{qp}}{H} > 0, \qquad (2.57)$$

$$\tau^{00} = \frac{D_Z E_{qp} R_{pK}}{H} > 0. \qquad (2.58)$$

Hence, opposite to conventional wisdom, the presence of tourism in the economy supports positive rates of tariffs and investment taxes. This is again due to the favorable tourism terms-of-trade effect induced by the consumption-substitution effect between the importable good Y and the non-traded good Z if $E_{qp} > 0$ in (2.57) and (2.58).

The jointly optimal tariffs and investment taxes, t^{00} and τ^{00}, are depicted at point E in Figure 2.5.[15] From (2.52) and (2.55), an increase in the tourism activity via a larger D_Z shifts the t^0 schedule to the right, while leaving the τ^0 schedule unchanged. This yields a new equilibrium at E′, which shows higher optimal rates for both tariffs and investment taxes. Hence, contrary to common belief, more protection of goods trade and factor flows is desirable as tourism expands. This result will be verified by numerical simulation in the next section.[16]

---

[15] In Figure 2.5, the slope of the t^0 schedule is $d\tau/dt|_t = R_{pK} + R_{KK}H/R_{pK}(E_{qq} + \partial D_Z/\partial q - R_{qq}) > 0$, and the slope of the τ^0 schedule is $d\tau/dt|_\tau = R_{pK} > 0$. These give that the slope of the t^0 schedule is larger than the slope of the τ^0 schedule.

[16] It should be more interesting to examine the change in tourists' expenditure T on t^{00} and τ^{00} in (2.57) and (2.58). However, it is analytically infeasible because the change in T affects not only D_Z but also H. Therefore, we rely on simulations, provided in Table 2.1, to obtain the effects of changes in T on t^{00} and τ^{00}.

2.3.2   *Simulations for optimal tariffs and capital taxes*

In this section, we calibrate the impact of international tourism on optimal tariffs and capital taxes; we specify functional forms for the utility and production functions. The production functions of the traded and non-traded goods are assumed to possess the Cobb–Douglas (CD) forms:

$$X = AL_X^\delta, \tag{2.59}$$

$$Y = BL_Y^\alpha K^\beta S^{1-\alpha-\beta}, \tag{2.60}$$

$$Z = GL_Z^\gamma V^{1-\gamma}, \tag{2.61}$$

where A, B, and G are the technology factors, and δ, α, β, and γ are the respective factor shares in the production of goods X, Y, and Z. Since the factors S and V are exogenously fixed, we set $S = V = 1$. Total employment for sectors X, Y, and Z in the economy is given by $L = L_X + L_Y + L_Z$. Given the relative prices, wage rate, and capital rental, profit maximization yields the equilibrium allocation of labor and demand for capital:

$$\frac{\delta X}{L_X} = \frac{p\alpha Y}{L_Y} = \frac{q\gamma Z}{L_Z} = w, \tag{2.62}$$

$$\frac{p\beta Y}{K} = r. \tag{2.63}$$

On the demand side of the economy, we assume a CD-CES (constant elasticity of substitution) utility function in which the non-traded and importable goods are substitutes:

$$U = \frac{C_X^\alpha \left[b^{1/(1+\sigma)} C_Y^{\sigma/(1+\sigma)} + \bar{b}^{1/(1+\sigma)} C_Z^{\sigma/(1+\sigma)} \right]^{\bar{\alpha}(1+\sigma)/\sigma}}{\left[b^{1/(1+\sigma)} + \bar{b}^{1/(1+\sigma)} \right]^{\bar{\alpha}(1+\sigma)/\sigma}}, \tag{2.64}$$

where a, b, $\bar{a}$, $\bar{b} > 0$ and $a + \bar{a} = b + \bar{b} = 1$. The elasticity of substitution between the consumption of the non-traded good and the manufacturing good is captured by $1 + \sigma$, where $\sigma > -1$. Utility maximization yields the following demand functions for goods X and Y:

$$C_X = \left(\frac{a}{\bar{a}}\right) \left[1 + \left(\frac{b}{\bar{b}}\right) \left(\frac{q}{p}\right)^\sigma \right] q C_Z, \tag{2.65}$$

$$C_Y = \left(\frac{b}{\bar{b}}\right) \left(\frac{q}{p}\right)^{1+\sigma} q C_Z. \tag{2.66}$$

Substituting (2.65) and (2.66) into the utility function in (2.64) yields:

$$U = \frac{\bar{b}^{\bar{a}/\sigma} \left(\frac{aq}{\bar{a}}\right)^a \left[1 + \left(\frac{b}{\bar{b}}\right)\left(\frac{q}{p}\right)^\sigma\right]^{1+\bar{a}/\sigma} C_Z}{[b^{1/(1+\sigma)} + \bar{b}^{1/(1+\sigma)}]^{\bar{a}(1+\sigma)/\sigma}}. \qquad (2.67)$$

The model is closed by considering the market-clearing condition for the non-traded good Z:

$$C_Z + D_Z = Z, \qquad (2.68)$$

where the demand for the non-traded good by tourists is specified as

$$D_Z = \frac{T}{q^\eta}. \qquad (2.69)$$

Note that η, the price elasticity of demand for good Z by tourists, measures the extent to which tourists substitute goods in consumption as the price of the non-traded good rises in the host country.

Finally, the budget constraint of the economy is:

$$C_X + p^*C_Y + qC_Z = X + p^*Y + qZ - r^*K. \qquad (2.70)$$

This implies the balance of trade condition $(X - C_X) + qD_Z = p^*(C_Y - Y) + r^*K$, such that the total value of exports of good X and tourism equals the total value of imports from good Y and capital inflows.

We proceed to solve the system of equations in (2.59)–(2.70). Given $p(=p^* + t)$ and $r(= r^* + \tau)$, we can obtain $X = A^{1/(1-\delta)}(\delta/w)^{\delta/(1-\delta)}$ and $L_x = \delta X/w$ from (2.59) and (2.62), $Y = [B(\alpha/w)^\alpha(\beta/r)^\beta p^{\alpha+\beta}]^{1/(1-\alpha-\beta)}$, $K = \beta pY/r$ and $L_Y = \alpha pY/w$ from (2.60)–(2.63), and $Z = G^{1/(1-\gamma)}(\gamma q/w)^{\gamma/(1-\gamma)}$ and $L_Z = \gamma qZ/w$ from (2.61) and (2.62). By setting $I = X + p^*Y + qZ - r^*K$ and using (2.65), (2.66), and (2.70), we obtain: $C_Z = \bar{a}\bar{b}\, I/q\{1 - b[1 - (q/p)^\sigma(p^* + at)/p]\}$ and hence C_X and C_Y in (2.65) and (2.66). Therefore, we can compute welfare U in (2.67), and furthermore, w and q are solved from the two equations $L = L_X + L_Y + L_Z$ and $C_Z + D_Z = Z$.

We start by assigning the values for the main endogenous variables of the reference equilibrium of the model: $X = 2$, $Y = 2$, $Z = 6$, $L_X = 2$, $C_Y = 3$, $C_Z = 5$, $r^* = 0.1$, $p^* = 1$, $q = 1$, $t = 0$ and $\tau = 0$, and the values for the elasticity parameters: $\alpha = 0.6$, $\beta = 0.2$, $\gamma = 0.6$, $\delta = 0.6$ and $\sigma = 3$. When tourism is absent in the economy $(T = 0)$, the optimal policy is free trade in goods and no taxes on capital ($t^{00} = 0$ and $\tau^{00} = 0$) and the utility is: $U^{00} = 3.4416$ (indicated in Table 2.1).

We consider next a case in which $T = 1$; that is, tourism revenue is 10% of the gross domestic product (GDP).[17] For an inelastic tourists' demand function ($\eta = 0.5$) in (2.65), we have the values of the variables: $p = 1$, $D_Z = 1$, $w = 0.6$, $L_Y = 2$, $L_Z = 6$, $K = 4$, $L = 10$, $C_X = 1.6$, and $r = 0.1$. The values of the scale parameters are: $A = 1.3195$, $B = 1$, and $G = 2.0477$. The values of the parameters are: $b = 0.375$ and $a = 0.1667$. In addition, we have the households' utility: $U(0,0) = 3.4566$ at free trade in goods and no taxes on capital.

Nevertheless, in the presence of tourism, the welfare of domestic households can be further increased by imposing tariffs and investment taxes. In calibration, we increase them from their free trade levels. The consequent welfare profile under $T = 1$ and $\eta = 0.5$ is plotted in Figure 2.6, in which the utility function is concave in the space of tariffs and investment taxes. The optimal tariff and tax rates are $t^{00} = 34.03\%$ and $\tau^{00} = 3.79\%$, and the corresponding utility is $U^{00} = 3.4962$. These optimal policies raise welfare by 1.15%, which confirms that free trade is not optimal for a small open economy with tourism.

We next increase the tourism activity T from 1 to 1.5 (i.e., tourism revenue is 15% of GDP) under $\eta = 0.5$. In this case, the optimal tariff and investment tax are: $t^{00} = 66.33\%$ and $\tau^{00} = 6.95\%$. Hence, an increase in the tourism activity gives higher optimal tariff and investment tax. This raises welfare of domestic households by 2.88% from the free trade level.

It is noted that the price elasticity of tourist demand for the non-traded good (η) can be used as a measure for the intensity of the competition from other destinations. Table 2.1 gives a sensitivity analysis for the optimal policies to the different price elasticities of tourist demand. When the demand by tourists becomes less elastic (smaller η) and hence less competitive from other destinations, the optimal tariffs and investment taxes become larger

---

[17]This ratio of tourism revenue to GDP can be illustrated by the Hong Kong economy. In 2004, total tourism expenditure associated to inbound tourism was HK$91.85 billion, or 7.12% of Hong Kong's GDP, while GDP was HK$1,290.81 billion. The service sectors related to tourism and non-traded goods, including restaurants and hotels, wholesale and retail trades, transport and communications, financing, real estate and business services, and community, social and personal services, account for roughly 54.17% of GDP. See the website of the Hong Kong Tourism Board (www.tourism.gov.hk), and *Hong Kong Monthly Digest of Statistics*, Census and Statistics Department, Hong Kong Special Administrative Region, January 2006, p. 223.

Table 2.1   Sensitivity analysis for tourism.

T	η	t^{00} (%)	τ^{00} (%)	U^{00}	$U(0,0)$	Change in U
0	3	0.00	0.00	3.4416	3.4416	0.00
1	3	14.14	1.64	3.4718	3.4566	0.44
1.5	3	17.40	1.99	3.4942	3.4701	0.69
0	1	0.00	0.00	3.4416	3.4416	0.00
1	1	25.14	2.85	3.4863	3.4566	0.86
1.5	1	38.13	4.19	3.5353	3.4737	1.77
0	0.5	0.00	0.00	3.4416	3.4416	0.00
1	0.5	34.03	3.79	3.4962	3.4566	1.15
1.5	0.5	66.33	6.95	3.5750	3.4749	2.88
0	0.2	0.00	0.00	3.4416	3.4416	0.00
1	0.2	47.37	5.15	3.5077	3.4566	1.48
1.5	0.2	244.6	22.35	3.6812	3.4758	5.91

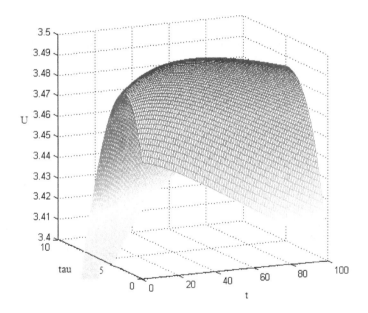

Figure 2.6   Welfare profile of tariffs and investment taxes.

and the levels of utility rise. When this price elasticity approaches to zero
(say, $\eta = 0.2$), utility can be raised by 5.91% when tourism revenue is 15%
of GDP ($T = 1.5$).

Incorporating the demand for the non-traded good by tourists into a
general equilibrium model, we have examined the welfare effects of tariffs and investment taxes for the economy with inbound tourism. Inbound

tourism converts local non-traded goods into tradable and hence generates a tourism terms-of-trade effect upon the economy. Due to this favorable expenditure-shifting effect on foreign tourists, we have found that increases in import tariffs and investment taxes can actually improve welfare of domestic households when the non-traded and importable goods are substitutes in consumption. This suggests that for a small open economy with tourism, free trade is not the first-best policy. Hence, the impact of the tourism-induced terms of trade should be considered in designing the tariff and investment tax policies for the economy with tourism. Thus, in tourism-dependent economies, import tariffs are useful in raising the welfare of domestic residents as they correct a foreign distortion arising from the movements in the tourism terms of trade.

This proposed mechanism for using tariffs and investment taxes to improve welfare has been numerically verified. This calibrated model has also shown that the optimal tariffs and investment taxes become larger when the economy faces less competition from other tourist destinations.

Chapter 3

TRIMs, Environmental Taxes, and Foreign Investment

3.1 Introduction

There have long been debates about the role of foreign investment in promoting the economic growth of a nation, especially for developing countries. Conventional reasons put forward to explain why foreign capital inflows provide the motivation for foreign firms to circumvent or "jump over" existing tariff barriers have been extensively examined, as has the welfare impact of tariff-jumping foreign investment to host economies. The inflow of foreign capital expands the output of the protected sector, thereby exacerbating the distortion created by tariffs. As a result, welfare declines as long as the imports are capital-intensive. This view suggests that additional policy intervention may be warranted for mitigating the tariff distortion. In this context, Rodrik (1987) has shown that the use of export requirements on foreign investment can actually improve home welfare, because such requirements reduce the output of overproduced commodities. It is notable that the export requirement has become one of the most commonly used trade-related investment measures (TRIMs) by both the developed and the developing nations before the World Trade Organization (WTO) fully implements the elimination of TRIMs.[1]

---

[1] Greenaway (1992) provides detailed discussions on TRIMs, pointing out that TRIMs tend to be trade restrictive and distorting. Also see Trade-Related Aspects of Investment Measures: Preamble, the GATT Puta del Este Declaration in 1994. The existing literature on the effects of TRIMs is still scanty to date. Article 5 of the declaration states that each contracting nation of the General Agreement on Tariffs and Trade (GATT) shall eliminate all TRIMs within certain time periods, depending on its development stage. However, the Declaration does not explicitly forbid the use of export performance requirements. The GATT was replaced by the WTO in 1995, which provides a forum for trade negotiations on reducing and eliminating trade obstacles.

On the other hand, there has been a growing interest about the linkage between trade liberalization, foreign direct investment (FDI), and the environment. Pethig (1976) and Siebert (1977) argue that strict environmental standards diminish the competitive position of a country's pollution-intensive industry. McGuire (1982) further shows that environmental regulations cause firms in a pollution-intensive industry to relocate their plants to countries with lax environmental policies. Copeland and Taylor (1997) find that capital mobility tends to cause world pollution to rise, as pollution-intensive production shifts to countries with fewer environmental regulations.[2]

Although theoretical relationships between the environment and foreign investment are plausible, empirical evidence linking environmental regulations to foreign investment is mixed and inconclusive. Tobey (1990), Grossman and Krueger (1993), and Antweiler (1996) find that stringent environmental controls do not significantly alter production composition and patterns of trade.[3] Levinson (1996) finds that choice of locations by US manufacturers is not responsive to environmental regulations. A few studies, however, indicate that pollution policy may affect producers' output and locational choices. An earlier survey by Epping (1986) reveals that businessmen considered favorable pollution laws important when deciding where to locate new plants. Gray (1997) finds a significant negative connection between new plants and state environmental regulatory measures for US manufacturing firms in the period 1963 to 1987. In view of the mixed empirical results, the issue is yet to be settled, since it remains a major topic of discussion at various workshops on trade and the environment.

In this chapter we focus on the design of jointly optimal policies in the presence of trade restrictions. Instead of analyzing the reforms on tariffs and quotas in a polluted open economy,[4] we examine the individual

---

[2]Markusen (1975) shows that the pollution level may affect the determination of the optimal tariff, and the optimal pollution tax may depend on the terms-of-trade effect. See also Krutilla (1991).

[3]Jaffe *et al.* (1995) also find little evidence that capital has moved in response to environmental regulations. Grossman and Krueger (1993) argue that air quality deteriorates with economic growth in poor countries with per capita income less than $4,000, and air quality can actually improve with economic output when per capita income level reaches $5,000.

[4]See Copeland (1994) for examining welfare-improving policy reforms when imports are subject to tariffs and/or quotas, as well as factors that are internationally mobile or immobile.

and joint effects of TRIMs, that is, export requirements imposed on foreign investment, in addition to environmental taxes. The welfare effects of export requirements have been examined by Rodrik (1987) and Chao and Yu (1994a) under tariffs and quotas, respectively. However, it is of analytical interest to study jointly optimal policies for export requirements in conjunction with other policies on foreign investment, for example, environmental taxes. Given that jointly optimal policies can serve as a benchmark for setting up policy targets in multilateral trade and investment negotiations among Asia-Pacific Economic Cooperation (APEC) and WTO participating countries, identifying such jointly optimal policies becomes a main objective of this chapter. Furthermore, the trade regimes studied are quantitative restrictions, such as quotas and voluntary export restraints (VERs), in addition to tariffs, while only the latter are commonly considered in the literature, with the exception of Copeland (1994).

This chapter is organized as follows. In Section 3.2 we set up a general equilibrium model incorporating export performance and environmental taxes for a polluted, small, open economy. In Section 3.3 we examine the case for tariffs based on the resource allocation and welfare effects of changes resulting from both types of regulation. The case of quantitative restrictions is studied in Section 3.4, where individually and jointly optimal policies are also derived and discussed. Concluding remarks are provided in Section 3.5.

3.2 The Model

In this section, we provide a simple general equilibrium model for a small open economy with measures on foreign investment and environmental taxes. There are two sectors in the host country, the polluting and the non-polluting, producing importable and exportable goods, respectively. The preexisting trade restrictions on imports, plus lax regulation of the environment, induce foreign capital flows into the host country.

To sharpen the analysis, we assume that foreign capital moves into a host country's polluting industries only. The non-polluting sector produces good Y by using labor and land, and the corresponding revenue function is $R(1, L) = \max\{Y : Y = Y(L, \overline{V})\}$, where L and $\overline{V}$ denote the labor and fixed land employed. Choosing good Y as the numeraire, its price equals unity. For simplicity, we suppress the fixed domestic land endowment in the revenue function. By Shephard's lemma, $R_L(= \partial R/\partial L)$ represents the wage rate of workers in sector Y.

The polluting firms produce good X by using domestic labor, domestic capital, $\overline{K}$, and foreign capital, K_f. Suppose the country imports good X with restrictions in the form of either an import tariff, t, or a quantitative control, M.[5] The trade restrictions render the domestic price of good X, denoted by p, higher than its world price, p^*. Note that p is fixed to $p^* + t$ under tariff, whereas p is flexible and endogenously determined under quantitative restriction. To bypass trade restrictions, foreign firms may choose to invest directly in the host country. In this chapter, we consider export-share requirements (ESRs) à la Rodrik (1987) and Chao and Yu (1994c). The requirements specify that a certain percentage, say α, of the output produced by using foreign capital has to be exported at the world price p^*. Therefore, the effective price facing firms in sector X is $p_e = \alpha p^* + (1-\alpha)p$, which is less than p but greater than p^*.

As foreign investment leads to an expansion in the production of polluting sector X, the environment deteriorates with a higher level of pollution, denoted by Z. Following Copeland (1994), pollution is modeled as a byproduct of producing good X in the host country.[6] In this chapter, a pollution tax is imposed on the production of good X to protect the environment. When both export requirements and pollution taxes are in place, the revenue function for sector X is $R^f(P_e, s, \overline{L} - L, K_f) = \max\{p_e X - sZ \colon (X, Z) \in T(\overline{L} - L, \overline{K} + K_f)\}$, where $T(\cdot)$ represents the production technology for good X. Note that $\overline{L}$ denotes the labor endowment in the host country, and hence $\overline{L} - L$ is the labor employed in sector X. The foreign capital, K_f, in addition to domestic fixed capital, $\overline{K}$, is used by the polluting industries. For notational simplicity, $\overline{K}$ is suppressed in the revenue function. Note that s denotes the rate of pollution tax. By Shephard's lemma, the level of pollution, Z, is obtained from:

$$R^f_s(p_e, s, \overline{L} - L, K_f) = -Z, \tag{3.1}$$

where $R^f_s = \partial R^f / \partial s$.

Turning to the factor markets, we assume that labor is perfectly mobile between the two sectors. In equilibrium, the wage rates are identical between the domestic and foreign sectors:

$$R_L(1, L) = R^f_L(p_e, s, \overline{L} - L, K_f), \tag{3.2}$$

where $R^f_L = \partial R^f / \partial(\overline{L} - L)$, denoting the wage rate in sector X.

---

[5]Trade barriers exist in the first place to protect the importable sector.

[6]Alternatively, pollution can be modeled as an input. See Yu and Ingene (1982) and Copeland and Taylor (1997).

We further assume that foreign capital is perfectly mobile internationally. Foreign capital flows in until its rate of return equals the world capital rate, r^*:

$$R_K^f(p_e, s, \overline{L} - L, K_f) = r^*, \tag{3.3}$$

where $R_K^f = \partial R^f / \partial K_f$, and r^* is given according to the small-country assumption.

On the demand-side, goods X and Y are consumed by the amounts of C_X and C_Y. The minimum expenditure needed in the host country to attain a given utility level u, facing the relative price p of good X and the level of pollution Z is: $E(p, 1, Z, u) = \min\{pC_X + C_Y : u(C_X, C_Y, Z) \geq u\}$, with respect to C_X and C_Y. The presence of pollution at the level of Z, which causes damage to consumers, implies the existence of an environmental distortion. Note that $E_p = \partial E / \partial p$, being the consumers' compensated demand for good X, and $E_z = \partial E / \partial Z > 0$, denoting the amount of pollution-caused marginal damage. It is assumed that $E_{pZ} = \partial C_X / \partial Z < 0$, namely, good X and pollution Z are substitutes in consumption; demand for good X declines as the pollution level rises.[7]

In equilibrium, the home country's expenditure equals GDP (production revenues from domestic and foreign sectors) plus domestic retention of rent accrued from trade restrictions and revenue collected from pollution taxes minus the returns paid to foreign capital repatriated to the foreign country:

$$E(p, 1, Z, u) = R(1, L) + R^f(p_e, s, \overline{L} - L, K_f)$$
$$+ (1 - \omega)(p - p^*)M + sZ - r^* K_f, \tag{3.4}$$

where M denotes the imports of good X. Note that ω with values between 0 and 1 is the rent leakage parameter denoting the fraction of the rent from trade restrictions accrued by foreigners.[8] Specifically, $\omega = 0$ in the cases of tariffs and quotas, since all tariff revenues and quota rents are retained at home; $\omega = 1$ with voluntary export restraints (VERs) under which foreigners receive all the rental revenue; and $\omega \in (0, 1)$ with combinations of quotas and VERs. We assume that the revenues collected from trade restrictions

---

[7]Copeland (1994) provides an example to illustrate the case that $E_{pZ} < 0$. Pollution may destroy wilderness and thus lead to a reduction in the demand for hiking shoes. In fact, the conditions for the negative E_{pZ} are $\partial^2 u / \partial C_X \partial Z < 0$, and $\partial^2 u / \partial C_Y \partial Z < 0$. Good X and pollution Z can also be complements in consumption, for example, higher pollution induces greater use of air conditioning or masks.

[8]See Anderson and Neary (1992) for an analysis of fractional rent retention.

and pollution taxes are returned to consumers in a non-distorting lump-sum fashion.

As for the goods market, the imports of good X equal the difference between domestic consumption and its local supply:

$$M = E_p(p, 1, Z, u) - (1 - \alpha)R_p^f(p_e, s, \overline{L} - L, K_f), \qquad (3.5)$$

where, $R_p^f = \partial R^f / \partial p_e = X$, denoting the quantity produced in the home country. With ESRs in effect, only the $(1 - \alpha)$ portion of the output of good X is allowed to be sold domestically. The excess demand for good X will be met by imports. The level of imports, M, in (3.5) is endogenously determined in the case of tariffs, whereas M is fixed in the case of quotas.

The small, capital-importing economy we considered is depicted by (3.1)–(3.5), which determine the values of the five endogenous variables, Z, L, K_f, u, and M or p, as functions of the policy variables, α and s, in the presence of preexisting tariffs, t, or quantitative controls, M.[9] In this chapter, we focus on the effects of policy changes on resource allocation and national welfare; the welfare effect can be obtained by totally differentiating (3.4) to yield:

$$E_u du = -tR_p^f d\alpha + (1 - \omega)t dM - \omega M dp + (s - E_z)dZ, \qquad (3.6)$$

where $E_u = \partial E / \partial u$, expressing the inverse of the marginal utility of income. The right-hand side of the welfare expression in (3.6) captures the four distortions in the economy associated with: (a) ESRs on sector X; (b) trade restrictions such as tariffs or quantitative controls; (c) the consequent rent leakage ω; and (d) environmental externality regarding pollution taxes and the marginal social damage of pollution.

Equation (3.6) is revealing about the first-best optimum. For a small open economy with the environmental externality, the first-best policy is free trade in goods and factors ($p = p^*$ and $t = 0$), along with a Pigouvian tax ($s = E_Z$) on pollution. Free trade renders $\alpha = 0$, since foreign capital would not flow in. This is a well-known result where the Pigouvian tax fully internalizes the marginal damage from pollution in the absence of other distortions (i.e., free trade) in the economy.

The first-best setting of free trade, nevertheless, remains a goal to be achieved by virtually every nation on earth. Although average tariff rates have been substantially reduced through the GATT and WTO negotiations in the past years, the use of non-tariff barriers, especially quantitative

---

[9] ω is treated as a parameter, which is not a policy of concern in this chapter.

restrictions, has become widespread.[10] This chapter sets out to address the following question: What would be the welfare effects of investment-related measures and environmental taxes in a second-best environment with irremovable trade restrictions? And what would be the appropriate policy prescriptions for various trade regimes?

3.3 Tariff Restrictions

Consider, first, that trade is restricted by import tariffs. Two scenarios will be examined: (a) investment measures or environmental taxes are applied in isolation; (b) both regulations are adopted simultaneously.

Under tariffs, the domestic price, p, is fixed by $p^* + t$, and the home country receives all the tariff revenue (i.e., $\omega = 0$). The change in welfare in (3.6) becomes

$$E_u du = -tR_p^f d\alpha + tdM + (s - E_Z)dZ. \tag{3.7}$$

To evaluate (3.7), the changes in imports can be obtained by differentiating (3.5):

$$dM = R_p^f d\alpha - (1 - \alpha)[R_{pK}^f dK_f - R_{pL}^f dL] + E_{pZ}dZ + E_{pu}du, \tag{3.8}$$

where $R_{pK}^f = \partial X/\partial K_f$ and $R_{pL}^f = \partial X/\partial(\overline{L} - L)$. It is noted that $X = R_p^f$ and hence $dX = R_{pK}^f dK_f - R_{pL}^f dL$, denoting the changes in the production of good X caused by changes in factor usages in sector X.[11] In addition, recall that $E_{pZ} < 0$ by assumption. The first two terms in (3.8) denote the local supply effect on imports, while the last two terms represent the demand effect through the pollution and income changes. When we substitute (3.8) into (3.7), the welfare expression can be rewritten as

$$(E_u - tE_{pu})du = -t(1 - \alpha)dX + tE_{pZ}dZ + (s - E_Z)dZ, \tag{3.9}$$

where the term in the parentheses on the left-hand side is positive by the normality assumption, and the inverse of the term is called the tariff multiplier.[12]

---

[10]Neary (1995) provides a detailed account.

[11]Because the production of good X depends directly on labor $(\overline{L} - L)$ and capital (K_f), we have $R_{pp}^f = 0$ and $R_{ps}^f = 0$ in deriving (3.8). See Rodrik (1987) for a related explanation.

[12]Jones (1969) provides an earlier analysis involving the tariff multiplier, which is also referred to as shadow prices. See Chao and Yu (1995) for an example.

The welfare expression in (3.9) clearly depends on the changes in the production of good X, as well as the changes in the emission of pollution Z. As pointed out by Rodrik (1987), the larger the output of the importable good X, the greater the trade distortion in the presence of irremovable tariffs. An expansion of the importable sector lowers welfare. This is indicated by the first term on the right-hand side of (3.9). Note that the coefficient of this term depends on the value of $1 - \alpha$. Thus, ESRs could be used as an investment measure to mitigate the distortion created by tariffs. In addition, the preexisting tariff lowers the consumption of good X from its optimal level. This consumption distortion would be further exacerbated by an increase in the level of pollution, since $E_{pZ} < 0$, thereby further worsening welfare, as expressed by the second term in (3.9). Nevertheless, higher pollution has one positive welfare effect, an increase in revenue resulting from the pollution taxes, as shown in the last term of (3.9).

3.3.1 *Optimal export-share requirements*

The welfare effect of ESRs in isolation can be deduced from (3.9). The effect hinges upon the resource allocation effect of changes in the policy measure. Basically, an increase in the ESR on the goods made by sector X lowers the effective price of good X, thereby causing a reduction in the production of good X and hence a fall in the emission of pollution Z; that is $\partial X/\partial \alpha < 0$ and $\partial Z/\partial \alpha < 0$. Detailed derivations are provided in Appendix A.1.

By (3.9), the welfare effect of the changes in the ESRs is:

$$(E_u - tE_{pu}) \left(\frac{du}{d\alpha} \right)$$

$$= -t(1 - \alpha) \left(\frac{\partial X}{\partial \alpha} \right) + [s - (E_Z - tE_{pZ})] \left(\frac{\partial Z}{\partial \alpha} \right). \qquad (3.10)$$

As α increases, the output of good X decreases, thereby partially offsetting the existing tariff-inflicted production distortion. The distortion-mitigating effect improves welfare. In the meantime, the resulting reduction in pollution generates dual effects on welfare: a fall in the pollution-tax revenue and a decrease in environmental damage. The former effect is welfare reducing, while the latter is welfare improving. Thus, the welfare effect of export requirements is, in general, indeterminate, depending particularly on the magnitude of the pollution tax. Consider the case of low pollution taxes, that is, $s < E_Z - tE_{pZ}$. An increase in the ESRs is always welfare improving, and hence its optimal level, denoted by α°, is 1. On the contrary, for a large value of s, the loss in tax revenue may be serious enough to lower welfare. Specifically, when $s > s_c$, we have $du/d\alpha < 0$, where $s_c = E_Z - tE_{pZ} + t(1 - \alpha)(\partial X/\partial \alpha)/(\partial Z/\partial \alpha)$. This implies that the optimal export share, α^o, is 0, so that all goods X produced by sector X are for domestic consumption. For $E_Z - tE_{pZ} < s < s_c$, however, the optimal α has a value between 0 and 1 and is derived by setting $du/d\alpha = 0$ in (3.10):

$$\alpha^o = 1 + (E_Z - tE_{pZ})\frac{\left(\frac{\partial Z}{\partial \alpha}\right)}{t\left(\frac{\partial X}{\partial \alpha}\right)} - \left[\frac{\left(\frac{\partial Z}{\partial \alpha}\right)}{t\left(\frac{\partial X}{\partial \alpha}\right)}\right]s. \tag{3.11}$$

The optimal export share, α^o, clearly depends upon the level of s for a given t. Since $\partial Z/\partial \alpha < 0$ and $\partial X/\partial \alpha < 0$, the relation between α^o and s is monotonically decreasing and can be plotted as the schedule α^o in Figure 3.1. This schedule shows that there is a trade-off between the two policies for attaining a maximum welfare level. Namely, the higher the pollution tax, the lower the export share, and vice versa.

Following the technique developed by Neary (1993b, 1995), we substitute α^o of (3.11) into (3.10) to yield the welfare effect of a change in α:

$$(E_u - tE_{pu})\left(\frac{du}{d\alpha}\right) = t\left(\frac{\partial X}{\partial \alpha}\right)(\alpha - \alpha^o). \tag{3.12}$$

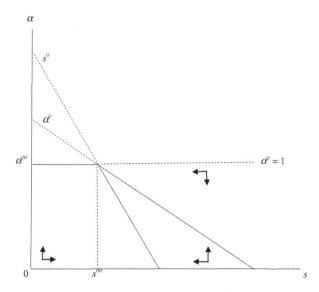

Figure 3.1 Optimal policies under tariffs.

Given $\partial X/\partial \alpha < 0$, we have $du/d\alpha > (<)0$, since $\alpha < (>)\alpha^o$. That is, if α is not equal to α^o initially, movements in α toward α^o lead to welfare increases. This implies that a rise (fall) in α will improve welfare for any given s when α lies below (above) α^o. This result has policy implications for a country facing negotiations over trade measures with APEC and WTO. The movements in α toward α^o for achieving higher welfare are denoted by vertical arrows in Figure 3.1. Since $\alpha \in [0,1]$, the α^o schedule consists of three segments: a horizontal part with $\alpha^o = 1$, followed by a downward-sloping line, and then again a horizontal part with $\alpha^o = 0$.

3.3.2 *Optimal environmental taxes*

Let us turn to the welfare effect of changes in environmental protection in terms of pollution taxes. The output effect of pollution taxes resembles that of ESRs. An increase in pollution taxes lowers the net producers' prices of good X, thereby causing a fall in the production of good X and hence a fall in the emission of pollution Z; that is, $\partial X/\partial s < 0$ and $\partial Z/\partial s < 0$.

By using (3.9), the welfare effect of the changes in pollution taxes is

$$
(E_u - tE_{pu})\left(\frac{du}{ds}\right) = -t(1-\alpha)\left(\frac{\partial X}{\partial s}\right) + [s - (E_Z - tE_{pZ})]\left(\frac{\partial Z}{\partial s}\right),
$$
(3.13)

where the first term on the right-hand side of (3.13) is positive, and the sign of the second term is indeterminate, depending on the value of s. As an increase in pollution taxes leads to a contraction of the protected good X, pollution taxes, similar to ESRs, yield a "double dividend" in that the taxes not only create a cleaner environment but also mitigate the tariff-induced production distortion.[13]

In the presence of a preexisting tariff, the (third-best) optimal choice of s, s^o, for any given ESR is obtained by setting $du/ds = 0$ in (3.13):

$$
s^o = E_Z - tE_{pZ} + t\frac{\left(\frac{\partial X}{\partial s}\right)}{\left(\frac{\partial Z}{\partial s}\right)} - \left[\frac{t\left(\frac{\partial X}{\partial s}\right)}{\left(\frac{\partial Z}{\partial s}\right)}\right]\alpha,
$$
(3.14)

which is positive, since $\alpha \leq 1$. Given the trade distortion, there is a third-best optimal pollution tax and the effect of an increase in pollution depends on whether or not the initial pollution tax is too high or too low.

---

[13]See a related discussion in Bovenberg and de Mooij (1994).

It is clear from (3.14) that s^o is dependent upon α. Since $\partial X/\partial s < 0$ and $\partial Z/\partial s < 0$, s^o is negatively related to α, as illustrated by the s^o schedule with a positive intercept in Figure 3.1. For a given α, an adjustment in s toward s^o improves welfare. This can be deduced by substituting (3.14) into (3.13):

$$(E_u - tE_{pu})\left(\frac{du}{ds}\right) = \left(\frac{\partial Z}{\partial s}\right)(s - s^o). \qquad (3.15)$$

Since $\partial Z/\partial s < 0$, we have $du/ds > (<)0$, since $s < (>)s^o$. This indicates the direction in which pollution taxes should be adjusted in order to move the economy closer to the third-best optimum. If $s > s^o$, then s should be reduced; if $s < s^o$, it should be increased. The desired adjustments in s are shown by the horizontal arrows in Figure 3.1.

3.3.3   Jointly optimal investment measures and environmental taxes

We are now ready to examine the welfare effect of simultaneous changes in both policies. By combining (3.12) and (3.15), we obtain:

$$(E_u - tE_{pu})du = t\left(\frac{\partial X}{\partial \alpha}\right)(\alpha - \alpha^o)d\alpha + \left(\frac{\partial Z}{\partial s}\right)(s - s^o)ds. \qquad (3.16)$$

In the presence of the existing tariff, the relationship between α^o and s^o is of interest because it sheds light on the second-best optimum. By solving (3.11) and (3.14) simultaneously, we obtain the jointly optimal s and α, expressed by:

$$s^{oo} = E_z - tE_{pZ}, \qquad (3.17)$$

$$\alpha^{oo} = 1. \qquad (3.18)$$

Generally, E_{pZ} can take any sign. The above result is stated as a proposition.

Proposition 3.1 *When imports are subject to irremovable tariffs, ESR measures and environmental taxes can be applied jointly to achieve the second-best optimum. If the goods protected and pollution are substitutes (complements) in consumption, the pollution tax rate has to be set to exceed (fall short of) the Pigouvian tax rate, and the ESR on foreign firms has to be set at 100%.*

These results are depicted in Figure 3.1, where the iso-welfare contours can be represented by a map of half-ellipses (not shown) and the jointly optimal α^{oo} and s^{oo} are given by the intersection of the α^o and s^o schedules. This second-best optimum can be explained as follows. Facing irremovable tariffs, foreign capital moves into a host country, resulting in an expansion of the protected sector and hence a worsening welfare. A strict investment measure, such as 100% export requirement, works to offset the detrimental overproduction effect caused by the tariff. The 100% export requirement in the current framework does not fully discourage foreign investment, so long as there exist relatively lax environmental regulations. Furthermore, a high pollution tax leads to a lower level of pollution Z, thereby raising the consumption of good X (assuming $E_{pZ} < 0$ to alleviate the tariff-inflicted consumption distortion). A higher pollution tax provides not only a cleaner environment but also a larger tax revenue. Both counts are welfare improving.[14]

3.4   Quantitative Restrictions

Under quantitative restrictions, the volume of the import of good X is fixed (i.e., $dM = 0$, while its price, p, is determined in the goods market). In contrast to the tariff case, the home country may receive only partial rent (i.e., $\omega \in [0,1]$) generated from restricting imports. Therefore, the welfare effect in (3.6) becomes:

$$E_u du = -(p - p^*)R_p^f d\alpha - \omega M dp + (s - E_Z)dZ, \qquad (3.19)$$

where the second term represents the rent loss from the rise in the domestic price of good X.

By utilizing the equilibrium condition of the goods market in (3.5), we obtain the changes in p:

$$E_{pp}dp = -R_p^f d\alpha + (1 - \alpha)dX - E_{pu}du - E_{pZ}dZ, \qquad (3.20)$$

where $E_{pp} = \partial C_X/\partial p < 0$ and $E_{pu} = \partial C_X/\partial u > 0$. The first two terms on the right-hand side of (3.20) stand for the supply effect, arising from the changes in export shares and the domestic production of good X. The last

---

[14]In this chapter, there are two incentives for FDI: tariff-jumping and pollution shifting. Here, we assume that the receiving country's environmental regulation is less stringent than the originating nation.

two terms correspond to the demand effect, stemming from both the income response to the welfare change and the shift in environmental quality.

Note that as p is endogenous under quantitative restrictions, the changes in X and Z in (3.19) and (3.20) depend on p, in addition to α and s. Thus, unlike the earlier case of tariffs, a two-stage procedure is warranted to solve for the impacts of investment measures and environmental taxes on welfare. In the first stage, we need to solve for the price-induced resource allocation effect. This can be done by using (3.1)–(3.3) to obtain $\partial X/\partial p > 0$ and $\partial Z/\partial p > 0$ (see Appendix). In the second stage, we use (3.19) and (3.20) to obtain the price and welfare effects.

Before proceeding, it may be worthwhile to explore the issue of equivalence between tariffs and quotas. Given α and s, the welfare effect of changes in tariffs or quotas can be obtained from (3.6) as $E_u\,du = (p - p^*)dM + (s - E_Z)dZ$. Consider a tariff that yields the same level of imports as a quota (i.e., dM is the same under both the tariff and the quota; so is dp by [3.20]). This gives $E_u(du/dM) = (p - p^*) + (s - E_Z)(dZ/dp)(dp/dM)$, implying that tariffs and quotas are equivalent in the context of other given policies. Assuming competitive foreign supply and perfect competition in domestic production, the equivalence should prevail.

Nevertheless, when the initial tariff and quota are fixed, the welfare effects of changes in other policies, such as ESRs or environmental taxes, are not identical under the tariff and quota regimes. The difference arises because domestic prices are unaffected in the case of tariffs, whereas the prices are induced to change in the presence of quotas, triggering a further resource allocation effect and an additional impact on welfare. This scenario will be analyzed in detail in subsequent sections.

3.4.1 *Optimal environmental taxes*

We begin by examining the welfare effect of pollution taxes. For a given ESR, substituting dp from (3.20) into (3.19) yields:

$$D\left(\frac{du}{ds}\right) = -\omega M\left[E_{pZ}\left(\frac{\partial Z}{\partial s}\right) - (1 - \alpha)\left(\frac{\partial X}{\partial s}\right)\right]$$

$$-(s - E_Z)\left[A(1 - \alpha) + E_{pp}\left(\frac{\partial Z}{\partial s}\right)\right], \qquad (3.21)$$

where $D = -E_u[E_{pp}-(1-\alpha)(\partial X/\partial p)+E_{pZ}(\partial Z/\partial p)]-E_{pu}(s-E_Z)(\partial Z/\partial p)$, which is positive by the stability condition as shown in the Appendix, and

$A = (\partial Z/\partial p)(\partial X/\partial s) - (\partial X/\partial p)(\partial Z/\partial s)$, capturing the output effect of a pollution tax via price changes.[15]

The fist bracketed term on the right-hand side of (3.21) stands for the rent-leakage effect, which lowers welfare, owing to the higher rent captured by the foreign country, since a pollution tax raises the price of good X. The second term represents the tax effect on the environmental distortion. The higher tax on pollution erodes the tax base (i.e., $\partial Z/\partial s < 0$). This may lower tax revenue and reduce the pollution-inflicted social damage. Apparently, the net effect depends on the relative magnitudes of s and E_Z. The indeterminacy of du/ds in (3.21) implies the existence of a non-zero optimal pollution tax rate (s^o), which can be solved by letting $du/da = 0$ as

$$s^o = E_z - \omega M \frac{\left[E_{pz}\left(\frac{\partial Z}{\partial s}\right) - (1-\alpha)\left(\frac{\partial X}{\partial s}\right)\right]}{\left[E_{pp}\left(\frac{\partial Z}{\partial s}\right) + A(1-\alpha)\right]}. \qquad (3.22)$$

Note that ω represents the quota rent leakage. If the home country gets all the quota revenue, then $s^o = E_Z$, the pollution tax simply internalizes the marginal social damage (see Copeland, 1994). With quota rent leakage, $s^o < E_Z$, since the second term on the right-hand side is negative. The optimal pollution tax is lower than its marginal social damage. This can be explained as follows. The existing quantitative control of imports distorts the domestic market by pushing up the price of goods. The pollution taxes exacerbate the price distortion by further raising the domestic price of goods.[16] Thus, the optimal pollution tax rate lies below the Pigouvian tax.

Substituting (3.22) into (3.21), we obtain:

$$D(du) = -\left[A(1-\alpha) + E_{pp}\left(\frac{\partial Z}{\partial s}\right)\right](s - s^o)ds. \qquad (3.23)$$

This implies that when $s > (<)s^o$ initially, the pollution tax should be set lower (higher) than s^o, since a higher pollution tax diminishes (raises) welfare.

---

[15]Using the comparative statics results in the Appendix, we can show that $(\partial Z/\partial p)(\partial X/\partial s) - (\partial X/\partial p)(\partial Z/\partial s) = (1-\alpha)R_{LL}R_{KK}^f(R_{sL}^f R_{pK}^f - R_{sK}^f R_{pL}^f)^2/D^2$. Note that in deriving (3.21), we have used $dX = (\partial X/\partial p)dp + (\partial X/\partial s)ds$ and $dZ = (\partial Z/\partial p)dp + (\partial Z/\partial s)ds$.

[16]This can be shown from (3.19), evaluated at s^o (i.e., $du/ds = 0$) : $dp/ds = [(1-\alpha) (\partial X/\partial s) - E_{pZ}(\partial Z/\partial s)]/[E_{pp} - (1-\alpha)(\partial X/\partial p) - E_{pZ}(\partial Z/\partial p)]$, which is positive.

3.4.2   *Optimal export-share requirements*

The welfare effect of changes in ESRs for a given pollution tax can be obtained by solving (3.19) and (3.20) as:

$$D\left(\frac{du}{d\alpha}\right) = -R_p^f B\left(\frac{dp}{d\alpha}\right) + \omega M\left[(1-\alpha)\left(\frac{\partial X}{\partial \alpha}\right) - E_{pZ}\left(\frac{\partial Z}{\partial \alpha}\right)\right]$$

$$-(s - E_Z)E_{pp}\left(\frac{\partial Z}{\partial \alpha}\right), \tag{3.24}$$

where $B = -t[E_{pp} - (1-\alpha)(\partial X/\partial p) + E_{pZ}(\partial Z/\partial p)] + \omega M - (s - E_Z)(\partial Z/\partial p)$. The sign of B can be inferred from the optimum level of imports, M°. Using (3.19) and (3.20), we obtain:

$$D\left(\frac{du}{dM}\right) = -(1-\omega)t\left[E_{pp} - (1-\alpha)\left(\frac{\partial X}{\partial p}\right) - E_{pZ}\left(\frac{\partial Z}{\partial p}\right)\right]$$

$$+ \omega M - (s - E_Z)\left(\frac{\partial Z}{\partial p}\right)$$

$$= B + \omega t\left[E_{pp} - (1-\alpha)\left(\frac{\partial X}{\partial p}\right) + E_{pZ}\left(\frac{\partial Z}{\partial p}\right)\right]. \tag{3.25}$$

M° can be obtained by letting $du/dM = 0$ in (3.25).[17] Here, we consider the meaningful case that quantitative control on imports in place is restrictive relative to the optimal level, that is, $M < M^\circ$, so that $du/dM > 0$. This requires that $B > 0$, since the second term in (3.25) is negative.

The interpretation of (3.24), which has three terms on the right-hand side, is as follows. The first term expresses the direct revenue loss as a consequence of raising the ESRs. The second term captures the rent loss from the rise in the prices of good X. The third term stands for the erosion of the tax base and its impact on tax revenue.

The welfare effect of ESRs in (3.24) nevertheless depends on the initial values of s. If initially $s > E_Z$, the erosion of the tax base, and hence the tax revenue loss, lowers welfare in addition to the first two detrimental effects

---

[17]The second-order condition of maximization requires $d^2u/dM^2 = \{\omega - (1-\omega)(dp/dM)\{[E_{pp} - (1-\alpha)(\partial X/\partial p) + E_{pZ}(\partial Z/\partial p)] + (\partial Z/\partial p)[E_{pZ}(dp/dM) + E_{ZZ}(dZ/dM)]\}/D < 0$, by ignoring the higher-order terms. This holds when $\omega > (dp/dM)[E_{pp} - (1-\alpha)(\partial X/\partial p)] - E_{ZZ}(\partial Z/\partial p)(dZ/dM)]/H$, where $H = 1 + (dp/dM)\{[E_{pp} - (1-\alpha)(\partial X/\partial p) + E_{pZ}(\partial Z/\partial p)] > 0$. Here, $dp/dM < 0$ and $dZ/dM = (\partial Z/\partial p)(dp/dM) < 0$. The values of ω are thus dependent on $E_{ZZ} : \omega > 0$ when $E_{ZZ} > 0$, and $\omega \geq 0$ when $E_{ZZ} < 0$. Therefore, welfare maximization under quotas (i.e., $\omega = 0$) is possible when $E_{ZZ} < 0$.

in (3.24). Hence, the optimal ESR, α^o, is 0. On the other hand, if $s < E_Z$, we have $du/d\alpha \gtrless 0$, implying:[18]

$$\alpha^o \in (0,1]. \tag{3.26}$$

This can be interpreted as follows. The lower the pollution level, the higher the ESR. The X sector will accrue more rent, however, owing to the higher prices of good X, evaluated at the level of α^o (i.e., $du/d\alpha = 0$). This can be seen from:

$$\frac{dp}{d\alpha} = \frac{-R_p^f + (1-\alpha)\left(\frac{\partial X}{\partial \alpha}\right) - E_{pZ}\left(\frac{\partial Z}{\partial \alpha}\right)}{E_{pp} - (1-\alpha)\left(\frac{\partial X}{\partial p}\right) + E_{pZ}\left(\frac{\partial Z}{\partial \alpha}\right)}, \tag{3.27}$$

which is positive. Hence, the optimal ESR lies between 0 and 1.[19]

3.4.3 *Jointly optimal export shares and environmental taxes*

We now consider the jointly optimal policies of ESRs and environmental taxes in the presence of quantitative restrictions. Since with rent leakage $s^o < E_Z$ in (3.22), and by using (3.26), we have the second-best optimal policies for ESRs and pollution taxes, denoted by α^{oo} and s^{oo}, as

$$\alpha^{oo} \in (0,1), \tag{3.28}$$

$$s^{oo} = \frac{E_Z - \omega M\left[E_{pZ}\left(\frac{\partial Z}{\partial s}\right) - (1-\alpha^{oo})\left(\frac{\partial x}{\partial s}\right)\right]}{\left[E_{pp}\left(\frac{\partial Z}{\partial s}\right) + A(1-\alpha^{oo})\right]}. \tag{3.29}$$

Note that $s^{oo} < E_Z$, reflecting that $M < M^o$ in (3.25). That is, when strict quantitative restrictions are in place, the distorted domestic prices of good X are relatively high.

To avoid exacerbating the existing distortion, the optimal pollution tax rate should be set lower than its Pigouvian rate. Concurrently, an ESR short of 100% can reduce the loss of rent to foreigners. The following proposition is immediate.

Proposition 3.2 *In the presence of strict quantitative restrictions, the second-best policies involve a smaller rate of pollution tax relative to its Pigouvian rate and a less than 100% ESR.*

---

[18] When $s < E_Z - \{R_p^f B - \omega M[(1-\alpha)(\partial X/\partial \alpha) - E_{pZ}(\partial Z/\partial \alpha)]\}/E_{pp}(\partial Z/\partial \alpha)$, we have $\alpha^o = 1$.

[19] The explicit expression for α^o is quite complicated.

Consider now a special type of quantitative restriction in the form of import quotas, for which all quota rents are retained at home; that is, $\omega = 0$. Using (3.29), we have:

$$s^{oo} = E_Z. \tag{3.30}$$

The optimal pollution tax here is exactly equal to the Pigouvian rate. This result can be understood by inspecting (3.19) and (3.20):

$$p^{oo} - p^* = -\frac{(s - E_Z)\left(\frac{\partial Z}{\partial p}\right)}{\left[E_{pp} - (1 - \alpha)\left(\frac{\partial X}{\partial p}\right) + E_{pZ}\left(\frac{\partial Z}{\partial p}\right)\right]}, \tag{3.31}$$

which implies that $p^{oo} = p^*$ and that the pollution tax would not affect the price of good X, thereby exerting no impact on the quota distortion. Hence, the optimal pollution tax equals the Pigouvian rate.

Substituting $\omega = 0$ and (3.30) into (3.24), we obtain

$$E_u\left(\frac{du}{d\alpha}\right) = -tR_p^f, \tag{3.32}$$

which is always negative. This implies that $\alpha^{oo} = 0$; the optimal policy here is to eliminate ESRs. This result extends the finding in Chao and Yu (1994a) to the case of environmental pollution. It is worthwhile to note that earlier Dei (1985a) provided an intuition for a somewhat different quota setting. Considering the case in which the domestic rate of capital return exceeds the world given rate (i.e., $r > r^*$ for an exogenous capital inflow), Dei found that additional foreign capital inflow is welfare improving, owing to lower payments for foreign capital via the fall in r. In the present framework, however, in which the domestic rate on capital return is fixed by the world rate ($r = r^*$) under internationally perfect mobility of capital, the channel for transmitting the policy effect on the return of foreign capital is cut off. Nevertheless, increasing ESRs in the presence of quotas leads to higher domestic prices for good X, thereby giving rise to the negative welfare effect via the over-production of the distorted sector. Hence, the policy is undesirable.[20] The following proposition is immediate.

Proposition 3.3 *When import quotas are in place, the optimal policies consist of adopting a pollution tax at a rate equal to the marginal damage of pollution coupled with a zero ESR.*

---

[20]See a relevant discussion in Chao and Yu (1994), which, however, deals only with export requirements under quotas.

3.5   Concluding Remarks

We have considered several optimal policy mixes of export performance
and environmental taxes affecting the inflow of foreign capital when trade
restrictions exist initially in the host country. It has been shown that the
optimal policy mix depends crucially on the types of trade restrictions.
Under import tariffs, strict policies for a pollution tax (i.e., higher than
its Pigouvian rate) and full export requirements (i.e., 100%) can alleviate
the consumption and production distortions created by tariffs. In contrast,
foreign investment can improve welfare when imports are subject to quotas.
The optimal investment policy involves a zero export requirement. This
leads to an equilibrium equivalent to one attainable by using the policy
mix of free trade in goods, coupled with Pigouvian taxes for internalizing
the environmental externality. When some quota rents leak to foreigners,
as in the case of VERs, however, optimal policies involve a laxer pollution
tax (i.e., lower than the Pigouvian rate), resulting in lower goods prices and
less rent paid to foreigners. Moreover, it is desirable for a host country to
impose appropriate ESRs to deter the inflow of foreign capital.

In the present framework, we have demonstrated an equivalence in the
effects of tariffs versus quotas. Nevertheless, the welfare effects for changes
in other policies, in the presence of a given tariff or quota, are not identical.
Furthermore, the present simple framework does not seem able to identify
and compare different second-best optimal levels of welfare attainable with
appropriate policy measures under tariffs and quotas. This line of inquiry,
perhaps with the aid of simulation, appears to be a worthwhile topic for
future research.

In this chapter, it is assumed that the polluting sector is the import-
competing sector, so that ESRs are relevant. If the polluting sector is
the exportable sector, however, the pollution tax should be set below its
Pigouvian level to mitigate the trade distortion.

Appendix

A.1   *Comparative statics*

Totally differentiating (3.2) and (3.3) yields:

$$(R_{LL}^f + R_{LL})dL - R_{LK}^f dK_f = -tR_{pL}^f d\alpha + R_{sL}^f ds + (1 - \alpha)R_{pL}^f dp$$

$$-R_{LK}^f dL - R_{KK}^f dK_f = tR_{pK}^f d\alpha - R_{sK}^f ds - (1 - \alpha)R_{pK}^f dp,$$

where $R^f_{LL} < 0$, $R^f_{KK} < 0$, $R^f_{LK} > 0$, $R^f_{pL} > 0$, $R^f_{pK} > 0$, $R^f_{sL} > 0$ and $R^f_{sK} < 0$. There, resource allocation effects of changes in α, s, and p can be solved, as follows:

$$\frac{\partial L}{\partial \alpha} = \frac{-t(R^f_{pL}R^f_{KK} - R^f_{pK}R^f_{LK})}{\Delta} > 0$$

$$\frac{\partial K_f}{\partial \alpha} = \frac{-t[R^f_p(R_{LL} + R^f_{LL}) + R^f_{pL}R^f_{LK})]}{\Delta} < 0$$

$$\frac{\partial L}{\partial s} = \frac{[R^f_{sL}R^f_{KK} - R^f_{sK}R^f_{LK})]}{\Delta} > 0$$

$$\frac{\partial K_f}{\partial s} = \frac{[R^f_{sL}R^f_{LK} - R^f_{sK}(R^f_{LL} + R^d_{LL})]}{\Delta} < 0$$

$$\frac{\partial L}{\partial p} = \frac{(1 - \alpha)[(R^f_{pL}(R^f_{KK} + R^f_{LK}R^f_{pK})]}{\Delta} < 0$$

$$\frac{\partial K_f}{\partial p} = -\frac{(1 - \alpha)[(R^f_{pK}(R^f_{LL} + R_{LL}) - R^f_{pL}R^f_{LK})]}{\Delta} > 0,$$

where $\Delta = R_{LL}R^f_{KK} + [R^f_{LL}R^f_{KK} - (R^f_{LK})^2] > 0$. Note that $R^f_{LL}R^f_{KK} - (R^f_{LK})^2 = 0$, owing to constant returns to scale technology in producing good X.

Using the results that $R^f_p = X$ and $R^f_s = -Z$, we can obtain:

$$\frac{\partial X}{\partial \alpha} = -R^f_{pL}\left(\frac{\partial L}{\partial \alpha}\right) + R^f_{pK}\left(\frac{\partial K_f}{\partial \alpha}\right) < 0$$

$$\frac{\partial Z}{\partial \alpha} = R^f_{sL}\left(\frac{\partial L}{\partial \alpha}\right) - R^f_{sK}\left(\frac{\partial K_f}{\partial \alpha}\right) < 0$$

$$\frac{\partial X}{\partial s} = -R^f_{pL}\left(\frac{\partial L}{\partial s}\right) + R^f_{pK}\left(\frac{\partial K_f}{\partial s}\right) < 0$$

$$\frac{\partial Z}{\partial s} = R^f_{sL}\left(\frac{\partial L}{\partial s}\right) - R^f_{sK}\left(\frac{\partial K_f}{\partial s}\right) < 0$$

$$\frac{\partial X}{\partial p} = -R^f_{pL}\left(\frac{\partial L}{\partial p}\right) + R^f_{pK}\left(\frac{\partial K_f}{\partial p}\right) > 0$$

$$\frac{\partial Z}{\partial p} = R^f_{sL}\left(\frac{\partial L}{\partial p}\right) - R^f_{sK}\left(\frac{\partial K_f}{\partial p}\right) > 0.$$

A.2   The tariff case

For comparing the intercepts and slopes of the s^o schedule and the α^o schedule, we rewrite the s^o schedule in (3.14) as:

$$\alpha = 1 + (E_Z - tE_{pZ})\frac{\left(\frac{\partial Z}{\partial s}\right)}{t\left(\frac{\partial X}{\partial s}\right)} - \left[\frac{\left(\frac{\partial Z}{\partial \alpha}\right)}{t\left(\frac{\partial X}{\partial \alpha}\right)}\right]s^o,$$

where the first two terms represent the intercept of the s^o schedule in the space of (s, α), as illustrated in Figure 3.1. The s^o schedule has a larger intercept than the α^o schedule, since:

$$(E_Z - tE_{pZ})\left[\frac{\left(\frac{\partial Z}{\partial s}\right)}{t\left(\frac{\partial X}{\partial s}\right)} - \frac{\left(\frac{\partial Z}{\partial \alpha}\right)}{t\left(\frac{\partial X}{\partial \alpha}\right)}\right]$$

$$= (E_Z - tE_{pZ})\frac{\left[\left(\frac{\partial X}{\partial \alpha}\right)\left(\frac{\partial Z}{\partial s}\right) - \left(\frac{\partial X}{\partial s}\right)\left(\frac{\partial Z}{\partial \alpha}\right)\right]}{t\left(\frac{\partial X}{\partial \alpha}\right)\left(\frac{\partial X}{\partial s}\right)}$$

$$= \frac{t(E_z - tE_{pZ})R_{LL}R_{KK}^f(R_{sL}^f R_{pK}^f - R_{sK}^f R_{pL}^f)^2}{\Delta} > 0.$$

Similarly, we can show that the s^o schedule is steeper than the α^o schedule, as follows:

$$\left.\frac{d\alpha}{dS}\right|_s - \left.\frac{d\alpha}{dS}\right|_\alpha = \frac{\left[\left(\frac{\partial X}{\partial s}\right)\left(\frac{\partial Z}{\partial \alpha}\right) - \left(\frac{\partial X}{\partial \alpha}\right)\left(\frac{\partial Z}{\partial \alpha}\right)\right]}{t\left(\frac{\partial X}{\partial \alpha}\right)\left(\frac{\partial X}{\partial s}\right)}$$

$$= -\frac{tR_{LL}R_{KK}^f(R_{sL}^f R_{pK}^f - R_{sK}^f R_{pL}^f)^2}{\Delta}.$$

A.3   Quantitative restrictions

Following Dei (1985b), the adjustment process for the goods market is $\dot{P} = aQ(p)$, where the dot is the time derivative, a is a positive constant, and $Q = E_p(p, 1, Z, u) - (1 - \alpha)R_p^f(P_e, s, \overline{L} - L, K^f) - M$ is the excess demand for good X. From (3.4), we can obtain that u is a function of p for a given α and s. By keeping M constant, we can take a linear approximation of the above adjustment process around the equilibrium point p^e as $\dot{P} = a(dQ/dp)(p - p^e)$. Following (3.19) and (3.20), we obtain $dp/dZ = p/D$. Hence, $dQ/dp < 0$ requires $D < 0$.

PART II
Export-Share Requirements

Chapter 4

Export-Share Requirements and Quota Protection

4.1 Introduction

Prior to the World Trade Organization (WTO) implementation of Agreements on phasing out trade-related investment measures (TRIMs), the policy of export-share requirements (ESRs) has been adopted by many countries, notably Mexico and Venezuela on their automobile industries in the 1980s,[1] and China on its garment, electronics, toy, and automobile sectors.[2] The original purpose of the policy, which requires foreign-owned multinational firms to export a certain fraction of their outputs, is to restrict the monopolistic power of global firms as well as to protect the domestic importable sectors. The policies were used to improve trade balances for host countries (Herander and Thomas, 1986) or to mitigate welfare losses caused by foreign inflows (Rodrik, 1987).

In this chapter we focus on the welfare issue of ESRs. The effects of policy-induced foreign capital inflows are now well known in the literature. A main motive for multinational firms to invest in foreign countries is to extend their product markets to host countries by circumventing trade

---

[1]See Herander and Thomas (1986) and Rodrik (1987) for related discussions.

[2]Article 9 of China's Joint-Venture Law states that "a joint venture is encouraged to market its product outside China." Export-share ratios are negotiated between Chinese government and foreign firms and are written into formal contractual documents. Personal interviews with a dozen foreign investors in China confirm that China's use of export-share policy is in fact extensive. While China welcomes foreign investment, virtually all foreign firms are subject to varying degrees of export performance requirements. Foreign enterprises in China producing automobiles, garments, electronics, and toys face stiff domestic competition. Hence, the use of the policy by China appears to be motivated by three factors: (a) protecting the domestic importable sectors; (b) improving employment of domestic labor; and (c) earning foreign exchanges.

barriers such as import tariffs and/or quotas (also see Bhagwati, 1973; Hamada, 1974; Minabe, 1974). Brecher and Diaz Alejandro (1977) show that tariff-induced foreign capital inflows are immiserizing if importables are capital-intensive. Rodrik (1987) proposes that the welfare loss can be mitigated if host countries implement ESRs, because the policy dampens the output of the overproduced importable goods. It is notable that for a given tariff adopted by a small country, tariff-jumping foreign capital inflows do not trigger domestic price-induced effects on resource allocation and national welfare.

Regarding quota protection, the impacts of foreign capital inflows are radically different from those under tariffs.[3] Dei (1985a) shows that foreign capital inflows are welfare improving via a reduction in the returns to foreign capital. Since ESRs on quota-jumping foreign firms discourage foreign investment, one may logically conjecture that the requirements in the presence of quotas are welfare reducing. In this chapter we show that the conjecture is correct. When the foreign firms are located only in specific economic activity zones typically identified with the import-competing sector, an introduction of or an increase in ESRs forces foreign firms to export a portion of their output, thereby pushing up the domestic price of the importables and hence reducing welfare via the higher price-induced payments to foreign capital.

The chapter is structured as follows. Section 4.2 presents a simple general equilibrium model of ESRs in the presence of import quotas. Utilizing the model, the impacts of ESRs on domestic welfare are examined in Section 4.3. Section 4.4 offers concluding remarks.

4.2 The Model of Export Requirements with Import Quotas

This section develops a model for examining the welfare effects of ESRs. The framework used is built upon the standard one of a competitive, small, open economy, in which two goods (X, Y) are produced by employing domestic labor (L_i) and capital (K_i). The two goods may also be produced by domestic labor and foreign capital (K_i^*). The home country imposes import quotas.

---

[3] For sector-specific foreign capital inflow with non-traded goods, see Tanigaki (1988).

Let the domestic price of good Y (the importable) in terms of good X (the exportable) be p and the domestic price of good X be normalized to be equal to 1. The revenue function of domestic firms is as follows: $R(1, p, k, L) = \max\{X(L_X, K_X) + pY(L_Y, K_Y) | K = K_X + K_Y, L = L_X + L_Y\}$, where K is the stock of domestic capital and L is the employment of labor by domestic firms. By Shephard's lemma, the partial derivative of R with respect to p yields the output of good Y; that is, $R_2 = \partial R / \partial p = Y$. The partial derivatives of R with respect to K and L yield the respective factor returns; that is $R_K = r$ and $R_L = w$, where w and r denote the returns to labor and domestic capital, respectively.

Let the world price of good Y be p^*. The import quotas create a discrepancy between the domestic price, p, and the world price of good Y such that $p > p^*$.[4] To circumvent quota restrictions, foreign firms may choose to invest directly in the host country.[5] In exchange for permission to invest in the host country, foreign firms consent to an ESR, namely that a share α of the output of good Y produced by foreign firms be mandated to be exported.[6] For simplicity it is assumed that, when instituted, the ESR applies retroactively to the foreign firms already established in the host country. So the effects of an introduction of the requirement ($\alpha = 0$ initially and $d\alpha > 0$) are analytically equivalent to an increase in the requirement ($\alpha > 0$ initially and $d\alpha > 0$). Note that for a given α, the effective producer price p_e facing foreign firms in sector Y is $p^* + (1 - \alpha)p$, which is less than the domestic price for domestic firms, $p > p_e > p^*$.

Given perfect competition and constant returns to scale, foreign firms can produce either exportables and/or importables. Hence, the revenue function for foreign firms is: $R^*(1, p_e, K^*, \overline{L} - L) = \max\{X^*(L_X^*, K_X^*) + p_e Y^*(L_Y^*, K_Y^*) : K^* = K_X^* + K_Y^*, \overline{L} - L = L_X^* + L_Y^*\}$, where K^* is the use of foreign capital in both sectors, $\overline{L} - L$ is the employment of domestic labor by foreign firms, and $\overline{L}$ denotes the nation's endowment of labor. It is

---

[4]Although protection in the form of import tariffs also creates a discrepancy between p and p^*, the domestic price under a tariff is fixed by p^* and the tariff rate. However, the domestic price under an import quota is not restricted; p can vary as a result of a change in the ESR. Thus, protection in the form of quota is essential for obtaining the price-induced effects of ESRs. A similar reason can be found in Almansi (1989).

[5]See Mundell (1957), Markusen (1983), and Svensson (1984) on the substitution between factor trade and goods trade.

[6]Since nothing impedes exports, the domestic and foreign prices of good X are identical. Hence, an ESR imposed on foreigners who invest in the export sector would not create a wedge in prices, and the policy is immaterial. The ESR on foreign firms investing in the export sector may be higher than the free trade ratio of exports to domestic production.

assumed that while the outputs of domestic and foreign firms are perfect substitutes, foreign firms do not use domestic capital and domestic firms do not hire foreign capital.

To examine the impact of export requirements on domestic welfare, we need to specify the demand side of the economy. The social demand can be represented by an expenditure function, $E(1, p, u) = \min(D_X + pD_Y)$, with respect to the demand for the two goods, D_X and D_Y, subject to a strictly quasi-concave utility function $u(D_X, D_Y) \geq u$.

With import quotas, the economy's budget constraint is given by:

$$E(1, p, u) = R(1, p, K, L) + R^*(1, p_e, K^*, \overline{L} - L)$$
$$- r^* K^* + (p - p^*)Q, \tag{4.1}$$

where Q denotes the import quotas and r^* is the rental of foreign capital. Equation (4.1) states that national expenditure equals national net revenue, which equals the values of both domestic and foreign firm production net of the returns to foreign capital plus the quota rent. The latter is assumed to be redistributed to the private sector in a non-distortionary lump-sum fashion.

Since foreign firms are required to export a share α of good Y, which they produce, the goods market equilibrium conditions require:

$$E_2(1, p, u) = R_2(1, p, K, L) + (1 - \alpha)R_2^*(1, p_e, K^*, \overline{L} - L) + Q, \tag{4.2}$$

where $E_2 = \partial E(1, p, u)/\partial p = D_Y$ is the demand for good Y; R_2, as noted earlier, is the domestic output of good Y; and $R_2^* = \partial R^*/\partial p_e$ is the output of good Y produced by the foreign firms. The right-hand side of (4.2) indicates the total supply of good Y.

The model is completed by specifying the factor market equilibrium conditions. Free mobility of labor yields equal wages between sectors, and between the domestic and foreign firms:[7]

$$R_L(1, p, K, L) = R_L^*(1, p_e, K^*, \overline{L} - L), \tag{4.3}$$

where $R_L = \partial R/\partial L$ and $R_L^* = \partial R/\partial(\overline{L} - L)$ denote the marginal products of labor in domestic and foreign firms in both sectors, respectively. Finally, the market equilibrium condition for foreign capital requires:

$$r^* = R_K^*(1, p_e, K^*, \overline{L} - L), \tag{4.4}$$

---

[7]Note that domestic labor is more productive in the foreign sector but is paid the same wage; there would be an additional incentive for foreign firms to invest in the home country.

where $R_K^* = \partial R^*/\partial K^*$. Note that either r^* or K^* can be determined in (4.4) depending upon the planning horizon considered: K^* is fixed and r^* is endogenous for the short run, whereas K^* is endogenous and r^* is given by the world capital rental rate in the longer run. We focus only on the short-run analysis in the text and relegate the longer-run results to footnote 20.

Differentiating (4.1) and utilizing (4.2)–(4.4), we obtain the welfare effects of changes in ESRs:

$$E_u du = -R_2^*(p - p^*)d\alpha - K^* dr^*. \tag{4.5}$$

There are two parts to the welfare effects: a direct welfare loss and an induced welfare impact via changes in the repatriation of earnings of foreign capital. The first term on the right-hand side of (4.5) captures such a direct welfare loss as α rises. A quota raises the domestic price of good Y above its world price. An ESR, however, forces the foreign firms to sell an α share of the output of good Y abroad at a lower world price, thereby resulting in a revenue loss.[8] In addition, the second term in (4.5), $K^* dr^*$, represents induced changes in the full repatriation of foreign-capital earnings.

Note that, unlike the case of tariffs examined by Rodrik (1987), the resource reallocation effect does not appear in (4.5). Under tariff protection, a rise in ESRs reduces the inflow of foreign capital, causing labor migration into the domestic firms. This result dampens the output of the overproduced importable goods so long as imports are relatively capital-intensive, thereby improving welfare through a reduction in production loss. Under quota protection, however, the volume of imports is fixed, and hence the linkage between resource reallocation and domestic welfare is cut off.[9] The latter effect constitutes a basic difference between the impact of ESRs in the presence of tariffs and quotas.

4.3 Export Requirements and Welfare

Equation (4.5) is the key expression for analyzing the welfare impact of ESRs in the presence of quotas. Foreign capital may produce the importable and/or exportable. So the issue is what product foreign capital produces. It can be easily shown that given perfect competition, constant returns to

---

[8]This point becomes clear if we recall that $p_e = \alpha p^* + (1 - \alpha)p = p - \alpha(p - p^*)$. A 1% increase in α results in a revenue loss by the amount of $R_2^*(p - p^*)$.

[9]A similar reasoning can be found in Buffie (1985), Dei (1985a), and Tanigaki (1988).

scale, and identical production functions for domestic and foreign firms, the export-share policy has no effect on domestic welfare if foreign firms can locate in both the exportable and the importable sector initially.[10] The intuition for this result is simple. Since the rental to capital is the same in both sectors, foreign capital can evade the export requirements by relocating from the importable sector to the exportable sector and repatriating its earnings in units of the importable.

In contrast, when foreign firms can locate only in the import-competing sector, the export-share policy affects welfare. This case is of real-world relevance, since in several developing countries foreign capital is allowed to locate only in special economic activity zones, such as industrial parks and export-processing zones, where generally only the import-competing goods are produced.[11]

Consider the latter case in which foreign firms produce only import-competing goods. The unit-cost functions in sector X and Y are $\gamma(w, r)$ and $\phi(w, r)$, respectively, and the price-cost relationships for domestic firms are:

$$\gamma(w, r) = 1 \tag{4.6}$$

$$\phi(w, r) = p. \tag{4.7}$$

The price-cost relationship for foreign firms is:

$$\phi(w, r^*) = p_e. \tag{4.8}$$

By comparing (4.7) and (4.8), we obtain that the return to foreign capital (r^*) is linked but not equal to the return to domestic capital (r). From (4.8), r^* depends on both w and p_e. Since w depends on p, and p_e depends on α, it follows that r^* is a function of both α and p. That is, $r^* = r^*(\alpha, p)$. As shown below, p itself can also be solved as a function of α. So we can write $r^* = r^*(\alpha, p(\alpha))$. Using the decomposition technique,

---

[10]Detailed proof of this result is available upon request from the authors. The method of proof parallels that of Rodrik (1987).

[11]See Miyagiwa (1986) and Marjit (1990) for related discussions. To attract foreign capital into the special economic zones, investment incentives such as tax holidays, freedom for remittance on capital income, etc., are generally provided. However, a certain percentage of the commodities produced in the zones are required to be exported. For example, 80% of the products manufactured by foreign firms in Malaysia have to be exported; see Spinanger (1984).

we differentiate r^* with respect to α to obtain:[12]

$$\frac{dr^*}{d\alpha} = \frac{\partial r^*}{\partial \alpha} + \left(\frac{\partial r^*}{\partial p}\right)\left(\frac{dp}{d\alpha}\right). \tag{4.9}$$

The first term on the right-hand side of (4.9) captures the direct effect of ESRs on foreign capital returns at constant p, and the second term is the effect on r^* induced by a change in p as a result of a change in α.

To solve for $\partial r^*/\partial \alpha$ and $\partial r^*/\partial p$ in (4.9), we need to use the market-clearing conditions for labor and capital. By Shephard's lemma, the factor demand for the unit output in sector i can be denoted by the partial derivative of the unit-cost function. Full employment in the competitive factor markets implies:

$$\gamma_w(w,r)X + \phi_w(w,r)Y + \phi_w(w,r^*)Y^* = \bar{L} \tag{4.10}$$

$$\gamma_r(w,r)X + \phi_r(w,r)Y = K \tag{4.11}$$

$$\phi_r(w,r^*)Y^* = K^*, \tag{4.12}$$

where, as noted earlier, $Y = R_2$ and $Y^* = R_2^*$.

Equations (4.6)–(4.8) and (4.10)–(4.12) describe the cost side of the submodel. There are six endogenous variables — w, r, r^*, X, Y, and Y^* — and one policy variable, α. This submodel is a mixture of the Heckscher–Ohlin model and the factor-specific model,[13,14] which is block recursive, since the factor returns, w, r, and r^*, can be solved solely from (4.6)–(4.8). Sectoral outputs can then be determined by the remaining equations (4.10)–(4.12) in terms of the factor returns. The domestic price of good Y, p, is treated as a given here and will be determined in a complete model that integrates the demand-side conditions.

By relegating the mathematics on the comparative statics to Appendix A.3, we present here only the interpretation of the results. Assuming the stability condition that sector Y is capital-intensive relative

---

[12]This decomposition technique is well known in the trade literature; see Batra and Scully (1971).

[13]Rodrik (1987) uses the Ricardo–Viner model, in which capital is specific to each sector. This constitutes another difference in addition to quotas versus tariffs between the present study and the Rodrik analysis.

[14]This production structure is originally due to Gruen and Corden (1970), and its general equilibrium properties have been extensively studied in Jones and Marjit (1992). For related studies on this model, see, among others, Batra and Casas (1976), Miyagiwa (1986), Marjit (1990), and Beladi and Marjit (1992).

to sector X, the famous Stolper–Samuelson result prevails. Namely, an increase in the price of good Y raises the return to domestic capital, $\partial r/\partial p > 0$, and lowers the wage for labor, $\partial w/\partial p < 0$. Thus, higher returns to foreign capital ($\partial r^*/\partial p > 0$) are necessary to ensure zero profits for foreign firms. Further, the price-output responses are normal under the stability condition.

The returns to labor and domestic capital should not be directly affected by the ESRs, because the requirements are imposed only on foreign firms. However, when foreign firms are located only in the importable sector, an introduction of or an increase in the ESR reduces the return to foreign capital. The lower r^* results from the lower effective producer price for foreign firms at a given p. This result can be easily seen by differentiating (4.8) to obtain:

$$\frac{\partial r^*}{\partial \alpha} = -\frac{r^*(p - p^*)}{p_e \theta^*_{KY}} < 0, \tag{4.13}$$

where $\theta^*_{KY} = r^* \phi_r/\phi$ signifies the distributive share of capital in foreign firms. Moreover, the lower effective producer price leads to a cutback in the production of Y^*, and some workers thus are released for domestic firms. Since good Y is assumed to be capital-intensive relative to good X, the Rybczynski effect prevails: The production of X rises and that of Y falls.

To ascertain the sign of $dr^*/d\alpha$ in (4.9), we need to determine the sign of $dp/d\alpha$, which can be derived as follows:[15]

$$\frac{dp}{d\alpha} = -\frac{\left\{ p\left[\frac{\partial Y}{\partial \alpha} + (1 - \alpha)\left(\frac{\partial Y^*}{\partial \alpha}\right) - Y^*\right] + m\left[R_2^*(p - p^*) + K^*\left(\frac{\partial r^*}{\partial \alpha}\right)\right] \right\}}{\Delta}, \tag{4.14}$$

where $m = pE_{2u}/E_u$ is the marginal propensity to consume good Y, and $\Delta = Q(c + s) + mK^*(\partial r^*/\partial p) > 0$ by the stability conditions.

Clearly, an introduction of or an increase in the ESRs generates two effects on the price of good Y. The first term on the right-hand side of (4.14) is the supply response to the export-share policy. The higher requirement reduces the effective price for foreign firms and hence a contraction in their output. In view of the Rybczynski effect, as foreign firms release labor the output of good Y supplied by domestic firms will also fall under the stability condition that good Y is relatively capital-intensive. With cutbacks

---

[15]See the Appendix for derivations.

in the outputs of the importable goods by both foreign and domestic firms and with imports restricted by the quota, the domestic price of Y will tend to rise.

The second term in (4.14) captures the demand response to the requirements via the income effect, which can be obtained by differentiating income, $I = R + R^* - r^*K^* + (p - p^*)Q$, with respect to α: $\partial I/\partial \alpha = -R_2^*(p - p^*) - K^*(\partial r^*/\partial \alpha)$. There are two offsetting effects of an increase in α on income. An increase in α leads to an income loss, owing to the reduction in the revenue for foreign firms, $-R_2^*(p - p^*)$, as well as a gain arising from the cutback in the repatriated earnings to foreign capital, $-K^*(\partial r^*/\partial \alpha)$. It is noteworthy that by virtue of the zero-profit condition (4.8), the loss in revenue is completely offset by the cutback in the payments to foreign capital. It follows that the income effect is zero,[16] and only the abovementioned supply effect prevails. Hence, an increase in the ESR always raises the domestic price ratio of the importable good, $dp/d\alpha > 0$.[17]

Referring to (4.9) and recalling from the Appendix that $\partial r^*/\partial \alpha < 0, \partial r^*/\partial p < 0$ and $dp/d\alpha > 0$, we obtain $dr^*/d\alpha \gtrless 0$. An increase in ESRs directly reduces the returns to foreign capital but indirectly raises the returns via a higher price of the importable good mainly caused by the reduced domestic supply of good Y.[18] Here, if the rise in the return to foreign capital outweighs the fall, an increase in the ESRs benefits the foreign firms at the expense of domestic welfare.

Now we can use (4.5) and (4.9) to deduce the welfare effect of an increase in the ESR in the presence of import quotas:

$$\frac{E_u du}{d\alpha} = -R_2^*(p - p^*) - K^*\left(\frac{\partial r^*}{\partial \alpha}\right) - K^*\left(\frac{\partial r^*}{\partial p}\right)\left(\frac{dp}{d\alpha}\right). \qquad (4.15)$$

Although the effect of the export-share policy on the returns to foreign capital is ambiguous, the welfare effect of the policy is unequivocal because the first two terms in (4.15) cancel out, owing to the zero direct-income effect, as noted earlier. The welfare effect thus depends solely on the price-induced payments to foreign capital.[19] A rise in the ESR unambiguously reduces

---

[16] By utilizing (4.13) and $\theta_{KY}^* = r^*\phi_r/\phi$, we can obtain $R_2^*(p - p^*) + K^*(\partial r^*/\partial \alpha) = 0$.

[17] This contrasts to the tariff case in which a change in α has no effect on p, since p under tariff is restricted to $p^*(1 + t)$, where t represents the tariff rate.

[18] Note that this price-induced additional effect of a higher return to foreign capital does not exist in the presence of a tariff.

[19] Note that by inducing a higher domestic price for the importable, the case of a quota precipitates a change that is similar to a deterioration in the terms of trade.

welfare when the return to foreign firms is endogenous.[20] The monotonic, negative relationship between the export ratio and social welfare in the presence of a quota implies that the optimal ESR is zero.[21]

Finally, it is of interest to note that if the object of the export-share policy is to protect the domestic importable, the policy may not be effective. The output of the domestic importable, Y, is a function of α and p. Hence, the effect of the export-share policy on Y is:

$$\frac{dY}{d\alpha} = \frac{\partial Y}{\partial \alpha} + \left(\frac{\partial Y}{\partial p}\right)\left(\frac{dp}{d\alpha}\right), \qquad (4.16)$$

where $\partial Y/\partial p > 0$, recalling the normal price-output responses. Note that $\partial Y/\partial \alpha < 0$ according to the Rybczynski effect: A rise in α lowers the effective price for foreign firms, leading to a reduction in Y and a release of workers to domestic firms. Since good Y is capital-intensive relative to good X, the production of X rises and that of Y falls. Recalling that $dp/d\alpha > 0$, the effect of the export-share policy on the output of the domestic importable is indeterminate. If the negative Rybczynski effect dominates the positive price-output response, the export-share policy results in a reduced output of the domestic importable, thereby defeating the intended purpose of protection.[22]

4.4   Concluding Remarks

In this chapter, we have developed a model for analyzing the effects of ESRs imposed on foreign firms when quota protection is in place. We have shown that, when foreign capital is located only in specific economic zones characterized by import-competing industries, the policy reduces welfare, owing

---

[20] As for the longer run, the foreign capital rental is fixed at the world capital-rental rate, so that $dr^* = 0$. Hence, similar to the short-run case, an increase in the ESR is welfare reducing via a direct revenue loss.

[21] This result contrasts to that of Rodrik (1987), who has shown that $du/d\alpha \gtrless 0$ in the presence of tariffs, and thus the non-zero optimal α exists.

[22] From (4.16), $dY/d\alpha > 0$ can occur if the price-induced rise in Y outweighs the direct reduction in output caused by a rise in α. That is, $dY/d\alpha > 0$ when $dp/d\alpha > -(\partial Y/\partial \alpha)(\partial Y/\partial p)$, where $dp/d\alpha$ is given in (4.14). By inspecting (4.14), this inequality will be satisfied when, for example, $c = 0$ and $m = 0$ along with $\partial[(1-\alpha)Y^*]/\partial p < \partial[(1-\alpha)Y^*]/\partial \alpha$. The latter condition states that the supply of good Y by foreign firms in the home market responds more to α relative to p, which is true when initial Y^* is large.

to the price-induced higher payments to foreign capital. Hence, the export-share policy under quota protection is detrimental to domestic welfare.

The welfare effects of the export-share policy in the presence of quotas, when the foreign firms are located only in the importable sector, are almost completely opposite to those under tariff protection obtained by Rodrik (1987). The differential welfare effects in the presence of a quota versus a tariff appear to result from the fact that under a quota, the domestic price ratio can increase in response to a higher export-share ratio, whereas under a tariff, the domestic price ratio is restricted to the world price and the tariff rate. Under a quota, the higher domestic prices give rise to the negative welfare effects, rendering the policy less desirable than under a tariff.

Appendix

A.1 *The price effect*

Totally differentiating (4.1) and (4.2) yields:

$$E_u du + K^* \left(\frac{\partial r^*}{\partial p} \right) dp = - \left[R_2^*(p - p^*) + K^* \left(\frac{\partial r^*}{\partial \alpha} \right) \right] d\alpha$$

$$E_{2u} du - (c + s) \left(\frac{Q}{p} \right) dp = \left[\frac{\partial Y}{\partial \alpha} + (1 - \alpha) \left(\frac{\partial Y^*}{\partial \alpha} \right) - Y^* \right] d\alpha,$$

where $E_u = \partial E / \partial u$ and $E_{2u} = \partial E_2 / \partial u$. We define $c = -(p/Q)(\partial E_2/\partial p) > 0$ and $s = (p/Q)[\partial Y/\partial p + (1 - \alpha)(\partial Y^*/\partial p)]$. Solving the above equations, we obtain (4.14) in the text:

$$\frac{dp}{d\alpha} = - \frac{\left\{ p \left[\frac{\partial Y}{\partial \alpha} + (1 - \alpha) \left(\frac{\partial Y^*}{\partial \alpha} \right) - Y^* \right] + m \left[R_2^*(p - p^*) \left(\frac{\partial r^*}{\partial \alpha} \right) \right] \right\}}{\Delta},$$

where $m = pE_{2u}/E_u$ is the marginal propensity to consume good Y and $\Delta = Q(c + s) + mK^*(\partial r^*/\partial p) > 0$ by the stability conditions.

A.2 *Stability*

Following Dei (1985b), the adjustment process for the goods market is $\dot{p} = aZ(p)$, where the dot is the time derivative, a is a positive constant, and $Z = E_2(1, p, u) - R_2 - (1 - \alpha)R_2^* - Q$ is the excess demand for good Y. From (4.5), we can obtain that u is a function of p for a given α. By keeping

α and Q constant, we can take a linear approximation of the above adjust-ment process around the quilibrium point p^e as: $\dot{p} = a(dZ/dp)(p - p^e)$. The necessary and sufficient condition for the stability is $dZ/dp < 0$. From the differentiations of (4.1) and (4.2), we obtain $dp/dZ = -p/\Delta$. Hence, $dZ/dp < 0$ requires that $s > 0$ and $\partial r^*/\partial p > 0$. As shown below, the assumption that good Y is strongly capital-intensive relative to good X implies $s > 0$ and $\partial r^*/\partial p > 0$.

A.3 *Comparative statics*

Let a hat over the variable denote the percentage change. Following Jone's (1965) notations, $\theta_{LX} = w\gamma_w/\gamma$ and $\theta_{KX} = r\gamma_r/\gamma$, for example, are the distributive share of labor and capital, respectively, in sector X, and $\lambda_{LX} = \gamma_w X/\overline{L}$ and $\lambda_{KK} = \gamma_r X/K$ are the fraction of labor and capital, respectively, employed in sector X. An asterisk denotes the case for foreign firms. From (4.6)–(4.8), we can solve for:

$$\frac{\widehat{w}}{\widehat{p}} = -\frac{\theta_{KX}}{\theta_{KY} - \theta_{KX}} < 0$$

$$\frac{\widehat{r}}{\widehat{p}} = \frac{\theta_{LX}}{(\theta_{KY} - \theta_{KX})} > 0$$

$$\frac{\widehat{r}^*}{\widehat{p}} = \frac{[\theta_{LY}^* \theta_{KX} + k(1 - \alpha)(\theta_{KY} - \theta_{KX})]}{\theta_{KY}^* (\theta_{KY}\theta_{KX})} > 0$$

$$\frac{\widehat{w}}{\widehat{\alpha}} = \frac{\widehat{r}}{\widehat{\alpha}} = 0$$

$$\frac{\widehat{r}^*}{\widehat{\alpha}} = -\frac{(k - 1)}{\theta_{KY}^*} \lesseqgtr 0,$$

and from (4.10), (4.11) and (4.12), we can solve for

$$\frac{\widehat{X}}{\widehat{p}} = \frac{A\lambda_{KY} - B\lambda_{LY} - C\lambda_{KY}\lambda_{LY}^*}{H} < 0$$

$$\frac{\widehat{Y}}{\widehat{p}} = -\frac{A\lambda_{KX} - B\lambda_{LX} - C\lambda_{KX}\lambda_{LY}^*}{H} > 0$$

$$\frac{\widehat{Y}^*}{\widehat{p}} = C > 0$$

$$\frac{\widehat{X}}{\hat{\alpha}} = \frac{D\lambda_{KY} - F\lambda_{KY}\lambda^*_{LY}}{H} > 0$$

$$\frac{\widehat{Y}}{\hat{\alpha}} = -\frac{D\lambda_{KX} - F\lambda_{KX}\lambda^*_{LY}}{H} < 0$$

$$\frac{\widehat{Y}^*}{\hat{\alpha}} = F < 0,$$

where $k = p/[p - \alpha(p - p^*)] \geq 1, S_{Li} = \sigma_i\lambda_{Li}\theta_{Ki}, S_{Ki} = \sigma_i\lambda_{Ki}\theta_{Li}, S_L = S_{LX} + S_{LY} + S^*_{LY}, S_K = S_{KX}S_{KY}$ and $S^*_K = \sigma^*_Y\theta^*_{LY}$, and

$$A = S_L\left(\frac{\widehat{w}}{\hat{p}}\right) - (S_{LX} + S_{LY})\left(\frac{\hat{r}}{\hat{p}}\right) - S^*_{LY}\left(\frac{\hat{r}^*}{\hat{p}}\right) < 0$$

$$B = -S_K\left(\frac{\widehat{w}}{\hat{p}}\right) + S_K\left(\frac{\hat{r}}{\hat{p}}\right) > 0$$

$$C = -S^*_K\left(\frac{\widehat{w}}{\hat{p}}\right) + S^*_K\left(\frac{\hat{r}^*}{\hat{p}}\right) > 0$$

$$D = S_L\left(\frac{\widehat{w}}{\hat{\alpha}}\right) - (S_{LX} + S_{LY})\left(\frac{\hat{r}}{\hat{\alpha}}\right) - S^*_{LY}\left(\frac{\hat{r}^*}{\hat{\alpha}}\right) > 0$$

$$E = -S_K\left(\frac{\widehat{w}}{\hat{\alpha}}\right) + S_K\left(\frac{\hat{r}}{\hat{\alpha}}\right) = 0$$

$$F = -S^*_K\left(\frac{\widehat{w}}{\hat{\alpha}}\right) + S^*_K\left(\frac{r^*}{\hat{\alpha}}\right) < 0.$$

Here σ_i denotes the factor substitution in the ith sector. Note that $\partial r^*/\partial p > 0$ and $s > 0$ require $H = \lambda_{LX}\lambda_{KY} - \lambda_{KX}\lambda_{LY} = \lambda_{KY}(1 - \lambda^*_{LY}) - \lambda_{LY} > 0$ and $\theta_{LX}\theta_{KY} - \theta_{KX}\theta_{LY} = \theta_{KY}\theta_{KX} > 0$; that is, good Y is strong capital intensive relative to good X.

Chapter 5

Export-Share Requirements, Trade Balances, and Welfare: A Two-Period Analysis

5.1 Introduction

From a historical perspective, the rules and articles of the now-expired institution GATT (General Agreement on Tariffs and Trade) have guided the formulation of trade policies of all its signatory nations over half a century before the setup of the World Trade Organization (WTO) in 1995. Basically, the general obligations of the member countries of GATT revolve around tariff liberalization in merchandise trade. And little attention has been given to the policies that do not directly restrict trade in merchandise but may nevertheless significantly affect such trade in an indirect manner. A good example of such policies is "performance requirements," which include export-share requirements (ESRs), local content specifications, and so on. These non-tariff policies, which had been commonly adopted by countries in the presence of distortions (e.g., tariffs), in dealing with multinational firms, are known as the trade-related investment measures (TRIMs). It has been argued that TRIMs indirectly discourage foreign direct investment (FDI) and can result in a restricted and distorted pattern of trade flows. Responding to this phenomenon, the Uruguay Round GATT negotiations in 1994 reached a landmark agreement that each contracting nation of GATT should eliminate all TRIMs.[1]

Several studies have been conducted on the welfare effects of TRIMs.[2] Aside from its welfare effect of the policy of export requirements as

---

[1]See the agreement on Trade-Related Aspects of Investment Measures, Article 5: Notification and Transitional Arrangements contained in the Punta del Este Declaration, 1994.

[2]Richardson (1993) provides a theoretical study of TRIMs in the form of content protection in the presence of foreign capital.

studied in Chapter 4, TRIMS were a popular instrument adopted by many developing countries for improving their trade imbalance difficulties. The trade balance implications of ESRs were studied by Chao and Yu (1998a). The main purpose of this chapter is to show how the export-share policy would affect the current account of the host country. To model the impact of the Uruguay Round agreement of the GATT, this chapter analyzes the case of two-period adjustments: an increase in the ESR in the first period followed by its removal in the second period on foreign firms. We obtain a crisp result that such an increase in the export requirement only in the first period always improves the trade balance in that period.

The chapter is structured as follows. Section 5.2 presents a two-period model incorporating non-traded goods. The presence of non-traded goods is useful in that changes in equilibrium real exchange rates become a key intertemporal channel through which the export-share policy affects the trade balance. Section 5.3 works out the model explicitly, and Section 5.4 offers concluding remarks.

5.2   The Model

A two-period, three-sector, general equilibrium model is used to examine the trade balance and welfare effects of ESRs for a small open economy.[3] We assume that domestic and foreign firms operate in the home country in both periods. Period 1 can be simply considered as the period prior to joining the GATT,[4] when domestic firms produce two types of goods (an exportable, X_1^1, and a non-traded good, X_2^1), and the home country imports good X_3^1, where the superscript stands for time period and the subscript for goods. Foreign firms in the home country produce only the importable goods for two reasons: first, foreign firms are strongly discouraged to produce products similar to and competitive with domestic products, as the firms are subject to extremely high production taxes imposed by the home country in Period 1 for protecting the domestic firms.[5] Second, facing high

---

[3]The two-period, general equilibrium framework is adapted from Lopez and Rodrik (1991).

[4]The policy of ESRs was used by many economies, which are obligated to the general elimination of TRIMs as a condition to join the GATT under the Uruguay Round decision in 1994.

[5]For instance, Brazil imposes extremely high taxes on foreign firms that produce similar goods in that country. Therefore, local production of goods 1 and 2 by foreign firms ceases to be profitable. There is a growing literature on the impacts of foreign investment. See,

import tariffs, foreign firms desire to bypass the tariff wall by producing the importable goods, X_3^1, inside the home country. Foreign investment can cause balance of trade difficulties. To alleviate trade-deficit problems, the home country adopts ESRs directed toward foreign-owned firms, i.e., a certain percentage, say α, of X_3^1 is mandated for export.[6] In Period 2, which can be thought of as after the country joins the GATT, all trade restrictions, including taxes, tariffs and ESRs, will be completely removed. Consequently, foreign firms can form joint ventures with domestic firms in producing domestic goods. That is, foreign firms can produce all three goods.

The exportable good is chosen to be numeraire in both periods; so P_1^i is normalized to unity $(i = 1, 2)$. The constrained revenue function of domestic firms in Period 1 is given by $R^1(1, q^1, L^1, \overline{K}, \overline{V}) = \max[X_1^1 + q^1 X_2^1 : \{X_j^1\} \in T^1(L^1, \overline{K}, \overline{V})]$ with respect to $X_j^1, j = 1, 2$, where L^1 is the total employment of labor in the domestic sectors, $\overline{K}$ and $\overline{L}$ are, respectively, the fixed endowments of domestic capital and other factors if any,[7] and $T^1(\cdot)$ represents the available technology set. By Shephard's lemma, the output of X_2^1 is $R_2^1(= \partial R^1/\partial q^1) = X_2^1$ and the rate of return on labor is $R_L^1 = \partial R^1/\partial L^1$.

Let the foreign price of the importable good be 1 and the tariff rate be t; then the producers' price of the importable in the presence of the exportable-share requirements in Period 1 is $p^1 = \alpha + (1 - \alpha)(1 + t)$, which is the weighted average of the foreign price and the domestic price with the weights being determined by α. However, the producers' price of the importable in Period 2 becomes $p^2 = 1$ since $t = \alpha = 0$ in the second period. The constrained revenue function for foreign-owned firms in Period 1 is $R^*(p^1, \overline{L} - L^1, k^*) = \max[p^1 X_3^1 : X_3^1 \in T^*(\overline{L} - L^1, k^*)]$, where $\overline{L} - L^1$ is the labor employment in the foreign-owned sector ($\overline{L}$ denotes the fixed labor endowment) and k^* is the inflow of foreign capital in Period 1. Here we have the usual results: $R_p^*(= \partial R^*/\partial p^1) = X_3^1$ and $R_L^*(= \partial R^*/\partial(\overline{L} - L)$.

Given the inflow k^* of foreign capital and using the revenue functions of both the domestic and foreign-owned firms, the gross domestic product

---

for example, Batra (1986), Casas (1985), Jones (1967, 1987), Khan (1982b), and Neary (1988), among others.

[6]Guisinger and Associates (1985) report in their study that 38 out of 74 investment cases are subject to export and/or other requirements.

[7]The vector $\overline{V}$ can be interpreted as specific factors to the domestic sectors.

(GDP) function for the host country can be written as:[8] $\pi^1(1, q^1, p^1, k^*) = \max[R^1(1, q^1, L^1, \overline{K}, \overline{V}) + R^*(p^1, \overline{L} - L^1, k^*)]$, where the home endowments of labor, capital, and other factors are suppressed. The outputs are $\pi^1_2(= \partial\pi^1/\partial q^1) = X^1_2$ and $\pi^1_3 = X^1_3$, and the host country's rate of return to foreign capital is $\pi^1_k(= \partial\pi^1/\partial k^*)$. It is assumed that in Period 1, while all firms use domestic labor, foreign firms do not use domestic capital and domestic firms do not hire foreign capital (i.e., joint ventures are not allowed). Given that foreign capital is internationally mobile, the domestic rate of return to foreign capital at equilibrium is equated to its world rate of return, r^*:

$$\pi^1_k(1, q^1, p^1, k^*) = r^*, \tag{5.1}$$

where r^* by the small-country assumption is exogenously given in the world capital market. Therefore, we can solve for k^* as a function of q^1 and p^1; i.e., $k^* = k^*(q^1, p^1)$ with $\partial k^*/\partial q^1 = -\pi^1_{k2}/\pi^1_{kk} > 0$ and $\partial k^*/\partial p^1 = -\pi^1_{k3}/\pi^1_{kk}$,[9] where the second subscript in the GDP function denotes the second partial derivative.

As noted earlier, all trade restrictions, such as taxes, import tariffs, and ESRs, are removed in Period 2 and foreign capital can flow into domestic industries. Hence, the producers' price of the importable in Period 2 is simply $p^2 = 1$. To reflect the perfect mobility of foreign capital, the host country's GDP function in Period 2 is modified as: $\pi^2(1, q^2, 1, K^*) = \max[X^2_1 + q^2 X^2_2 + X^2_3 : \{X^2_j\} \in T^2(\overline{L}, \overline{K} + K^*, \overline{V})]$, where K^* is Period 2's foreign capital. Note that K^* is equal to k^* plus new inflows of foreign capital in Period 2.[10] We assume that the world rate of return to capital in Period 2 remains the same as in Period 1, i.e.:

$$\pi^2_K(1, q^2, 1, K^*) = r^*. \tag{5.2}$$

Therefore, $K^* = K^*(q^2)$ from (5.2) with $dK^*/dq^2 = -\pi^2_{k2}/\pi^2_{KK} > 0$.

The production side needs to be matched by the demand side of the economy. Let $\delta = 1/(1 + r^*)$ be the intertemporal discount factor. The economy-wide demand information can be represented by the following two-period expenditure function: $E(1, q^1, 1 + t, \delta, \delta q^2, \delta, u) = \min[D^1_1 + q^1 D^1_2 + (1 + t)D^1_3 + \delta D^1_1 + \delta q^2 D^2_1 + \delta D^3_1]$ with respect to the

---

[8]Rodrik (1987) and Richardson (1993) use two separate restricted revenue functions for domestic and foreign-owned sectors.

[9]The explicit expressions of π^i_{jk} s are presented in Appendix A.1.

[10]For sharpening the analysis, we assume that the domestic labor, capital, and other factors do not grow over the two periods.

demand for goods, D_j^i, subject to a strictly quasi-concave utility function $u(D_1^1, D_2^1, D_3^1, \delta D_1^1, D_1^2, D_1^3) \geq u$. By Shephard's lemma, we have $E_2(= \partial E/\partial q^1) = D_2^1$ etc., and $E_u = \partial E/\partial u$ is the marginal utility of income.

We close the two-period model by noting the economy's intertemporal budget constraint, i.e., the present value of the consumer expenditure is constrained by the present values of production and tariff revenues net of returns to foreign capital. Thus, we can write:

$$E(1, q^1, 1 + t, \delta, \delta q^2, \delta, u) = \pi^1(1, q^1, p^1, k^*) - r^* k^* + t M^1$$
$$+ \delta[\pi^2(1, q^2, 1, K^*) - r^* K^*], \qquad (5.3)$$

where M^1 denotes the imports of goods X_3^1 in Period 1. It is assumed that the tariff revenue is returned to the private sector in a lump-sum fashion and the foreign capital earnings are repatriated wholly to the foreign countries.

Taking into account that foreign firms are mandated to export a share α of their products in Period 1, the first-period imports of foreign goods are:

$$M^1 = E_3(1, q^1, 1 + t, \delta, \delta q^2, \delta, u) - (1 - \alpha)\pi_3^1(1, q^1, p^1, k^*), \qquad (5.4)$$

where E_3 is the first-period demand for the importable goods and π_3 is the first-period local production of the importable goods by foreign firms, in which an α portion is exported.

In addition, market clearing for the non-tradables in Periods 1 and 2 requires:

$$E_2(1, q^1, 1 + t, \delta, \delta q^2, \delta, u) = \pi_2^1(1, q^1, 1, K^*), \qquad (5.5)$$

$$E_5(1, q^1, 1 + t, \delta, \delta q^2, \delta, u) = \pi_2^2(1, q^2, 1, K^*). \qquad (5.6)$$

These imply that the prices of the non-tradables in Periods 1 and 2, q^1 and q^2, are endogenous.

Equations (5.1)–(5.6) constitute the basic model of the host country, which can be used to solve for the six unknowns, k^*, K^*, M^1, u, q^1 and q^2, for the policy variable α. We can then use the results to examine the effect of the export-share policy on the trade balance. The current account balance in Period 2 is given by:

$$B^2 = [\pi_2^1(\cdot) - E_4(\cdot)] - [E_6(\cdot) - \pi_3^2(\cdot)] - r^* K^*, \qquad (5.7)$$

where E_4 and E_6 are the demand for the exportable and the importable in Period 2, respectively. The first (second) bracketed term represents exports (imports) of the exportable importable, while the last term is the second-period payments to foreign capital. Since the intertemporal trade balance requires $B^1 + \delta B^2 = 0$, for a given δ an improvement in the current account balance in Period 2 necessarily implies a δ-weighted equivalent deterioration in the balance in Period 1 and vice versa:

$$dB^1/d\alpha = \delta(E_{4u} + E_{6u})(du/d\alpha) + \delta(E_{42} + E_{62})(dq^1/d\alpha)$$

$$+ (q^2\pi_{22}^2 + \delta E_{45} + \delta E_{65})(dq^2/d\alpha) + q^2\pi_{k2}^2(dK^*/d\alpha). \quad (5.8)$$

In deriving (5.8), the linear homogeneity of π^2, $q^2\pi_{22}^2 = -(\pi_{12}^2 + \pi_{32}^2)$, is used. The values of $du/d\alpha$, $dq^1/d\alpha$, $dq^1/d\alpha$, and $dK^*/d\alpha$ will be derived from (5.1)–(5.6) in the next section. Equation (5.8) clearly shows that the effect of the export-share policy on the first-period trade balance is determined by the effects of the policy on welfare, the non-tradable prices, and the inflow of foreign capital.

5.3   Effects of Export Requirements

Totally differentiating the budget constraint (5.3) and utilizing conditions (5.1)–(5.3) and (5.6), we obtain the welfare expression for ESRs in the presence of the preexisting tariff:

$$E_u du = t\pi_3^1 d\alpha + tdM^1, \quad (5.9)$$

where $E_u > 0$. The first term in (5.9) captures the loss in income arising in the foreign-owned sector of the export-share policy due to the lowered producer price to foreign firms, and the second term stands for the volume-of-trade effect. Differentiating the import equation in (5.4) totally and then substituting the result into (5.9), we obtain:

$$(E_u - tE_{3u})du = t[E_{32}dq^1 + \delta E_{35}dq^2 - (1 - \alpha)dX_3^1], \quad (5.10)$$

where the second subscript in the expenditure function denotes the second partial derivative. On the left-hand side of (5.10), $(E_u - tE_{3u}) > 0$ when goods are normal in consumption.[11]

The tariff in Period 1 provides an incentive for foreign firms to set up plants in the home country in the first place. The welfare effect of the export-share policy is then determined on the basis of how effective the policy is in mitigating the loss from preexisting tariffs via the increase

---

[11] By linear homogeneity of $E(\cdot)$ in prices, $E_u = E_{1u} + q^1 E_{2u} + (1 + t)E_{3u} + \delta E_{4u} + \delta E_{5u} + \delta E_{6u}$. So, $E_u - tE_{3u} > 0$.

in imports, which are already too low. The level of imports depends on substitutability in demand between the importable and the non-tradables, as well as on the supply of the importable by foreign-owned firms, X_3^1, in (5.10). Since $X_3^1 = \pi_3^1(1, q^1, p^1, k^*(q^1, p^1))$, and $p^1 = p^1(\alpha)$, it is immediate that $dX_3^1 = (\partial X_3^1/\partial q^1)dq^1 + (\partial X_3^1/\partial \alpha)d\alpha$, where $\partial X_3^1/\partial q^1 > 0$ and $\partial X_3^1/\partial \alpha < 0$, as shown in the Appendix. The welfare expression of the export-requirement policy in (5.10) can therefore be rewritten as:

$$(E_u - tE_{3u})du = t \left[E_{32} - (1 - \alpha) \left(\frac{\partial X_3^1}{\partial q^1} \right) \right] dq^1$$

$$+ \delta t E_{35} dq^2 - t(1 - \alpha) \left(\frac{\partial X_3^1}{\partial \alpha} \right) d\alpha. \qquad (5.11)$$

The welfare depends on the (non-traded) price-induced output effects in both periods and the (export share) policy-induced production effect. The changes in q^1 and q^2 can be solved from the market-clearing conditions in (5.5) and (5.6). Differentiating them yields:

$$E_{2u}du + \left(E_{22} - \frac{\partial X_2^1}{\partial q^1} \right) dq^1 + \delta E_{25}dq^2 = \left(\frac{\partial X_2^1}{\partial \alpha} \right) d\alpha, \qquad (5.12)$$

$$E_{5u}du + E_{52}dq^1 + \left(\delta E_{55} - \frac{\partial X_2^2}{\partial q^2} \right) dq^2 = 0, \qquad (5.13)$$

where $\partial X_2^1/\partial q^1 > 0$ and $\partial X_2^1/\partial \alpha^1, < 0$, and $\partial X_2^2/\partial q^2 > 0$ (see the Appendix). Note that the change in X_2^1, $dX_2^1 = (\partial X_2^1/\partial q^1)dq^1 + (\partial X_2^1/\partial \alpha)d\alpha$ is used to obtain (5.12).

By using (5.11)–(5.13), we can solve for the effect of the export-requirement policy on the prices of the non-traded goods in both periods:

$$\frac{dq^1}{d\alpha} = \frac{\left\{ \left(\frac{\partial X_2^1}{\partial \alpha} \right) \left[A - (E_u - tE_{3u}) \left(\frac{\partial X_2^2}{\partial q^2} \right) \right] \right.}{\left. + t(1 - \alpha) \left(\frac{\partial X_3^1}{\partial \alpha} \right) \left[E_{2u} \left(\delta E_{55} - \frac{\partial X_2^2}{\partial q^2} \right) - \delta E_{5u} E_{25} \right] \right\}}{\Delta}, \qquad (5.14)$$

$$\frac{dq^2}{d\alpha} = \frac{\left\{ \left(\frac{\partial X_2^1}{\partial \alpha} \right) [E_{52}(E_u - tE_{3u}) + tE_{5u}E_{32}] \right.}{\left. + t(1 - \alpha) \left(\frac{\partial X_3^1}{\partial \alpha} \right) [E_{2u}E_{52} - E_{5u}E_{22}] + E_{5u}C) \right\}}{\Delta}, \qquad (5.15)$$

where $A = \delta[(E_u - tE_{3u})E_{35} + tE_{5u}E_{35}] < 0,$[12] and, as defined in the Appendix, $C < 0$ under the assumption of non-complementarity in consumption ($E_{jk} \geq 0, j \neq k$). In addition, $\Delta > 0$ by the stability condition, shown in the Appendix. There are two parts to determine the price effect: the first terms on the right-hand sides of (5.14) and (5.15) denote the supply effect and the second terms capture the demand effect. An increase in ESRs reallocates labor from foreign-owned firms to the domestic sectors, which reduces the production of X_2^1 through the Rybczynski effect,[13] thereby resulting in higher prices of the non-tradables. In addition, the policy leads to a decreased local supply of the importable and hence, increases in the imports of foreign goods. This results in a higher tariff revenue which increases q^1 and q^2 by the income effect. Thus, the demand effect reinforces the supply effect, causing the non-tradable prices in (5.14) and (5.15) to move up in both periods. Defining the real exchange rate (ei) as the domestic relative price of tradable goods to non-tradable goods ($e^i = p^i/q^i$), the price effect of the export-share policy implies an appreciation in the real exchange rates for both periods.

We turn next to the welfare effect of the export-share policy. From (5.10) we obtain:

$$(E_u - tE_{3u})\left(\frac{du}{d\alpha}\right)$$

$$= tE_{32}\left(\frac{dq^1}{d\alpha}\right) + \delta tE_{35}\left(\frac{dq^2}{d\alpha}\right) - t(1 - \alpha)\left(\frac{dX_3^1}{d\alpha}\right). \qquad (5.16)$$

Since $dq^1/d\alpha > 0$ and $dq^2/d\alpha > 0$ by (5.14) and (5.15), the first two terms on the right-hand side of (5.16) are positive if the importable and non-traded goods are intra- and intertemporal substitutes ($E_{32} > 0$, $E_{35} > 0$). That is, welfare improves when rises in q^1 and q^2 lead to a higher tariff revenue via more imports. The third term in (5.16) expresses the production effect of foreign-owned firms. In general, $dX_3^1/d\alpha$ is ambiguous because of the negative direct impact ($\partial X_3^1/\partial \alpha$) together with the positive price-induced effect ($\partial X_3^1/\partial q^1$)($dq^1/d\alpha$). Nevertheless, by combining the three

---

[12]Since $E_u(\cdot)$ and $E_5(\cdot)$ are, respectively, homogenous of degree 1 and 0 in prices, $A < 0$.
[13]The stability condition, shown in the Appendix, requires that X_2^1 is capital-intensive to X_1^1.

terms in (5.16), we obtain a crisp result:

$$\Delta\left(\frac{du}{d\alpha}\right) = -t\left\{(1-\alpha)\left(\frac{\partial X_3^1}{\partial \alpha}\right)\left[\delta G - E_{22}\left(\frac{\partial X_2^2}{\partial q^2}\right)\right] - \delta\left(E_{55} - \frac{\partial X_2^2}{\partial q^2}\right)\right.$$
$$\left. \times \left[(1-\alpha)C + E_{32}\left(\frac{\partial X_2^1}{\partial \alpha}\right)\right] + \delta E_{52}E_{35}\left(\frac{\partial X_1^2}{\partial \alpha}\right)\right\}, \quad (5.17)$$

which $G = E_{22}E_{55} - E_{25}E_{52} > 0$ by concavity of the $E(\cdot)$ function. That is, by (5.17), $du/d\alpha > 0$ when goods are normal and substitutable in consumption. The following proposition is immediate.

Proposition 5.1 *In the presence of import tariffs, a temporary increase in ESRs under the assumption of substitutability in consumption causes equilibrium real exchange rates to appreciate in both periods and, hence, renders the welfare to improve. Thus, in the short run, the optimal policy is 100% ESR on foreign-owned firms.*

As regards the trade balance effect of the export-share policy, using (5.14), (5.15), and (5.17) we obtain $dB^1/d\alpha > 0$ in (5.8) if goods are normal and substitutable.

Proposition 5.2 *A temporary increase in ESRs always improves the trade balance in the short run, if goods are normal and substitutable in consumption.*

The explanation for this result is as follows. Tightening the export-share policy has a direct impact on boosting export. The policy also has a negative impact on foreign-owned firms in Period 1; consequently, labor is released from the foreign-owned importable sector and partly absorbed by the exportable sector. This helps to improve the trade balance of Period 1. In addition, the tightened policy causes a rise in the non-tradable prices in both periods, thereby raising the Period 2's demand for the exportable and importable goods. This interperiod consumption-substitution effect further improves Period 1's trade balance which will offset the fall in Period 2's trade balance.

We have derived the above results under a "general" specification of production. The model can be used for considering special cases of factor market structures. Here we consider only a mobile-factor case, i.e., labor and capital are mobile between the domestic sectors, and there are no other specific factors ($\overline{V} = 0$) in production. Let $c_j(\cdot)$ be the unit-cost function for good j in both periods. Equilibrium conditions for the goods markets require that: (a) $c_1(w^i, r^i) = 1$; (b) $c_2(w^i, r^i) = q^i$; and (c) $c_3(w^i, r^*) \geq p^i$ for Period i. Since $\alpha = t = 0$ in Period 2, we have $p^1 > p^2 = 1$. This implies that $c_3(w^2, r^*) \geq p^2$ and hence, $X_3^2 = 0$ with $X_1^2 > 0$ and $X_2^2 > 0$.[14] Because capital is perfectly mobile between sectors in Period 2, we have $r^2 = r^*$. Therefore, w^2 and q^2 are respectively determined by (a) and (b), thereby yielding $dq^2/d\alpha = 0$. On the other hand, due to the Heckscher–Ohlin structure in the domestic sectors for Period 1, q^1 depends only upon factor returns (w^1 and r^1) which are functions of α alone. Hence, $dq^1/d\alpha > 0$ if X_2^1 is capital-intensive relative to X_1^1. The general results obtained in Propositions 5.1 and 5.2 hold for the mobile factor case.

5.4   Concluding Remarks

In this chapter, we have developed a two-period model for analyzing the effects of a temporary increase in ESRs on equilibrium real exchange rates, national welfare, and the trade balance. The analysis suggests that the export-share policy improves the trade balance in the short run. This result is consistent with the real-world observation that many developing countries have used this policy in the past to tackle their trade balance difficulties during the early stages of development.

As a result of the 1994 Uruguay Round of trade negotiations, the GATT and the WTO member nations reached an agreement to eliminate trade-distorting TRIMs within two, five, and seven years for developed, developing, and least-developed contracting countries, respectively. On the one hand the abolition of TRIMs would facilitate international investment and fair competition between domestic and foreign firms, and the use of TRIMs protects domestic industries and improve trade balances, especially of developing nations. On the other hand, it is worthwhile to conduct more detailed analysis and empirical estimation to ascertain the efficiency of the WTO agreement to abolish the TRIMs. The present chapter makes a modest contribution toward this end.

---

[14]See Rodrik (1987) for a similar result.

Appendix

A.1   *Resource allocation in period 1*

From the labor market equilibrium condition, $R^1_L(1, q^1, L^1, \overline{K}, \overline{V}) = R^*_L(p^1, \overline{L} - L^1, k^*)$, we have:

$$\frac{\partial L^1}{\partial \alpha} = -\frac{t R^*_{Lp}}{R^1_{LL} + R^*_{LL}} > 0,$$

$$\frac{\partial L^1}{\partial q^1} = -\frac{R^1_{L2}}{R^1_{LL} + R^*_{LL}} < 0, \quad \text{if } R^1_{L2} < 0,$$

$$\frac{\partial L^1}{\partial k^*} = \frac{R^*_{Lk}}{R^1_{LL} + R^*_{LL}} < 0.$$

Utilizing this information, we can obtain the following:

$$\pi^1_{22} = R^1_{22} + R^1_{2L}\left(\frac{\partial L^1}{\partial q^1}\right) > 0,$$

$$\pi^1_{23} = \pi^1_{32} = -\left(\frac{R^1_{2L}}{t}\right)\left(\frac{\partial L^1}{\partial \alpha}\right) = -R^*_{pL}\left(\frac{\partial L^1}{\partial q^1}\right) > 0,$$

$$\pi^1_{33} = R^*_{pp} + \left(\frac{R^*_{pL}}{t}\right)\left(\frac{\partial L^1}{\partial \alpha}\right) > 0, \quad \text{where } R^*_{pp} = 0,$$

$$\pi^1_{k2} = \pi^1_{2k} = -R^*_{kL}\left(\frac{\partial L^1}{\partial q^1}\right) = R^1_{2L}\left(\frac{\partial L^1}{\partial k^*}\right) > 0,$$

$$\pi^1_{k3} = \pi^1_{3k} = R^*_{kp}\left(\frac{R^*_{kL}}{t}\right)\left(\frac{\partial L^1}{\partial \alpha}\right) = R^*_{pk}R^*_{pL}\left(\frac{\partial L^1}{\partial k^*}\right) > 0,$$

$$\pi^1_{kk} = R^*_{kk} - R^*_{kL}\left(\frac{\partial L^1}{\partial k^*}\right) = \frac{R^1_{LL}R^*_{kk}}{(R^1_{LL} + R^*_{LL})} < 0.$$

So, we can show that:

$$\frac{\partial X_3^1}{\partial q^1} = \pi_{32}^1 - \left(\frac{\pi_{3k}^1}{\pi_{kk}^1}\right) \pi_{k2}^1 > 0,$$

$$\frac{\partial X_3^1}{\partial \alpha} = -t \left[\pi_{33}^1 - \left(\frac{\pi_{3k}^1}{\pi_{kk}^1}\right) \pi_{k3}^1\right] < 0,$$

$$\frac{\partial X_2^1}{\partial q^1} = \pi_{22}^1 - \left(\frac{\pi_{2k}^1}{\pi_{kk}^1}\right) \pi_{k2}^1 > 0,$$

$$\frac{\partial X_2^1}{\partial \alpha} = -t \left[\pi_{23}^1 - \left(\frac{\pi_{2k}^1}{\pi_{kk}^1}\right) \pi_{k3}^1\right] < 0,$$

$$\frac{\partial X_2^2}{\partial q^2} = \pi_{22}^2 - \frac{(\pi_{k2}^2)^2}{\pi_{kk}^2} > 0,$$

where $C = (\partial X_3^1/\partial \alpha)(\partial X_2^1/\partial q^1) - (\partial X_2^1/\partial \alpha)(\partial X_3^1/\partial q^1) < 0$ and $H = \pi_{22}^1 \pi_{33}^1 - (\pi_{23}^1)^2 = (R_{22}^1 R_{pL}^*/t)(\partial L^1/\partial \alpha) > 0$.

A.2 *Stability*

Since the goods markets of the non-tradables are always cleared in both periods, the adjustment processes for them are:

$$\dot{q}^1 = a_1 Z^1(q^1, q^2),$$
$$\dot{q}^2 = a_2 Z^2(q^1, q^2),$$

where the dot is the time derivative, α_1 is a positive constant, and $Z^1 = E_2(\cdot) - \pi(\cdot)$ and $Z^2 = E_2(\cdot) - \pi(\cdot)$ are, respectively, the excess demands for the non-tradables in Periods 1 and 2. From (5.11), we can obtain that u is a function of q^1 and q^2 for a given α. We take a linear approximation of the above adjustment processes around the equilibrium (q_e^1, q_e^2) as:

$$\dot{q}^1 = a_1 \left[\left(\frac{\partial z^1}{\partial q^1}\right)(q^1 - q_e^1) + \left(\frac{\partial Z^1}{\partial q^2}\right)(q^2 - q_e^2)\right],$$

$$\dot{q}^2 = a_2 \left[\left(\frac{\partial z^2}{\partial q^1}\right)(q^1 - q_e^1) + \left(\frac{\partial Z^2}{\partial q^2}\right)(q^2 - q_e^2)\right].$$

A sufficient condition for stability of the above system is:

$$\frac{\partial Z^1}{\partial q^1} + \frac{\partial Z^2}{\partial q^2} < 0.$$

From (5.11)–(5.13), we can solve for:

$$\frac{\partial q^1}{\partial Z^1} = \frac{\left[A - (E_u - tE_{3u})\left(\frac{\partial X_2^2}{\partial q^2}\right)\right]}{\Delta},$$

$$\frac{\partial q^2}{\partial Z^2} = \frac{\left[S - (E_u - tE_{3u})\left(\frac{\partial X_2^1}{\partial q^1}\right) - tE_{2u}(1 - \alpha)\left(\frac{\partial X_3^1}{\partial q^1}\right)\right]}{\Delta},$$

where $A < 0$, $S = (E_u - tE_{2u})E_{22} + tE_{2u}E_{32} < 0$, and Δ denotes the determinant of the coefficient matrix of (5.11)–(5.13). Hence, $\Delta > 0$ is sufficient for $\partial Z^1/\partial q^1 < 0$ and $\partial Z^2/\partial q^2 < 0$. Note that $R_{2L}^1 < 0$ is required for $\partial X_3^1/\partial q^1 > 0$ since $\partial X_3^1/\partial q^1 = \pi_{32}^1 - \pi_{2k}^1\pi_{3k}^1/\pi_{kk}^1$.

Chapter 6

Export Requirements, Investment Quotas, and Welfare in a Dynamic Economy

6.1 Introduction

To circumvent widespread existing tariff barriers in commodity trade, firms have resorted to relocating a part or all of their production activities from home bases to foreign locations. This is known as the "tariff-jumping" motive of foreign direct investment (FDI).[1] Tariff-jumping foreign investment, however, tends to reduce the host country's welfare for two reasons. First, foreign capital inflow exacerbates the existing tariff distortion through "overproduction" of the importable goods, in which the country has a comparative disadvantage.[2] Second, foreign investment may crowd out a substantial amount of domestic investment, thereby slowing down the accumulation of domestic capital.

To mitigate the tariff distortionary effect of foreign capital inflows, Rodrik (1987) argues for the use of an export-performance policy. As mentioned in Chapters 4 and 5, this policy specifies that a portion of the output produced by foreign firms in the host country must be exported at world prices (which are lower than the tariff-inclusive domestic prices). The subsequent fall in the effective prices leads to a lower return to foreign capital and hence a smaller output. The contraction in the protected sector corrects the distortion exacerbated by foreign investment, rendering the policy of export requirements to be welfare improving.[3]

---

[1] The other purpose of foreign investment is globalization of the production process to take advantage of an international division of labor. See Ethier (1986) for details.

[2] This argument was presented by Brecher and Diaz Alejandro (1977).

[3] Chao and Yu (1994c) analyzed the welfare effect of export-share requirements under quotas.

Alternatively, foreign capital inflows may be restricted to a certain level to avoid crowding out domestic investment. Foreign investment restrictions can be imposed in the form of quantity controls (i.e., foreign investment quotas) and/or by confirming foreign investment in certain sectors where domestic investment is deficient. Although there have been extensive studies on the welfare effect of exogenous inflows of foreign capital in static models,[4] little attention has been given to the crowding-out effect of capital inflows and the effects of the export performance policy in a dynamic setting.

In the agreements reached in the Uruguay Round of the General Agreement on Tariffs and Trade (GATT) in 1994, the export-performance requirements, input import limitations, and other policy interventions were lumped together under the generic heading "trade-related investment measures" (TRIMs).[5] By now, TRIMs have been phased out by the member nations of the WTO due to the agreement reached. However, in this chapter, for analytical and policy interest we examine two welfare issues relating to TRIMs. First, what is the optimal level of foreign-investment quotas in the presence of a tariff? Second, what is the optimal ratio of export requirements for correcting the tariff distortion exacerbated by foreign capital? To answer these two questions, an intertemporal model is developed in Section 6.2, in which the short-run and the steady-state equilibrium will be analyzed. Section 6.3 examines the crowding-out and the welfare effects of foreign investment quotas and export-share requirements (ESRs) on foreign firms. In addition, individually and jointly optimal policies will be derived and discussed. Section 6.4 contains concluding remarks.

6.2　The Model

In this section we describe the setup of an intertemporal model in which both domestic and foreign firms operate in the home country. By using labor and sector-specific factors, domestic firms produce two types of goods: an importable manufacturing good X and an exportable agricultural good Y. The production functions are given by: $X = X(L_X, K)$ and $Y = Y(L_Y, V)$, where L_i denotes labor employed by domestic firms in sector $i(i = X, Y)$, and K and V, respectively, are capital and land-specific to manufacturing

---

[4]See Batra and Ramachandran (1980), Batra (1986), and Beladi and Marjit (1993), among others.

[5]Greenaway (1992) provides a detailed list of TRIMs.

and agricultural production.[6] Assume that the home country is small and thus cannot affect the world goods prices. Let good Y be the numeraire, and hence the domestic relative price of good X is p. To protect domestic firms in the importable sector, a specific tariff, τ, is imposed so that $p = p^* + \tau$, where p^* is the exogenously given world price. The production structure of domestic firms can be summarized by their revenue function as: $R(1, p, L, K) = \text{maximum } \{pX(L_X, K) + Y(L_Y, V): L = L_X + L_Y\}$, where L denotes total workers employed in domestic firms. We suppress for simplicity the fixed factor V in the above revenue function. By Shephard's lemma, the partial derivative of the revenue function with respect to the goods price (input) provides the output (factor price), i.e., the output of X is $X = R_p(=\partial R/\partial p)$, the wage rate to labor in the domestic sectors is $w = R_L$, and the rate of return to domestic capital is $r = R_K$.

To bypass the tariff barrier, foreign firms can relocate their plants in the host country to produce the manufacturing good: $X_f = X^f(L_X^f, K_f)$, where L_K^f is the domestic workers employed in foreign firms and K_f is foreign capital. It is assumed that goods X and X_f are identical.

As pointed out earlier, foreign capital can crowd out domestic capital. To address the problem of crowding out, the domestic country adopts the policy of imposing quotas on foreign investment.[7] In the presence of tariffs, more capital inflow by loosening quota restrictions on foreign investment can, however, reduce welfare. Eliminating or lowering the tariff rate enhances welfare for a small country, but the policy may not be viable. Thus, we follow Rodrik (1987) by considering a politically more feasible policy of TRIMs, such as ESRs for foreign firms. The requirement specifies that a certain percentage, say α, of foreign firms' output be mandated for export. When the requirement is implemented, the effective goods price facing foreign firms is: $p_e = \alpha p^* + (1 - \alpha)p$, which is a weighted average of the foreign price and the domestic price with the weights equal to α and $1 - \alpha$. The revenue function for foreign firms is: $R^f(p_e, \overline{L} - L, K_f) = \text{maximum } \{p_e X^f(L_K^f, K_f): L_K^f - \overline{L} - L\}$, where $\overline{L}$ is the endowment of labor in the host country. Here we have the usual dual properties: $X_f = R_p^f(=\partial R^f/\partial p_e)$ and $w = R_L^f(=\partial R^f/\partial(\overline{L} - L))$ under perfect labor mobility between sectors. It is noted that $r_f = R_K^f(=\partial R^f/\partial K_f = p_e(\partial X^f/\partial K_f))$ is the domestic return to foreign capital. In view of the

---

[6]See Jones (1971) for a lucid exposition of the specific-factor model.

[7]This is referred to as placing limitations on input imports, classified under input-based TRIMs. See Greenaway (1992) for a detailed discussion.

direct control of foreign investment, we can reasonably assume $r_f/p_e > r^*$, where r_f/p_e is the *per-dollar* return to foreign capital and r^* denotes the world rate of return to foreign bonds (its price is equal to 1).[8] The higher domestic rate of capital return can provide another incentive, aside from tariff-jumping, for attracting foreign investment to the host country.

The above production information can be represented by the cost–price relation. We assume that firms are perfectly competitive and operate under constant returns to scale technologies. Zero profits prevail in equilibrium; unit cost, $c^i(\cdot)$, of a product must equal its price in each sector:

$$c^X(w,r) = p, \tag{6.1}$$

$$c^Y(w,v) = 1, \tag{6.2}$$

$$c^f(w,r_f) = p_e = \alpha p^* + (1-\alpha)p, \tag{6.3}$$

where v, r, and r_f are, respectively, the rate of return to land, domestic capital, and foreign capital. Since domestic agents are allowed to hold foreign bonds, the per-dollar return to domestic capital, r/p, is pinned down to r^* in steady state, as shown below. Thus, the wage rate, w, and the rate of return to foreign capital, r_f, are determined respectively by (6.1) and (6.3) as functions of α alone. This implies that in the steady state the factor returns are independent of the stocks of domestic and foreign capital. However, in the short run, r/p may be not equal to r^*, causing insufficient numbers of equations in (6.1)–(6.3) to determine four unknowns — r, w, v and r_f — under the specific-factor model. Additional equilibrium conditions for the factor markets are therefore needed. This is a notable feature of the present model.

Turn next to the demand side of the model. Domestic agents, endowed with a fixed supply of labor, accumulate two kinds of assets: foreign bonds and domestic capital. The agents use revenues from domestic and foreign firms, plus the interest income from foreign bond, to finance spending in the consumption of two goods $(C_i, i = X, Y)$, domestic investment (I) and payments to foreign capital $(r_f K_f)$. Hence, the accumulation of foreign assets (b) is:

$$\dot{b} = R(1, p, K, L) + R^f(p_e, K_f, \overline{L} - L) + r^* b$$

$$- (pC_X + C_Y) - p[I + \phi(I)] - r_f K_f + T, \tag{6.4}$$

where T is the government lump-sum transfer payment to tariff revenue.

---

[8] We consider a "corn" type economy, in which good X can be either consumed or reinvested. The price of capital is p at home and p^* abroad.

It is assumed that good X can be used either for domestic consumption or for investment. Installation or adjustment costs, $\phi(I)$, have to be incurred for sustaining investment at the level of I. Following Turnovsky and Sen (1991), the adjustment cost is a convex function of I : $\phi' > 0$ and $\phi'' > 0$ with $\phi(0) = 0$ and $\phi'(0) = 0$. The rate of the accumulation of domestic capital is:

$$\dot{K} = I. \tag{6.5}$$

Here we ignore depreciation for the sake of convenience.

The agents' decision is to choose the levels of consumption, labor allocation, and domestic investment to maximize the intertemporal utility function:

$$Max_{\{C_i, L, I\}} W = \int_0^\infty U(C_X, C_Y) e^{-r^* t} dt, \tag{6.6}$$

subject to (6.4), (6.5), and initial stocks of assets, $b(0) = b_0$ and $K(0) = K_0$, where $U(\cdot)$ is the instantaneous utility function and the foreign interest rate, r^*, serves as the rate of time preference. The two goods are normal in consumption, and the instantaneous utility function is concave.

This is a standard optimization problem, which can be analyzed through its first-order optimality conditions with respect to the decision variables, C_X, C_Y, L and I, as follows:

$$U_X(C_X, C_Y) = \lambda_1 p, \tag{6.7}$$

$$U_Y(C_X, C_Y) = \lambda_1, \tag{6.8}$$

$$R_L(1, p, K, L) = R_L^f(p_e, K_f, \overline{L} - L), \tag{6.9}$$

$$\lambda_1 p [1 + \phi'(I)] = \lambda_2, \tag{6.10}$$

where λ_1 and λ_2, the costate variables associated with (6.4) and (6.5), are respectively the shadow values of wealth (held in the form of foreign bonds) and domestic capital. Equations (6.7) and (6.8) describe the consumption behavior regarding the two goods: C_i depends on λ_1 alone for a given p by a small country assumption. The labor allocation between domestic and foreign firms is determined in (6.9) by equating marginal product of labor. Equation (6.10) sets out the equilibrium condition for an optimal mix of investment between foreign bonds and domestic capital.

In addition, the costate variables λ_1 and λ_2 move according to the paths depicted by:

$$\dot{\lambda}_1 = 0, \tag{6.11}$$

$$\dot{\lambda}_2 = \lambda_2 r^* - \lambda_1 R_K(1, p, K, L). \tag{6.12}$$

The world interest rate r^* is assumed to be constant. It then follows from (6.11) that the shadow value of foreign assets λ_1 is always at its steady-state value $\overline{\lambda}_1$ (to be determined below).

Finally, there are the transversality conditions:

$$\lim_{t\to\infty} e^{-r^*t}\lambda_1 b(t) = \lim_{t\to\infty} e^{-r^*t}\lambda_2 K(t)0, \qquad (6.13)$$

for meeting the intertemporal budget constraint. The first expression in (6.13) warrants that consumers cannot borrow indefinitely to repay past debts, while the second term ensures that $K(t)$ grows at a rate less than r^* if λ_2 is constant.

The intertemporal economy can be described by the temporary equilibrium, dynamics, and steady-state equilibrium, where the adjustment paths are the shadow value of domestic capital (λ_2), the domestic capital (K), and the current account balance (b). Our analysis will proceed accordingly.

6.2.1   *Temporary equilibrium*

For given domestic and foreign capital stock and foreign bonds in the short run, a temporary equilibrium is characterized by the optimal solutions of consumption, labor allocation, and investment in (6.7)–(6.10), along with an equilibrium condition for foreign firms. Since foreign capital inflow is under strict quantity control, K_f is fixed and its return in the host country, r_f, is determined by:

$$r_f = R_K^f(p_e, K_f, \overline{L} - L). \qquad (6.14)$$

Here we assume that r_f exceeds the capital return in the source country, as foreign capital flows into the host nation to seek better returns until the quota is used up.

Since $\overline{\lambda}_1$ is given by (6.11), the model contains a dichotomy in the short run. The demand side of (6.7) and (6.8) is separated from the supply side of (6.9), (6.10), and (6.14); that is, (6.7) and (6.8) determine C_X and C_Y as functions of $\overline{\lambda}_1$ alone, while (6.9), (6.10), and (6.14) determine L, I, and r_f. We first define Tobin's $q = \lambda_2/\lambda_1$, which is the shadow price of investment. Investment is a function of q according to (6.10):

$$I = (\phi')^{-1}\left(\frac{q}{p-1}\right) \equiv H(q), \qquad (6.15)$$

where $H' > 0$ and $H(p) = 0$.

Secondly, in the specific-factor model, the short-run sectoral allocation of labor (L) in response to a change in α, K or K_f can be derived by differentiating (6.9): $dL/d\alpha > 0, dL/dK > 0$, and $dL/dK_f < 0$. That is, labor employment in domestic firms increases when: (a) ESR against foreign firms is tightened; (b) more domestic capital is used; or (c) less foreign capital is employed. These results are intuitively clear. Furthermore, the reallocation of labor in favor of domestic sectors results in, as expected, a lower rate of return to foreign capital: $dr_f/d\alpha < 0, dr_f/dK < 0$ and $dr_f/dK_f < 0$.[9]

6.2.2 *Steady-state equilibrium*

The steady-state equilibrium of the economy can be characterized by the optimal solutions of consumption in (6.7) and (6.8), investment in (6.15), along with neither capital gains nor losses ($\dot{q} = 0$ in [6.12]) and no changes in the stock of foreign assets [$\dot{b} = 0$ in (6.4)]:

$$U_X(\widetilde{C}_X, \widetilde{C}_Y) = \overline{\lambda}_1 p, \tag{6.16}$$

$$U_Y(\widetilde{C}_X, \widetilde{C}_Y) = \overline{\lambda}_1, \tag{6.17}$$

$$\widetilde{q} = p, \tag{6.18}$$

$$R_K[1, p, \widetilde{K}, L(\alpha, \widetilde{K}, K_f)] = r^* p, \tag{6.19}$$

$$r^* b + R(1, p, \widetilde{K}, L(\alpha, \widetilde{K}, K_f)) + R^f(p_e, K_f, \overline{L} - L(\alpha, \widetilde{K}, K_f))$$
$$-(p\widetilde{C}_X + \widetilde{C}_Y) - p[H(\widetilde{q}) + \phi(H(\widetilde{q})] - r_f(\alpha, \widetilde{K}, K_f)K_f + T = 0, \tag{6.20}$$

where "$\sim$" over a variable denotes its steady-state value. Note that tariff revenue is: $T = \tau[\widetilde{C}_X + H(\widetilde{q}) + \phi(H(\widetilde{q})) - R_p - (1 - \alpha)R_p^f]$. In addition, the transversality condition in (6.13) yields the relationship between b and K:

$$b_0 - \widetilde{b} = \left[\frac{\Omega}{(\mu_1 - r^*)}\right](K_0 - \widetilde{K}), \tag{6.21}$$

where, as shown in Appendix A.2, the sign of Ω is ambiguous.

Equations (6.16)–(6.21) can be used to solve the steady-state values of $\widetilde{C}_X, \widetilde{C}_Y, \widetilde{q}, \widetilde{K}, \widetilde{b}$, and $\overline{\lambda}_1$ for given policy instruments of K_f and α. We will analyze the welfare implications of these two policies. The analysis sheds light on the current discussion of ongoing trade liberalization endeavor. Did

---

[9]The short-run, comparative static results and dynamic adjustments are provided in the Appendix.

the complete elimination of TRIMs by the WTO member nations improve their national welfare? This question will be addressed in the next section.

6.3 Welfare Effects of Foreign Investment Quotas and Export Requirements

The welfare implications of policy changes can be analyzed through the intertemporal utility function in (6.6). Following Turnovsky and Sen (1991), we linearize the instantaneous utility function around steady state and the welfare in (6.6) can be expressed by:

$$W \approx \frac{U(\widetilde{C}_X, \widetilde{C}_Y)}{r^*} + \frac{U_X(C_X(0) - \widetilde{C}_X)}{(r^* - \mu_1)} + \frac{U_Y(C_Y(0) - \widetilde{C}_Y)}{(r^* - \mu_1)}. \quad (6.22)$$

The first term in (6.22) represents the presented value of the steady-state utility, while the remaining two terms denote the adjustments of consumption toward steady-state equilibrium. Using the equilibrium conditions (6.16) and (6.17), the welfare change in (6.22) becomes:

$$dW = -\left[\frac{U_Y}{(r^* - \mu_1)} \right] \left\{ \left(\frac{\mu_1}{r^*} \right) \left[pd\widetilde{C}_X + d\widetilde{C}_Y \right] - \left[pdC_X(0) + dC_Y(0) \right] \right\}, \quad (6.23)$$

where the first term and the second term represent, respectively, the changes in steady state and initial consumption of goods X and Y.

6.3.1 *A loosening in foreign investment quotas*

The impacts on the steady-state variables of a loosening of foreign investment quotas (i.e., a rise in K_f) can be examined by using the cost–price structure in (6.1)–(6.3). Since domestic capital and foreign bonds are perfect substitutes, the rate of return to domestic capital is fixed to the world interest rate at steady state by (6.19). For the given domestic relative price of good X, the steady-state wage rate w is fixed by (6.1). This implies that the rate of return to foreign capital, r_f, depends only on α, not on K_f. Therefore, the effect of changes in K_f upon the host country works through the labor reallocation effect; an increase in K_f raises local production by foreign firms, and more domestic workers are employed in the foreign sector. This relocation of labor leads to a contraction in domestic production and hence a crowding out of domestic investment:

$$\frac{d\widetilde{K}}{dK_f} = \frac{R_{KL}\left(\frac{\partial L}{\partial K_f}\right)}{\left[R_{KK} + R_{KL}\left(\frac{\partial L}{\partial K}\right)\right]} < 0. \tag{6.24}$$

Since the domestic goods price is fixed, this crowding out of domestic investment affects welfare only through the income effect. By using (6.16), (6.17) and (6.20), the effects of changes in capital controls on the consumption of goods X and Y in steady state are:

$$\frac{d\widetilde{C}_X}{dK_f} = -\frac{A_K(U_{XY} - pU_{YY})}{\Delta}, \tag{6.25}$$

$$\frac{d\widetilde{C}_Y}{dK_f} = -\frac{A_K(pU_{XY} - U_{XX})}{\Delta}, \tag{6.26}$$

where $U_{XX} < 0, U_{YY} < 0, U_{XY} > 0$ and $\Delta = U_{XX} + pp^*U_{YY} - (p + p^*)$ $U_{XY} < 0$. It is noted that $A_K = -\tau\{(1-\alpha)R_{pK}^f + [R_{pL} - (1-\alpha)R_{pL}^f]G_K\}$, being the income effect via the change in tariff revenue. For a given tariff, the change in tariff revenue is mainly contributed by the change in the domestic supply of good X, which comes from the direct and the indirect production effect as shown in the first and the second term in A_K. Also note that $G_K = \partial L/\partial K_f + [\mu_1/(\mu_1 - r^*)](\partial L/\partial K)(d\widetilde{K}/dK_f) < 0$: the labor-reallocation and the crowding-out effect. An increase in foreign capital raises foreign firms' local production of good X but lowers the domestic firms' production. The former reduces tariff revenue whereas the latter increases it. The sign of A_K depends, therefore, on the value of α. For a small α (i.e., $R_{pL} < (1 - \alpha)R_{pL}^f$), the loss of tariff revenue from the increase in foreign firms' output dominates the gain from the reduction in domestic firms' output. This implies that a loosening (tightening) of capital controls is always welfare decreasing (improving). However, when α gets larger and $R_{pL} > (1 - \alpha)R_{pL}^f$, the tariff-revenue gain from the reduction in domestic output may be so strong that loosening capital controls becomes welfare improving.[10]

In summary, the welfare effect of foreign capital controls depends on the sign of A_K. The optimal level of foreign capital is obtained by setting

---

[10]Using (6.7) and (6.8), the effects of changes in foreign capital on consumption are: $dC_i/dK_f = (dC_i/d\lambda_1)(d\lambda_1/dK_f)$, where $dC_i/d\lambda_1 < 0$. Note that $d\bar{\lambda}_1/dK_f = A_K[U_{XX}U_{YY} - (U_{XY})^2]/\Delta$ from (6.16), (6.17) and (6.20). Hence, dC_i/dK_f depend on the sign of A_K. A similar result applies to the initial effect on consumption.

$A_K = 0$. Since A_K is not explicitly expressed in terms of K_f, the optimal level is determined by a critical level of export share, α_K:

$$\frac{dW}{dK_f} \lessgtr 0 \quad \text{as } \alpha \gtrless \alpha_K \qquad (6.27)$$

where $\alpha_K = 1 - G_K R_{pL}/(G_K R_{pL}^f - R_{pK}^f) < 1$ by noting that $R_{pL} < R_{pL}^f$).[11] The following proposition is immediate.

Proposition 6.1 *For a tariff-ridden, small open economy, a loosening of foreign investment quotas increases (reduces) tariff revenue and hence improves (deteriorates) the welfare of the economy if the ESR on foreign firms is higher (lower) than the critical level α_K.*

Specifically, the optimal level of foreign capital is zero when $\alpha < \alpha_K$. This is a generalization of immiserizing inflows of foreign capital obtained by Brecher and Diaz Alejandro (1977) under zero ESRs. When $\alpha = \alpha_K$, some inflows of foreign capital are optimal. However, when $\alpha > \alpha_K$, the optimal inflow of foreign capital is identified with the situation where all labor is employed only in the foreign sector. The entire relationship is plotted in Figure 6.1, where the optimal levels of foreign capital are represented by the K_f^0 schedule, a step function in the policy space of (α, K_f). The horizontal arrows indicate the welfare-improving adjustments in capital controls. Adjustment in welfare in the policy space is depicted in Figure 6.1, adapted from the graphical representation of iso-welfare contours in Neary (1993, 1995).

6.3.1.1 *A reduction in export-share requirements*

Consider now a reduction in ESRs on foreign firms. Such a reduction causes labor to relocate from domestic to foreign firms, resulting in a fall in the steady-state domestic capital. By using (6.19), we have:

$$\frac{d\tilde{K}}{d\alpha} = -\frac{R_{KL}\left(\frac{\partial L}{\partial \alpha}\right)}{\left[R_{KK} + R_{KL}\left(\frac{\partial L}{\partial K}\right)\right]} > 0. \qquad (6.28)$$

---

[11]By (6.9), we have $p(\partial X/\partial L_X) = p_e(\partial X_f/\partial L_X^f)$, which gives $\partial X/\partial L_X \leq \partial X_f/\partial L_X^f$ because $p_e \leq p$. Using Shephard's lemma, we obtain $R_{pL} = (\partial X/\partial L_X)(dL_X/dL) < \partial X/\partial L_X \leq \partial X_f/\partial L_X^f = R_{pL}^f$.

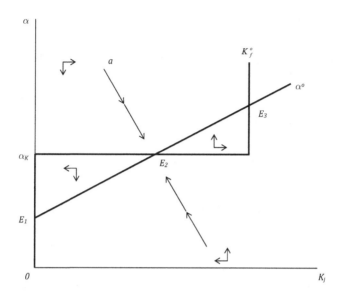

Figure 6.1   Joinly optimal policies.

By utilizing (6.16), (6.17), and (6.20), the steady-state effects of the change in the export shares on the consumption of goods X and Y can be similarly obtained as in the earlier case of capital controls, except for the income effect: $A_\alpha = -\tau[R_{pL} - (1 - \alpha)R_{pL}^F]G_\alpha - K_f(\partial r_f/\partial \alpha)$, where $G_\alpha = \partial L/\partial \alpha + [\mu_1/(\mu_1 - r^*)](\partial L/\partial K)(d\tilde{K}/d\alpha) > 0$, capturing the labor-reallocation and crowding-out effects. Similar to the A_K expression, the first term in A_α contains changes in tariff revenue. In addition, there is a term on the rate of return on foreign capital, which is absent in the case of capital controls. This A_α expression of the income effect is a generalization of Rodrik (1987, Equation 11), in which the crowding-out effect is absent due to the static nature of his model.

In essence, the effect of ESRs on welfare depends on the level of α. By setting $A_\alpha = 0$, we obtain the optimal ESR, α^0, as follows:

$$\alpha^0 = \left(1 - \frac{R_{pL}}{R_{pL}^f}\right) - \left[\frac{\left(\frac{\partial r_f}{\partial \alpha}\right)}{\tau R_{pL}^f G_\alpha}\right] K_f. \qquad (6.29)$$

Since $\partial r_f/\partial \alpha < 0$, α^0 is positively related to K_f. Substituting α^0 into A_α, we obtain:

$$\text{sign}\left(\frac{dW}{d\alpha}\right) = \text{sign } A_\alpha = -\text{sign } [\tau R_{pL}^f G_\alpha(\alpha - \alpha^0)]. \qquad (6.30)$$

When $\alpha < (>)\alpha^0$, a rise (fall) in α improves welfare according to (6.30). The α^0 schedule expressed by (6.29) is plotted in Figure 6.1 with an intercept $(1 - R_{pL}/R_{pL}^f)$ less than 1 and a positive slope. The vertical arrows in Figure 6.1 indicate the welfare-improving movements of ESRs. Thus, the following proposition is immediate.

Proposition 6.2 *For a tariff-ridden, small, open economy, a non-zero optimal ESR exists for each quota of foreign investment. Furthermore, the larger the foreign investment, the higher the optimal ESR.*

6.3.2 *Jointly optimal policies*

As shown above, when a tariff exists in a country, some TRIMs, such as foreign investment quotas and/or export requirements, may be welfare improving. Therefore, as long as preexisting distortions remain, analytically TRIMs would be a useful instrument for the host country, although they are now disallowed. An interesting question thus arises: In the presence of a preexisting tariff, what would be the jointly optimal policies regarding foreign capital controls and ESRs?

The jointly optimal levels of policies, denoted by α^{00} and K_f^{00}, can be easily identified and explained with the help of Figure 6.1, in which the two schedules showing optimal α^0 and K_f^0 intersect three times at E_1, E_2, and E_3. These intersection points represent the second-best policy alternatives the government can choose. It turns out that only the alternative E_2 is economically meaningful. This can be seen as follows. The policy alternative E_1 denotes $K_f^{00} = 0$ and α^{00} at the intercept of the α axis, implying that foreign firms do not exist so that there is no need to implement export requirements. This is a hypothetical case irrelevant for the present analysis. On the other hand, point E_3 represents the case that all domestic labor is employed in the foreign sector and the domestic sectors vanish, implying that the country becomes completely specialized in producing the importable good X_1 only. This is a highly unrealistic case and would be deleted from the choice set by the government. Therefore, we will focus on analyzing the interior point E_2, denoting the only viable policy alternative. From (6.27) and (6.29), we can solve for point E_2:

$$\alpha^{00} = 1 - \frac{G_K R_{pL}}{(G_K R_{pL}^f - R_{pK}^f)}, \qquad (6.31)$$

$$K_f^{00} = \frac{\tau G_\alpha R_{pL} R_{pK}^f}{\left[\left(\frac{\partial r_f}{\partial \alpha} \right) \left(G_K R_{pL}^f - R_{pK}^f \right) \right]} > 0. \tag{6.32}$$

Note that the jointly optimal export requirement ratio, α^{00}, is less than 1. The positive relationship between the tariff rate and the level of foreign capital in (6.32) justifies the tariff-jumping capital inflow. If the preexisting tariff policy responsible for attracting foreign investment were removed (i.e., $\tau = 0$), "TRIMs would simply wither on the vine," as aptly pointed out by Greenaway (1992, p. 156). Moreover, the optimal level of foreign capital is inversely related to G_K in (6.32), capturing the crowding-out effect on domestic capital; the more the crowding out, the tighter the optimal foreign-investment quota.

Suppose initially the economy is characterized by a tight foreign investment quota together with a restrictive ESR, such as the situation depicted by point "a" in Figure 6.1. The host country would benefit by loosening the quota on foreign investment and relaxing the requirement on export shares. As a result, point "a" moves to point E_2, and along the movement the host country's welfare improves, as verifiable from the non-depicted map of potato-shaped iso-welfare contours à la Neary (1995) in the (α, K_f) space.

Proposition 6.3 *In the presence of a preexisting tariff on the importable goods, the jointly optimal policy is a quota on foreign capital together with an ESR on foreign firms.*

The presumption for this proposition is the existence of tariffs. In the face of recent trade liberalization, tariffs have been reduced but not completely removed. For example, according to an agreement between China and the US on China's entry into the WTO, China reduces tariffs on automobiles to 25% in 2006 from the 80 to 100% before China joined the WTO. Hence, when the preexisting distortions are too politically difficult to be completely removed, the use of TRIMs appears to provide a second-best solution in that TRIMs offset some of the adverse consequences of the preexisting distortions. Of course, welfare would be higher if the preexisting tariff could be removed. Under free trade in goods, $\tau = 0$ in (6.32), foreign firms cease to locate production activities abroad ($K_f = 0$), and, hence, there will be no need to impose ESRs ($\alpha = 0$) by (6.29).[12]

---

[12]It may be noted that jointly optimal policies do not necessarily exist, if the α^0 schedule is located far below the K_f^0 schedule in Figure 6.1 so that the two loci do not intersect.

6.4   Concluding Remarks

This chapter has developed an intertemporal model with accumulations of domestic capital and foreign bonds. The preexisting tariff barrier attracts foreign investment, and hence domestic and foreign firms co-exist in the host country. To protect domestic firms, TRIMs, such as foreign-investment quotas and ESRs, are used against foreign firms. We have analyzed the intricate interactions between foreign-investment quotas and ESRs and the various welfare impacts of these foreign investment-related measures. In the presence of tariff, the second-best policy is a foreign-investment quota together with an ESR on foreign firms. Although tariffs have been recently reduced to relatively low levels under the auspices of the WTO and/or by some regional trade agreements, completely eliminating TRIMs as agreed upon in the 1994 Uruguay Round of GATT negotiations would not be optimal for a country if the existing distortions (say, tariffs), cannot be totally abolished for political or other reasons.

   In this chapter, we have focused on the jointly optimal policies of foreign-investment quotas and ESRs in the steady state. Nevertheless, the sequencing issue of implementing these two policies is not considered. This is an interesting topic for future research.

Appendix

A.1   *Short-run comparative statics*

From (6.9), we have:

$$\frac{dL}{d\alpha} = -\frac{\tau R_{Lp}^{f}}{(R_{LL} + R_{LL}^{f})} > 0,$$

$$\frac{dL}{dK} = -\frac{R_{LK}}{(R_{LL} + R_{LL}^{f})} > 0,$$

$$\frac{dL}{dK_{f}} = \frac{R_{LK}^{f}}{(R_{LL} + R_{LL}^{f})} < 0,$$

where $R_{LL} = \partial R_{L}/\partial L < 0$, $R_{LK} = \partial R_{L}/\partial K > 0$, $R_{Lp}^{f} = \partial R_{L}^{f}/\partial P_{e} > 0$, and so on.

Also, from (6.14), we obtain:

$$\frac{dr_f}{d\alpha} = -\tau R_{Kp}^f - R_{KL}^f \left(\frac{dL}{d\alpha}\right) < 0,$$

$$\frac{dr_f}{dK} = -R_{KL}^f \left(\frac{dL}{dK}\right) < 0,$$

$$\frac{dr_f}{dK_f} = R_{KK}^f - R_{KL}^f \left(\frac{dL}{dK_f}\right) = \frac{R_{LL} R_{KK}^f}{(R_{LL} + R_{LL}^f)} < 0.$$

In deriving the above results, the condition that $R_{KK}^f - R_{LL}^f - (R_{LK}^f)^2 = 0$ under a constant returns to scale technology for foreign firms is utilized.

A.2   *Dynamics and solutions*

The dynamic system of the economy consists of $\dot{q}$, $\dot{K}$, and $\dot{b}$ in (6.12), (6.5), and (6.4), respectively. Since the adjustments of q and K are independent of b, we can linearize (6.12) and (6.5) around the steady states of q and K, denoted by $\tilde{q}$ and $\tilde{K}$, to yield:

$$\begin{bmatrix} \dot{q} \\ \dot{K} \end{bmatrix} = \begin{bmatrix} r^* & -R_{KK} - R_{KL}\left(\frac{\partial L}{\partial K}\right) \\ H'(\tilde{q}) & 0 \end{bmatrix} \begin{bmatrix} q - \tilde{q} \\ K - \tilde{K} \end{bmatrix}, \qquad (A.1)$$

where the determinant of the coefficient matrix is $D = H'(\tilde{q})[R_{KK} + R_{KL}(\partial L/\partial K)]$ and all partial derivatives are evaluated at their steady-state values. Note that $R_{KK} = pX_{KK}, X_{KK} = \partial^2 X/\partial K^2$, and so on. Under constant returns to scale, $X_{KK}X_{LL} - (X_{KL})^2 = 0$. Using this condition, we have $R_{KK}R_{LL} - (R_{KL})^2 = p^2 X_{KK}X_{LL}(dL_X/dL) - p^2(X_{KL})^2(dL_X/dL)^2 = p^2 X_{KK}X_{LL}(dL_X/dL)(1 - dL_X/dL) > 0$, where $0 < dL_X/dL < 1$ due to the specific-factor structure in the domestic sectors. Then, we obtain: $D = H'(\tilde{q})\{[R_{KK}R_{LL} - (R_{KL})^2] + R_{KK}R_{LL}^f\}/(R_{LL} + R_{LL}^f) < 0$. This implies that the steady-state equilibrium is a saddle point with one negative and one positive eigenvalue, denoted by $\mu_1 < 0$ and $\mu_2 > 0$. By using the initial condition of K_0, the stable solutions to the differential equations in (A.1) are given by:

$$K = \tilde{K} + (K_0 - \tilde{K})e^{\mu_1 t}, \qquad (A.2)$$

$$q = \tilde{q} + \left[\frac{\theta}{(\mu_1 - r^*)}\right](K_0 - \tilde{K})e^{\mu_1 t}, \qquad (A.3)$$

where $\theta = -[R_{KK} + R_{KL}(\partial L/\partial K)] > 0$.

Next, substituting tariff revenue T into (6.4) and linearizing it around the steady state, and then using (A.2) and (A.3) yields:

$$\dot{b} = r^*(b - \widetilde{d}) + \Omega(K_0 - \widetilde{K})e^{\mu_1 t}, \tag{A.5}$$

where $\Omega = -p^*\theta H'(q)/(\mu_1 - r^*) + \{R_K - \tau R_{pK} - t[R_{pL} - (1 - \alpha) R_{pL}^f](\partial L/\partial K)\} \gtrless 0$. The solution to the differential equation in (A.5) is:

$$b = \widetilde{b} + \left[\frac{\Omega(K_0 - \widetilde{K})}{(\mu_1 - r^*)}\right] e^{\mu_1 t} + \left[b_0 - \widetilde{b} - \frac{\Omega(K_0 - \widetilde{K})}{(\mu_1 - r^*)}\right] e^{r^* t}, \tag{A.6}$$

where b_0 is the initial stock of foreign bonds. Applying the transversality condition in (6.13) to (A.6) yields (6.21) in the text.

Chapter 7

The Impact of
Export-Share Requirements
Under Production Uncertainty

7.1 Introduction

With the increasing importance of foreign direct investment (FDI) to the
world economy, economists have devoted considerable attention to a broad
class of governmental intervention policies that were intended to enhance
welfare in the host country. As mentioned in earlier chapters, one such
form of intervention that has attracted academic attention is export-share
requirements (ESRs) imposed on FDI. These ESRs require the foreign direct
investor to export some portion of its output. Many countries had adopted
an ESR policy prior to its being disallowed by the World Trade Organization (WTO) agreement. It is, therefore, socially relevant as well as
intellectually interesting to inquire whether such requirements can achieve
their intended aim. The theoretical evidence is mixed. In the context of a
general equilibrium setting, Rodrik (1987) argued that ESRs *may* improve
welfare by lessening production of an overproduced, tariff-protected good.
Chao and Yu (1994a) extended Rodrik's conclusion to a three-sector, general equilibrium economy characterized by sector-specific unemployment.
In contrast, in the presence of import quotas, Chao and Yu (1994b) argue
that ESRs are generally welfare reducing. Thus, the theoretical evidence is
distinctly mixed. It is noteworthy that all these studies were confined to the
case of certainty. The implications of uncertainty for the efficacy of ESRs
should be explored. Such exploration may be of societal value both because
the world is characterized by the presence of uncertainty and because policymakers in developing economies often imposed ESRs on FDI before the
mid-2000s.

Generally speaking, the analyses of uncertainty for trade issues have built upon Batra's (1972) pioneering introduction of uncertainty into a two-sector, two-factor general equilibrium model. Noteworthy is the welfare analysis of tariffs versus quotas with a random international price of the imported good (Choi and Beladi, 1993).[1] This chapter, drawing on Chao *et al.* (2004), also builds on Batra's analytical approach, although within the context of a three-sector model. (Our reasoning for employing a third sector is developed below.) The broad conclusion that has emerged from the introduction of uncertainty is that while some results of international trade theory under certainty extend to the case of uncertainty, other results may be reversed. This deduction also applies to our results.

The chapter is organized as follows. Section 7.2 develops a three-sector model of ESRs under production uncertainty. Section 7.3 analyzes the factor price and resource allocation effects of ESRs in both the short run and the long run. Section 7.4 offers concluding remarks.

7.2   The Model

In a simple general equilibrium model of international trade, an economy consists of a primary sector (agriculture, denoted as Sector 1) and a secondary sector (manufacturing, denoted as Sector 2). Rodrik (1987) has observed that it is not unusual for the agricultural good to be exported while domestic production of the manufactured good is supplemented by imports. Additionally, the manufacturing sector is often protected by an import tariff of $\tau\%$. Provided the economy under investigation is sufficiently small relative to the world economy, it can be treated as a price-taker on world markets. Under such a scenario the domestic price of the manufactured good is $(1 + t)\hat{p}_2$, where $\hat{p}_2$ is the world price of the manufactured good.

As Rodrik (1987) has noted, one of the (intended) results of tariff protection is that it induces firms that export to the country to circumvent the import duty by investing in the host country. Such investment causes a subtle but fundamental alteration in the simple general equilibrium model described above. In particular, while "foreign-owned" manufacturing competes for labor, it generally brings its own capital; that is, it does not compete for capital in the host country. Thus, in a modeling sense

---

[1]They fixed the wage and capital–rental rates; but, to maintain mathematical tractability, they allowed resources to be unemployed.

"foreign-owned" manufacturing is not a subset of Sector 2 but is itself a separate, secondary sector (denoted as Sector 3). To sharpen the analysis, we assume that goods produced by foreign-owned manufacturing firms are perfectly substitutable for goods produced by domestic manufacturers.

Attempts by foreign-owned firms to circumvent the import duty may be at least partially countered by the host government through the imposition of an ESR of $\beta\%$ of the output produced by foreign-owned firms, with $0 \leq \beta \leq 1$. This causes the effective price for the foreign-owned manufacturing firms to be a weighted average of the price obtained from the required export sales and the price obtained from sales in the host country: $\hat{p}_3 = \beta\hat{p}_2 + (1-\beta)(1+\tau)\hat{p}_2 = (1 + (1-\beta)\tau)\hat{p}_2$. Note that domestic manufacturing (Sector 2) receives a greater effective per-unit price than does foreign-owned manufacturing (Sector 3): $(1+\tau)\hat{p}_2 > \hat{p}_3 > \hat{p}_2$. Both sectors obtain a higher price than do manufacturers selling only on the world market — this is ultimately the inducement for foreign-owned manufacturing to construct facilities in the host country.

While uncertainty can occur in any sector, we shall assume that only agricultural goods are subject to production uncertainty. Weather volatility is an obvious reason for such uncertainty. We also assume, as is typical in trade models, that the production function for the ith sector ($i \in (1,2,3)$) is linearly homogenous and concave and that all sectors may be characterized by perfect competition intrasectorally. Thus we write total output in each sector as:

$$Q_1 = \alpha F_1(K_1, L_1) = \alpha L_1 f_1(k_1) \tag{7.1}$$

$$Q_j = F_j(K_j, L_j) = L_j f_j(k_j) \quad j \in (2,3), \tag{7.2}$$

where α is a random variable with $E[\alpha] \equiv \mu$. In the preceding equations K_i and L_i denote the aggregate employment of capital and labor in the ith sector ($i \in (1,2,3)$), and $k_i \equiv K_i/L_i$ is the ith sector's capital–labor ratio. Note that due to the assumptions of linear homogeneity and convexity we have $f'_i > 0 > f''_i$. While labor is perfectly mobile between sectors, capital is mobile only between the domestic Sectors 1 and 2 since foreign firms are assumed to use only foreign capital. Such capital is further assumed to display attributes regarding management and marketing not readily available from domestic capital; thus, Sectors 2 and 3 are depicted as having their own, unique production functions.

Full employment of labor and domestic capital implies:

$$L_1 + L_2 + L_3 = \overline{L} \tag{7.3}$$

and

$$K_1 + K_2 = \overline{K} \tag{7.4}$$

where $\overline{L}$ and $\overline{K}$ are the fixed stocks of labor and capital in the host country. Combining (7.3) and (7.4) yields a condensed expression for full employment of resources:

$$L_1(k_1 - k_2) + k_2(\overline{L} - L_3) = \overline{K}. \tag{7.5}$$

Let the aggregate profit level in the ith sector be π_i and let the ith sector's wage and capital-rental rates be denoted by w_i and r_i, respectively. Using the first good as numeraire, the profit level in the agricultural sector can be written as:

$$\pi_1 = Q_1 - (w_1 L_1 + r_1 K_1) = L_1[\alpha f_1(k_1) - w_1 - r_1 k_1]. \tag{7.6}$$

Profits in the domestic and foreign-owned manufacturing sectors are:

$$\pi_2 = (1 + \tau)p_2 Q_2 - (w_2 L_2 + r_2 K_2)$$
$$= L_2[(1 + \tau)p_2 f_2(k_2) - w_2 - r_2 k_2, \tag{7.7}$$

and

$$\pi_3 = p_3 Q_3 - (w_3 L_3 + r_3 K_3)$$
$$= L_3[(1 + (1 - \beta)\tau)p_2 f_3(k_3) - w_3 - r_3 k_3]. \tag{7.8}$$

We have written $p_j \equiv \hat{p}_j/p_1$ in reflection of the first good being taken as numeraire.

Since the production function in the first sector is subject to uncertainty, agricultural producers maximize their expected utility from profit: $E[U] \equiv E[U(\pi_1)]$ where E is the expectation operator. First-order conditions for a maximum are:

$$E[U'\{\alpha f_1' - r_1\}] = 0 \tag{7.9}$$

and

$$E[U'\{\alpha(f_1 - k_1 f_1') - w_1\}] = 0. \tag{7.10}$$

First-order profit-maximizing conditions for domestic manufacturing are:

$$(1 + \tau)p_2 f_2' - r_2 = 0 \tag{7.11}$$

and

$$(1 + \tau)p_2(f_2 - k_2 f_2') - w_2 = 0, \tag{7.12}$$

Similarly, first-order profit-maximizing conditions for foreign-owned manufacturing are:

$$[1 + (1 - \beta)\tau]p_2 f_3' - r_3 = 0 \tag{7.13}$$

and

$$[1 + (1 - \beta)\tau]p_2(f_3 - k_3 f_3') - w_3 = 0, \tag{7.14}$$

where f_j' and $(f_j - k_j f_j')$ are the marginal products of capital and labor, respectively.

Assuming perfect competition in the factor markets, factor rewards are identical across sectors. Thus, the factor-market equilibrium conditions are:

$$\frac{(f_1 - k_1 f_1')E[U'\alpha]}{E[U']} = (1 + \tau)p_2(f_2 - k_2 f_2'), \tag{7.15}$$

$$\frac{f_1' E[U'\alpha]}{E[U']} = (1 + \tau)p_2 f_2', \tag{7.16}$$

and

$$(1 + t)(f_2 - k_2 f_2') = [1 + (1 - \beta)\tau](f_3 - k_3 f_3'). \tag{7.17}$$

Equations (7.15)–(7.17) represent the equality between wage rates in agriculture and domestic manufacturing, rental rates in agriculture and domestic manufacturing, and the wage rates in domestic and foreign-owned manufacturing. The expression $E[U'\alpha]/[U']$ is the risk margin — the marginal rate of substitution between a unit of uncertain claim to profit and units of sure claim to profit (for an elaboration, see Batra, 1975).

While the rental rate is equalized across Sectors 1 and 2 by virtue of capital mobility, the adjustment mechanism in foreign-owned manufacturing operates differently. In the short run r_3 may be above the international cost of capital (r_3^*) since the amount of capital devoted to the third sector is fixed at $\overline{K}_3$. In particular, the short-run capital-rental rate is defined by the expression: $r_3 \equiv p_3 f_3'(\frac{\overline{K}_3}{L_3}) \equiv p_3 f_3'(\bar{k}_3)$. Any change in $\bar{k}_3$ is due to a change in labor employed: $d\bar{k}_3 = -\bar{k}_3 dL_3/L_3$. It follows that the capital-rental rate in foreign-owned manufacturing rises or falls according to the formula:

$$dr_3 = p_3 f_3'' d\bar{k}_3 + f_3' \left\{ \frac{p_3 dp_2}{p_2} + (1 - \beta)p_2 d\tau - \tau p_2 d\beta \right\}. \tag{7.18}$$

In the long run, international mobility of capital assures that r_3 will equal the international cost of capital; specifically, we must have $p_3 f_3'(k_3') = r_3^*$. In this expression k_3^* is the capital–labor ratio that will assure a return on capital in the host country equal to the international cost of capital at the producer's price level p_3.

This completes our discussion of the fundamental model underlying our analysis of ESRs. The preceding model depicts the production side of a general equilibrium structure; its key equations are (7.15)–(7.17) and (7.5). These comprise four unknowns — L_1, k_1, k_2, and L_3 — and five parameters $(\overline{K}, \overline{L}, p_2, t, \text{ and } \beta)$.

7.3 Analysis

Following the procedure developed in detail by Batra (1975), we analyze the basic system of four equations in order to determine the effect of changes in the parameters upon the endogenous variables. In light of our focus upon ESRs we simplify our presentation by only considering changes in the ESR — that is, changes in β. The effect of changes in the other parameters may be analyzed in the same manner. Differentiating (7.15)–(7.17) and (7.5) provides the basic system:

$$
\begin{bmatrix}
\Omega A & B_1 & C_1 & 0 \\
A & B_2 & C_2 & 0 \\
0 & 0 & -\frac{r\gamma_2}{\sigma_2} & -\frac{r_3\gamma_3 k_3}{\sigma_3 L_3} \\
k_1 - k_2 & L_1 & L_2 & -k_2
\end{bmatrix}
\begin{bmatrix}
dL_1 \\
dk_1 \\
dk_2 \\
dL_3
\end{bmatrix}
=
\begin{bmatrix}
0 \\
0 \\
\frac{\tau p_2 w}{p_3} \\
0
\end{bmatrix}
d\beta. \qquad (7.19)
$$

In the preceding system we have used the following definitions:

$$\Omega \equiv \frac{w_i}{r_i} = \frac{f_i - k_i f_i'}{f_i'} > 0 \quad i \in (1,2)$$

$$\sigma_i \equiv -\frac{f_i'(f_i - k_i f_i')}{k_i f_i f_i''} > 0$$

$$h \equiv (\alpha f_1' - r_2) = (\alpha f_1' - (1+t)p_2 f_2')$$

$$\gamma_1 \equiv \frac{w L_1}{Q_1} > 0$$

$$A \equiv (\Omega + k_1)E[U''h^2] < 0$$

$$\gamma_2 \equiv \frac{wL_2}{1 + \tau p_2 Q_2} > 0$$

$$B_1 \equiv \{\Omega L_1 E[U''h^2] - k_1 f_1'' E[U'\alpha]\} \gtreqless 0$$

$$\gamma_3 \equiv \frac{wL_3}{1 + (1 - \beta)\tau p_2 Q_3} > 0$$

$$B_2 \equiv \{L_1 E[U''h^2] + f_1'' E[U'\alpha]\} < 0$$

$$C_1 \equiv (1 + \tau)p_2 f_2'' \{k_2 E[U'] + \Omega L_1 (k_2 - k_1) E[U''h]\} \gtreqless 0$$

$$C_2 \equiv (1 + \tau)p_2 f_2'' \{-E[U'] + L_1 (k_2 - k_1) E[U''h]\} \gtreqless 0. \qquad (7.20)$$

Note that σ_i is the elasticity of substitution in the ith sector and that γ_i is labor's share of output in the ith sector. We have defined the common wage rate as $w \equiv w_1 = w_2 = w_3$ and the common rental rate on domestic capital as $r \equiv r_1 = r_2$. In order to sign the terms in (7.20) we have utilized a proof due to Batra (1975) that under non-increasing absolute risk aversion $E[U''h] \geq 0 \geq E[U''h^2]$ and $E[U'\alpha] > 0$. This merely states that as wealth increases, risk aversion does not increase.

It is useful to make some mathematical simplifications before proceeding further. Define the following expressions:

$$B \equiv (B_1 - \Omega B_2) = -f_1''(\Omega + k_1)E[U'\alpha] = \frac{wE[U']}{k_1\sigma_1} > 0$$

$$C \equiv (\Omega C_2 - C_1) = -(1 + \tau)p_2 f_2''(\Omega + k_2)E[U'] = \frac{wE[U']}{k_2\sigma_2} > 0$$

$$J \equiv (B_1 C_2 - C_1 B_2)$$

$$= -\frac{rf_2''}{f_2'}f_2'[L_1(\Omega + k_2)E[U']E[U''h^2] + f_1''(k_2 - k_1)E[U'\alpha]G]$$

$$= \frac{r\gamma_2 E[U']\{K_1\sigma_1(\Omega + k_2)A - w(k_2 - k_1)G\}}{k_1 k_2 \sigma_1 \sigma_2 (\Omega + k_1)} < 0 \quad \forall k_2 \geq k_1$$

$$\qquad (7.21)$$

where:

$$G \equiv \{E[U'] + L_1(\Omega + k_1)E[U''h]\} > 0. \qquad (7.22)$$

In light of the observation of Hazari and Sgro (1992) that in lesser-developed economies manufacturing has a higher capital–labor ratio than does agriculture, we henceforth restrict our analysis to the case of $k_2 > k_1$.

The determinant (Δ) of the coefficient matrix (7.19) may be written as:

$$\Delta \equiv \frac{B(Z_1 + Z_2)}{k_2\sigma_2} \tag{7.23}$$

where:

$$Z_1 = \frac{\gamma_2\gamma_3 r_3 k_3 (k_2 - k_1)^2 G}{L_3\sigma_3(\Omega + k_1)} > 0$$

$$Z_2 \equiv -A\gamma_2 r_2 k_2^2 + \gamma_3 r_3 k_3 \frac{(K_2\sigma_2 + K_1\sigma_1)}{L_3\sigma_3}$$

$$+ \gamma_2 K_1\sigma_1\Omega(k_2 - k_1) > 0. \tag{7.24}$$

In light of $G > 0 > A$ and $k_2 \geq k_1$ we have $\Delta > 0$.

In order to be able to demonstrate the effect of uncertainty upon the efficacy of ESRs we now present the immediately preceding results in the absence of uncertainty. The determinant ($\equiv \Delta^c$) becomes:

$$\Delta^c \equiv \frac{wrr_3 k_3 \gamma_2\gamma_3(k_2 - k_1)^2}{k_1 k_2\sigma_1\sigma_2\sigma_3 L_3(\Omega + k_1)} > 0. \tag{7.25}$$

The superscript "C" denotes certainty. Values of the key definitions in the system are:

$$
\begin{aligned}
&A^C = 0 = h^C && G^C = 1 \\
&B_1^C = -k_1 f_1'' > 0 && C_1^C = (1 + \tau)p_2 k_2 f_2'' < 0 \\
&B_2^C = f_1'' < 0 && C_2^C = -(1 + \tau)p_2 f_2'' > 0 \\
&B^C = \frac{w}{k_1\sigma_1} > 0 && C^C = \frac{w}{k_2\sigma_2} > 0 \\
&J^C = -1(1 + \tau)p_2 f_1'' f_2''(k_2 - k_1) \leq 0 && \forall k_2 \geq k_1.
\end{aligned}
\tag{7.26}
$$

We shall make use of these certainty values in the comparative analyses below.

We apply Cramer's rule to (7.19) and (7.23) so as to conduct comparative static analyses of the effects of shifts in parametric values. Here we only deal with changes in the ESR (i.e., β).

We begin with an analysis of the capital–labor ratios:

$$\frac{dk_1}{d\beta} = \xi k_2 AC < 0 \qquad (7.27)$$

$$\frac{dk_2}{d\beta} = \xi k_2 AB < 0 \qquad (7.28)$$

where $\xi \equiv \frac{tp_2 w}{p_3 \Delta} = \frac{tw}{[1+(1-\beta)\tau]\Delta} > 0$. An increase in the ESR lowers the capital–labor ratio in both domestic sectors in the presence of uncertainty. In contrast, in the absence of uncertainty, $A^C = 0$; thus we observe $\frac{dk_1^C}{d\beta} = 0 = \frac{dk_2^C}{d\beta}$. We may state that uncertainty lowers the capital–labor ratio in both domestic sectors. This is explained by a fall in the wage–rental ratio as ESR increases; below we derive and discuss this phenomenon.

Now consider the effect of a change in β on labor utilization in the foreign-owned manufacturing sector:

$$\frac{dL_3}{d\beta} = \xi[A(BL_2 + CL_1) + (k_2 - k_1)J] < 0. \qquad (7.29)$$

An increase in β lowers the effective price realized by the third sector since $p_2 < (1 + \tau)p_2$: the manufacturers recognize less revenue per unit from export sales than they do from domestic sales. Note that in the absence of uncertainty the absolute magnitude of the decrease in labor utilization is smaller. The interesting question is whether, under full employment, labor shifts toward agriculture, domestic manufacturing, or both. We begin our answer by solving for β's impact on agricultural employment:

$$\frac{dL_1}{d\beta} = -k_2 \xi J > 0. \qquad (7.30)$$

Clearly at least some of the third sector's workers move to the first sector whether or not there is uncertainty in the agricultural sector. What happens to labor employment in domestic manufacturing? Combining (7.27) and (7.28) with (7.3) reveals:

$$\frac{dL_2}{d\beta} = \xi[k_1 J - A(BL_2 + CL_1)] \gtreqless 0. \qquad (7.31)$$

The effect is ambiguous, although in the absence of uncertainty the effect is clearly negative. What is not ambiguous is the impact on total employment in manufacturing. Adding (7.29) and (7.31) yields:

$$\sum_{j=2}^{3} \frac{dL_j}{d\beta} = \xi k_2 J < 0. \qquad (7.32)$$

Total manufacturing employment declines as a result of an increase in the
ESR; with full employment, agricultural employment rises by a comparable
amount (see [7.30]).

Note that in the absence of uncertainty (i.e., $A^C = 0$) labor shifts
into agriculture from *both* domestic and foreign-owned manufacturing. In
contrast, with uncertainty, domestic manufacturing employment may rise
even though total manufacturing employment $(L_2 + L_3)$ falls in response to
an increase in β. Therefore, uncertainty may induce an employment shift
toward domestic manufacturing.

Now consider the effects of a change in the ESR upon the level of cap-
ital employed. Recall that we have defined $K_i \equiv k_i L_i$, so $dK_i = k_i dL_i + L_i dK_i (i \in (1,2))$; this implies:

$$\frac{dK_1}{d\beta} = \xi k_2 (ACL_1 - k_1 J) \gtreqless 0 \qquad (7.33)$$

$$\frac{dK_2}{d\beta} = \xi k_2 (k_1 J - ACL_1) \lesseqgtr 0$$

$$= -\frac{dK_1}{d\beta}. \qquad (7.34)$$

In the absence of production uncertainty we obtain $\frac{dK_1^C}{d\beta} > 0 > dK_2^C/d\beta$.
Capital clearly shifts from domestic manufacturing to agriculture. However,
in the presence of uncertainty, increases in the ESR may encourage investment in domestic manufacturing at the expense of agricultural investment.
This result is consistent with that found by Das (1977), who showed that
the Rybczynski effect may not hold in the presence of production uncertainty. In particular, a rise in β *may* increase the production of domestic
manufacturing through higher labor employment in the second sector (see
[7.31]). If it does increase, it may raise demand for capital in the second
sector (see [7.34]). This result can also be seen by differentiating $k_2 (\equiv \frac{K_2}{L_2})$
to yield:

$$\frac{dK_2}{d\beta} = \left(\frac{L_2 dk_2}{d\beta} + \frac{k_2 dL_2}{d\beta} \right) \gtreqless 0. \qquad (7.35)$$

The ambiguity in the sign of $dK_2/d\beta$ is due to the fact that under uncertainty an increase in β induces an ambiguous effect on the level of labor
employed in the second sector. In light of (7.35), in conjunction with the
preceding analyses, we state the following proposition.

Proposition 7.1 *The presence of production uncertainty (in comparison
to the case of certainty) has the following effects upon resource allocation*

in response to an increase in the ESR (β) for foreign-owned manufacturing firms. First, an increase in β may result in more labor and more capital for domestic manufacturing, although the capital–labor ratio will decline. Second, an increase in β may result in less capital in the agricultural sector, although the capital–labor ratio will decline. If less capital is employed in agriculture due to an increase in β, then (a) more capital will be employed in domestic manufacturing, and (b) more labor will be employed in domestic manufacturing and in agriculture. If an increase in β lowers labor employment in domestic manufacturing, then it will also lower capital utilization in that sector, but will raise labor utilization and capital utilization in the agricultural sector.

In order to ascertain the effect of a change in β on factor rewards we differentiate (7.11) and (7.12) to obtain:

$$\frac{dr}{d\beta} = -\frac{\xi r \gamma_2 AB}{\sigma_2} > 0 \tag{7.36}$$

$$\frac{dw}{d\beta} = -k_2 \frac{dr}{d\beta} < 0. \tag{7.37}$$

An increase in the ESR raises the return to domestic capital at the expense of labor's remuneration. Factor rewards are unaffected by a change in the ESR when there is certainty: $\frac{dr^C}{d\beta} = 0 = dw^C/d\beta$. In the presence of uncertainty, an increase in the ESR financially benefits capital while adversely affecting the reward to labor. As a result the wage–rental ratio falls. This can be seen through analysis of the wage–rental ratio (Ω):

$$\frac{d\Omega}{d\beta} = -\frac{f_i f_i''}{f_i'^2} \xi k_2 AC = -\frac{f_i f_i''}{(f_i')^2} \frac{dk_i}{d\beta} < 0, \quad i \in (1,2). \tag{7.38}$$

Of course, under certainty a change in the ESR has no impact on the ratio of factor rewards ($\frac{d\Omega}{d\beta} = 0$).

Economic intuition for the results can be understood by recognizing that, given free mobility of resources between the two domestic sectors, Sectors 1 and 2 constitute a subsystem of the Heckscher–Ohlin model. Increasing the ESR means a fall in the producer's price in the foreign-owned manufacturing sector. Thus the policy $d\beta > 0$ discourages foreign capital inflows. As a result, labor moves from the third sector into the first sector; it may also move into the second sector. For the subsystem defined by these sectors this labor inflow represents a Rybczynski effect.

Factor rewards are solely determined by output prices in the standard Heckscher–Ohlin subsystem; hence, they cannot be affected by ESRs. This "independence result" does not hold in the presence of uncertainty. Increasing the ESR discourages foreign capital inflows. As the labor supply for the domestic sectors increases, it also raises the capital-rental rate while lowering the wage rate (but not necessarily the rate of labor utilization).

What is the effect of a change in the ESR on the capital-rental in the third sector? In the short run, $r_3 = p_3 f_3'(\bar{k}_3)$; recalling $d\bar{k}_3 = -\bar{k}_3 dL_3/L_3$ reveals:

$$\frac{d\bar{k}_3}{d\beta} = \frac{\bar{k}_3}{L_3}\frac{dL_3}{d\beta} > 0. \tag{7.39}$$

Because the sectoral stock of capital is fixed, the only possible response to the forced increase in exports is to decrease its use of labor (see [7.29]); this raises the short-run capital–labor ratio.

Utilizing (7.17) — while holding p_2 and τ constant — yields insight into the short-run capital-rental rate in the third sector:

$$\frac{dr_3}{d\beta} = p_3 f_3''\frac{d\bar{k}_3}{d\beta} + f_3'\frac{dp_3}{d\beta} = \frac{p_3\gamma_3}{L_3\sigma_3}\frac{dL_3}{d\beta} - \tau p_2 f_3' < 0. \tag{7.40}$$

An increase in the ESR drives down the capital-rental rate in foreign-owned manufacturing in the short run through its negative impacts upon both labor employment and the effective price of sectoral output.

In the long run the level of foreign capital is endogenously determined while r_3 is exogenously given as r_3^*. Since $r_3^* = p_3 f_3'(k_3^*)$, it immediately follows that $dr_3^* = 0 = (p_3 f_3'' dk_3^* - tp_2 f_3' d\beta)$. After making the usual substitutions we obtain the impact of a change in β on the long-run capital–labor ratio in the third sector:

$$\frac{dk_3^*}{d\beta} = -\frac{\tau p_2 k_3^* \sigma_3}{p_3\gamma_3} < 0. \tag{7.41}$$

In the long run, the capital–labor ratio is inversely related to a change in the ESR. This, of course, is the opposite directional impact from that obtained in the short run. The long-run result is intuitively obvious because an increase in β lowers the effective price p_3, thereby lessening the marginal product of capital. The appropriate managerial response is to decrease the amount of capital employed, thereby lowering the capital–labor ratio and raising the marginal product of capital. In particular, making use of $K_3^* \equiv k_3^* L_3$ yields the change in the long-run level of capital employed in the third sector:

$$\frac{dk_3^*}{d\beta} = k_3^* \frac{dL_3}{d\beta} + L_3 \frac{dk_3^*}{d\beta} < 0. \tag{7.42}$$

These results hold even in the absence of uncertainty, provided domestic manufacturing is relatively more capital-intensive than the agricultural sector. Thus we may state the following proposition.

Proposition 7.2 *In the presence of production uncertainty, an increase in the ESR (β) has several effects on factor rewards*:

- *It raises the domestic capital-rental rate.*
- *It creates a concomitant fall in the wage rate.*
- *In the third sector an increase in the ESR has a dampening effect on the foreign capital-rental rate in the short run.*
- *In the long run this capital-rental rate must equalize with the international cost of capital.*

Differentiating the expected output of the agricultural sector while utilizing equations (7.29)–(7.31) yields:

$$\frac{dE[\Omega_1]}{\mathrm{d}\beta} = \frac{\xi\mu\gamma_2 r f_1'(k_2 - k_1)BG}{\sigma_2} \geq 0 \quad \forall\, k_2 \geq k_1. \tag{7.43}$$

Provided the agricultural sector is *not* relatively capital-intensive, its expected output rises in response to an increase in the ESR imposed on the third sector. This result, replicating that obtained in a certainty environment, reflects an increased level of labor employment dominating a decline in the capital–labor ratio — and even a possible decline in the absolute level of capital employed in agriculture.

Turning to domestic manufacturing we obtain:

$$\frac{dQ_2}{d\beta} = -\xi f_2'[ABL_2\Omega + (\Omega + k_2)(ACL_1 - k_1 J)] \gtrless 0. \tag{7.44}$$

As noted earlier, the Rybczynski effect fails to hold in an economy characterized by production uncertainty. The ambiguous reallocation of labor and capital for the second sector gives rise to the indeterminate output change in Q_2. Under certainty this ambiguity disappears: $\frac{dQ_2^C}{d\beta} < 0$. In the presence of uncertainty, a change in the ESR generally affects output of the domestic manufacturing sector, although the directional impact of this effect is itself of uncertain sign in the absence of knowledge of specific values for the parameters.

Finally, differentiating (7.2) enables us to solve for the effect of a change in the ESR upon output from the foreign-owned manufacturing sector. In the short run, with capital fixed at $\overline{K}_3$, we have:

$$\frac{dQ_3}{d\beta} = \frac{(f_3 - \bar{k}_3 f_3')dL_3}{d\beta} < 0. \tag{7.45}$$

In the long run we obtain:

$$\frac{dQ_3}{d\beta} = L_3 f_3' \frac{dk_3^*}{d\beta} + (f_3 - k_3^* f_3')\frac{dL_3}{d\beta} < 0. \tag{7.46}$$

Note that $dL_3/d\beta < 0$ by (7.29) and, in the long run, $\frac{dk_3^*}{d\beta} < 0$ by (7.41). An increase in the ESR will lower output of the third sector independent of uncertainty in the agricultural sector — although uncertainty increases the magnitude of this effect because producers are risk averse. We state the following proposition.

Proposition 7.3 *The presence of production uncertainty can cause an increase in the ESR to have an impact on the magnitude of output produced by the first and the third sectors. The negative effect of an increase in β on the domestic manufacturing sector's output under certainty may be negated, or reversed, under uncertainty.*

This section outlines a model for studying the welfare effects of ESRs in the presence of production uncertainty in the agricultural sector. The demand side of the economy is represented by an expenditure function that can be expressed as $H(1, (1 + \tau)p_2, \tilde{W}) = min[\tilde{C}_A + (1 + \tau)p_2 C_M : U(\tilde{C}_A C_M) = \tilde{W}]$. In this expression, $\tilde{C}_A$ is the uncertain level of Hicksian demand for the agricultural product, C_M is the certain level of Hicksian domestic demand for the manufactured good, and $\tilde{W}$ is the uncertain level of welfare achieved when domestic prices are $(1 + \tau)p_2$ for the manufactured good (the agricultural good is treated as numeraire so its price is set to unity). We assume that the social welfare function is quasi-concave: $U(\tilde{C}_A, C_M) \geq \tilde{W}$. Implicit in this formulation is that agricultural producers are unable to diversify risk.

The country's budget constraint requires that expenditures on goods equal revenue from production and tariffs (net of payments to foreign capital):

$$H(1, (1 + \tau)p_2, \tilde{W})$$

$$= Q_1 + (1 + \tau)p_2 Q_2[1 + (1 - \beta)\tau]p_2 Q_3 + \tau p_2 I - r_3 K_3. \tag{7.47}$$

The first three terms on the right-hand side of (7.47) represent gross national product (GNP). The term "I" denotes imports of the manufactured good so that tariff revenue from imports is $\tau p_2 I$. We assume that the total tariff revenue is returned to domestic consumers in a lump-sum payment. The final term in (7.47) is rental payments to foreign capital; we assume that it is repatriated to the foreign country. Note that in (7.47) welfare is uncertain because agricultural output is uncertain.

Under the tariff regime the amount of the manufactured good imported is determined endogenously as domestic demand minus domestic supply:

$$I = C_M - Q_2 - (1 - \beta)Q_3. \tag{7.48}$$

Note that $C_M = \partial H(1, (q + t)p_2, \tilde{W})/\partial p_2 \equiv H_p$ by Shephard's lemma.

We differentiate (7.47) and (7.48) to obtain the welfare impact of a change in ESRs and combine the results[2] to obtain:

$$(H_w - \tau p_2 H_{pW})\frac{d\tilde{W}}{d\beta}$$

$$= h\frac{dK_1}{d\beta} + \Omega\frac{dL_1}{d\beta} - \tau p_2\frac{dQ_2}{d\beta} + (1 - \beta)\frac{dQ_3}{d\beta} - K_3\frac{dr_3}{d\beta}, \tag{7.49}$$

where $H_w \equiv \partial H/\partial \tilde{W}$ and $H_{pW} \equiv \partial H_p/\partial \tilde{W}$. Note[3] that $(H_W - tp_2 H_{pW}) > 0$. We observe that the three preexisting distortions in the economy affect the impact of a change in the ESR on national welfare. Those distortions are: (a) production uncertainty, captured in the first term of (7.49) by $h \equiv (\alpha f_1' - r_2)$; (b) the tariff distortion, captured by τ in the second term; and (c) changes in payments to foreign capital, captured by the third term.

In order to establish a benchmark we first consider the case of certainty. In this situation $h = 0$ so the first term in (7.49) disappears. We have $\frac{dQ_2}{d\beta} < 0$ and $\frac{dQ_3}{d\beta} < 0$ by (7.1), (7.44), and (7.45). Furthermore, $\frac{dr_3}{d\beta} < 0$ in the short run (per [7.40]) whereas $\frac{dr_3}{d\beta} = 0$ for the long run. This is sufficient to assure that, under certainty in agricultural production, an increase in the ESR *increases* national welfare in both the short run and the long run. Intuitively this occurs because the rise in export requirements mitigates the distortion of overproduction of the manufactured good by both domestic

---

[2]Because $h \equiv (\alpha f_1' - r_2)$, we obtain $dQ_1 + (1 + t)p_2 dQ_2 + [1 + (1 - \beta)t]p_2 dQ_3 = hdK_1 + \Omega hdL_1$.

[3]Since $H_p = C_M$, the marginal propensity to consume may be defined as $0 \leq m \equiv [\frac{(1+t)p_2 H_{pW}}{H_W}] \leq 1$. This implies $(H_W - tp_2 H_{pW}) = H_W(1 + t - tm)/(1 + t) > 0$.

and FDI producers. Further, it reduces rental payments to foreign capital in the short run. It follows that the optimal ESR for foreign-owned firms is 100% from the perspective of the home country. This result echoes those obtained by Rodrik (1987) and Chao and Yu (1994b).

The introduction of uncertainty in the production of the agricultural product will modify the preceding result. Specifically, since $h < 0$, an agricultural expansion induced by an increase in the ESR imposed on the manufacturing sector[4] can diminish the effectiveness of the export-requirement policy. This implies that the optimal level of required exports is below 100% under uncertainty. In the most extreme case, the ESR *could* be zero if the impact of production uncertainty is sufficiently large. In light of recent meteorological observations concerning El Niño, it seems clear that current agricultural production may have higher variance than was the case earlier. The optimal ESR for a country of a given year may well differ from its optimal value ten or twenty years ago.

7.4   Concluding Remarks

We have constructed a three-sector, general equilibrium framework with production uncertainty. In our model the third sector is foreign-owned manufacturing; this sector "imports" its own capital but relies upon domestic labor. Within this context we have studied the implications of ESRs for resource allocation, sectoral outputs, factor rewards, and national welfare. By way of summary, several results that are unaffected by changes in the ESR under certainty actually have non-zero signs in the presence of uncertainty, namely the capital–labor ratio in both domestic sectors and the rewards to both capital and labor. In addition, several results that are definitively signed in a world of certainty are ambiguously signed in a world of uncertainty. These ambiguities are primarily focused upon the domestic manufacturing sector. From the viewpoint of public policy officials, the most important fact is that ESRs *may* be welfare reducing when the world is characterized by uncertainty even though they are, at the margin, welfare enhancing in a world of certainty.

Agricultural producers strive to maximize their expected utility from profits in this model. A set of welfare functions could be used for each group (in lieu of a single national welfare function) in order to allow for differential

---

[4]We refer to $dL_1/d\beta$ and $dK_1/d\beta$ in Eqs. (7.30) and (7.33), respectively.

risk-bearing ability across groups. This model could also be used to study the effects of changes in: (a) the stock of labor or capital; (b) the world price of the traded good; (c) the long-run price of international capital; or (d) the impact of governmental policy variables such as tariffs or wage subsidies.[5] In a similar vein other types of uncertainty (e.g., price uncertainty) can be studied in an appropriately modified version of the framework presented here.

---

[5]For example, see Marjit (1991) for a study of wage subsidies.

PART III

Content Protection, Equity Controls, and Foreign Investment

Chapter 8

Content Protection, Urban Unemployment, and Welfare

8.1 Introduction

The policy of domestic content protection was popular among semi-industrialized nations for many years, especially before the World Trade Organization (WTO) enforcement of the agreements on eliminating any trade-related investment measure (TRIM) that is inconsistent with Article XI of the General Agreement on Tariffs and Trade's (GATT) 1994 Uruguay Round. Resource-limited economies have relied on the use of foreign materials to achieve growth. Intermediate goods are imported for further processing, and final products are exported. While increasing use of imported materials helps to spur growth in the domestic final product sector, it nevertheless also brings about the undesirable effect of lowering the domestic value added to the final product. A domestic content requirement thus is evolved to protect domestic producers of intermediate goods by specifying that a certain percentage of domestic intermediates be used in the production of final products. This policy appears to be inconsistent with the TRIMs agreement of GATT and WTO on foreign investors' right to use imported inputs.

At the theoretical level, various aspects of content protection have been explored by trade theorists. Earlier analyses include Johnson (1963b), Wonnacott and Wonnacott (1967), and Munk (1969). It is noteworthy that Corden (1971) and Grossman (1981) examine the resource allocation effect of content protection in a partial equilibrium setting. Mussa (1984), Hollander (1987), and Vousden (1987) extend the Corden–Grossman analysis to settings involving imperfect market structures. Richardson (1989), however, adopts a general equilibrium approach to study the welfare consequences of content protection.

This chapter, drawing on Chao and Yu (1993), also develops a general equilibrium framework to explore the resource allocation and welfare effects of content protection. Our study differs from that of Richardson in two significant respects. First, Richardson considers a full-employment economy; the economy in this chapter suffers from unemployment. Second, Richardson's approach parallels the work of Rodrik (1987) on export-performance requirement; our vintage of analysis is more in line with the content protection literature. Within our framework we are able to establish several new results. In particular, we show that when the agricultural sector has a higher labor–land ratio than the economy as a whole, a higher domestic content requirement leads to a decrease in the output and the price of the domestic intermediate, the import of the foreign intermediate, and the urban unemployment ratio. Furthermore, a tightening of content protection results in a lower welfare.

The remainder of this chapter is organized as follows. Section 8.2 presents a three-sector, general equilibrium model incorporating sector-specific unemployment. Section 8.3 examines the effects of content protection on prices of goods, unemployment, and resource allocation. The welfare effects of content protection are explored in Section 8.4. Section 8.5 offers concluding remarks.

8.2   A Three-Sector Model

A three-sector, general equilibrium model is developed for exploring the impacts of content protection. Consider a semi-industrialized or a developing economy characterized by urban-specific unemployment, à la Harris and Todaro (1970). The original Harris–Todaro model consists of two sectors with sector-specific unemployment.[1] For our purpose, the Harris–Todaro model is expanded to include three sectors: the intermediate good (M), the agricultural (Y), and the manufacturing (X). Both M and Y are produced in the rural area by utilizing labor and land, and X is produced in the urban area with the help of labor and intermediate goods.[2] The intermediates are

---

[1] For studies on the various facets of the Harris–Todaro framework, see Khan (1980), Neary (1981), Khan and Naqvi (1983), Batra and Naqvi (1987), Parai and Batra (1987), Beladi (1988), and Chao and Yu (1990).

[2] The assumption that the production of intermediates is located away from the areas where the inputs are used is not particularly stringent. There are real-world counterparts to this assumption. For example, rubber and tin production in Malaysia is located in rural

either imported or domestically produced. It is assumed that these two types of intermediates are perfect substitutes. Final goods X and Y are traded internationally at the externally determined world prices.

The production functions are assumed to be linearly homogeneous. They are expressed by:

$$M = M(L_M, T_M)$$

$$Y = Y(L_Y, T_Y)$$

$$X = X(L_X, M + M^*), \qquad (8.1)$$

where L_i ($i = M, Y, X$) denotes the labor employment in sector i, T_j ($j = M, Y$) represents the land employment in sector j, and M^* is the imported intermediate good. To simplify the analysis, inputs in sector X are assumed to be used in fixed proportions to output, so that one unit of the intermediate goods along with one unit of labor is used to produce one unit of X.[3] That is, no substitutions between labor and intermediates are permitted. By choosing good X as the numeraire, the relative price of good Y is denoted by p. Given the assumption of a small country, p is exogenously determined.

Let q be the relative price of the domestic intermediate good, which is determined endogenously, and let q^* be the world price of the imported intermediates. If $q < q^*$, firms in the X sector will use only the domestic intermediate. This case is of limited interest, since content protection is not needed. Thus, it is assumed that $q > q^*$ throughout the analysis.[4],[5] It follows that if there is no content protection, sector X would not purchase the domestic component. The domestic intermediate-good sector would be forced to close down, thereby generating severe unemployment. To protect the workers in the M sector, sector X is required by law to use a certain minimum quantity of domestic intermediates, specified at the $k\%$ of the total quantity of the physical unit of the intermediates. That is:

$$k = \frac{M}{(M + M^*)}, \qquad (8.2)$$

---

areas, whereas products using rubber and tin as major inputs are generally manufactured in metropolitan areas. Also, the food-processing industry is usually located in urban areas, whereas the ingredients used are produced in rural areas.

[3]This implies $X = M + M^* = L_X$. This assumption was used by Corden (1971) and Vousden (1987). Also, see Jones and Spencer (1989) for a related study.

[4]See Grossman (1981) for a detailed discussion.

[5]The case where $q = q^*$ will be discussed in Section 8.3.

where k is referred to as the domestic content requirement defined in the physical sense.[6] As pointed out by Grossman (1981), the effective price of the intermediate inputs (q_e) is simply the weighted average of their domestic price and the world price, with the weights being k and $(1-k)$, respectively:

$$q_e = kq + (1 - k)q^*.$$

Consider the equilibrium in the labor market. While workers can freely move between the urban and the rural area, the urban wages (w_X) are institutionally set at levels higher than the market-clearing wages; hence urban unemployment emerges. Following Harris–Todaro (1970), it is hypothesized that at the labor market equilibrium, the rural wage, w, is equal to the expected urban wage, which is w_X times the probability of employment in the urban area:

$$w_X = w(1 + \lambda), \qquad (8.3)$$

where $\lambda = L_u/L_X$ is the urban unemployment ratio and $1/(1+\lambda)$ serves as an index for the probability of finding a job. Here, L_u represents the level of urban unemployment. Note that under perfect competition labor is paid according to the value of its marginal product:

$$w_X = X_L \left(= \frac{\partial X}{\partial L} \right),$$
$$w = pY_L = qM_L. \qquad (8.4)$$

Denoting the total endowment of labor by L, we can write:

$$(1 + \lambda)L_X + L_Y + L_M = L. \qquad (8.5)$$

By utilizing the fixed-coefficient production function of X, (8.5) can be rewritten as:

$$(1 + \lambda)X + L_Y + L_M = L. \qquad (8.6)$$

Denoting the land endowment in the rural area by T, full utilization of land implies:

$$T_Y + T_M = T. \qquad (8.7)$$

---

[6]Since it is assumed that domestic and foreign intermediates are homogeneous, an analysis of physical content requirements appears relevant. The use of physical content requirements can be found in the real world. For example, Taiwan's food-processing industry was required to use at least 30% of the rice that is domestically produced. Another example is the Australian tobacco industry (Vousden 1990). For an interesting exposition on the alternative value-added content requirement, see Grossman (1981).

The rental (t) is paid by the value of its marginal product:

$$t = pY_T = qM_T. \tag{8.8}$$

The production side of the model described above can be easily analyzed through its duality. Let $\alpha(w_X, q_e)$, $\beta(w,t)$, and $\gamma(w,t)$ be the unit-cost functions for sectors X, Y and M, respectively. By Shephard's lemma, the partial derivative of the ith unit-cost function provides the factor demand for the unit output of sector i. For example, $\beta_w(w,t)Y$ denotes the labor employment in sector Y. Here the subscript indicates the partial derivative. Thus, the production structure (8.1) through (8.8) can be represented by:

$$1 = \alpha(w_X, q_e) = w_X + q_e \tag{8.9}$$

$$p = \beta(w,t) \tag{8.10}$$

$$q = \gamma(w,t) \tag{8.11}$$

$$w_X = (1 + \lambda)w \tag{8.12}$$

$$(1 + \lambda)X + \beta_w(w,t)Y + \gamma_w(w,t)M = L \tag{8.13}$$

$$\beta_t(w,t)Y + \gamma_t(w,t)M = T \tag{8.14}$$

$$kX = M \tag{8.15}$$

$$(1 - k)X = M^*. \tag{8.16}$$

Equations (8.9) and (8.11) reflect the assumption of constant returns to scale and perfect competition in sectors X, Y, and M that unit cost must equal output price in equilibrium. Equation (8.12) denotes the Harris–Todaro labor market equilibrium condition. Equations (8.13) through (8.16) are the employment conditions of labor, land, domestic, and imported intermediates, respectively.

Note that the foregoing system consists of eight equations containing eight endogenous variables — q, w, t, λ, X, Y, M, and M^* — and one policy variable, k. That is, all the endogenous variables are functions of k. However, the system is block recursive: the agricultural and the intermediate-good sector in the rural area form a 2×2 Heckscher–Ohlin subsystem. That is, w and t can be solved first by (8.10) and (8.11) as functions of q. Then, from (8.9), q itself is a function of k.

Therefore, for analytical convenience, the effects of content protection are decomposed into two effects: the direct effect at the constant relative price of the domestic intermediate, and the price-induced effect.[7] That is, from (8.12)–(8.16), we can solve for λ, X, Y, M, and M^* as functions of k and q, where q captures the price-induced effect. In the next section we shall utilize this method to examine the effects of content protection on the urban unemployment ratio, the production of the domestic intermediate, and the import of the foreign intermediate.

8.3 Content Protection and Resource Allocation

We begin our analysis by examining the direct effect of content protection at a constant q. It is noteworthy that from (8.10) and (8.11), $\partial w/\partial k = \partial t/\partial k = 0$. A change in k will not directly affect the rural wage and the rental rate because they are solely determined in the Heckscher–Ohlin subsystem of Y and M, and in such a subsystem factor prices are related only to output prices. From (8.12) and recalling that w_X is exogenously given, it is clear that λ also is not affected by k, $\partial\lambda/\partial k = 0$. Content protection has no direct impact on the urban unemployment ratio.

For the given q, however, an increase in the content requirement raises the effective cost of the intermediates and thus renders a loss for the firms in sector X. As a result, some firms are forced to close down, thereby releasing workers to be partially relocated to the rural region. The supply of rural labor increases accordingly. The Rybczynski result thus will ensue in the Heckscher–Ohlin subsystem. As shown in Appendix A.1, the system is stable whether the agricultural sector is land-intensive or strongly labor-intensive (i.e., a higher labor–land ratio in the agricultural sector than the economy as a whole) relative to the intermediate-good sector. It is not unreasonable to assume for our analysis, however, that the agricultural sector is strongly labor-intensive. Then it is immediately apparent that $\partial Y/\partial k > 0$ and $\partial M/\partial k < 0$. Content protection raises the agricultural output at the expense of the intermediate output at the constant q.

That $\partial M/\partial k < 0$ at the constant q is an interesting result and deserves elaboration. Differentiating (8.15) yields:

$$\frac{\partial M}{\partial k} = X + k\left(\frac{\partial X}{\partial k}\right) = X\left(\frac{1+\hat{X}}{\hat{k}}\right), \tag{8.17}$$

---

[7]This decomposition technique is well known in the trade literature; see Batra and Scully (1971), among others.

where a hat denotes the percentage change of variables. The first term in (8.17) states that a tightening of content protection, that is, a higher k, immediately forces the firms in sector X to use more domestic intermediates. The second term captures the output-reduction effect on the use of domestic intermediates due to the exit of firms. As noted earlier, $\partial M/\partial k < 0$, it follows that $\hat{X}/\hat{k} < -1$, signifying a more than proportional contracting impact on X.

Consider next the price-induced effect on content protection. Assuming that Y is strongly labor-intensive relative to M, by virtue of the Stolper–Samuelson theorem we have $\partial w/\partial q < 0$ and $\partial t/\partial q > 0$ for the subsystem of the rural sectors Y and M. That is, a fall in the price of domestic intermediates leads to a higher rural wage and a lower land rental. Moreover, in view of the results of comparative statics relegated to the Appendix, we have $\partial X/\partial q > 0$, which implies $\partial M/\partial q > 0$ and $\partial Y/\partial q < 0$. Normal price-output responses prevail in this economy.

A refreshing result is that $\partial\lambda/\partial q > 0$; that is, the urban unemployment ratio rises as the price of the domestic intermediate increases. The reason for this result is as follows. A rise in q leads to a fall in the rural wage, which induces rural to urban migration, thereby causing the urban unemployment ratio to rise. This can be easily verified by (8.3).

To ascertain the overall impacts of content protection, we now turn to assess the effect of an increase in k on the price of the domestic intermediate. Conceivably, q may initially be greater than, equal to, or less than q^*. As mentioned earlier, the case that $q > q^*$ is of limited interest because content protection is not warranted. When $q = q^*$ initially, by virtue of the zero-profit condition expressed by (8.9), a change in k cannot affect q. The producers in the X sector are indifferent to using domestic or foreign intermediates. The demand for labor and intermediates by the X sector remains unaffected, and its output stays unchanged. It can be seen from (8.13) and (8.14) that the outputs of sectors Y and M also remain unaffected. Tightening of content protection, that is, k increases from its initial value, does not generate any effect on resource allocation. Thus, the case of $q = q^*$ initially is also of limited interest.

The case of genuine interest is that q exceeds q^* initially. Tightening content protection now generates two offsetting effects on the price of domestic intermediates. A direct increase in the demand for M raises its price. Meanwhile, the exit of firms from sector X results in a decrease in the demand for M, thereby dampening q. However, the reduction of M due to the contraction of the X sector outweighs the increase in the demand for M

directly resulting from a tightening of content protection. This implies that the net effect of content protection on the use of domestic intermediates is determinate: a rise in k lowers the total demand for M ($\partial M/\partial k < 0$) and hence its price. This result can be confirmed by differentiating (8.9) and using $q_e = kq + (1 - k)q^*$ to yield: $dp/dk = -(q - q^*)/k < 0$.

Combining the various direct and indirect effects of a change in k, we can derive the following results.

Proposition 8.1 *For q exceeds q^* initially, tightening the domestic content requirements leads to a decrease in the output of the domestic intermediates, the import of the foreign intermediate, and the urban unemployment ratio, if the agricultural sector is assumed to be strongly labor-intensive relative to the intermediate-good sector.*

Proof We have already shown $\partial X/\partial q > 0$, $\partial \lambda/\partial q > 0$, $\partial \lambda/\partial k = 0$, and $dq/dk < 0$. By using these results, we need to show $dM/dk < 0$, $dM^*/dk < 0$ and $d\lambda/dk < 0$. Since $M = kX$ $(k, q(k))$ and $M^* = (1 - k)X(k, q(k))$, the output effect of the domestic intermediate and the import of the foreign intermediate can be expressed, respectively, as:

$$\frac{dM}{dk} = X + k\left(\frac{\partial X}{\partial k}\right) + k\left(\frac{\partial X}{\partial q}\right)\left(\frac{dq}{dk}\right), \qquad (8.18)$$

and

$$\frac{dM^*}{dk} = -X + (1 - k)\left(\frac{\partial X}{\partial k}\right) + (1 - k)\left(\frac{\partial X}{\partial q}\right)\left(\frac{dq}{dk}\right). \qquad (8.19)$$

Because $\partial X/\partial q > 0$, $dq/dk < 0$, and $\partial M/\partial k = X + k(\partial X/\partial k) < 0$, we conclude that $dM/dk < 0$. An increase in k results in a reduction of M production. Similarly, $dM^*/dk < 0$. An increase in k, as expected, reduces the import of M^*.

As for urban unemployment, we have:

$$\frac{d\lambda}{dk} = \frac{\partial \lambda}{\partial k} + \left(\frac{\partial \lambda}{\partial q}\right)\left(\frac{dq}{dk}\right). \qquad (8.20)$$

Since $\partial \lambda/\partial q > 0$, $dq/dk < 0$ and $\partial \lambda/\partial k = 0$, we obtain $d\lambda/dk < 0$, confirming that an increased k reduces the urban unemployment ratio. $\square$

It is of interest to compare our result in (8.18), $dM/dk < 0$, with that derived by Grossman (1981). Grossman has shown, in a partial equilibrium setting, that $dM/dk > 0$ for small increases from its free trade value in k and dM/dk may turn negative for successively larger increases in k. Our result, derived in a general equilibrium framework, is apparently much stronger. Our crisp result hinges crucially upon the fact that the reduction in the demand for M, as a result of the exit of firms from sector X, outweighs the initial increase in the use of M due to small increases in k from its initial value. The corresponding reduction in the supply of M in the general equilibrium model follows from the Rybczynski effect triggered by the reverse migration of labor from the urban to rural region. The Rybczynski effect is reinforced by the price-induced adverse effect on M as $\partial M/\partial k = k(\partial X/\partial q) > 0$ and $dq/dk < 0$. It is noteworthy that the reverse migration of labor does not result from rigidity in the urban wage. If there is no rigid urban wage, perfect mobility of labor leads to wage equalization among sectors. The equilibrium wage, however, is solely determined within the Heckscher–Ohlin subsystem of Y and M, and thus the wage is not directly related to k. Therefore, regardless of the rigid urban wage, an increase in k immediately pushes up q_e and hence the unit cost in producing good X above its price, thereby causing firms to exit from sector X. The influx of released workers into the rural region leads to an expansion of the Y sector at the expense of the M sector. And the contraction of the M sector is accentuated by the drop in its goods price.

8.4 Content Protection and Welfare

Let us now turn to the examination of the welfare effect of the domestic content requirement. A duality approach popularized in the trade literature is used. Let the demand side of the economy be represented by an expenditure function:

$$E(1, p, u) = \min(D_X + pD_Y), \tag{8.21}$$

with respect to the demand for the two final commodities, D_X and D_Y, subject to a strictly quasi-concave utility function $u(D_X, D_Y) = u$.

The economy's budget constraint is given by:

$$E(1, p, u) = X + pY - q^*M^*, \tag{8.22}$$

which states that national expenditures equal the final gross revenues of sectors X and Y, less the returns to the foreign intermediate.

Taking total differentiation in (8.22) and defining the welfare change by $dW = E_u du$, we obtain:

$$dW = X_L dL_X + X_{M+M^*}(dM + dM^*)$$
$$+ pY_L dL_Y + pY_T dT_Y - q^* dM^*. \qquad (8.23)$$

By recalling (8.3), (8.4), and (8.8), and noting that $X_{M+M*} = kq + (1-k)q^*$, (8.23) can be simplified to:

$$\frac{dW}{dk} = -wL_X \left(\frac{d\lambda}{dk}\right) - (1-k)(q - q^*)\left(\frac{dM}{dk}\right)$$
$$+ k(q - q^*)\left(\frac{dM^*}{dk}\right). \qquad (8.24)$$

The urban unemployment ratio, the production of the domestic intermediates, and the import of the foreign intermediates all appear to play crucial roles in determining national welfare.

The first term on the right-hand side of (8.24) denotes the employment effect induced by content protection. An increase in content protection lowers the price of the domestic intermediate. Since the agricultural sector is relatively labor-intensive, the rural wage will be pushed up according to the Stolper–Samuelson result. The higher rural wage will slow down or even reverse the migration from the rural to the urban area, thereby reducing the urban unemployment ratio. The employment effect is conducive to welfare.

The second term captures the welfare impact of the production of the domestic intermediate good. Note that the domestic content requirement mandates that the final-product producers use a certain amount of the relatively more expensive domestic intermediate. This requirement generates a distortion of resource misallocation, thereby lowering production efficiency. An increase in content protection, however, reduces the distortion because a higher k raises the cost of the intermediate inputs for sector X, which will lower its production of good X and reduce its derived demand for the domestic intermediate. A cutback in the production of M constitutes a production gain, which enhances welfare.

Finally, the last term indicates the impact of the import of the foreign intermediate. An increase in the domestic content requirement results in a lower production of good X, and hence reduced import demand for the relatively cheaper foreign intermediate. This is detrimental to national welfare.

In view of the conflicting effects in (8.24), it appears that dW/dk may take any sign. Nevertheless, by using (8.5), (8.7), (8.15), (8.18), and (8.19), along with the Euler identity of the production function of M (i.e., $qM = wL_M + tT_M$) and the expression of $\partial\lambda/\partial q$ in the Appendix, we can rewrite (24) as:[8]

$$\frac{dW}{dk} = A\left[\frac{(\lambda_{LY} - \lambda_{TY})}{(\theta_{LY} - \theta_{LM})}\right]\left(\frac{dq}{dk}\right), \qquad (8.25)$$

where $A = wtLT/\beta qY > 0$, λ_{ij} is the fraction of factor i employed in sector j, and θ_{ij} is the distributive share of factor i employed in sector j. By recalling that $dq/dk = -(q - q^*)/k < 0$ for $q > q^*$, we can conclude $dW/dk < 0$ under the stability condition that $\lambda_{LY} > \lambda_{TY}$ and $\theta_{LY} > \theta_{LM}$. The following proposition is immediate.

Proposition 8.2 *An increase in the domestic content requirement unambiguously lowers national welfare, if the agricultural sector is strongly labor-intensive relative to the intermediate-goods sector.*

Proposition 8.2 implies that, in a stable system, the loss resulting from the reduction in using cheaper foreign intermediates caused by local content protection outweighs the total gains arising from higher employment and the decreased use of expansive domestic intermediates.

Note that this proposition holds for a full-employment economy in which the employment effect naturally vanishes. Thus, content protection worsens national welfare for the full-employment economy more than that for the unemployment economy. Our analysis suggests that abolition of content protection or non-implementation of content protection is the optimal policy for an economy with or without unemployment.

8.5 Concluding Remarks

In the foregoing analysis we have shown that an increase in local content protection reduces the urban unemployment ratio, the production of the domestic intermediates, and the import of the foreign intermediates. On the basis of these effects, we have delineated the welfare impacts of content

---

[8]Equivalently, the economy's budget constraint can be expressed in terms of factor incomes: $E(1, p, u) = w_X L_X + w L_Y + w L_M + t T_Y + t T_M = wL + tT$. By differentiating this constraint and then using the expressions of $\partial w/\partial q$ and $\partial t/\partial q$ in the Appendix, we can also obtain (8.25).

protection: despite the favorable employment effect of content protection, a higher content requirement will be unambiguously welfare reducing.

It is worth noting that the present model, which is in the Stolper–Samuelson tradition, is inadequate for studying gains or losses to the domestic intermediate sector, because zero profit prevails in that industry and no industry-specific factors would benefit or suffer from content protection. To examine the role for industry-aligned lobbies, a specific-factor version of the present model would be appropriate. We shall develop such a version for studying the lobbying issue in the future.

It is also noteworthy that the intermediate-goods sector is assumed to be located in the rural area, whereas the final product is manufactured in the urban area. This assumption serves to render our analysis tractable by preserving the Heckscher–Ohlin subsystem in the rural region. The assumption, however, is not without real-world counterparts. Of course, one may consider the alternative case in which the intermediate-goods sector is located in the urban area. Such an analysis is expected to be fairly complex. It may be further remarked that if the pattern of trade consists of good X being exported and good Y being imported, content protection resulting in a reduction in the output of good X, a fall in the import of M^*, and a rise in the output of good Y implies a shrinkage in the volume of trade.

Appendix

A.1 *Stability*

Following Chang (1981), the dynamic adjustment process at any given k is specified as follows:

$$\dot{Y} = a_1\{p - \beta(w,t)\}$$

$$\dot{X} = \left(\frac{1}{k}\right)$$

$$\dot{M} = a_2\{q - \gamma(w,t)\}$$

$$\dot{w} = -\left[\frac{w}{(1+\lambda)}\right]$$

$$\dot{\lambda} = a_3\{(1+\lambda)X + \beta_w(w,t)Y + \gamma_w(w,t)M - L\}$$

$$\dot{t} = a_4\{\beta_t(w,t)Y + \gamma_t(w,t)M - T\},$$

where a dot over the variable is the time derivative and a_i is the speed of the adjustment that is assumed to be positive.

Let $\theta_{LY} = w\beta_w/\beta$ and $\theta_{TY} = t\beta_t/\beta$ be the distributive share of labor and land in sector Y, and $\lambda_{LY} = \beta_w Y/L$ and $\lambda_{TY} = \beta_t Y/T$ be the fraction of labor and land employed in sector Y, and so on.[9] Linearization of the differential equations around the equilibrium values gives:

$$
\begin{bmatrix} \dot{Y} \\ \dot{X} \\ \dot{w} \\ \dot{t} \end{bmatrix} = \begin{bmatrix} 0 & 0 & -a_1\theta_{LY} & -a_1\theta_{TY} \\ 0 & 0 & -a_2\theta_{LM} & -a_2\theta_{TM} \\ a_3\lambda_{LY} & a_3[\lambda_{LM}+\lambda_{LX}(1+\lambda)] & -a_3[s_1+\lambda_{LX}(1+\lambda)] & a_3s_1 \\ a_4\lambda_{TY} & a_4\lambda_{TM} & a_4s_2 & -a_4s_2 \end{bmatrix} \begin{bmatrix} \hat{Y} \\ \hat{X} \\ \hat{w} \\ \hat{t} \end{bmatrix}.
$$

The D-stability (for all speeds of adjustment) of the original non-linear system requires that every principal minor of the coefficient matrix of even order is non-negative, and every principal minor of odd order is non-positive (see Quirk and Saposnik, 1968). Let J_i denote the ith principal minor. Then, we have $J_1 = J_2 = J_3 = 0$, and $J_4 = a_1a_2a_3a_4(\lambda_{LY} - \lambda_{TY})(\theta_{LY} - \theta_{LM})$.

The stability conditions thus require $J_4 > 0$. By using the definitions, it is apparent that $\lambda_{LY} - \lambda_{TY} = (T_Y/L)(L_Y/T_Y - L/T)$. Thus, $\lambda_{LY} - \lambda_{TY} >$ $(<) \, 0$ if and only if sector Y has a higher (lower) labour–land ratio than the economy as a whole. Furthermore, $\lambda_{LY} - \lambda_{TY} = \lambda_{LY} - \lambda_{LY}\lambda_{TY} - \lambda_{TY} +$ $\lambda_{LY}\lambda_{TY} = \lambda_{LY}\lambda_{TM} - \lambda_{TY}(1 - \lambda_{LY}) = (T_M T_Y/TL)[L_Y/T_Y - L_M/T_M -$ $(1+\lambda)L_X/T_M]$. In other words, $\lambda_{LY} - \lambda_{TY} > 0$ if sector Y is strongly labor-intensive (i.e., $L_Y/T_Y > L_M/T_M + (1+\lambda)L_X/T_M$), whereas $\lambda_{LY} - \lambda_{TY} < 0$ if and only if sector Y is land-intensive relative to sector M.

Hence, the stability conditions are met whether the agricultural sector is land-intensive or strongly labor-intensive relative to the intermediate-goods sector. It is reasonable to assume, however, that the agricultural sector is strongly labor-intensive relative to the intermediate-goods sector in the rural area, that is, $\lambda_{LY} > \lambda_{TY}$, which implies $\theta_{LY} > \theta_{LM}$. For example, rice production in a typical developing country is strongly labor-intensive relative to cotton production.

A.2   Comparative statics

The effects of a change in k and q on the endogenous variables can be derived by differentiating (8.10) through (8.15). Let a hat denote the rate

---

[9]See Jones (1965) for a detailed discussion.

of change of a variable. By assuming that Y is labor-intensive relative to M, we can obtain:

$$\frac{\hat{w}}{\hat{q}} = -\frac{\theta_{TY}}{(\theta_{LY} - \theta_{LM})} < 0$$

$$\frac{\hat{t}}{\hat{q}} = \frac{\theta_{LY}}{(\theta_{LY} - \theta_{LM})} > 0$$

$$\frac{\hat{\lambda}}{\hat{q}} = \frac{(1 + \lambda)\theta_{TY}}{\lambda(\theta_{LY} - \theta_{LM})} > 0$$

$$\frac{\hat{X}}{\hat{q}} = \frac{\{s_1\lambda_{TY} + s_2\lambda_{LY} + \theta_{TY}\lambda_{LX}\lambda_{TY}(1 + \lambda)\}}{(\theta_{LY} - \theta_{LM})(\lambda_{LY} - \lambda_{TY})} > 0$$

$$\frac{\hat{Y}}{\hat{q}} = -\frac{[s_1\lambda_{TM} + s_2(1 - \lambda_{LY}) + \theta_{TY}\lambda_{LX}\lambda_{TM}(1 + \lambda)]}{(\theta_{LY} - \theta_{LM})(\lambda_{LY} - \lambda_{TY})} < 0$$

$$\frac{\hat{w}}{\hat{k}} = \frac{\hat{t}}{\hat{k}} = \frac{\hat{\lambda}}{\hat{k}} = 0$$

$$\frac{\hat{X}}{\hat{k}} = \frac{-1 - \lambda_{LX}\lambda_{TY}(1 + \lambda)}{(\lambda_{LY} - \lambda_{TY})} < -1$$

$$\frac{\hat{Y}}{\hat{k}} = \frac{\lambda_{LX}\lambda_{TM}(1 + \lambda)}{(\lambda_{LY} - \lambda_{TY})} > 0,$$

where $s_1 = \sigma_Y\theta_{TY}\lambda_{LY} + \sigma_M\theta_{TM}\lambda_{LM} > 0$ and $s_2 = \sigma_Y\theta_{LY}\lambda_{TY} + \sigma_M\theta_{LM}\lambda_{TM} > 0$. Here $\sigma_Y = \beta\beta_w t/\beta_w\beta_t$ and $\sigma_M = \gamma\gamma_{wt}/\gamma_w\gamma_t$ signify the factor substitution in sectors Y and M, respectively.

Chapter 9

Local Content Requirements, Welfare, and Trade Balance

9.1 Introduction

The trade-related investment measure (TRIMs) agreement of the General Agreement on Tariffs and Trade (GATT) and World Trade Organization (WTO) aims at eliminating the use of TRIMs for promoting competition. Broadly speaking, there are two types of TRIMs: output based and input based.[1] Historically, among the input-based TRIMs, local content protection (CP) had become the most commonly used by both the developed and developing countries.[2] Under the CP scheme, foreign-owned firms are required to employ a minimum amount of domestic inputs in their production. Local content requirements were particularly prevalent in the automobile industry of Australia and a good number of industries in Canada, Peru, India, Korea, and China, among other nations.

The effects of the CP scheme have been studied extensively in the trade literature dating back to the earlier descriptive work of Johnson (1963a), Munk (1969), and Corden (1971), followed by a more analytical investigation by Grossman (1981). These studies, however, are mainly partial equilibrium in nature, and the intersectoral resource allocation effect and related issues are understandably not tackled. To remedy this limitation, Chao and Yu (1993) utilize a general equilibrium setting to demonstrate in a four-sector model with urban unemployment, that higher local CP is unambiguously welfare reducing. Gu and Yabuuchi (2003), however, show

---

[1] Greenaway (1992) provides detailed discussion on TRIMs. Some case studies are given in Guisinger and Associates (1985).

[2] Among output-based TRIMs, export-share requirements (ESRs) are the most commonly employed. Chao and Yu (1998a) examine the effects of a temporary increase in ESRs to foreign-owned firms on the trade balance and national welfare.

that CP can be welfare improving, dependent on where the intermediate-goods sector is located. The analysis is extended to a setting by allowing variable labor supply by Fung (1994).[3]

To promote trade liberalization in a progressive manner, an agreement to remove TRIMs, including CP, was reached in the 1994 Uruguay Round GATT negotiation. The North American Free Trade Agreement (NAFTA) and the WTO go beyond the GATT agreement by disallowing most major items of TRIMs, including CP. Linking performance requirements to investment incentives is also prohibited. However, it is customary for a country to attract foreign firms by initially offering investment incentives and/or instituting import restrictions. After the foreign firms set up operations inside the host country, TRIMs may be adopted to either counter the monopoly power of the foreign firms and/or to protect domestic firms. In this connection, in the past CP was used to protect the domestic intermediate-goods sector. It is thus of academic interest to analyze the consequences of the policy of CP and to determine the conditions for each occurrence so as to shed light on the WTO agreement and the policy recommendations.

The setting we deploy in this chapter is the following. Fierce foreign competition resulting from increasing liberalization of trade in both final and intermediate goods over the past decades has endangered the survival of domestic raw-material producers in many countries. To compel firms to use domestic raw materials, local content requirements rather than tariffs are implemented. While CP is imposed in Period 1, it will be eliminated in the subsequent period due to trade liberalization and the WTO agreement. Note that the two periods in the model are connected through the balance of trade, which is also a major concern for policymakers. We will show that such a temporary one-period rise in CP can worsen the trade balance via declines in both intertemporal welfare and real exchange rates. This result arises from the possibility that a slight tightening of a given CP regime can yield an undesirable effect on resource allocation. Our analysis of CP is reminiscent of the argument of infant industry protection.

This chapter is organized as follows. Section 9.2 presents a two-period, four-sector, general equilibrium model, in which the two periods are linked mainly through the trade balance. Section 9.3 examines the effects of a change in CP in the first period only on the real exchange rate, welfare, and the trade balance. Some concluding remarks are provided in Section 9.4.

---

[3] Other relevant studies on content requirements can be found in Kim (1997) and Lahiri and Yano (2003).

9.2   The Model

Consider a two-period economy that produces four goods: an importable processed good X, an exportable good Y, a non-tradable good Z, and a raw material M_d. We introduce the non-tradable good in the model for determining the real exchange rate, which is the inverse of the non-tradable price (López and Rodrik, 1991). The production of good X requires raw material M, which can be supplied by domestic and foreign producers, M_d and M_f, and a set of specific factors, K_X.[4] The production function of good X over the two periods is: $X^i = X^i(M^i, K_X)$, where $M^i = M_d^i + M_f^i$ and the superscript, $i = 1, 2$, denotes the time period. It is assumed that there is no growth in the production factors, so the time index for K_X can be conveniently suppressed. Regarding the domestic production of raw materials and the exportable good, it is assumed for simplicity's sake that only labor inputs are needed: $M_d^i = M_d^i(L_M^i)$ and $Y^i = Y^i(L_Y^i)$. For the production of the non-traded good, it is specified as: $Z^i = Z^i(L_Z^i, K_Z)$, where L_Z^i and K_Z are labor and specific factors used by sector Z. Note that labor is the only mobile factor in the economy.

By choosing good Y as the numeraire, the prices of domestic and foreign raw materials are denoted by p^i and p^*, respectively. Since the home country is a small open economy, the price of the importable good X is given exogenously and normalized to 1. Moreover, the prices of the non-traded good, denoted by q^i, are endogenously determined in the economy. Letting w^i be the wage rate, the unit-cost functions for producing good Y and raw-material M_d can be expressed by $c_Y(w^i)$ and $c_M(w^i)$. In equilibrium, unit price must equal unit cost for each sector. Thus, we have: $1 = c_Y(w^i)$ and $p^i = c_M(w^i)$. This gives a constant w^i and thus a constant p^i (and, therefore, we can drop the superscript i for wage rates and domestic material prices).[5]

We assume for concreteness that the home technology is comparatively inferior or the home wage cost is higher. The domestic material cost and

---

[4]The discussions of the specific-factor model can be found in Jones (1971). Also see, for example, Batra and Beladi (1990) and Beladi and Marjit (1992) for applications.

[5]In the general equilibrium analysis, changes in wages yield repercussions on labor allocation between sectors. Nonetheless, in this chapter, the flexible price q^i of the non-traded good serves this purpose for giving induced changes in labor allocation and thereby affecting welfare and the trade balance. Studies on labor choice and the price of the non-traded good can be found, for example, in Hatzipanayotou and Michael (1995), Hsieh *et al.* (1998), and Yabuuchi and Beladi (2001).

hence the price exceeds the corresponding foreign price, i.e., $p > p^*$. To sustain the domestic raw-material sector in Period 1, local CP is implemented. Under this protection scheme, it becomes mandatory for the producers of good X to use a minimum of, say, $\alpha\%$ of raw materials which is domestically made,[6] i.e., $M_d^1 = \alpha M^1$. The effective material cost per unit of good X in Period 1, p_e^1, is then the weighted average of p and p^* with the weights equal to α and $(1-\alpha)$, respectively; that is, $p_e^1 = \alpha p + (1-\alpha)p^*$ and apparently $p^* < p_e^1 < p$. The difference between p_e^1 and p^* is the increase in the material cost per unit of the processed good as a result of the mandatory use of the domestic component. However, trade is liberalized in the second period and CP is eliminated in accordance with the WTO agreement, and hence no domestic raw materials would be used at all. This gives $p_e^2 = p^*$ as $\alpha = 0$.

The above production activities and their implications can be expressed by the revenue functions. For Period 1, due to the requirement of local CP, it is revealing for us to construct the revenue functions separately for sector X and sectors Y and Z.[7] For a given L_M^1, the *constrained* revenue function for sector X is: $R^* (1, L_M^1, M_f^1) = X[M_d^1(L_M^1) + M_f^1, K_X]$; the revenue function for sectors Y and Z combined is: $R^1 (1, q^1, \overline{L} - L_M^1) = \max\{Y^1(L_Y^1) + q^1 Z^1 (L_Z^1, K_Z) : L_Y^1 + L_Z^1 = \overline{L} - L_M^1\}$, where $\overline{L}$ is the labor endowment in the economy. Note that $R_L^* = p_e^1 (\partial M_d^1 / \partial L_M^1) = (p_e^1/p)w$ and $R_L^1 = w$. Since $p_e^1 < p$, we have: $R_L^* < R_L^1$. This implies that local CP causes a loss to the economy because the resulting contribution of labor to the processed good (via the production of domestic raw materials) is lower than that to the non-traded good. However, in Period 2, local CP is eliminated, and hence the home processed-good industry uses only the foreign materials to produce good X. The domestic raw-material sector ceases to exist. Period 2's national revenue function becomes: $R^2(1, 1, q^2, M_f^2) = \max\{X^2(M_f^2, K_X) + Y^2(L_Y^2) + q^2 Z^2(L_Z^2, K_Z) : L_Y^2 + L_Z^2 = \overline{L}\}$.

Using the properties of the revenue functions, the equilibrium conditions for the labor and raw material markets can be specified as follows:

$$R_L^*(1, L_M^1, M_f^1) = \left(\frac{p_e^1}{p}\right) R_L^1(1, q^1, \overline{L} - L_M^1), \qquad (9.1)$$

---

[6]Content protection can be defined in terms of either the quantity and/or the value of raw materials. Here, we only analyze the former.

[7]The separate, constrained revenue functions are useful in depicting the individual sectors. Such frameworks are used in Rodrik (1987).

$$R_M^*(1, L_M^1, M_f^1) = p_e^1, \tag{9.2}$$

$$R_M^2(1, q^2, M_f^2) = p^*, \tag{9.3}$$

where the subscripts in the revenue functions denote the partial derivatives. Note that using the definition of $R_M^*(\cdot)$, we have: $R_M^* = (\partial X^1/\partial M^1)$ $(\partial M^1/\partial M_f^1) = p_e^1$.

Turn to the demand side of this two-period economy. Total expenditure is: $E(1, 1, q^1, \delta, \delta, \delta q^2, u) = \min\{D_X^1 + D_Y^1 + q^1 D_Z^1 + \delta D_X^2 + \delta D_Y^2 + \delta q^2 D_Z^2 :$ $u(D_X^1, D_Y^1, D_Z^1, D_X^2, D_Y^2, D_Z^2) \geq u\}$, where D_j^i is the demand for good j in period i, u is the aggregate welfare measure, and δ is the discount factor reflecting consumers' time preference. The national budget constraint requires that the present value of total expenditure equals the present value of total income:

$$E(1, 1, q^1, \delta, \delta, \delta q^2, u) = R^*(1, L_M^1, M_f^1) + R^1(1, q^1, \overline{L} - L_M^1) - p^* M_f^1$$
$$+ \delta \left[R^2(1, 1, q^2, M_f^2) - p^* M_f^2 \right], \tag{9.4}$$

where total income equals production revenues minus the payments for the imports of foreign materials over the two periods.

To complete the model, we need to introduce the market-clearing condition for the non-tradable in each period:

$$E_3(1, 1, q^1, \delta, \delta, \delta q^2, u) = R_2^1(1, q^1, \overline{L} - L_M^1), \tag{9.5}$$

$$E_6(1, 1, q^1, \delta, \delta, \delta q^2, u) = R_3^2(1, 1, q^2, M_f^2), \tag{9.6}$$

where $E_3 = \partial E/\partial q^1$ and $R_2^1 = \partial R^1/\partial q^1$, denoting the demand and supply of the non-tradable in Period 1. Similarly, $E_6 = \partial E/\partial \delta q^2$ and $R_3^2 = \partial R^2/\partial q^2$ for Period 2.

The two-period system in (9.1)–(9.6) consists of six unknowns — $L_M^1, M_f^1, M_f^2, u, q^1$, and q^2 — with a CP policy instrument, α. To facilitate tracing out the economic intuitions, we solve the system in a stepwise manner: the resource allocation effect and the welfare effect can be obtained from (9.1)–(9.3) and (9.4), respectively, as functions of α, q^1, and q^2, and then the price effects from (9.5)–(9.6) as functions of α. Using the price effects, we can obtain the reduced-form, overall impact of a change in the local content ratio on domestic welfare.[8]

---

[8]The impacts of the domestic content ratio can be also simultaneously solved from (9.1)–(9.6). However, the stepwise solution procedure is better for tracing out the underlying economic intuitions than the simultaneous solution procedure. Note that this stepwise solution technique is used by Batra and Scully (1971) in a different context.

A secondary purpose of this study is to examine the effect of the change in CP on the trade balance. Though the trade balance does not directly affect welfare in the present model, it is nonetheless a major policy concern of an economy. This is because deteriorations in the trade balance lower gross domestic product (GDP) and hence indirectly affect welfare via falls in consumption. Note that the trade balance in Period 2 is given by:

$$B^2 = [R_2^2(1, 1, q^2, M_f^2) - E_5(1, 1, q^1, \delta, \delta, \delta q^2, u)]$$
$$-[E_4(1, 1, q^1, \delta, \delta, \delta q^2, u) - R_1^2(1, 1, q^2, M_f^2)] - p^* M_f^2. \quad (9.7)$$

The first two terms on the right-hand side of (9.7) represent the value of exports of good Y, the next two terms denote the imports of good X, and the last term is the value of imports of foreign materials. Since trade balance in the present intertemporal setting requires: $B^1 + \delta B^2 = 0$, we have $dB^1/d\alpha = -\delta(dB^2/d\alpha)$.[9] Totally differentiating (9.7) yields:

$$\frac{dB^1}{d\alpha} = \delta(E_{4u} + E_{5u})\left(\frac{du}{d\alpha}\right) + \delta(E_{43} + E_{53})\left(\frac{dq^1}{d\alpha}\right)$$
$$+ \delta[R_{33}^2 q^2 + \delta(E_{46} + E_{56})]\left(\frac{dq^2}{d\alpha}\right) + \delta q^2 R_{3M}^2\left(\frac{dM_f^2}{d\alpha}\right). \quad (9.8)$$

Note that, due to the price effect, a slight change in CP in Period 1 can affect Period 2's demand for foreign materials in (9.8). This can be seen by differentiating (9.3) and solving to yield: $dM_f^2/d\alpha = -(R_{3M}^2/R_{MM}^2)(dq^2/d\alpha)$. Substituting this into (9.8), the change in the trade balance can be expressed by:

$$\frac{dB^1}{d\alpha} = \delta(E_{4u} + E_{5u})\left(\frac{du}{d\alpha}\right) + \delta(E_{43} + E_{53})\left(\frac{dq^1}{d\alpha}\right)$$
$$+ \delta\left[\frac{R_{33}^2 q^2 + \delta(E_{46} + E_{56}) - q^2(R_{3M}^2)^2}{R_{MM}^2}\right]\left(\frac{dq^2}{d\alpha}\right). \quad (9.9)$$

The trade balance effect of a temporary rise in local CP in Period 1 clearly depends on its impacts on u, q^1, and q^2. These effects of the change in CP on welfare and the prices of the non-tradable goods in both periods will be examined in the next section.

---

[9]This two-period framework is adapted from López and Rodrik (1991) and utilized by Chao and Yu (1998a).

9.3   Effects of Content Protection

We examine first the resource allocation effect of a slight tightening of a given CP. The production of raw materials is to meet the derived demand by the processed-good sector. For a given output of good X, local CP initially raises the demand for the domestic material component to substitute the imported foreign materials. However, CP increases the effective price of raw materials, leading to a reduction in the production of good X. The cutback in the output results in a lower demand for both the domestic and foreign materials. Except for the neighborhood of zero output of good X, the adverse output effect of CP dominates the favorable substitution effect on the demand for domestic materials by sector X. This can be confirmed by solving (9.1) and (9.2) to obtain $\partial L_M^1/\partial\alpha < 0$, or equivalently $\partial M_d^1/\partial\alpha < 0$, and $\partial M_f^1/\partial\alpha < 0$.[10] So, the local CP is not a viable policy in the present framework to protect the domestic raw-material sector. Analogously, a rise in the price of good Z expands the non-tradable sector at the expanse of the processed-good sector, thereby giving: $\partial L_M^1/\partial q^1 < 0$ and $\partial M_f^1/\partial q^1 < 0$ (see Appendix A.1).

Turn next to the welfare effect of a slight change in local CP. Totally differentiating the budget constraint in (9.4), and then utilizing (9.1)–(9.3), (9.5), and (9.6) yields:

$$E_u du = (p_e^1 - p^*)dM_f^1 - \left(\frac{1-p_e^1}{p}\right)R_L^1 dL_M^1, \qquad (9.10)$$

where $E_u = \partial E/\partial u$ is the inverse of marginal utility of income and is normalized to 1. The welfare effect of the change in local CP depends on the divergences among the intermediate goods prices p^*, p_e^1, and p, and the CP-induced price distortion leads to the resource allocation effect via changes in M_f^1 and L_M^1. Since M_f^1 and L_M^1 are functions of α and q^1, the change of welfare in (9.10) can be compactly expressed by:

$$du = \left(\frac{\partial u}{\partial\alpha}\right)d\alpha + \left(\frac{\partial u}{\partial q^1}\right)dq^1, \qquad (9.11)$$

where $\partial u/\partial\alpha = (p_e^1 - p^*)(\partial M_f^1/\partial\alpha) - (1-p_e^1/p)R_L^1(\partial L_M^1/\partial\alpha) \gtrless 0$, denoting the direct welfare effect of the change in local CP, and $\partial u/\partial q^1 = (p_e - p^*)(\partial M_f^1/\partial q^1) - (1 - p_e^1/p^1)R_L^1(\partial L_M^1/\partial q^1)$, representing the non-tradable price-induced welfare effect.

---

[10]See the Appendix for derivations.

It is instructive to examine the conditions for signing the direct welfare effect, $\partial u / \partial \alpha$. A slight rise in local CP unequivocally raises the material cost in the production of the processed good, and its per-unit rate of increase can be measured by: $\alpha = (p_e^1 - p^*)/(p - p^*)$, a "direct cost" of protection. This implies that in the standard supply/demand diagram CP causes an upward shift in the supply curve of good X, thereby resulting in a smaller quantity of X produced and, hence, a direct revenue loss. Accompanying the revenue loss in the processed-good sector are the reductions in the demand for labor by the domestic raw material sector and for foreign materials, measured respectively by $R_L^1(\partial L_M^1/\partial \alpha)$ and $p^1(\partial M_f^1/\partial \alpha)$. Since $R_L^* < R_L^1$ (as the value added of labor is less in the processed sector), reallocation of labor from sector X to the other sectors generates a marginal allocative gain. We define this "marginal gain of labor reallocation" caused by an increment in CP (MGLR) as:

$$\text{MGLR} = \frac{R_L^1 \left(\frac{\partial L_M^1}{\partial \alpha} \right)}{\left[R_L^1 \left(\frac{\partial L_M^1}{\partial \alpha} \right) + p \left(\frac{\partial M_f^1}{\partial \alpha} \right) \right]},$$

which is between 0 and 1. In sum, the direct welfare effect of a slight rise in CP is negative (positive) when the direct cost of the rise in CP is larger (smaller) than its marginal gain of labor reallocation; namely, $\partial u / \partial \alpha < (>)0$ when $\alpha > (<)\text{MGLR}$.[11]

As for the price-induced welfare effect, we need first to determine the change in the non-tradable prices caused by the change in CP. Differentiating the market-clearing conditions in (9.5) and (9.6), we obtain:

$$E_{3u}du + \left[E_{33} - R_{22}^1 + R_{2L}^1 \left(\frac{\partial L_M^1}{\partial q^1} \right) \right] dq^1 + \delta E_{36} dq^2 = -R_{2L}^1 \left(\frac{\partial L_M^1}{\partial \alpha} \right) d\alpha,$$

$$(9.12)$$

$$E_{6u}du + E_{63}dq^1 + \left[\frac{\delta E_{66} - R_{33}^2 + (R_{M3}^2)^2}{R_{MM}^2} \right] dq^2 = 0, \tag{9.13}$$

where $E_{ju} > 0$, being the marginal propensity to consume good j, and $E_{jk} > 0$, assuming goods are inter- or intratemporal substitutes. Solving

---

[11]Using the definition of p_e^1, we can rewrite $\partial u / \partial \alpha$ as: $\partial u / \partial \alpha = (1 - p^*/p^1)$ $\{\alpha[p(\partial M_f^1/\partial \alpha) + R_L^1(\partial L_M^1/\partial \alpha)] - R_L^1(\partial L_M^1/\partial \alpha)\}$.

(9.12) and (9.13) yields the CP-caused changes in Period 1's non-tradable price:

$$\frac{dq^1}{d\alpha} = \frac{\left[AR^1_{2L}\left(\frac{\partial L^1_M}{\partial\alpha}\right) + (\delta E_{36}E_{6u} + AE_{3u})\left(\frac{\partial u}{\partial\alpha}\right)\right]}{\Delta}, \tag{9.14}$$

where $A = -[\delta E_{66} - R^2_{33} + (R^2_{M3})^2/R^2_{MM}] > 0$, and $\Delta > 0$ by the stability condition, as shown in the Appendix. The effect of the slight rise in CP on the non-tradable price in (9.14) is determined jointly by the supply and demand forces. As indicated by the first term on the right-hand side of (9.14), an increase in CP leads to reallocation of labor from the raw-material sector to the non-tradable sector. This increases the supply of good Z and lowers its price in Period 1. The second term captures the demand effect via the direct CP effect, $\partial u/\partial\alpha$, which is negative if the direct cost of CP, α, exceeds its marginal gain of labor reallocation. If this happens, the demand effect reinforces the supply effect, causing the non-tradable price in (9.14) to move downward (i.e., real exchange rate depreciation) in Period 1. Otherwise, a slight tightening of a given CP regime may result in an appreciation of the real exchange rate in Period 1. Clearly, this occurs when the demand effect outweighs the supply effect in the non-tradable market.[12]

Similarly, using (9.12) and (9.13), we can obtain the change in Period 2's non-tradable price:

$$\frac{dq^2}{d\alpha} = \frac{\left\{E_{63}R^1_{2L}\left(\frac{\partial L^1_M}{\partial\alpha}\right) + [E_{3u}E_{63} - E_{6u}(E_{33} - R^1_{2L})]\left(\frac{\partial u}{\partial\alpha}\right) - CE_{6u}R^1_{2L}\right\}}{\Delta}, \tag{9.15}$$

where $C = (\partial u/\partial\alpha)(\partial L^1_M/\partial q^1) - (\partial u/\partial q^1)(\partial L^1_M/\partial\alpha) > 0$.[13] While the first two terms on the right-hand side of (9.15) resemble the supply-and-demand effects in (9.14), the third term captures an additional demand effect through the change in the period's non-tradable price. When $\partial u/\partial\alpha < 0$, the fall in q^1, shown in (9.14), causes in the second period a reversal in labor reallocation from the non-tradable to the raw-material sector, resulting in a loss in income. This production loss together with the supply-and-demand effects leads to a reduction in Period 2's non-tradable price.

---

[12]By using the definition of MGLR and the expression of $\partial u/\partial\alpha$, the condition for real appreciation in (9.14) is: $\alpha < (1 - b)$MGLR, where $b = pAR^1_{2L}/(p - p^*)(\delta E_{36}E_{6u} + AE_{3u})R^1_L$. That is, a smaller α is needed to make a larger positive $\partial u/\partial\alpha$ and hence a positive $dq^1/d\alpha$ in (9.14).

[13]The proof is provided in the Appendix.

We turn next to the welfare effect of the slight rise in CP. From (9.11), we obtain:

$$\frac{du}{d\alpha} = \frac{-\left\{[A(E_{22} - R_{22}^1) + \delta E_{63} E_{36}]\left(\frac{\partial u}{\partial \alpha}\right) + AC R_{2L}^1\right\}}{\Delta}, \qquad (9.16)$$

which depends on the direct income effect, $\partial u / \partial \alpha$, as well as the q^1-induced unfavorable labor-reallocation effect in Period 2, captured by the C term in (9.16). The overall welfare effect is hence negative when $\partial u / \partial \alpha$ is negative.[14] However, the welfare effect may be positive when $\partial u / \partial \alpha$ is positive. The latter occurs for a small content requirement ratio. Therefore, the slight tightening of a given CP may improve the welfare only when the requirement is small.

Combining the implications directly deducible from (9.9) and (9.14)–(9.16), we can state the following.

Proposition 9.1 *In a two-period model with non-tradable goods, a temporary slight rise in the domestic content requirements leads to lower intertemporal welfare, depreciation in the real exchange rate, and hence worsening of the first-period trade balance, when the content requirement ratio exceeds the marginal gain of labor reallocation arising from content protection.*

This result can be explained as follows. Given that the content requirement ratio is high, the protection leads to an expansion of the non-tradable sector at the expense of the exportable sector for Period 1, thereby resulting in a lower non-tradable price and a depreciation of the corresponding real exchange rate in Period 1. The contraction in the exportable sector causes deterioration in the first-period trade balance. In addition, the subsequent fall in the non-tradable price in Period 2 raises the relative price of the exportable good, thereby expanding its production and inducing a switch in the consumption toward the cheaper non-traded good. This improves Period 2's trade balance, and, by implication of (9.7), the first-period trade balance must decline. Note that a slight increase in CP in the first period lowers the imports of foreign materials. But this effect can partially offset the deterioration in the trade balance.

---

[14]By using the definition of A, we have: $AE_{33} + \delta E_{36} E_{63} = -\delta(E_{33}E_{66} - E_{36}E_{63}) + E_{33}[R_{33}^2 - (R_{M3}^2)^2 / R_{MM}^2] < 0$ since $E_{33}E_{66} - E_{36}E_{63} \geq 0$ for the concave expenditure function in prices.

9.4   Concluding Remarks

Using a two-period general equilibrium model, this chapter examines the various effects of a slight tightening of a given CP regime for a small open economy with a non-traded good. A temporary rise in domestic content requirements can worsen the trade balance and national welfare, when the relative cost of protection exceeds its marginal gain from labor reallocation.

To promote liberalization of world trade in a progressive manner, the WTO member countries have been required to remove their trade-related investment measures (TRIMs), notably local CP, within two years for developed and five years for developing contracting parties. This chapter has shown that the WTO agreement appears meaningful because the elimination of CP over the periods can improve a country's trade balance, in addition to reducing the trade-restrictive and distorting effects.

Appendix

A.1   *Resource allocation*

Totally differentiating (9.1) and (9.2), and then solving them yields:

$$\frac{\partial L_M^1}{\partial \alpha} = -\left[\frac{(p - p^*)}{p}\right]\frac{(pR_{LM}^* - R_L^1 R_{MM}^*)}{D} < 0,$$

$$\frac{\partial M_f^1}{\partial \alpha} = -\left[\frac{(p - p^*)}{p}\right]\frac{(R_L^1 R_{LM}^* - pR_{LL}^* - p_e^1 R_{LL}^1]}{D} < 0,$$

$$\frac{\partial L_M^1}{\partial q^1} = \left(\frac{p_e^1}{p}\right)\frac{R_{Lq}^1 R_{MM}^*}{D} < 0,$$

$$\frac{\partial M_f^1}{\partial q^1} = -\left(\frac{p_e^1}{p^1}\right)\frac{R_{Lq}^1 R_{ML}^*}{D} < 0,$$

where $D = (p_e^1/p)R_{LL}^1 R_{MM}^* + [R_{LL}^* R_{MM}^* - (R_{ML}^*)^2] > 0$. Using the above results, we can obtain: $C = (\partial u/\partial \alpha)(\partial L_M^1/\partial q^1) - (\partial u/\partial q^1)(\partial L_M^1/\partial \alpha) = \alpha(p_e^1/p)R_{Lq}^1(p - p^*)^2/D > 0$.

A.2   *Stability*

Since the non-tradable markets are always cleared in both periods, the adjustment processes are:

$$\dot{q}^1 = a_1 H^1(q^1, q^2),$$
$$\dot{q}^2 = a_2 H^2(q^1, q^2),$$

where the dot is the time derivative, a_i is a positive constant, and $H^1 = E_3(\cdot) - R_2^1(\cdot)$ and $H^2 = E_6(\cdot) - R_3^2(\cdot)$ are, respectively, the excess demand for the non-tradable in Period 1 and 2. We take a linear approximation of the above adjustment processes around the equilibrium $(\tilde{q}^1, \tilde{q}^2)$ for a given α as:

$$\dot{q}^1 = a_1 \left[\left(\frac{\partial H^1}{\partial q^1} \right) (q^1 - \tilde{q}^1) + \left(\frac{\partial H^1}{\partial q^2} \right) (q^2 - \tilde{q}^1) \right],$$

$$\dot{q}^2 = a_2 \left[\left(\frac{\partial H^2}{\partial q^1} \right) (q^1 - \tilde{q}^1) + \left(\frac{\partial H^2}{\partial q^2} \right) (q^2 - \tilde{q}^1) \right].$$

A sufficient condition for stability of the above system is: $\partial H^1/\partial q^1 < 0$ and $\partial H^2/\partial q^2 < 0$. From (9.11)–(9.13), we can solve for:

$$\frac{\partial q^1}{\partial H^1} = \frac{\left[\frac{\delta E_{66} - R_{33}^2 + (R_{M3}^2)^2}{R_{MM}^2} \right]}{\Delta},$$

$$\frac{\partial q^2}{\partial H^2} = \frac{\left[\left(\frac{\partial u}{\partial q^1} \right) E_{3u} + E_{33} - R_{22}^1 + R_{2L}^1 \left(\frac{\partial L_M^1}{\partial q^1} \right) \right]}{\Delta},$$

where Δ is the determinant of the coefficient matrix of (9.11)–(9.13). Hence, $\Delta > 0$ is sufficient for $\partial H^1/\partial q^1 < 0$. The condition that $\partial u/\partial q^1 < -[E_{33} - R_{22}^1 + R_{2L}^1(\partial L_M^1/\partial q^1)]/E_{3u}$ is also needed for $\partial H^2/\partial q^2 < 0$.

Chapter 10

Wholly Foreign-Owned Enterprises or Joint Ventures

10.1 Introduction

International investment by multinational firms has grown rapidly over the past three decades. The resource allocation and welfare effects of foreign investment in a general equilibrium setting have been studied by trade theorists, dating back to Jones (1967, 1984), and subsequently by Batra and Ramachandran (1980), Batra (1986), Neary (1988), Hill and Mendez (1992), and Chao and Yu (1996), among others. A major purpose of multinational firms is to circumvent trade barriers by directly producing and selling the products in the host country. To counter the monopoly power of the global firms, host countries resorted to various measures of performance requirements, notably export-share requirements (ESRs) and local equity controls. Other policies include local content protection, import ceilings, and so on. (See Chapters 4 to 9 for related studies.) For example, Colombia required multinational firms involved in the petrochemical industry to export a minimum of 80% of their product in order to be granted 100% ownership. (See Guisinger and Associates [1985, p. 292] for a detailed discussion.) The joint-venture law of China not only encourages foreign firms to sell their products outside China, but also promotes local participation of equity of global firms.

Given that the global firms attempt to penetrate the market of the host country, while the host country strives to protect the domestic producers, the interest of the global firms is apparently in conflict with the national interest of the host country. The solution to this conflict of interest seems to lie in the trade-off between releasing (gaining) equity control by global firms in exchange for permission to sell more (less) inside the host country. Our analysis, however, suggests fairly straightforward policy choices regarding the optimal combinations of local equity controls and export shares.

This chapter develops a framework for examining the effects of ESRs and local equity controls of multinational firms as well as ascertaining the jointly optimal combinations of these two policies for a small open host economy in the presence of tariffs. A key result to emerge from the analysis is that wholly foreign-owned enterprises (i.e., 100% foreign ownership by global firms), coupled with an ESR, constitute the optimal policy for the host country. Our analysis of the welfare impact of permitting wholly foreign-owned enterprises has an important bearing on policymaking by capital-importing developing nations. For example, China adopted open-door economic policies more than three decades ago. The main method of foreign firms making direct investment in China has been equity joint ventures, which involve the sharing of the capital investment between a foreign firm and a local partner. Recently, foreign firms have been allowed to make direct investments in China without any local participation. Both Hong Kong Bank and Citibank, as well as Merck Sharp & Dohme (marketers of pharmaceutical products), among other firms, have been allowed to establish wholly-owned branches and operations inside China. Although the wholly foreign-owned firms are still limited in number, such firms and operations are nevertheless on the rise.[1] This chapter provides an economic explanation for the shift in the policy from strong local equity controls to allowing 100% foreign ownership.

A general equilibrium model dealing with equity controls and ESRs is introduced in Section 10.2. Utilizing the model, we examine the effect of export requirements and local equity controls on resource allocation and welfare in Section 10.3. The individual and jointly optimal policies are also explored in this section. The concluding remarks are presented in Section 10.4.

10.2 The Model

At the outset we provide a general equilibrium, specific-factor model to examine the optimal policies of export requirements and local equity controls of multinational firms in a small, capital-importing, open economy.

---

[1]According to a news article in *Ming Pao* on March 3, 1993, China allows 100% foreign ownership of power stations in order to tackle the serious energy shortage.

In this economy, the domestic firms produce two goods: an importable good X and an exportable good Y. While nothing interferes with trade in the exportable good, the host country imposes a tariff on the import of good X to protect the domestic importable sector. To circumvent this tariff protection, foreign firms choose to invest in the home country's importable sector.

The production functions of the domestic and multinational firms are $Y = Y(L_Y, T)$, $X_l = X^l(L_l, K_l)$ and $X_m = X^m(L_m, K_m)$, where X_l and X_m are outputs of X produced by the local and multinational firms, respectively, and L_i represents the domestic labor employed in firm i. While labor is perfectly mobile among all firms, capital (K_i) is specific for sector X and land (T) is specific for sector Y. (See Jones, 1971, for a discussion of the specific-factor model.) Hill and Mendez (1992), using a general equilibrium model, consider the effect of local equity controls on labor employment. A local equity-share policy means that a certain percentage of total equity in the multinational firms (say β), is held by domestic residents. Thus, for the multinational firms, we posit the following relations: $K_m^d = \beta K_m$ and $K_m^f = (1 - \beta)K_m$, where K_m^d, and K_m^f are, respectively, the domestic and foreign capital used in the multinational firms.

We assume that the domestic labor, capital, and land are fully employed: $L_Y + L_l + L_m = \bar{L}$, $K_l + K_m^d = \bar{K}$ and $T = \bar{T}$, where $\bar{L}$, $\bar{K}$, and $\bar{T}$ are the given endowments of the domestic labor, capital, and land. Note that we shall use $L = L_Y + L_l$ to denote the total labor employed by the domestic firms in both sectors.

The production side of the model can be efficiently summarized by the revenue functions. Let the exportable good Y be the numeraire so that the price of Y is normalized to unity. Due to the small country assumption, the tariff-inclusive domestic price of good X, p is determined by the foreign price p^* and the specific tariff rate t as $p = p^* + t$. Consider first the revenue function of domestic firms which is given by $R(1, p, L, \bar{K}, -\beta K_m) = \max\{Y(L_Y, T) + pX^l(L_l, K_l) : L = L_Y + L_l, K_l = \bar{K} - \beta K_m\}$ with respect to L_Y, L_l, and K_l. Because land is given, we suppress T in the above revenue function. By Shephard's lemma, the partial derivative of R with respect to the goods' price yields the output of good X by the local firms, i.e., $R_p = \partial R/\partial p = X_l$. Also, the partial derivatives of R with respect to labor and capital indicate, respectively, the returns to labor and capital, i.e., $R_L = \partial R/\partial L$ and $R_K = \partial R/\partial(\bar{K} - \beta K_m)$.

To circumvent the tariffs, foreign capital flows into the domestic importable sector. In the context of the present model, the multinational firms are subject to two requirements, namely the local equity control and the export-share ratio. The export requirement specifies that a share α of the output of good X_m produced by multinational firms be exported. For a given α, the effective producer price of good X, p_e, facing the multinational firms, is simply: $p_e = \alpha p^* + (1-\alpha)p$, which is necessarily less than the domestic price for domestic firms. Thus the ESR results in a wedge between the prices of domestic firms and global firms in the importable sector. Since $p^* < p_e < p$, an increase in α implies a decrease in p_e, and hence a larger wedge between p_e and p. (See Rodrik, 1987, for a detailed discussion of ESRs.) The revenue function for multinational firms can be written as: $R^m(p_e, \bar{L} - L, K_m) = p_e X^m(L_m, K_m)$, where $L_m = \bar{L} - L$. By virtue of the usual properties of the revenue function, we have $R_p^m = \partial R^m / \partial p_e = X_m$, $R_L^m = \partial R^m / \partial (\bar{L} - L)$ and $R_K^m = \partial R^m / \partial K_m$.

Due to perfect mobility of labor between sectors, the wage rates are equalized between the domestic and multinational firms:

$$R_L(1, p, L, \bar{K} - \beta K_m) = R_L^m(p_e, \bar{L} - L, K_m). \qquad (10.1)$$

Given that the multinational firms are constrained by the local ESR, the effective rental rate to their capital is the weighted average of the domestic and foreign rental rates:

$$R_K^m(p_e, \bar{L} - L, K_m) = \beta R_K(1, p, L, \bar{K} - \beta K_m) + (1 - \beta)r^*, \qquad (10.2)$$

where R_K is the rental cost of domestic capital and r^* the cost for foreign capital. We assume that the domestic rental rate is higher than the foreign rate, $R_K > r^*$, so that the host country imports capital.

Turning to the demand side of the economy, the social demand can be represented by an expenditure function, $E(1, p, u) = \text{minimum}(D_Y + pD_X)$ with respect to the demand for the two goods, D_Y, and D_X, subject to a strictly quasi-concave utility function $u(D_Y, D_X) \geq u$. Note that $E_p = \partial E(1, p, u)/\partial p = D_x$ is the demand for good X, and $E_u = \partial E(1, p, u)/\partial u$ denotes the marginal utility of income. Consumer expenditure is constrained by production and tariff revenues net of rental payments to foreign capital. Thus, the economy's budget constraint can be written as:

$$E(1, p, u) = R(1, p, L, \bar{K} - \beta K_m) + R^m(p_e, \bar{L} - L, K_m)$$

$$- (1 - \beta)r^* K_m + tQ, \qquad (10.3)$$

where Q denotes the import of good X. Equation (10.3) equates national expenditure to national net revenue, which equals the values of production of goods X and Y minus the returns to foreign capital plus tariff revenue.

It is assumed that the foreign capital returns are totally repatriated to the source country, and the tariff revenue is redistributed to the private sector in a lump-sum fashion.

Taking into account that multinational firms are mandated to export a share α of their produce, we can state the goods-market equilibrium conditions as:

$$Q = E_p(1, p, u) - R_p((1, p, L, \bar{K} - \beta K_m) - (1 - \alpha)R_p^m(p_e, \bar{L} - L, K_m),$$
(10.4)

where E_p, as noted earlier, is the demand for good X, R_p is the domestic output of good X, and R_p^m is the output of good X produced by the multinational firms.

The model consists of (10.1)–(10.4), which contain four endogenous variables — u, L, K_m, and p — and two policy variables, α and β, in the presence of a preexisting tariff rate, t. The tariff generates a price distortion relative to the world price, and the distortion results in a welfare loss in a small open economy. The welfare effects of export requirements and local equity controls are then determined partly on the basis of how they mitigate or reinforce the loss from tariff (examined in the next section).

10.3   The Resource Allocation and Welfare Effects

Totally differentiating the budget constraint (10.3) and utilizing (10.1), (10.2), and (10.4), we obtain the welfare expression for assessing the effects *ceteris paribus* of changes in the requirements of the export share and local equity share of multinational firms:

$$(E_u - tE_{pu})du = t^2(1 - \alpha)R_{pp}^m d\alpha - [(R_K - r^*) - tR_{pK}]K_m d\beta$$

$$+ t\{(1 - \alpha)R_{pL}^m - R_{pL}]dL$$

$$- [(1 - \alpha)R_{pK}^m - \beta R_{pK}]dK_m,$$
(10.5)

where the second subscript in the revenue and expenditure functions denotes the second-order partial derivative. Note that on the left-hand side of (10.5), $E_u - tE_{pu} > 0$ if both goods are normal. On the right-hand side, the first term captures the direct effect of an increase via a higher tariff revenue caused by a reduction in the production of multinational firms. Since $R^m(p_e, K_m, \bar{L} - L) = p_e X^e(L_m, K_m)$, we obtain $R_{pp}^m = 0$ for given L_m and K_m. Hence, the direct effect vanishes.

The second term on the right-hand side of (10.5) shows the direct effect resulting from strengthening local equity control. Here $(R_K - r^*)$ captures the higher production cost paid by the multinational firms as a result of the increased use of domestic capital, whereas tR_{pK} indicates the increase in the tariff revenue as the volume of import of good X increases. The third and the fourth terms in the parentheses capture the resource reallocation effects (among the domestic and foreign firms as well as the inflows of foreign capital) of the two policies.

As shown by the welfare expression (10.5), the effects of export requirements and equity controls depend crucially upon the direct impact of such policies as well as the policy-induced gains and losses resulting from reallocation of capital and labor. The resource reallocation effects thus deserve further elaboration (derivations are relegated to the Appendix). Recall that an increase in the export-share ratio lowers the effective goods price for the multinational firms. The lower product price leads to a reduction in the production of X_m, thereby reducing the global firms' demand for both capital and labor. Thus, we have $\partial L_m / \partial \alpha < 0$ and $\partial K_m / \partial \alpha < 0$, which is the output effect. Given full employment of labor, $\partial L_m / \partial \alpha < 0$ readily implies $\partial L / \partial \alpha > 0$ for a given β.

While the export-share policy has a clear-cut effect on resource allocation, the policy of local equity control nevertheless results in an indeterminate shift in resource allocation. This asymmetry can be explained as follows. A tightened control of local equity results in a higher capital cost for both the global and the local firms and hence labor, substituting for capital for producing a given output. This factor-substitution effect is absent in the case of export-share policy. Furthermore, the output effect is also present here. If the global firms are strongly capital-intensive relative to the local firms within the X sector, the output effect further dampens the demand for capital in the multinational firms but amplifies the demand for labor in the local firms. Thus, the factor-substitution effect reinforces the output effect, thereby rendering $\partial K_m / \partial \beta < 0$ and $\partial L / \partial \beta > 0$. On the other hand, if the multinational firms are not strongly capital-intensive, the factor-substitution effect offsets the output effect, and hence we obtain ambiguous effects of equity controls on the demand for labor and capital, i.e., $\partial K_m / \partial \beta \gtrless 0$ and $\partial L / \partial \beta \gtrless 0$.

We are now ready to examine the welfare effects of the policies. Consider first the effect of a marginal change in the export requirements in the presence of a given local equity share for multinational firms. Setting $d\beta = 0$ in (10.5) and recalling $R_{pp}^m = 0$, we can obtain:

$$(E_u - tE_{pu})\frac{du}{d\alpha} = t\left\{ [(1 - \alpha)R_{pL}^m - R_{pL}]\left(\frac{\partial L}{\partial \alpha}\right) \right.$$

$$\left. - [(1 - \alpha)R_{pK}^m - \beta R_{pK}]\left(\frac{\partial K_m}{\partial \alpha}\right)\right\}, \qquad (10.6)$$

$$= -t\left\{ \frac{\partial X_l}{\partial \alpha} + (1 - \alpha)\left(\frac{\partial X_m}{\partial \alpha}\right)\right\}, \qquad (10.7)$$

where $\partial X_l/\partial \alpha = R_{pL}(\partial L/\partial \alpha) - \beta R_{pK}(\partial K_m/\partial \alpha) > 0$ and $\partial X_m/\partial \alpha = -R_{pL}^m(\partial L/\partial \alpha) + R_{pK}^m(\partial K_m/\partial \alpha) > 0$. From (10.7), for a given tariff, the welfare effect of export requirements works through the output impact of a change in α on the domestic supply of the importable good, which includes the production of purely local firms plus the $(1 - \alpha)$ portion of the supply of multinational firms. Hence, increasing the export requirement mitigates (amplifies) the cost of the tariff if it decreases (increases) the domestic output of the importable good.

In the neighborhood of a zero-export requirement, $\alpha = 0$, (10.6) can be expressed as $(E_u - tE_{pu})(du/d\alpha) = t\{[R_{pL}^m - R_{pL}](\partial L/\partial \alpha) - [R_{pK}^m - \beta R_{pK}](\partial K_m/\partial \alpha)\} \geq 0$, where $R_{pL}^m \geq R_{pL}$ and $R_{pK}^m \geq \beta R_{pK}$.[2] An introduction of export requirements results in a decrease in the domestic supply of the importable good. With a given tariff rate, a consequent rise in imports means a higher tariff revenue and, hence, an improved domestic welfare. On the other hand, when $\alpha = 1$, (10.7) reduces to $(E_u - tE_{pu})du/d\alpha = -t\{\partial X_l/\partial \alpha\}$, which is always negative. Clearly, a reduction of export requirements will then improve welfare.

In general, when α lies between 0 and 1, the welfare effect of changes in export requirements is ambiguous. The second-best choice of α, α^0, for

---

[2]From the first-order condition of maximizing the domestic revenue function, we obtain $R_{pL} = (\partial X_l/\partial L_l)(dL_l/dL) = p(\partial X_l/\partial L_l)$ and $R_{pK} = \partial X_l/\partial K_l$, where $p = dL_l/dL = Y_{LL}/(Y_{LL} + pX_{LL}^l)$. Similarly, we have $R_{pL}^m = \partial X_m/\partial L_m$ and $R_{pK}^m = \partial X_m/\partial K_m$. From (10.1), we have $p(\partial X_l/\partial L_l) = p_e(\partial X_m/\partial L_m)$. Since $p \geq p_e$, we have $\partial X_m/\partial L_m \geq \partial X_l/\partial L_l$; that is, $R_{pL}^m \geq \partial X_l/\partial L_l \geq R_{pL}$. Also, $R_{pK} = \partial X_l/\partial K_l$ and $R_{pK}^m = \partial X_m/\partial K_m$. From (10.2), we have $p_e(\partial X_m/\partial L_m) \geq \beta p(\partial X_l/\partial K_l)$. This implies $R_{pK}^m \geq \beta R_{pK}$.

given β and t, can be obtained by setting (10.6) or (10.7) to zero:

$$\alpha^0 = 1 + \frac{\left[R_{pL}\left(\frac{\partial L}{\partial \alpha}\right) - \beta R_{pK}\left(\frac{\partial K_m}{\partial \alpha}\right)\right]}{\left(\frac{\partial X_m}{\partial \alpha}\right)}, \tag{10.8}$$

$$= 1 + \frac{\left(\frac{\partial X_l}{\partial \alpha}\right)}{\left(\frac{\partial X_m}{\partial \alpha}\right)}. \tag{10.9}$$

Note that the optimal export-share ratio depends upon the local equity ratio. For wholly foreign-owned enterprises (i.e., $\beta = 0$), $\alpha^o = [R_{pK}^m(\partial K_m/\partial\alpha) - (R_{pL}^m - R_{pL})(\partial L/\partial\alpha)]/(\partial X_m/\partial\alpha)$, which lies in the interval $(0, 1)$. When $\alpha = 0$, the factor-market equilibrium condition in (10.1) implies $\beta = 1$;[3] that is, when the global firm is wholly locally owned (or nationalized), the ESR is naturally not warranted. The relationship between α and α^0, however, is a bit complex. While α^0 increases as p decreases in the neighborhood of unity, the rest of the α^0 schedule in the space of α and β in Figure 10.1 can be either negatively or positively sloped. This diagrammatic technique is adapted from the one utilized by Neary (1993) in delineating the relationship between tariffs and taxation of foreign capital. Nevertheless, our main result that zero β is optimal holds regardless of whether the α^0 curve remains negative throughout.

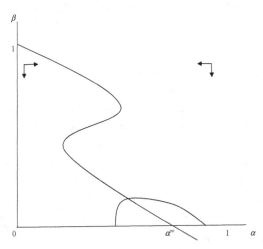

Figure 10.1 Optimal policies under a positive output response to local equity controls.

---

[3]When $\alpha^0 = 0$, we have $\partial X_m/\partial\alpha = -\partial X_m/\partial\alpha$. Since $\partial X_l/\partial\alpha = R_{pL}(\partial L/\partial\alpha) - \beta R_{pK}(\partial K_m/\partial\alpha)$ and $\partial X_m/\partial\alpha = -R_{pL}^m(\partial L/\partial\alpha) + R_{pK}^m(\partial K_m/\partial\alpha)$, we obtain $R_{pL} = R_{pL}^m$ and $\beta R_{pK} = R_{pK}^m$. Recall $p = p^e$, when $\alpha = 0$. This implies $\beta = 1$.

Equations (10.8) or (10.9) imply that the optimal α^0 exists such that, for a given β, a movement in α horizontally toward α^0, if $\alpha \neq \alpha^0$ initially, enhances welfare. This can be deduced by substituting (10.9) into (10.7):

$$(E_u - tE_{pu})\frac{du}{d\alpha} = t\left(\frac{\partial X_m}{\partial \alpha}\right)(\alpha - \alpha^0). \tag{10.10}$$

Since $\partial X_m/\partial \alpha < 0$, $du/d\alpha > (<)0$ as $\alpha < (>)\alpha^0$. Thus, a rise (fall) in α, as shown by the horizontal arrows in Figure 10.1, will enhance welfare for any given β, when α lies to the left (right) of α^0.

We turn next to the welfare effect of local equity controls in the presence of given ESRs. From (10.5), we have:

$$(E_u - tE_{pu})\frac{du}{d\beta}$$

$$= -(R_K - r^*)K_m + t\left\{R_{pK}K_m + [(1-\alpha)R_{pL}^m - R_{pL}]\right.$$

$$\left. \times \left(\frac{\partial L}{\partial \beta}\right) - [(1-\alpha)R_{pK}^m - \beta R_{pK}]\left(\frac{\partial K_m}{\partial \beta}\right)\right\}, \tag{10.11}$$

$$= -(R_K - r^*)K_m - t\left\{\frac{\partial X_l}{\partial \beta} + (1-\alpha)\left(\frac{\partial X_m}{\partial \beta}\right)\right\}, \tag{10.12}$$

where $\partial X_l/\partial \beta = R_{pL}(\partial L/\partial \beta) - \beta R_{pK}(\partial K_m/\partial \beta) - R_{pK}K_m \gtrless 0$ and $\partial X_m/\partial \beta = -R_{pL}^m(\partial L/\partial \beta) + R_{pK}^m(\partial K_m/\partial \beta) \gtrless 0$. Hence, the welfare effect of equity controls appears, in general, ambiguous, and the effect depends crucially on the impact of β on the output of the importable good.

Consider first the case in which the output response to local equity control is non-negative, i.e., $\partial X_l/\partial \beta + (1-\alpha)(\partial X_m/\partial \beta) \geq 0$. An increase in β reduces the imports of good X and lowers the tariff revenue (thus amplifying the production cost of the tariff). The smaller tariff revenue, along with the higher cost of capital, as shown in (10.12), reduces welfare. The larger the β ratio, the smaller the welfare. This implies that the optimal β ratio, β^0, is zero. Equivalently, wholly foreign-owned firms in the presence of an export-share ratio are socially optimal. This is illustrated in Figure 10.1, where the vertical arrows pointing down indicate a welfare-improving shift in β. The welfare increase is the greatest until β reaches the lines $\beta^0 = 0$. The iso-welfare contours are depicted by a map of inverted U-shaped curves. A representative contour is shown in Figure 10.1.

Given the individually optimal α^0 and β^0 curves, the jointly optimal combination of α and β is simply the intersection of α^0 and β^0 schedules. By utilizing (10.8) with $\beta^0 = 0$, we obtain:

$$\alpha^{00} = 1 + R_{pL}\frac{\left(\frac{\partial L}{\partial \alpha}\right)}{\left(\frac{\partial X_m}{\partial \alpha}\right)} \quad \text{and} \quad \beta^{00} = 0. \tag{10.13}$$

Clearly, the policy implication is that the global firms be wholly foreign-owned, coupled with the optimal export share, α^{00}. In this case, the welfare loss of the tariff is ameliorated only by a positive ESR on the foreign firm.

Consider the remaining case in which the output response to local equity control is negative, i.e., $\partial X_l/\partial \beta + (1 - \alpha)(\partial X_m/\partial \beta) <$. There are now two conflicting effects of local equity controls: strengthening local equity control increases the cost of producing X_m, as shown in the first term of (10.12), whereas the higher p increases the tariff revenue through a lower supply of good X. The welfare effect is ambiguous and depends on the export-requirement parameter. By setting $du/d\beta = 0$, in (10.12), we can obtain:

$$\beta_c = \frac{-(R^m_K - r^*)K_m}{t\left[\frac{\partial X_l}{\partial \beta} + (1 - \alpha)\left(\frac{\partial X_m}{\partial \beta}\right)\right]}. \tag{10.14}$$

However, this β_c gives a minimum instead of maximum welfare, because the welfare function is convex with respect to β.[4] Therefore, the optimal β is: $\beta^0 = 1$ when $du/d\beta > 0$, and $\beta^0 = 0$ when $du/d\beta < 0$. The β^0 schedule is depicted in Figure 10.2. By (10.12), the corresponding critical value of α to sign $du/d\beta$ is: $\alpha_c = 1 + [\partial X_l/\partial \beta + (R_K - r^*)(K_m/t)]/(\partial X_m/\partial \beta)$. That is, when $\alpha < \alpha_c$, we have $du/d\beta < 0$, and hence the optimal β is $\beta^0 = 1$, whereas when $\alpha > \alpha_c$, $du/d\beta < 0$, hence the optimal β is $\beta^0 = 0$. In addition, at $\alpha = \alpha_c$, $\beta^0 = 1$ when $\beta > \beta_c$ but $\beta^0 = 0$ when $\beta^0 < \beta_c$. Thus we have a piecewise discontinuous step function of β^0 with a break occurring at α_c in Figure 10.2.

Figure 10.2 reveals that there are in fact two jointly optimal policies: (a) $\alpha^{00} = 0$ and $\beta^{00} = 1$; and (b) $\alpha^{00} = 1 + R_{pL}(\partial L/\partial \alpha)/(\partial X_m/\partial \alpha)$ and $\beta^{00} = 0$. The first policy is of limited interest since foreign capital is not allowed in the host country. And the second policy is exactly the same as

---

[4]By using (10.12) and (10.14), we obtain: $(E_u - tE_{pu})(du/d\beta) = -(t/\beta)[\partial X_l/\partial \beta + (1 - \alpha)(\partial X_m/\partial \beta)](\beta - \beta_c)$. Since the coefficient of $(\beta - \beta_c)$ is positive, $du/d\beta > (<)\,0$ as $\beta > (<)\beta_c$.

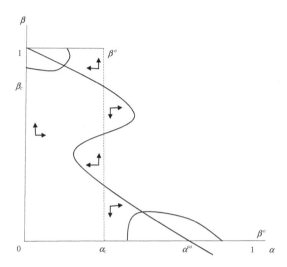

Figure 10.2   Optimal policies under a negative output response to local equity controls.

the one discussed previously. An ESR, coupled with 100% foreign ownership in multinational firms, is the jointly optimal policy. In sum, we may state the following proposition.

Proposition 10.1 *Wholly foreign-owned enterprises coupled with a positive export requirement are better than joint ventures for a small open economy under preexisting tariff protection.*

10.4   Concluding Remarks

In this chapter we have developed a model for analyzing the welfare effects of export requirements and local equity controls of multinational firms for a small open economy under tariff protection. Several results were derived. First, for a given local equity share of the multinational in the neighborhood of a zero-export requirement, increasing the requirement improves the welfare, whereas in the neighborhood of a full-export requirement, reducing the requirement enhances welfare. Second, if raising local equity increases the domestic supply of the importable good, then higher local equity leads to a decline in welfare. In this case, the optimal level of local equity is zero. If raising local equity leads to a fall in domestic supply of the importable good, then the welfare effect is *a priori* indeterminate. Nevertheless, between the two possible optimal policies, only one is relevant and interesting. The desirable policy involves the use of an export requirement coupled with wholly foreign-owned multinational firms.

Appendix: An Analysis of the Resource Reallocation Effects

Equity-share and export-share requirements affect resource allocations. To ascertain the effects, differentiating (10.1) and (10.2) yields:

$$\frac{\partial L}{\partial \alpha} = \frac{t[R^m_{pK}(\beta R_{LK} + R^m_{LK}) - R^m_{pL}(\beta^2 R_{KK} + R^m_{KK})]}{D} > 0,$$

$$\frac{\partial K_m}{\partial \alpha} = \frac{t[R^m_{pK}(R_{LL} + R^m_{LL}) - R^m_{pL}(\beta R_{LK} + R^m_{LK})]}{D} < 0,$$

$$\frac{\partial L}{\partial \beta} = \frac{[(R_K - r^*)(\beta R_{LK} + R^m_{LK}) + A K_m R_{KK} R^m_{KK}]}{D} \gtrless 0,$$

$$\frac{\partial K_m}{\partial \beta} = \frac{\begin{matrix}[(R_K - r^*)(R_{LL} + R^m_{LL}) \\ + A K_m R_{KK} R^m_{LK} - \beta K_m (R_{LL} R_{KK} - R^2_{LK})]\end{matrix}}{D} \gtrless 0,$$

where $A = \beta(K_m/L_m) - \rho(K_l/L_l)$ with $\rho = Y_{LL}/(Y_{LL} + pX^l_{LL})$. Because of diminishing returns of factors (i.e., $Y_{LL} = \partial^2 Y/\partial L^2 < 0$ and $X^l_{LL} = \partial^2 X_l/\partial L^2_l < 0$), we have $0 < \rho < 1$, and, hence $A \gtrless 0$. Clearly, $A > (<) 0$, if the multinational firm is strongly capital(labor)-intensive relative to the local firm within the X industry. Note that the denominator D is: $\beta^2(R_{LL}R_{KK} - R^2_{LK}) + [R^m_{LL}R^m_{KK} - (R^m_{LK})^2] + R_{KK}R^m_{KK}A^2 + (\rho - 1)R_{LK}R^m_{KK}(K_l/L_l)$. By assuming that the production functions display constant returns to scale, we have $R^m_{LL}R^m_{KK} - (R^m_{LK})^2 = 0$ for the multinational firms, and due to labor allocation in the domestic firms producing Y and X_l, we have $R_{LL}R_{KK} - R^2_{LK} = \rho p^2[X^l_{LL}X^l_{KK} - \rho(X^l_{LK})^2] > 0$ by assuming X_l gives constant returns to scale, where $R_{LL} = \rho p X^l_{LL}$, $R_{LK} = \rho p X^l_{LK}$ and $R_{KK} = p X^l_{KK}$ from the first-order conditions of the maximization of the domestic revenue function. Therefore, it follows that $D > 0$. The positive D assures the stability of the model.

Chapter 11

Domestic Equity Controls
of Multinational Enterprises

11.1 Introduction

In recent decades, foreign direct investment (FDI) by multinational firms
has played a vital role in promoting economic growth in developing and
newly industrialized nations. As domestic capital is generally insufficient
for sustaining growth of local production, foreign capital is much needed
for developing certain key sectors of the emerging economies. However,
many nations have restricted foreign investment out of fear of the awe-
some monopoly power of global firms and a concern for safeguarding
national sovereignty. As a result, numerous countries have adopted policies of restricting foreign ownership by requiring domestic equity shares in
multinational enterprises.[1] In view of the pertinent real-world observations,
questions of analytical interest readily arise. Do local equity regulations
imposed upon multinational firms help spur growth and promote welfare
of the host economy? Would the mobility of foreign capital and the type of
trade instrument in place affect the outcomes of equity regulations?

To answer these queries, we note at the outset that domestic equity
requirements mean a greater demand for local capital by multinational
firms. This, nevertheless, leads to contrasting output responses and welfare
consequences in varying time horizons. With fixed foreign capital in the
short run, the equity policy raises the local production of the multinational
firms. However, in the long run, the policy results in exit of foreign capital
and thus a reduction in output. Furthermore, the type of trade instrument

---

[1]For example, Guatemala has imposed a 30% local equity-share requirement on multinationals. The local equity controls were quite high in India and Peru with 60% and
51%, respectively. See Hill and Mendez (1992).

in place (i.e., tariffs versus quotas), also plays a key role in determining the output response to equity regulation. We will show that when quotas restrict imports, raising equity requirements improves welfare in the short run but reduces welfare in the long run. In contrast, when tariffs are in place, the policy lowers welfare in the short run but raises welfare in the long run.

11.2　General Equilibrium Analysis of Domestic Equity Controls

We refer to Chao and Yu (2000a) and consider a small open economy in which two goods are produced in the home country: the exportable Y and the importable X. The production functions for domestic firms are $Y = Y(L_Y, K_Y)$ and $X_l = X^l(L_l, K_l)$, where L_i and K_i denote labor and capital employment in sector i, and Y and X_l are the outputs of goods Y and X produced by domestic firms. Since labor and capital are perfectly mobile, these two domestic sectors form a Heckscher–Ohlin system of production.

The importable sector X is protected by import quotas or tariffs. Foreign enterprises, however, can partially bypass trade restrictions by undertaking direct investment and engaging in the production of good X, denoted by X_m, in the host country.[2] The production of X_m requires foreign capital and domestic capital, along with domestic labor L_m, as $X_m = X^m(L_m K_m)$, where K_m is the total capital used in the subsidiaries of the multinational firms. Although foreign firms are permitted to operate in the host country, they are often subject to a variety of performance standards and requirements, such as domestic equity ratios.[3] A local-equity-share policy

---

[2] For the literature on tariff-jumping foreign investment, see, for example, Kemp (1966), Jones (1967), Buffie (1985), Batra (1986), and Beladi and Marjit (1992). There are of course other motives for FDI, namely export orientation, ownership, location, or internalization so as to cope with global competition and the like. In this study, we abstract from the features (or complications) of increasing returns to scale technology and imperfect competition that characterize multinational enterprises.

[3] Other performance regulations for foreign multinationals include local content requirements, export-share requirements (ESRs), and so on. See Chao and Yu (1993) for an analysis of local content requirements, and Rodrik (1987) and Chao and Yu (1996b) for studies of ESRs. These performance regulations are the most commonly used instruments within the TRIMs (trade-related investment measures). See Greenaway (1992) for an excellent survey on TRIMs, and Yu and Chao (1998) for a related exposition.

aims at maintaining a certain, say β, percentage of total equity held by local partners. The equity-share relation for multinational firms is therefore $K_m^d = \beta K_m$ and $K_m^f = (1-\beta)K_m$, where K_m^d and K_m^f are, respectively, the domestic and foreign capital utilized in the multinational firms. We follow Rodrik (1987) and Hill and Mendez (1992) to assume that goods produced by the local and multinational firms are perfect substitutes.

In this chapter, full employment of the domestic labor and capital is assumed; i.e., $L_Y + L_l + L_m = \bar{L}$ and $K_Y + K_l + K_m^d = \bar{K}$, where $\bar{L}$ and $\bar{K}$ are the given endowments of the domestic labor and capital. We shall use $L = L_Y + L_l$ to denote the total labor employed by the domestic firms in both sectors. The production side of the model can be represented by the revenue function. Choosing good Y as the numeraire, the domestic price of good X is denoted by p. The revenue function of domestic firms is defined by $R(p, L, \bar{K} - \beta K_m) = \max\{Y(L_Y, K_Y) + pX^l(L_l, K_l) : L = L_Y + L_l, \bar{K} - \beta K_m = K_Y + K_l\}$ with respect to L_i and K_i. Using Shephard's lemma, $R_p(= \partial R/\partial p) = X_l$. Also, $R_L = \partial R/\partial L$ and $R_K = \partial R/\partial(\bar{K} - \beta K_m)$, denoting the rates of return to labor and capital, respectively.

To circumvent trade restrictions, foreign firms venture into the home importable sector to produce good X. The revenue function for the multinational firms can be written as $R^m(p, \bar{L} - L, K_m) = pX^m(L_m, K_m)$, where $L_m = \bar{L} - L$ and $K_m = K_m^d + K_m^f$. Notice that $R_p^m(= \partial R^m/\partial p) = X_m$, which is the output of good X produced by foreign firms, and $R_L^m = \partial R^m/\partial(\bar{L}-L)$ and $R_K^m = \partial R^m/\partial K_m$, denoting the rates of return to labor and capital, respectively, in foreign firms.

Because of intersectoral mobility of labor, the wage rates (w) in equilibrium are equalized between the domestic and multinational firms:

$$R_L(p, L, \bar{K} - \beta K_m) = w = R_L^m(p, \bar{L} - L, K_m). \qquad (11.1)$$

Since the multinational firms are constrained by the domestic equity-share requirements, the effective rental rate to their capital is the weighted average of the domestic and foreign rental rates:

$$R_K^m(p, \bar{L} - L, K_m) = \beta r + (1 - \beta)r^f, \qquad (11.2)$$

where $r = R_K(p, L, \bar{K} - \beta K_m)$, denoting the rental cost of domestic capital, and r^f is the cost of foreign capital in the host country. We assume that the domestic rental rate is higher than the foreign rate: $r > r^f \geq r^*$, where r^* is the rate of return in the world capital market.[4] Foreign capital cannot move in the short run, but it is movable in the long run.[5]

To complete the model, we need to specify the demand side of the economy, which can be captured by an expenditure function $E(p, u) = \min(D_Y + pD_X)$ with respect to the demand for the two goods D_Y and D_X, subject to a strictly quasi-concave utility function $u(D_Y, D_X) \geq u$. By Shephard's lemma, we have $E_p(= \partial E(p, u)/\partial p) = D_X$, the demand for good X. Aggregate expenditure is constrained by revenues from both production and import restrictions net of rental payments to foreign capital. The economy's budget constraint can be therefore written as:

$$E(p, u) = R(p, L, \bar{K} - \beta K_m) + R^m(p, \bar{L} - L, K_m)$$
$$+ (p - p^*)Q - (1 - \beta)r^f K_m, \qquad (11.3)$$

where Q denotes the imports of good X. The foreign capital returns are fully repatriated to the source country, and the revenue from tariffs or quota rents is redistributed to the private sector.

In equilibrium, the goods market satisfies the following condition:

$$Q = E_p(p, u) - R_p(p, L, \bar{K} - \beta K_m) - R_p^m(p, \bar{L} - L, K_m). \qquad (11.4)$$

where E_p is the demand for good X, and $R_p(R_p^m)$ is the output of good X produced by the local (multinational) firms. Equation (11.4) is simply a definition of import demand for good X.

Equations (11.1)–(11.4) delineate the constraints and the equilibrium conditions of the model. We shall utilize this framework to examine both the short-run and the long-run effects of domestic equity regulations on national welfare under import quotas or tariffs.

11.3   The Case of Quotas

Under the quota regime, the domestic price of the importable, p, is endogenous. Differentiating (11.3) and using (11.1), (11.2), and (11.4), the welfare

---

[4]Domestic firms and foreign firms are separated in the sense that foreign firms establish their own production plants in the host country, rather than invest in domestic firms. That is why $r > r^*$. This assumption is also made by Hill and Mendez (1992).

[5]To highlight the role of multinational firms, we follow Rodrik (1987) and use the mobility of foreign capital as a measure of time horizon. This is different from the usual definition of the short run versus the long run in terms of the mobility of capital between sectors (cf. Neary, 1978).

effect of domestic equity control can be obtained as:

$$E_u du = -(r - r^f)K_m d\beta - (1 - \beta)K_m dr^f, \tag{11.5}$$

where $E_u(= \partial E(p, u)/\partial u) > 0$, being the inverse of the marginal utility of income. The first term on the right-hand side of (11.5) is the first-order loss resulting from the required use of the more expensive local capital. The second term is the welfare effect induced via changes in payments to foreign capital. It is notable that, as is known from the literature on quotas,[6] the resource reallocation effect does not appear in (11.5). This is because the volume of imports is fixed under quotas and the link between resource allocation and welfare ceases to exist.

Before we proceed further, it is instructive to outline the various favorable and unfavorable causal impacts of domestic equity control, β, on domestic welfare, u. In (11.5), β can exert a direct, adverse effect on u. However, in the short run r^f is endogenous (i.e., $r^f = r^f(\beta, p)$ by [11.1] and [11.2]) and hence β also affects u indirectly via the changes in r^f. The welfare expression in (11.5) can be rewritten as:

$$E_u du = -(r - r^f)K_m d\beta - K_m(1 - \beta)\frac{\partial r^f}{\partial \beta}d\beta - K_m(1 - \beta)\frac{\partial r^f}{\partial p}dp. \tag{11.6}$$

Equation (11.6) reveals the three basic welfare effects of β under quotas: the first-order loss, the second-order effect via the direct impact on r^f, and the third-order effect via the price-induced change in r^f. Note that the value of $\partial r^f/\partial \beta$ can be derived from (11.1) and (11.2) as:[7]

$$\frac{\partial r^f}{\partial \beta} = -\frac{r - r^f}{1 - \beta}. \tag{11.7}$$

Here, $R^m_{LL}R^m_{KK} - (R^m_{LK})^2 = 0$ is used in view of the constant returns to scale technology in foreign firms. Substituting (11.7) into (11.6), it turns out that the second-order welfare gain just offsets the first-order loss. This

---

[6]See, for example, Dei (1985b) and Neary (1988) for discussions.

[7]Let $c^i(\cdot)$ be the unit-cost function of Section i. Under perfect competition, unit costs equal prices in equilibrium: (a) $c^Y(w, r) = 1$, (b) $c^l(w, r) = p$, and (c) $c^m[w, \beta r + (1 - \beta)r^f] = p$. This implies w and r are functions of p alone by the Heckscher–Ohlin structure in (a) and (b). So we simply differentiate $R^m_L = w$ and $R^m_K = \beta r + (1 - \beta)r^f$ in (11.1) and (11.2) to obtain $\partial r^f/\partial \beta$ in (11.7).

provides the change in welfare as:

$$E_u du = -K_m(1 - \beta)\frac{\partial r^f}{\partial p}dp, \qquad (11.8)$$

which depends only on the price-induced changes in p. The value of $\partial r^f/\partial p$ in (11.8) can be obtained from (11.1) and (11.2) as well:

$$\frac{\partial r^f}{\partial p} = R_{pK}^m - \beta R_{pK} - (R_{KL}^m + \beta R_{KL})\frac{\partial L}{\partial p}, \qquad (11.9)$$

where $\partial L/\partial p = (R_{pL}^m - R_{pL})/(R_{LL} + R_{LL}^m)$ with $R_{LL} < 0$ and $R_{LL}^m < 0$. From (11.9), the sign of $\partial r^f/\partial p$ depends upon the signs of both $R_{pK}^m - R_{pK}$ and $R_{pL}^m - R_{pL}$, which can be determined from the stability conditions (shown in the Appendix). The conditions require that: (a) $R_{pK} > 0$ and $R_{pL} < 0$,[8] i.e., good X is relatively capital-intensive compared with good Y in domestic sectors; and (b) $R_{pK}^m > R_{pK}$, i.e., foreign firms are more capital-sensitive than domestic firms for good X. Under stability, it is immediate that $\partial r^f/\partial p > 0$. This is reminiscent of the Stolper–Samuelson result. A rise in p leads to increases in the output of good X by multinational firms, yielding a higher demand for foreign capital that pushes up its rental rate shown in the first term of (11.9). However, the upward pressure is mitigated by the required use of domestic capital via equity controls as shown in the second term. Furthermore, the higher output promotes employment of labor by multinationals and subsequently renders a higher rental rate to foreign capital as indicated in the third term.

For the short run with fixed K_m^f, the price change dp in (11.9) can be obtained by differentiating the goods-market equilibrium condition (11.4):

$$E_{pu} du + \left[E_{pp} - R_{pp} + \frac{(R_{pL}^m - R_{pL})^2}{R_{LL} + R_{LL}^m}\right] dp = \left(\frac{\partial X_l}{\partial \beta} + \frac{\partial X_m}{\partial \beta}\right) d\beta, \qquad (11.10)$$

where $E_{pu} = \partial E_p/\partial u > 0$ by assuming that good X is normal and $\partial X_l/\partial \beta + \partial X_m/\partial \beta$ represents the change in the total supply of good X by domestic and multinational firms. Substituting (11.9) into (11.10) yields

---

[8]If good X is capital-intensive relative to good Y for domestic sectors, then $dL_1/dL < 0$ and hence $R_{pL} = (\partial X^1/\partial L_1)(dL_1/dL) < 0$.

the price response to domestic equity control:

$$\frac{dp}{d\beta} = \frac{\frac{\partial X_l}{\partial \beta} + \frac{\partial X_m}{\partial \beta}}{\Delta}, \tag{11.11}$$

where $\Delta < 0$ by the stability condition. Equation (11.11) suggests that the price effect depends only on the supply response, expressed by:

$$\frac{\partial X_l}{\partial \beta} + \frac{\partial X_m}{\partial \beta} = -K_m R_{pK} - (R_{pL}^m - R_{pL})\frac{\partial L}{\partial \beta} + (R_{pK}^m - \beta R_{pK})\frac{\partial K_m}{\partial \beta}, \tag{11.12}$$

which is positive under the stability conditions.[9] The reason for this result is straightforward. An increase in domestic equity requirements forces foreign firms, facing a fixed amount of foreign capital in the short run, to use more domestic capital. As a result, production of good X by the foreign firms increases at the expense of the outputs of the domestic firms. If the foreign firms are capital-sensitive relative to their counterpart domestic firms ($R_{pK}^m > R_{pK}$), then the increase in production of good X by the foreign firms outweighs the fall in production of good X by the domestic firms, thereby yielding a positive supply of good X in the host country.

From (11.11) and (11.12), a rise in domestic equity controls lowers the price of good X for the short run. This reduces rental payments to foreign firms and thus improves welfare according to (11.8). The crisp result that $du/d\beta > 0$ under stability in the short run, however, does not imply that the optimal policy is wholly domestic-owned multinational firms. Recalling that $r^f = r^f(\beta, p)$ with $\partial r^f/\partial \beta < 0$, $\partial r^f/\partial p > 0$, and $dp/d\beta < 0$ by (11.7), (11.9), and (11.11), this implies:

$$\frac{dr^f}{d\beta} = \frac{\partial r^f}{\partial \beta} + \frac{\partial r^f}{\partial p}\frac{dp}{d\beta} < 0. \tag{11.13}$$

A rise in β means a rise in the use of domestic and hence total capital in multinational firms, thereby reducing their marginal product of capital. However, the minimum r^f is the exogenously given world rental rate r^*. Therefore, the maximum level of β for the short run is β^0 which renders

---

[9]Using (11.1) and (11.2), we obtain $\partial L/\partial \beta = K_m R_{LK}^m/(1-\beta)R_{LL}^m < 0$. Also by using the definition of $K_m^f = (1-\beta)K_m$, we have $\partial K_m/\partial \beta = K_m/(1-\beta) > 0$ for a given K_m^f in the short run.

$r^f = r^*$; the optimal β by making use of the effective rental rate constraint in (11.2) is given by:

$$\beta^0 = \frac{R_K^m - r^*}{r - r^*}. \qquad (11.14)$$

Since $r > R_K^m > r^*$, it is immediate that $\beta^0 < 1$ in (11.14). In summary, we may state the following.

Proposition 11.1 *For the short run with a fixed amount of foreign capital inflows, raising the domestic equity ratio in multinational firms up to the optimal ratio given by (11.14) improves the welfare of the quota-ridden economy. Thus, the optimal policy is partial domestic ownership of the multinational firms.*

We turn to the long-run case, where foreign capital K_m^f is allowed to flow into the host country until its domestic rate of return r^f equals the fixed world rate r^*. Given $dr^* = 0$, (11.5) simplifies to:

$$E_u \left(\frac{du}{d\beta} \right) = -(r - r^*) K_m. \qquad (11.15)$$

That is, only the first-order welfare loss exists in the long run. We have $du/d\beta < 0$ and thus $\beta^0 = 0$. Hence, we state the following proposition.

Proposition 11.2 *In the long run, in which the domestic rate of return to foreign capital equals the world rate, raising local equity requirements under the quota regime is always welfare reducing, and the optimal policy is 100% of foreign ownership in multinational firms.*

The long-run result confirms Dei's (1985a) original insight that, in a quota regime, foreign capital inflows always improve welfare.[10]

11.4 The Case of Tariffs

In this section, we turn briefly to the welfare effects of equity controls under tariffs.[11] In this case, the quantity of imports, Q, is an endogenous

---

[10]The welfare results obtained are based on the assumption that there is a quota on the import-competing good. The best policy, however, is the removal of the original distortion.

[11]Although some welfare aspects of domestic equity controls and ESRs under tariffs have been examined in a somewhat different model by Chao and Yu (1996b), the study, nevertheless, does not consider the short-run case nor the issue of comparing short run versus long run.

variable. Let the rate of tariff on the imports of good X be $t = p - p^*$. Differentiating (11.3) and (11.4) yields the changes in welfare:

$$E_u du = -(r - r^f)K_m d\beta - (1 - \beta)K_m dr^f - t \left(\frac{\partial X_l}{\partial \beta} + \frac{\partial X_m}{\partial \beta} \right) d\beta.$$

$$(11.16)$$

In contrast to the quota case, the resource allocation effect appears in (11.16). For a given p under tariffs, r^f is a function of β alone, i.e., $r^f = r^f(\beta)$ with $\partial r^f/\partial \beta = -(r - r^f)/(1 - \beta) < 0$. The first two terms in (11.16) hence cancel out, and the welfare effect of domestic equity controls becomes:

$$(E_u - tE_{pu})\frac{du}{d\beta} = -t \left(\frac{\partial X_l}{\partial \beta} + \frac{\partial X_m}{\partial \beta} \right). \qquad (11.17)$$

Equation (11.17) states that the welfare effect of equity regulation depends only on the changes in tariff revenue.

As shown in (11.12), $\partial X_l/\partial \beta + \partial X_m/\partial \beta > 0$ in the short run with a given level of foreign capital K_m^f. Raising domestic equity requirements lowers tariff revenue owing to increases in the total supply of the importable good X in the host country. Therefore, domestic equity controls in the presence of tariff protection reduce welfare in the short run, implying that the optimal level of β is $\beta^0 = 0$.

As for the long run, foreign capital flows in when $r^f \geq r^*$. Denoting $c^m(\cdot)$ as the unit-cost function, the long-run equilibrium for foreign firms requires $r^f \geq r^*$ and $c^m[w, \beta r + (1 - \beta)r^f] = p$.[12] As a result of the Heckscher–Ohlin structure in domestic sectors, w and r are fixed and so is $\beta r + (1 - \beta)r^f$ under tariffs. This implies that, by (11.1) and (11.2), raising equity requirements will not affect the demand for labor and capital in foreign firms, i.e., $\partial L/\partial \beta = \partial K_m/\partial \beta = 0$. This further implies that $\partial X_m/\partial \beta = 0$. In addition, by (11.12) we have $\partial X_l/\partial \beta = -K_m R_{pK} < 0$. Equity controls lower the long-run supply of good X and thus raise welfare through the increase in tariff revenue. Since $\beta r + (1 - \beta)r^f (= R_K^m)$ is fixed, the optimal equity control is $\beta^0 = (R_K^m - r^f)/(r - r^f)$ for the long run. The following proposition is immediate.

---

[12]The "slackness" condition states that $X_m \geq 0$ as $c^m[w, \beta r + (1 - \beta)r^f] \gtrless p$. To assure the operation of the multinational firms in the host country, we rule out the case that $c^m(\cdot) > p$. See Rodrik (1987) for a detailed discussion.

Proposition 11.3 *When imports are subject to tariffs, raising equity controls lowers short-run welfare but increases long-run welfare. The optimal equity control is zero in the short run, whereas it is positive in the long run.*

11.5 Concluding Remarks

We have examined the welfare effects of domestic equity requirements on multinational firms in a general equilibrium framework. We have shown that the welfare effects of the policy are conditional on both the type of trade instrument in place and the mobility of foreign capital. Under quotas, the host country's welfare depends on changes in income accrued to foreign capital. On the other hand, when imports are subject to tariffs, local equity control affects domestic welfare through changes in tariff revenue. Based upon the different sources of income changes, dramatically contrary policy implications can be drawn. The short-run versus the long-run welfare effects of the equity policy under tariffs versus quotas may provide useful insight into trade policy formulation as well as whether or not to implement local equity requirements in regulating multinational firms.

Appendix: Stability

Following Dei (1985a), the adjustment for goods prices under quotas is assumed to follow:

$$\dot{p} = vZ(p),$$

where the dot over variables denotes the time derivative, ν is a positive adjustment coefficient, and $Z = E_p - R_p - R_p^m - Q$ is the excess demand for good X at home for any β.

Linearizing the adjustment process around the equilibrium value p_e yields:

$$\dot{p} = v\left(\frac{dZ}{dp}\right)(p - p_e).$$

A necessary and sufficient condition for stability under quotas requires a negative value of dZ/dp. From (11.8) and (11.10), we have:

$$\frac{dZ}{dp} = \frac{1}{\Delta},$$

where

$$\Delta = (E_{pp} - R_{pp}) + \frac{(R_{pL}^m - R_{pL})^2}{(R_{LL} - R_{LL}^m)} - \left(\frac{E_{pu}}{E_u}\right) K_m (1 - \beta)$$

$$\times \left\{ (R_{pK}^m - \beta R_{pK}) - \left[\frac{(R_{KL}^m + \beta R_{KL})(R_{pL}^m - R_{pL})}{(R_{LL} + R_{LL}^m)} \right] \right\}.$$

A sufficient condition for $\Delta < 0$ is that $R_{pL} < 0$ and $R_{pK}^m > R_{pK}$.

Chapter 12

Trade Liberalization, Foreign Ownership, and the Environment

12.1 Introduction

For the last three decades, inward foreign direct investment (FDI) has contributed a great deal to improving the economic performance of many countries. To attract foreign investment, various incentives, including low taxes, tax holidays, etc., have been provided.[1] However, many nations have also imposed restrictions on foreign-invested firms for a variety of reasons: to ameliorate fear of the monopoly power of multinational enterprises, to protect domestic firms, to tap into economic rents, and to preserve the environment. It is quite common for foreign firms to encounter domestic ownership requirements, environmental regulations, and other restrictions.[2]

In recent years, with an increasing number of countries, especially a major trading country such as China, joining the World Trade Organization (WTO), the liberalization of trade and investment has become a global trend. Both tariffs and non-tariff barriers are being reduced or eliminated to pave the way for more trade and foreign investment. For example, the issue of market access was a central theme in the negotiation for China's accession into the WTO. Since joining the WTO on December 11, 2001,

---

[1]In China, the average corporate income tax rates for domestic and foreign-owned firms are 30% and 11%, respectively.

[2]Conklin and Lecraw (1997) provide detailed discussion on the reasons and consequences of restricting foreign ownership in India, Morocco, the Philippines, and South Korea. Also see, for example, the survey article by Ching et al. (2004) on the commonly encountered restrictions for inward FDI in the Asia-Pacific region.

China has increasingly allowed more foreign ownership in various sectors.[3] The rise in the ratio of foreign ownership, through its effect on the inflows of FDI, would affect the economic performance and growth of the host country.

On the other hand, liberalization of investment can lead to an increase in pollution especially for developing countries, which generally have less stringent environmental standards. Lax regulations and low pollution taxes in these countries provide an incentive for polluting industries in industrialized countries to move there. This is often referred to as "pollution exporting" or "ecological dumping."[4]

Given that inward FDI plays a key role in promoting production and income and that the subsequent booming activities can lead to more pollution and environmental degradation, a policy issue which has been heatedly debated arises as to how a society can properly balance economic growth versus quality environment. The intricate link between foreign ownership and the environment and the resulting effect on national welfare is in need of scrutiny.[5] The purpose of this chapter is to examine why and how trade liberalization affects firm ownership and the environment. Drawing on Chao and Yu (2007), we use a general equilibrium framework for a small open economy, and derive the optimal policies regarding domestic versus foreign ownership and the extent of environmental measures. Our main finding is that the optimal policies can be reversed with increasing trade liberalization. In particular, when the tariff exceeds a certain rate, the optimal policy consists of a 100% domestic ownership requirement and a stringent pollution tax. However, when the tariff falls below that critical rate, the optimal policy involves 100% foreign ownership coupled with a lax pollution levy. These results appear to be borne out by casual observations that liberalizing trade via tariff reduction has caused increasing foreign ownership with deteriorations in the environment.

---

[3] According to the agreement, China permits foreign telecoms service suppliers to establish joint-venture enterprises with no more than 25% ownership. The foreign ownership is increased to 35 and 49% after one and two years of accession to the WTO.

[4] See Jaffe *et al.* (1993) for further discussion. Also see Khan (1996) and Neary (1999) for the theoretical work on trade and the environment.

[5] Chao and Yu (1996a) examine the welfare effect of domestic equity controls in conjunction with export-share requirements (ESRs). Chao and Yu (2000a) explore the welfare effect of domestic equity requirements in the presence of alternative types of trade restrictions and varying degrees of capital mobility are examined. Furthermore, Chao and Yu (2000b) study the individual and joint effects of ESRs and environmental taxes under quotas and voluntary export restraints. Also see Chao and Yu (2004).

This chapter is organized as follows. Section 12.2 presents a simple general equilibrium model with ownership restrictions and environmental pollution. Section 12.3 examines the welfare impact of altering ownership restrictions and pollution taxes for the economy. In addition, the individually and jointly optimal policies regarding ownership and pollution are derived in Section 12.3, and the consequent implications of trade liberalization on them are deduced. Section 12.4 provides some concluding remarks.

12.2   The Model

Consider a small open economy that produces two traded goods, X and Y, by using labor and capital. The production technologies for both goods are under constant returns to scale, and the production functions are: $X = X(L_X, K_X)$ and $Y = Y(L_Y, K_Y)$, where L_i and K_i denote, respectively, the amounts of labor and capital used in sector i. The production of good X, however, generates pollution emissions, Z, as a byproduct. Since pollution harms the public, a pollution tax, s, is imposed on pollution emissions.

We assume that the home country exports good Y and imports good X. While there are no impediments to the export of good Y, a specific tariff, t, is imposed on the import of good X. Choosing good Y as the numeraire, the domestic price of good X is equal to the foreign price plus the tariff, i.e., $p = p^* + t$.

On the economy's demand side, consumers demand good X and Y in the amounts D_X and D_Y. Given the tariff-inclusive price p of good X and the level of pollution Z, the minimum expenditure needed to attain a given utility u is: $E(p, 1, Z, u) = \min\{pD_X + D_Y : u(D_X, D_Y, Z) \geq u\}$, with respect to D_X and D_Y. Here, $E_p = \partial E/\partial p$, being the consumers' compensated demand for good X, and $E_Z = \partial E/\partial Z > 0$, expressing the marginal damage caused by pollution to consumers. Note that $E_{pZ} = \partial D_X/\partial Z$, representing the relationship between good X and pollution Z in consumption. For concreteness, they are assumed to be substitutes ($\partial D_X/\partial Z < 0$), i.e., consumption of good X declines as the pollution level increases.[6]

To facilitate an analysis of inward FDI, we assume that capital is mobile internationally, but labor is not. Tariffs are in place in the home country. To bypass the tariff barrier, foreign firms venture into the home country to

---

[6]Good X, for example, can be outdoor activities. The case that good X and pollution Z are complements ($\partial D_X/\partial Z > 0$) can be analogously considered. See Neary (1999) for discussion.

invest in the importable sector X.[7] Following Hill and Mendez (1992), the home government imposes an ownership requirement in the sector to protect domestic firms: $\xi\%$ of capital must be domestically owned, i.e., $K_X^d = \xi K_X$. This implies that the inflow of foreign capital is: $K_X^f = (1-\xi)K_X$. Assuming factor prices are flexible, domestic capital and labor are fully employed: $K = K_X^d + K_Y$ and $L = L_X + L_Y$, where K and L are the endowments of capital and labor in the home country. The net revenue functions for sectors X and Y can be written as: $R(p, s, L_X, K_X) = pX(L_X, K_X) - sZ$ and $H(1, L-L_X, K-\xi K_X) = Y(L_Y, K_Y)$. Note that $R_p(= \partial R/\partial p) = X$, being the domestic production of good X, and $R_s(= \partial R/\partial s) = -Z$, representing the (negative) pollution emissions.

As for the labor market, workers move between sectors X and Y until wages are equalized:

$$R_L(p, s, L_X, K_X) = H_L(1, L - L_X, K - \xi K_X), \qquad (12.1)$$

where $R_L = \partial R/\partial L_X$ and $H_L = \partial H/\partial L_Y$ are the wage rates in sectors X and Y, respectively.

Consider the capital market. Sector Y uses domestic capital only and its rate of return is: $H_K(= \partial H/\partial K_Y)$. However, sector X uses both domestic capital and foreign capital, the rate of return to capital is:

$$R_K(p, s, L_X, K_X) = \xi H_K(1, L - L_X, K - \xi K_X) + (1 - \xi)r^*, \qquad (12.2)$$

where r^* is the exogenously given world rate of return on foreign capital. It is reasonable to assume for this small open economy that $H_K > r^*$.

Turn next to the economy. The home country needs to satisfy the following budget constraint:

$$E(p, 1, Z, u) = R(p, s, L_X, K_X) + H(1, L - L_X, K_X)$$
$$+ sZ + tM - (1 - \xi)r^*K_X, \qquad (12.3)$$

where M is the import of good X. Equation (12.3) states that total expenditure is equal to revenue from production, plus pollution taxes and import tariffs, minus the payments to foreign capital. We assume that the pollution taxes and import tariffs are returned to the public in a lump-sum fashion. Further, the import of good X is defined as:

$$M = E_p(1, p, Z, u) - R_p(p, s, L_X, K_X), \qquad (12.4)$$

---

[7]See Brecher and Diaz Alejandro (1977) and Beladi and Marjit (1992) for tariff-jumping capital inflows.

which is the difference between domestic demand for and supply of good X. Recall that:

$$Z = -R_s(p, s, L_X, K_X) \tag{12.5}$$

represents the pollution emissions by firms in sector X.

The capital-importing economy described in (12.1)–(12.5) consists of five unknowns — L_X, K_X, u, M, and Z — together with three policy instruments, t, ξ, and s. We will examine the various effects of trade liberalization on the optimal ratio of foreign ownership and pollution tax rate.

12.3   Optimal Ownership and Environmental Policies

The model in (12.1)–(12.5) is block recursive: the resource allocation effect of changes in L_X and K_X can be solved from (12.1) and (12.2), and then the results can be used to obtain the welfare implications from (12.3)–(12.5). Differentiating (12.1) and (12.2), we obtain the resource allocation effect:

$$\frac{\partial L_X}{\partial s} = \frac{[R_{Ls}(R_{KK} + \xi^2 H_{KK}) - R_{Ks}(R_{LK} + \xi H_{LK})]}{G} < 0, \tag{12.6}$$

$$\frac{\partial K_X}{\partial s} = \frac{-[R_{Ls}(R_{KL} + \xi H_{KL}) - R_{Ks}(R_{LL} + \xi H_{LL})]}{G} < 0, \tag{12.7}$$

$$\frac{\partial L_X}{\partial \xi} = \frac{\left[(H_K - r^*)(R_{LK} + \xi H_{LK}) + K_X R_{KK} H_{KK}\left(\xi \frac{K_X}{L_X} - \frac{K_Y}{L_Y}\right)\right]}{G} < 0, \tag{12.8}$$

$$\frac{\partial K_X}{\partial \xi} = \frac{-\left[(H_K - r^*)(R_{LL} + H_{LL}) + K_X R_{KL} H_{KK}\left(\xi \frac{K_X}{L_X} - \frac{K_Y}{L_Y}\right)\right]}{G} < 0, \tag{12.9}$$

where $G = -R_{KK} H_{KK}(\xi K_X/L_X - K_Y/L_Y)^2 < 0$. It is noted that $R_{Ls} = -(\partial Z/\partial X)(\partial X/\partial L_X) < 0$ and $R_{Ks} = -(\partial Z/\partial X)(\partial X/\partial K_X) < 0$ by assuming that pollution Z is a byproduct in the production of good X (i.e., $\partial Z/\partial X > 0$). Using (12.6)–(12.9), we have: $\partial X/\partial s < 0$ and $\partial X/\partial \xi < 0$. As expected, a higher pollution tax or domestic ownership requirement in the foreign-invested polluting firm leads to a contraction in its output.

As for the change in welfare, we can differentiate (12.3)–(12.5) to obtain:

$$E_u du = -(H_K - r^*)K_X d\xi - (E_Z - s)dZ + tdM, \qquad (12.10)$$

where $E_u = \partial E/\partial u > 0$, being the inverse of the marginal utility of income. The change in welfare in (12.10) depends on the three policy measures in the economy: ownership restrictions, pollution taxes, and import tariffs. It is clear from (12.10) that the first-best policy is free mobility of capital $(H_K = r^*)$ and free trade in goods $(t = 0)$, combined with a Pigouvian tax on pollution emissions, i.e., $s = E_Z$, the tax is exactly equal to the marginal damage caused by pollution to consumers.

The "first best" serves as a good benchmark. In reality, the first-best conditions are generally not met.[8] Suppose at the outset there are import tariffs, ownership restrictions, and pollution taxes. For a given tariff, the welfare effects of restrictions on foreign capital and pollution taxes can be obtained from (12.10). To facilitate the analysis, we substitute the change in (12.4) into (12.10) to yield:

$$(E_u - tE_{pu})du = -(H_K - r^*)K_X d\xi - (E_Z - tE_{pZ} - s)dZ - tdX,$$
$$(12.11)$$

where $E_{pu}(= \partial D_X/\partial u) > 0$ by assuming that good X is normal in consumption.

12.3.1 *Optimal pollution tax*

We consider first the pollution tax. By setting $d\xi = 0$ in (12.11), the *ceteris paribus* welfare effect of a change in the pollution taxes is:

$$(E_u - tE_{pu})\left(\frac{du}{ds}\right) = -(E_Z - tE_{pZ} - s)\left(\frac{dZ}{ds}\right) - t\left(\frac{dX}{ds}\right), \quad (12.12)$$

where $dZ/ds < 0$ and $dX/ds < 0$. The first term in (12.12) states that a rise in the pollution taxes lowers pollution emissions. This improves environmental amenities for the public, but also reduces pollution tax revenue. In addition, the higher tax dampens domestic production of good X, thereby increasing imports and tariff revenue. The welfare effect of pollution taxes depends on both effects and is in general ambiguous. We can therefore

---

[8]See Choi and Beladi (1993) for a discussion on the optimal trade policies for a small open economy.

determine the optimal rate of pollution taxes, denoted by s^o, by setting $du/ds = 0$ in (12.12), as:

$$s^o = E_Z - tE_{pZ} + t\frac{\left(\frac{dX}{ds}\right)}{\left(\frac{dZ}{ds}\right)}, \tag{12.13}$$

where $E_{pZ} < 0$ by assumption. Equation (12.13) states that if free trade prevails $(t = 0)$, we have: $s^o = E_Z$, which is the Pigouvian tax rate. In the presence of tariffs, the optimal pollution tax exceeds the Pigouvian rate, because the existing tariffs induce more production of good X and hence aggravate pollution emissions. A larger pollution tax is therefore needed for correcting the distortions in consumption and production. Note that s^o is mainly determined by the tariff rate and is independent of ξ.

We can check whether welfare is locally maximized at the optimal pollution rate s^o. Substituting (12.13) into (12.12), the welfare expression in (12.12) can be rewritten as:

$$(E_u - tE_{pu})\left(\frac{du}{ds}\right) = \left(\frac{dZ}{ds}\right)(s - s^o). \tag{12.14}$$

Since $dZ/ds < 0$, we have $du/ds < (>) 0$ as $s > (<) s^o$. That is, the welfare will be improved when the pollution tax rate is adjusted toward the tax rate s^o, implying that s^o is a local maximum. We depict this result in a space of (s, ξ) in Figures 12.1 and 12.2. The s^o schedule, according to (12.13), is a vertical line; trade liberalization via a reduction in t results in a smaller s^o, thereby inducing the s^o schedule to shift to the left.[9]

12.3.2 Optimal domestic ownership

Consider next the welfare effect of a change in foreign ownership holding the pollution tax constant. From (12.11), we have:

$$(E_u - tE_{pu})\left(\frac{du}{d\xi}\right) = -(H_K - r^*)K_X$$

$$-(E_Z - tE_{pZ} - s)\left(\frac{dZ}{d\xi}\right) - t\left(\frac{dX}{d\xi}\right). \tag{12.15}$$

An increase in the ratio of domestic ownership raises the capital cost of producing good X, as indicated in the first term of (12.15). The higher capital cost of good X dampens its production, resulting in more imports and hence increased tariff revenue. The subsequently lowered pollution

---

[9]This diagrammatic technique is adapted from Neary (1993a).

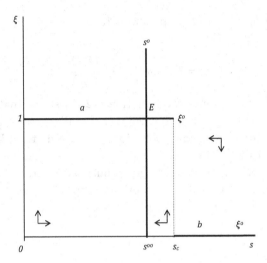

Figure 12.1   Optimal policies under large tariffs.

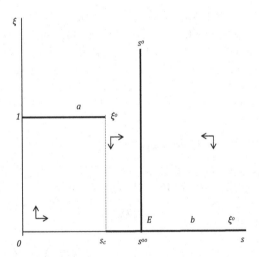

Figure 12.2   Optimal policies under small tariffs.

emissions improve environmental amenities for consumers, but pollution tax revenue falls. The welfare change in (12.15) again is ambiguous and its directional impact depends on the value of s. By setting $du/d\xi = 0$, we can determine the optimal ξ which depends upon the critical level of s, denoted by s_c, as:[10]

$$s_c = E_Z - tE_{pZ} + t\frac{\left(\frac{dX}{d\xi}\right)}{\left(\frac{dZ}{d\xi}\right)} + \frac{(H_K - r^*)K_X}{\left(\frac{dZ}{d\xi}\right)}. \tag{12.16}$$

That is, when $s < (>) s_c$, we have $du/d\xi > (<) 0$ because the gains from tariff revenue and consumer benefit from environmental improvements are larger (smaller) than the loss of pollution tax revenue. This can be seen by substituting (12.16) into (12.15) to obtain:

$$(E_u - tE_{pu})\left(\frac{du}{d\xi}\right) = \left(\frac{dZ}{d\xi}\right)(s - s_c), \tag{12.17}$$

where $dZ/d\xi < 0$. It is immediate that $du/d\xi > 0$ if $s < s_c$ and hence $\xi^o = 1$, implying 100% domestic ownership is optimal. In contrast, $du/d\xi < 0$ if $s > s_c$ and hence $\xi^o = 0$, indicating wholly foreign-owned enterprises are optimal. The ξ^o schedule, depicted in Figures 12.1 and 12.2, consists of two disjoint horizontal segments, a and b, with the jumping point s_c. Note that, from (12.11) and (12.13), a reduction in t shifts the value of s_c and s^o to the left.

12.3.3 *Jointly optimal policies*

Having studied the individually optimal policies, we can now determine the jointly optimal policies. This can be done by subtracting (12.13) from (12.16) to yield:

$$s_c - s^o = tA + \frac{(H_K - r^*)K_X}{\left(\frac{dZ}{d\xi}\right)}, \tag{12.18}$$

where $A > 0$.[11] The first term on the right-hand side of (12.18) is positive, while the second term is negative. The gap between the critical s_c and the optimal s^o crucially depends on the tariff rate, among other parameters. In particular, the critical rate of tariff is: $t_c = -(H_K - r^*)K_X/A(dZ/d\xi)$. For $t > t_c$, we have $s_c > s^o$, as depicted in Figure 12.1, in which the intersection between the ξ^o schedule and the s^o schedule at point E reveals the following

---

[10]Using $R_K = \xi H_K + (1-\xi)r^*$, we have: $\xi^o = K_X(R_K - r^*)/[(s - E_Z + tE_{pZ})(dZ/d\xi) - t(dX/d\xi)]$. Substituting this expression into (12.15), we have: $(E_u - tE_{pu})(du/d\xi) = [K_X(R_K - r^*)/\xi](\xi/\xi^o - 1)$. Since $K_X(R_K - r^*)/\xi > 0$, the welfare at ξ^o is at minimum, rather than maximum.

[11]$A = (dX/d\xi)/(dZ/d\xi) - (dX/ds)/(dZ/ds) = R_{ss}[R_{pL}(\partial L/\partial \xi) - R_{pK}(\partial K_X/\partial \xi)] > 0$.

jointly optimal policies: 100% domestic ownership ($\xi^o = 1$) together with
the pollution tax (s^{oo}). However, for $t < t_c$, we have $s_c < s^o$, as depicted
in Figure 12.2. Here a reduction of t causes shifts of both the s_c and s^o
schedules to the left, but with a larger shift in the s_c line. As illustrated in
Figure 12.2, the intersection at point E shows that 100% foreign ownership
($\xi^o = 0$) combined with a relatively lax pollution tax (s^{oo}) is jointly optimal.
Thus, we can state the following proposition.

Proposition 12.1 *In a small tariff-ridden economy, trade liberalization
via tariff reduction can result in a switch in ownership of a firm from
wholly domestic to wholly foreign, coupled with deterioration in environmental quality due to a lower pollution tax.*

12.4   Concluding Remarks

This chapter has examined the important effects of trade liberalization
on firms' ownership and the environment for a small open economy. The
linkages between foreign investment and environmental policies have been
explored. We derived the optimal policies separately for regulating pollution and foreign ownership as well as jointly for both issues. The main
result is that as tariffs fall below a critical level, the optimal ratio of foreign ownership can switch from zero to 100%, coupled with a loosening of
environmental standards.

Our analysis is consistent with the casual observations that trade liberalization, especially in developing nations, can lead to lax pollution regulations in the midst of rising foreign investment. The results appear to
be supportive of the prediction by the pollution-exporting hypothesis that
trade liberalization can result in environmental degradations in developing
nations.[12] It should nonetheless be pointed out that the estimates in several empirical studies (e.g., Grossman and Krueger, 1993, among others),
indicate that the increase in pollution subsequent to trade liberalization is,
however, relatively small. This may be partially explained by the use of
pollution-abating technology by foreign-invested firms. The role of abate-
ment in the optimal policies can be a topic of our future research.

---

[12]Also see the work by Beladi *et al.* (2000) on the relationship between foreign investment
and the environment in a North–South model.

Chapter 13

Optimal Foreign-Investment and Pollution Taxes

13.1 Introduction

Recently, strong environmental concern has been voiced and a variety of environmental protection measures have been implemented in many advanced industrialized countries. As a result, the costs of production in polluting industries in these nations have soared. In an effort to hold down production costs and to maintain a competitive edge, polluting industries have sought relocation of their plants to areas with lax environmental regulations within and/or outside the country. This phenomenon is known as "pollution exporting." On the national level, Gray (1997) examines the location of manufacturing firms in the US over the 1963–1987 period and finds a significant negative connection between new plants and state environmental regulatory measures.[1] This result supports the pollution-exporting hypothesis.

On the international level, less-developed countries (LDCs) have faced a severe shortage of domestic capital, and the lack of capital has constituted a major obstacle to their economic growth. To mitigate the problem, LDCs have resorted to a variety of investment incentives, such as relaxed environmental standards and/or investment-tax reductions for foreign firms.[2] As a result, polluting industries have been relocated from the US, European Union (EU) nations, and Japan to Mexico, China, and other developing Asian countries. Jaffe et al. (1995) provide an extensive survey and discussion on this issue.

---

[1]Previous empirical studies (e.g., Levinson, 1996b) find some small, negative effects of environmental regulations on manufacturing plant location.

[2]The welfare effect of investment taxes has been extensively studied. See, for example, Kemp (1966), Jones (1967, 1987), and Neary (1993b).

The relationship between free trade and the environment has been studied. Grossman and Krueger (1993) argue that trade liberalization may improve the environment because it raises incomes that create a demand for better enforcement of pollution regulations. On the other hand, Copeland and Taylor (1994) claim that free trade could worsen the environment because the policy leads to shifts of the most pollution-intensive industries to countries with the weakest pollution regulations.

While a free trade policy has been advocated by the number nations of the General Agreement on Tariffs and Trade (GATT) and World Trade Organization (WTO), trade barriers are still common, especially among LDCs.[3] Multinational firms seeking to bypass trade barriers and to expand their markets have made direct investments in developing nations. Foreign capital inflows in LDCs lead to the expansion of production and subsequent generation of more pollution, thereby exacerbating already undesirable environmental conditions. The trade-off between economic growth and maintaining environmental quality has become a heatedly debated policy issue. To shed some light on the debate, it is worthwhile exploring the intricate linkages between the environment and the ultimate impact of foreign investment on national welfare.[4] Using a North–South trade model, Copeland and Taylor (1997) find that international capital mobility may raise or lower world pollution depending on the pattern of trade. Their study is short of delineating the national policy issues arising from international capital mobility.

Recognizing that the existence of trade barriers, the expansion of multinational production activities, and the international relocation of production are simply matters of fact in the modem era, several issues of analytical interest and policy concern arise. Among those that we set out to explore in this chapter are the second-best optimal policies for a small open economy regarding foreign investment in conjunction with environmental preservation. While the inflow of foreign capital and pollution emission are subject to taxes/subsidies, two scenarios will be considered: (a) foreign-investment

---

[3]Hong Kong and Singapore are perhaps the only places that have adopted a nearly free trade policy. Nevertheless, tariffs are still imposed in these two city states on certain categories of imports, i.e., automobiles, cigarettes, and liquor.

[4]A few studies have examined the effects of tariffs and pollution taxes. See, for example, Copeland (1994).

policy and environmental policy are set independent of each other; and (b) the two policies are set jointly.

Our analysis is related to Bond (1991) and Copeland (1994). However, Bond does not study the pollution issue, and Copeland does not look at investment taxes. We examine the two policies in the absence of international tax credits followed by an analysis when such tax credits are available in the source country.[5] Note that in this chapter pollution is considered as a byproduct of production, and the pollution distortion can be partially corrected by pollution taxes.

The chapter is structured as follows. Section 13.2 sketches the benchmark model of a small capital-importing economy, and briefly discusses the welfare effects of foreign-investment and pollution policy. Section 13.3 examines the host country's optimal policies for foreign investment and pollution when investment tax credits are allowed in the source country. Section 13.4 provides conclusions.

13.2 A Benchmark Model

Consider a small, open, capital-importing country producing two traded goods, good 0 and good y in the amounts of y_0 and y, respectively, and one type of pollutant, z, by using more than two non-traded factors of production along with capital. While capital is internationally mobile, it is, nonetheless, subject to taxes/subsidies in both the host and source countries.

The country is endowed with the non-traded factors by a vector, v, and the supply of capital is $k = \bar{k} + k^*$, where $\bar{k}$ is the country's capital endowment and k^* is the inflow of foreign capital. The domestic consumption of good 0 and good y is, respectively, denoted by D_0 and D. It is assumed that the country exports good 0 and imports good y. While nothing interferes with the exports, immutable tariffs are imposed on the imports to protect the domestic import-competing sector. We choose good 0 as the numeraire and let p^* be the given world price and t the tariff rate. The domestic relative price of y is given by $p = p^* + t$.

---

[5] It is assumed that the home country is constrained by world trade in its choice of tariffs, but chooses pollution and investment taxes optimally to maximize national welfare.

We designate sector $y(y_0)$ the polluting (non-polluting) industry. Pollution is modeled as a byproduct of the production of y in the home country.[6] Pollution being a public detriment generates an adverse externality to consumers. For correcting the pollution distortion, pollution taxes, s are imposed on the producers of good y. The aggregate revenue function for the home economy is: $R(1, p, s, k) = \max\{y_0 + py - sz : (y_0, y, z) \in T(v, k)\}$, where $T(v, k)$ denotes the convex technology set. By the envelope theorem, the output of y is $y = R_p(= \partial R/\partial p)$, the pollutant is $z = -R_s$, and the return to foreign capital is $r = R_k$.

The demand side of the economy can be captured by the aggregate expenditure function: $E(1, p, z, u) = \min\{D_0 + pD : U(D_0, D, z) = u\}$, where U is the utility function and $E_u > 0$. Note that $\partial U/\partial z < 0$, as pollution adversely affects utility, and thus more spending on goods is needed, i.e., $E_z > 0$, for keeping the same level of utility.

By assuming that the revenues from tariffs and taxes are returned to consumers in a lump-sum manner, the equilibrium conditions for the economy are given by:

$$E(1, p, z, u) = R(1, p, z, k) - r(k - \bar{k}) + \tau(k - \bar{k}) + sz + tM, \quad (13.1)$$

$$M = E_p(1, p, z, u) - R_p(1, p, s, k), \quad (13.2)$$

$$R_k(1, p, s, k) - \tau - \tau^* = r^* - \tau^*, \quad (13.3)$$

$$R_s(1, p, s, k) = -z, \quad (13.4)$$

where $\tau(\tau^*)$ is the tax rate on capital in the host (source) country, r^* is a given rate of capital return in the source country, and M denotes the home country's imports of good y. Equation (13.1) states the home country's budget constraint: the value of consumption at domestic prices equals the gross domestic product (GDP) plus the tax revenues, accrued from foreign capital and pollution taxes, and tariff revenue. Equation (13.2) defines net imports, where $E_p = D$ is the demand for good y. Based on after-tax rates of return, the equilibrium level of capital inflows is determined by (13.3), in which foreign capital is subject to double taxation when $\tau > 0$. The case of tax credits will be analyzed below.

---

[6]Pollution can be modeled as a byproduct of the polluting industry (Yu, 1980; Copeland, 1994) or treated as an input in the production process (Yohe, 1979; Yu and Ingene, 1982; Khan, 1996).

The small open economy with a given tariff contains four unknowns – $u, k, z,$ and M and two policy instruments, τ and s. The welfare effects of changes in investment and pollution taxes can be obtained by differentiating (13.1) and (13.2) as:

$$(E_u - tE_{pu})\frac{du}{d\tau} = [s - (E_z - tE_{pz})]\left(\frac{dz}{d\tau}\right) + (\tau - tR_{pk})\left(\frac{dk}{d\tau}\right), \qquad (13.5)$$

$$(E_u - tE_{pu})\frac{du}{ds} = [s - (E_z - tE_{pz})]\left(\frac{dz}{ds}\right) + (\tau - tR_{pk})\left(\frac{dk}{ds}\right) - tR_{ps}, \qquad (13.6)$$

where $E_{pu} > 0$ and $E_u - tE_{pu} > 0$.[7] Note that $E_{pz} = \partial D/\partial z > (<)$, when D and z are complements (substitutes);[8] $D_{ps} = \partial y/\partial s < 0$, indicating that an increase in pollution taxes lowers the production of y; and by virtue of the Rybczynski effect, $R_{pk} = \partial y/\partial k > 0$, when y is capital-intensive relative to y_0.[9] In addition, from (13.3) and (13.4), $dk/d\tau < 0$, $dz/d\tau < 0$, $dz/ds < 0$ and $dk/ds < 0$.

The first term on the right-hand side of (13.5) or (13.6) indicates the effect of pollution distortions, which can be partially corrected by pollution taxes. The second term captures the effect of investment taxes and tariff distortions arising from the inflow of foreign capital. The additional term in (13.6) is the direct impact of pollution taxes on tariff distortions.[10] By setting (13.5) and (13.6) to zero, we obtain the optimal investment tax rates (τ^0) and the optimal pollution tax rates (s^0):

$$\tau^0 = \frac{\left\{\left[tR_{pk}\left(\frac{dk}{d\tau}\right) + (E_z - tE_{pz})\left(\frac{dz}{d\tau}\right)\right] - s\left(\frac{dz}{d\tau}\right)\right\}}{\left(\frac{dk}{d\tau}\right)}, \qquad (13.7)$$

$$s^0 = \frac{\left\{t\left[R_{ps} + R_{pk}\left(\frac{dk}{ds}\right)\right] + (E_z - tE_{pz})\left(\frac{dz}{ds}\right) - \tau\left(\frac{dk}{ds}\right)\right\}}{\left(\frac{dz}{ds}\right)}. \qquad (13.8)$$

---

[7]Defining the marginal propensity to consume y as $m = pE_{pu}/E_u$, we can rewrite $E_u - tE_{pu} = E_u(1 - tm/p)$, where the inverse of $(1 - tm/p)$ is the tariff multiplier. See Jones (1969) and Neary and Ruane (1988). Since $E_u = E_{1u} + (p^* + t)E_{pu}$ by homogeneity of E, $E_u - tE_{pu} = E_{1u} + p^*E_{pu} > 0$, for the normal-goods case.

[8]For example, Copeland (1994) assumes that $E_{pz} < 0$.

[9]See also the related discussion in Yu and Ingene (1982).

[10]See Appendix A.1 for the explicit expressions of dk and dz.

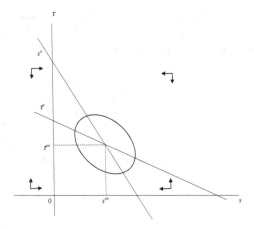

Figure 13.1 $\tau^{00} > 0$ and $s^{00} > 0$.

The optimal τ^0 in (13.7) depends negatively on the level of s, and s^0 in (13.8) varies inversely with τ. These relationships are plotted in Figure 13.1, in which movements in τ or s toward $\tau^0(s^0)$ improve welfare.

We consider next the jointly optimal solution of investment and pollution taxes, which is the intersection of the τ^0 and s^0 schedules. The iso-welfare contours are illustrated in Figure 13.1 by a map of ellipses. By solving (13.7) and (13.8) simultaneously, we obtain:

$$s^{00} = E_z - tE_{pz} - tR_{ps}R_{ss}^{-1}, \qquad (13.9)$$

$$\tau^{00} = t(R_{pk} - R_{ps}R_{ss}^{-1}R_{sk}). \qquad (13.10)$$

Under free trade ($t = 0$), the pollution tax alone is used for correcting the pollution damage, yielding $s^{00} = E_z$. However, with a preexisting tariff, the optimal pollution and investment taxes will be altered from their first-best levels in a direction that mitigates the tariff distortion.[11] Since $R_{ps} = \partial y/\partial s$ and $R_{ss} = -\partial z/\partial s$ in (13.9), we have $R_{ps}R_{ss}^{-1} = -\partial y/\partial z < 0$, reflecting the relationship of y to its byproduct, z, and hence $s^{00} > 0$. As for τ^{00}, it can be obtained by substituting $G_{pk} = \partial y/\partial k$, $G_{ps} = \partial y/\partial s$, $G_{ss} = -\partial z/\partial s$

---

[11]If there were no tariff, there would be no incentive to use taxes on foreign capital. A pollution tax alone would be called for dealing with pollution. However, with a tariff in place, policy must aim to alleviate the tariff distortion. Thus, a second instrument (the capital tax or subsidy) can be used to improve welfare.

and $R_{sk} = -\partial z/\partial k$ into (13.10) to yield:

$$\tau^{00} = t\left[\frac{\partial y}{\partial k} - \left(\frac{\partial y}{\partial s}\right)\left(\frac{\partial s}{\partial z}\right)\left(\frac{\partial z}{\partial k}\right)\right] \lessgtr 0. \tag{13.11}$$

The sign of τ^{00} depends on the relative magnitudes between the direct and indirect impacts of foreign capital on the output of good y. If the direct (indirect) effect dominates, the capital inflow results in over(under)-production of the import-competing sector, thus causing a decrease (an increase) in the volume of imports. Foreign investment will be taxed (subsidized), since imports are already below (above) the social optimal level with a tariff.

Proposition 13.1 *For a small open economy with a fixed tariff, the effect of the capital inflow on the level of pollution is dealt with by the pollution tax. However, the optimal policy on foreign investment is a tax or subsidy, depending on whether foreign capital has an expansionary or a contractionary effect on the output of the import-competing sector.*

Figure 13.1 illustrates the case of jointly optimal positive investment taxes, while Figure 13.2 depicts the case of jointly optimal negative investment taxes.[12]

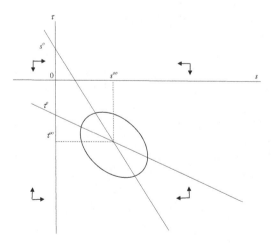

Figure 13.2 $\tau^{00} < 0$ and $s^{00} > 0$.

---

[12]This diagrammatic technique is adapted from Neary (1993b, 1995).

13.3 Investment Tax Credits and the Optimal Pollution Tax

The preceding analysis was conducted by assuming that international tax credits are not available, i.e., foreign investors pay taxes to the host country and the amount of taxes paid cannot be deducted from the tax liability in the source country.[13] The treatment of taxation without tax credits differs from the current tax systems in the US and in Organization for Economic Cooperation and Development (OECD) countries, where the tax liability in the source country can be reduced by the amount of taxes paid to the host country.

In this section, we follow Bond (1991) by incorporating the tax credit system into the economy. With investment tax credits, the effective tax rate applicable to foreign investment is $\max(\tau, \tau^*)$, and hence the after-tax rate of return to foreign capital in the host country becomes $R_k - \max(\tau, \tau^*)$. The equilibrium condition for inflows of foreign capital in (13.3) is now modified as:

$$R_k(1, p, s, k) - \max(\tau, \tau^*) = r^* - \tau^*. \qquad (13.12)$$

It is notable that if the host country gives subsidies to foreign capital, the source country would capture all the subsidies. The tax credits become irrelevant and, hence, would not affect the capital-market equilibrium condition as in (13.3), but $\tau < 0$.

Consider the welfare effect of each of two policies in isolation. From (13.12) or (13.3), the tax credit system in the source country has no direct impact on the host country's pollution policy, but the tax credit can affect the host country's capital-tax policy. Three cases can be considered. For $\tau < 0$ or $\tau > \tau^*$, the pre-tax capital returns, R_k, depend on the level of τ because $R_k - \tau = r^*$ by (13.3) or $\max(\tau, \tau^*) = \tau^*$ by (13.12), and hence the earlier results derived in the absence of tax credits hold qualitatively. On the other hand, for $0 \leq \tau \leq \tau^*$, we have $\max(\tau, \tau^*) = \tau^*$. The rate of return on foreign capital in the host country depends on the tax rate in the source country, and, furthermore, the foreign investors incur a tax liability of $\tau^* - \tau$ to the source country. It follows that the pre-tax R_k, is fixed to the rate of r^* as can be verified by (13.12), and changes in home tax rates will have no effect on the pre-tax rate of return on foreign capital

---

[13]The assumption of the absence of international tax credits is implicit in numerous studies; see Kemp (1966), Jones (1967), and Neary (1993b), among others.

once the tax credit is in place. This implies that $dk/d\tau = 0$ by (13.12) and $dz/d\tau = 0$ by (13.4). Thus, the welfare analysis differs from the earlier results derived without tax credits.

The analysis of tax credits on the host country's welfare for $0 < \tau < \tau^*$ can proceed as follows. When the source country introduces a tax credit system, the cost of foreign capital in the host country immediately falls by the amount of credit granted if the domestic tax rate is lower than that of the source country; specifically, the marginal cost of capital decreases from $(r^* + \tau)$ in (13.3) to r^* in (13.12). The tax credit causes a rise in the level of foreign capital in the host country, and the inflow of foreign capital yields a primary welfare gain through an increase in tax revenue as:

$$(E_u - tE_{pu})\left(\frac{\Delta u}{\Delta \tau}\right) = -\left(\frac{\partial k}{\partial \tau}\right)\tau^0. \tag{13.13}$$

Since the cost of foreign capital at home depends only on the source country's tax rate, the tax credit works as if the host country completely eliminates the tax rate on foreign capital (i.e., $\tau = 0$). Although the host government does not change the tax rate, the tax rate simply becomes irrelevant.

Once the tax credit is established abroad, we have $R_k = r^*$ in (13.12) when $0 \le \tau \le \tau^*$. To capture tax revenue from the source country, the host country can raise the domestic tax rate to match that of the foreign tax. The secondary welfare effect of the tax credit can be obtained by totally differentiating (13.1) and (13.2) as:

$$(E_u - tE_{pu})du = [s - (E_z - tE_{pz})]dz$$
$$+ (\tau - tR_{pk})dk - tR_{ps}ds + (k - \bar{k})d\tau. \tag{13.14}$$

The last term captures a fiscal externality of higher tax revenue by an increase in the home tax rate.

Recalling that $dz/d\tau = dk/d\tau = 0$ under $0 \le \tau \le \tau^*$ for the tax credit system, the secondary welfare effect of changes in the home tax rate is:

$$(E_u - tE_{pu})\left(\frac{du}{d\tau}\right) = k - \bar{k} > 0, \tag{13.15}$$

which captures a gain in tax revenue through a higher tax rate. Note that the host country can raise the tax rate on foreign investment up to τ^*

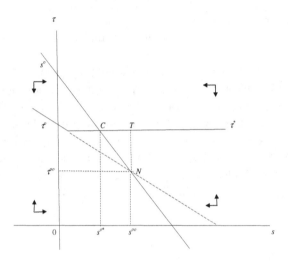

Figure 13.3   Optimal policies under tax credits with initial capital tax.

without incurring allocative losses in the presence of the tax credit system. The optimal tax rate for the home country for $0 \leq \tau \leq \tau^*$ under tax credits is: $\tau^0 = \tau^*$. Figure 13.3 illustrates this result; when $0 \leq \tau \leq \tau^*$ under tax credits, the optimal tax schedule rotates to the horizontal line τ^*, and when $\tau > \tau^*$, the optimal tax schedule follows through and coincides with the schedule τ^0.

As for the capital subsidy case, $\tau < 0$, the introduction of the tax credit by the source country does not result in primary welfare changes, as can be seen from (13.3). The welfare effect of the tax credit depends only on whether or not the home country responds to the foreign use of tax credits. If the host country does not respond to the tax credit, it is clear that $\partial u/\partial \tau < 0$ for $0 > \tau > \tau^0$, implying that the optimal policy must involve a capital subsidy. On the other hand, if the host government responds to the tax credit by switching from subsidizing foreign capital to imposing tax instead, we have in (13.15) $\partial u/\partial \tau > 0$ for $0 \leq \tau \leq \tau^*$ as discussed earlier. This suggests that the introduction of tax credits can generate a non-convexity in the optimal tax problem at $\tau = 0$ for the portion that $\tau^0 < 0$, as illustrated by the opposite movements of the vertical arrows in Figure 13.4. That is, the optimal tax/subsidy policy is not cut and dried; a small increase in subsidy to capital will increase welfare by raising revenue mainly from pollution taxes, as indicated in (13.5), whereas a small increase in the tax rate also improves welfare, in (13.15),

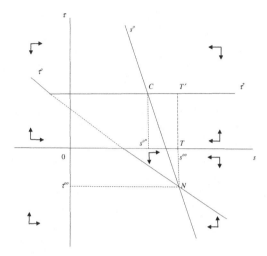

Figure 13.4   Optimal policies under tax credits with initial capital subsidy.

by capturing some tax revenue from the source country. Therefore, the optimal policy in this case will involve comparing whether welfare is higher at $\tau = \tau^*$ for responding to the tax credit or at negative τ^0s in (13.7) for not responding. Essentially, the host country has to choose between using the capital-subsidy policy to raise revenue from pollution taxes and deploying the capital-tax policy to capture revenue from the source country.

We turn next to the case where both policy variables are amenable to simultaneous changes. The jointly optimal policy depends upon the initial situation of the host economy. Consider first the situation in which a positive capital tax is used at the outset, as illustrated in Figure 13.3. The jointly optimal policy then depends upon the relative magnitudes of τ^* and τ^{00}. The jointly optimal investment tax will be τ^{00} when $\tau^* < \tau^{00}$, whereas it will be τ^* when $\tau^* \geq \tau^{00}$. In the latter case, the tax credit system is operational. As illustrated in Figure 13.3, the host country would be better off by raising its tax rate up to τ^* to capture the primary and secondary tax revenues from the source country. Replacing τ by τ^* in (13.8), the corresponding optimal pollution tax becomes:

$$s^{0*} = \frac{\left\{ t \left[R_{ps} + R_{pk} \left(\frac{dk}{ds} \right) \right] + (E_z - tE_{pz}) \left(\frac{dz}{ds} \right) - \tau^* \left(\frac{dk}{ds} \right) \right\}}{\left(\frac{dz}{ds} \right)}. \quad (13.16)$$

Since $\tau^* \geq \tau^{00}$, we have $s^{0*} \leq s^{00}$. This can be shown by comparing (13.16) with (13.9) to yield:[14]

$$s^{0*} - s^{00} = - \left[\left(\frac{dk}{ds} \right) \left(\frac{dz}{ds} \right) \right] (\tau^* - \tau^{00}).$$ (13.17)

Recalling that $dk/ds < 0$ and $dz/ds < 0$, we have $s^{0*} \leq s^{00}$ when $\tau^* \geq \tau^{00}$. This readily implies that when the home tax rate is smaller than the foreign rate, the introduction of a tax credit system by the source country can unexpectedly make the host country better off at the expense of the source country. This can happen if the host nation raises its tax rate to match the foreign rate, thereby capturing tax revenue from the source country. As a result, the host country can afford to be lax on its pollution policy directed toward foreign investment. The following proposition is immediate.

Proposition 13.2 *When a tax on foreign capital is initially in place in the host country and the foreign tax rate in the source country exceeds that of the host country, an introduction of tax credits in the source country will lead in the host country to an increase in the investment tax rate but a decrease in the pollution tax rate.*

A foreign investment tax credit system in the source country will induce the home country to raise its optimal investment tax from τ^{00} to τ^* and lower its optimal pollution tax from s^{00} to s^{0*}. Although for $0 \leq \tau \leq \tau^*$ the host country's tax rate has no allocative effects (i.e., $dk/d\tau = dz/d\tau = 0$), the levels of foreign capital and pollution emissions do change due to the primary effect of inflows of foreign capital and the secondary effect arising from the response to the tax credit:

$$\frac{\Delta k}{\Delta \tau} = \left. \frac{\Delta k}{\Delta \tau} \right|_{\tau = \tau^{00}} + \left(\frac{dk}{ds} \right) \left(\frac{\Delta s}{\Delta \tau} \right) > 0,$$ (13.18)

$$\frac{\Delta z}{\Delta \tau} = \left(\frac{\partial z}{\partial k} \right) \left(\frac{\Delta k}{\Delta \tau} \right) \bigg|_{\tau = \tau^{00}} + \left(\frac{dz}{ds} \right) \left(\frac{\Delta s}{\Delta \tau} \right) > 0,$$ (13.19)

where $dk/ds < 0$, $dz/ds < 0$, $\Delta s = s^{0*} - s^{00} < 0$ and $\Delta \tau = \tau^* - \tau^{00} > 0$. When the tax credit system is introduced in the source country, the

---

[14]In evaluating the parameters under tax credit relative to the benchmark (no tax credit) equilibrium, it is assumed that the values such as E_Z, E_{pZ}, and R_{ps} in (13.9) and (13.16) remain the same throughout the policy change.

cost of investing in the host country falls, causing an increase in foreign capital inflows and consequently a rise in the level of pollution. Furthermore, the tax credit will lead to a reduction in the optimal pollution tax, and hence a further deterioration in the environmental quality in the host nation.

The tax credit introduced in the source country will affect the welfare of the host country. Such a welfare effect can be obtained by substituting s^{0*} in (13.16) to (13.14), and then combining the result with (13.13) to obtain:

$$(E_u - tE_{pu}) \left(\frac{\Delta u}{\Delta \tau}\right)$$
$$= -\left(\frac{\partial k}{\partial \tau}\right)\tau^{00} + (k - \bar{k}) + \left(\frac{dz}{ds}\right)(s - s^{0*})\left(\frac{\Delta s}{\Delta \tau}\right), \quad (13.20)$$

where s^{00} is the pollution tax before the introduction of tax credits by the source country.

The welfare effect can be deduced from (13.20) with the aid of Figure 13.3. Before the introduction of a tax credit in the foreign country, the domestic economy is depicted by point N that characterizes the second-best mix of investment and pollution optimal taxes, τ^{00} and s^{00}, respectively. Aside from the primary welfare gain in the first term of (13.20), the use of tax credit in the source country leads to an increase in the investment tax τ^* to point T, thereby improving welfare through a secondary effect, as expressed by the second term of (13.20). Furthermore, the higher investment-tax rate causes the pollution tax, s, to fall from s^{00} to s^{0*} at point C. The fall in the pollution tax also improves welfare, as captured by the second term of (13.20). The following proposition is immediate.

Proposition 13.3 *For a small, capital-importing country, if the investment tax rate in the host country is less than that in the source country, the use of tax credit in the source country leads to an improvement in the host country's welfare, but a worsening in the host nation's pollution level.*

A caveat should be in order. The drop in the optimal pollution tax would be less, in view of the plausible case in which the willingness to pay for pollution reduction increases with the level of utility arising from a transfer of wealth from the source to the host country; that is, the parameter E_z may not remain constant.

A more interesting case involves the initial use of a subsidy on foreign capital, $\tau^{00} < 0$. As indicated above, for each policy in isolation, the optimal tax rate for the portion that $\tau^0 < 0$ is indeterminate. This implies that multiple equilibria may exist for jointly optimal tax and pollution tax policies. Specifically, Figure 13.4 shows the existence of two equilibria as indicated by point N in the absence of responses to tax credits and point C with responses to tax credits. The welfare comparison of these two equilibria can be obtained by tracing the movements from point N to T, followed by the movements from point T to T' and then to C. The former adjustment worsens welfare, whereas the latter shifts improve welfare. These welfare effects can be shown by using (13.20), except $\tau^{00} < 0$. While the second and third terms on the right-hand side of (13.20) remain the same, the first term, instead of showing the introductory effect, represents a secondary effect from responding to the tax credit by eliminating capital subsidy (the movement from point N to T). This subsidy removal results in a welfare loss due to a fall in foreign capital. If this loss is outweighed by the gains of increases in tax revenue (signified by the movements from point T to C), a tax on foreign capital, together with pollution taxes, becomes the jointly optimal policy; otherwise, capital subsidy remains the optimal policy. The following proposition is immediate.

Proposition 13.4 *When a subsidy to foreign capital is initially in place, the introduction of the tax credit in the source country may cause the host country to switch its capital subsidy to a tax policy. The switch in policy can induce the host country to cut pollution tax.*

Note that the switch may still improve the environment if the pollution reduction, due to a lower level of foreign capital caused by the removal of capital subsidy, dominates the rise in the level of pollution induced by the fall in the pollution tax.

13.4   Concluding Remarks

This chapter has analyzed the second-best policies for an economy with a preexisting tariff. Based on a small, capital-importing, general equilibrium model, we have examined the individual and the joint effects on pollution and capital tax policies when tax credits are absent or present in the source country. In the absence of tax credits, the joint optimal policy is a pollution tax along with a foreign investment tax or subsidy, depending on whether foreign capital inflows have an expansionary or a contractionary effect on the import-competing sector.

However, when the investment tax credits are allowed in the source country and the foreign tax rate exceeds that of the host country, the tax credit system will result in a higher investment tax rate but a lower pollution tax. The welfare of the host country increases by capturing some capital-tax revenue from the source country while environmental quality deteriorates in the host country. Moreover, the source country's tax credits can induce the host country to switch its initial policy from capital subsidy to capital tax. Although this policy switch induces a lower pollution tax, the environment may still be improved if capital taxes can lead to a significant contraction in the polluting industry.

Appendix

A.1 *Resource allocation*

From the differentiations of (13.3) and (13.4), we have:

$$dk = R_{kk}^{-1}d\tau - R_{kk}^{-1}R_{ks}ds,$$

$$dz = -R_{sk}R_{kk}^{-1}d\tau - (R_{ss} - R_{sk}R_{kk}^{-1}R_{ks})ds,$$

where $R_{ks} = -\partial z/\partial k <$ and $R_{ss} = -\partial z/\partial s > 0$. Therefore, $dk/d\tau < 0$, $dk/ds < 0$, $dz/ds < 0$, and $dz/d\tau < 0$.

A.2 *The τ^0 and s^0 schedules*

From (13.7), the τ^0 curve in the (s, τ) space is:

$$\tau^0 = \frac{\left[tR_{pk}\left(\frac{dk}{d\tau}\right) + (E_z - tE_{pz})\left(\frac{dk}{d\tau}\right)\right]}{\left(\frac{dk}{d\tau}\right) - s\left(\frac{dz}{d\tau}\right)\left(\frac{dk}{d\tau}\right)}$$

and from (13.8) the s^0 curve can be expressed as:

$$\tau = \frac{\left\{t\left[R_{ps} + R_{pk}\left(\frac{dk}{ds}\right)\right] + (E_z - tE_{pz})\left(\frac{dz}{ds}\right)\right\}}{\frac{\left(\frac{dk}{ds}\right) - s^0\left(\frac{dz}{ds}\right)}{\left(\frac{dk}{ds}\right)}}.$$

Then, we can obtain that the intercept of the s^0 curve is larger than that of the τ^0 curve:

$$\frac{\left\{t\left[R_{ps} + R_{pk}\left(\frac{dk}{ds}\right)\right] + (E_z - tE_{pz})\left(\frac{dz}{ds}\right)\right\}}{\left(\frac{dk}{ds}\right)}$$

$$- \frac{\left[tR_{pk}\left(\frac{dk}{d\tau}\right) + (E_z - tE_{pz})\left(\frac{dk}{d\tau}\right)\right]}{\left(\frac{dk}{d\tau}\right)}$$

$$= -[tR_{ps} - (E_z - tE_{pz})R_{ss}]\left(\frac{R_{kk}}{R_{ks}}\right) > 0,$$

which is positive, assuming good y is capital-intensive.

Analogously, we can compare the slopes of the two curves and show that the s^0 curve is steeper than the τ^0 curve:

$$-\frac{\left(\frac{dz}{d\tau}\right)}{\left(\frac{dk}{d\tau}\right)} + \frac{\left(\frac{dz}{ds}\right)}{\left(\frac{dk}{ds}\right)} = -\frac{R_{ss}R_{kk}}{R_{ks}} < 0,$$

which is negative, given good y is capital-intensive.

Chapter 14

Foreign Capital and the Economy Under Imperfect Competition

14.1 Introduction

The welfare effects of exogenous inflows of foreign capital in the presence of trade restrictions have been extensively studied. Brecher and Diaz Alejandro (1977) show that when imports are subject to tariffs, an introduction of foreign capital inflows accentuates the tariff distortion and hence reduces national welfare if the import-competing sector is relatively capital-intensive. In contrast, Dei (1985a) shows that when imports are restricted by quotas, foreign capital inflows in the presence of foreign-owned capital always improve welfare by depressing the rental and so lowering the payments to existing foreign-owned capital. Neary (1988), using a common framework for both tariffs and quotas, obtains more general results of foreign capital inflows; the welfare effect of such inflows depends crucially on whether foreign-owned capital exists initially in the home country.[1] In addition, Khan (1982b) and Grinols (1991) have examined the effects of foreign capital inflows for a generalized Harris–Todaro economy under tariff protection. Khan finds that the result by Brecher and Diaz Alejandro is still valid even in the presence of unemployment, whereas Grinols argues that increased foreign capital need not be detrimental to welfare if the opportunity costs of labor are sufficiently low.

Note that the models used by these authors are all based upon the premise of perfect competition along with constant returns to scale

---

[1]It may be noted that, unlike the case of tariffs, an inflow of foreign capital in the absence of existing foreign-owned capital has no effect on welfare when a quota is in place.

technology. Although perfect competition serves as a useful assumption in crystallizing theoretical insights, it nevertheless fails to depict many of the real-world phenomena. The real-world economy is characterized, to a large extent, by imperfect competition and economies of scale. The policy implications of imperfect competition and economies of scale have been examined in the literature (see, for example, Brander and Spencer, 1985), mostly dealing with developed economies.

In her survey, Krueger (1984) points out that although market imperfections exist in developed nations, the imperfections are far more serious and pervasive in developing countries. In an illuminating paper, Rodrik (1988) reports that most developing nations have very high four-firm concentration ratios.[2] He finds that a developing economy is typically characterized by: (a) restricted entry in manufacturing partly because of the absence of serious antitrust policies; (b) high protection of the manufacturing sector by quotas rather than tariffs; and (c) imperfect home capital markets and, thus, sluggish movements of capital among sectors.[3]

This chapter develops a model to incorporate these key features of imperfect competition characterizing a developing economy. In addition to the above-mentioned features as noted by Rodrik, we also introduce in our framework sector-specific unemployment frequently observed in a developing nation. The model will then be utilized to examine the welfare implications of foreign capital inflows. It will be shown that foreign capital inflows in the presence of a given quota may be detrimental to welfare in the short run in which capital is sector-specific; the inflows, however, are in the long run necessarily welfare improving with intersectoral capital mobility. Since perfect competition is a limiting case of imperfect competition modeled in this chapter, Dei's result regarding welfare-improving foreign capital can be viewed as a special case of the present analysis.

We construct a general equilibrium model to capture the key features of imperfect competition for developing economies in Section 14.2. The resource allocation effects of foreign capital inflows in the presence of quantitative restrictions are examined in Section 14.3. The welfare impact of foreign capital inflows is discussed in Section 14.4. Section 14.5 presents concluding remarks.

---

[2] The four-firm concentration ratios are 50% in Chile, 55% in India, 73% in Mexico, etc.

[3] Rodrik also noted that industrial power in many developing countries is in the hands of minority ethnic groups with an entrepreneurial spirit.

14.2 The General Equilibrium Model with Oligopolistic Competition

Consider a simple two-sector developing economy producing two types of goods: manufacturing (X) and agriculture (Y). Assume for simplicity that consumer tastes can be represented by a quasi-linear utility function, $U(D_X, D_Y) = u(D_X) + D_Y$, where D_i is the consumption demand for good $i(i = X, Y)$.[4] Utility maximization yields the inverse demand function for manufacturing as: $p_X = p_Y \phi(D_X)$, where $\phi(D_X) = du(D_X)/dD_X$ with $\phi'(D_X) < 0$. Note that the quasi-linear specification of demand suppresses the income effect on the demand for manufactures. This simplifying assumption serves to highlight the price effect and renders the analysis tractable.

We assume that the developing economy exports agricultural products and imports manufacturing goods. Then the domestic demand for manufacturing is comprised of the amount of the domestic production as well as the imports. The inverse demand function for manufacturing can therefore be expressed by:

$$p_X = p_Y \phi(X + Q), \tag{14.1}$$

where X is the level of home production and Q is the amount of imports. As noted by Rodrik (1988), developing countries generally impose quantitative restrictions, such as quotas, rather than tariffs on their imports for protecting their import-competing industries. We shall thus hereafter refer to Q as import quotas, and Q is treated as given.[5]

Let us turn to model the production facet of this two-sector economy. The agricultural product is produced by utilizing capital and labor with constant returns to scale technology. It is assumed that the agricultural sector is characterized by perfect competition, and hence there is zero profit for agriculture. Let $\alpha(\cdot)$ be the unit-cost function for agriculture. The zero-profit condition can then be expressed by:

$$\alpha(w_Y, r_Y) = p_Y, \tag{14.2}$$

where $w_Y(r_Y)$ are the wage rate (capital rental) in agriculture. By choosing agriculture as the numeraire, the price of Y, p_Y, can be normalized to unity.

---

[4]Konishi *et al.* (1990), among others, have utilized this utility function in their study of oligopolistic competition.

[5]Note that only quantity restrictions in trade, such as quotas, are consistent with the price-setting behavior by home firms; the analysis presented cannot be applied to the case of tariffs.

The manufacturing sector, on the other hand, is characterized by oligopolistic competition. The sector consists of n identical firms, where n is a relatively small number. The sector output is simply the sum of the outputs of the n firms, i.e., $X = \sum_{1}^{n} x$, where x denotes the output of each firm. Firms in the manufacturing sector use capital and labor to produce goods with increasing returns to scale technology. Barriers to entry into the manufacturing sector due to the lack of adequate financing and serious antitrust policies cause imperfections in the product market. Thus, profits exist for each manufacturing firm. The firm's profit function is:

$$\pi = p_X x - C(w_X, r_X, x)$$
$$= \phi\left(x + \sum x_{-i} + Q\right) x - C(w_X, r_X, x), \qquad (14.3)$$

where x_{-i} denotes the output of any other firm in sector X; w_X and r_X are the wage rate and rental rate in manufacturing, and $C(\cdot)$ denotes the firm's total cost function. We assume that $C(\cdot)$ is separable and consists of two parts:

$$C(w_X, r_X, x) = m(w_X, r_X)x + F(w_X, r_X), \qquad (14.4)$$

where $m(\cdot)x$ and $F(\cdot)$ represent the total variable and fixed costs, respectively, and $m(\cdot)$ is the marginal cost. The existence of the fixed costs generates scale economies for firms in sector X.

The first-order condition for profit maximization of (14.3) is:

$$\phi(X + Q) + \gamma x \phi'(X + Q) = m(w_X, r_X), \qquad (14.5)$$

where $X = nx$ for the symmetric equilibrium, and $\gamma = \partial X/\partial x = 1 + \sum \partial x_{-i}/\partial x$ captures the firm's exogenous conjecture on the market-supply response to a change in its own output for a given quota. Equation (14.5) simply states a conjectural variation solution to profit maximization, i.e., the *perceived* marginal revenue (MR) is equated with the marginal costs. Note that when $\gamma = 0$, $p_X = m$, implying perfect competition; $\gamma = 1$, $\phi + x\phi' = m$, indicating Cournot competition; $\gamma = n$, signifying a cartel; and $\gamma = n = 1$ for monopoly.[6]

---

[6]For simplicity, the conjectural variations used here are exogenously fixed and appear to lack microeconomic foundations. Versions of conjectural variations, e.g., consistent conjectural variations, which are a bit more complex, may also be used.

To carry out analysis in the general equilibrium setting, we need to specify equilibrium conditions for factor markets as well. By using the firm's cost function (13.4) and applying Shephard's lemma, demand for labor (L_i) and capital (K_i) for sector i can be expressed by:

$$L_X = m_w(w_X, r_X)X + nF_w(w_X, r_X), \quad L_Y = \alpha_w(w_Y, r_Y)Y,$$

$$K_X = m_r(w_X, r_X)X + nF_r(w_X, r_X), \quad K_Y = \alpha_r(w_Y, r_Y)Y,$$

where $m_w = \partial m/\partial w_X$, etc. Note that $m_w X(m_r X)$ denotes the amount of labor (capital) used as a variable input in the manufacturing sector.

For capturing the duality and imperfection in the labor market in developing countries, we follow Harris and Todaro (1970) and assume that the wage rate in manufacturing is set above the market-clearing wage $(w_X = \bar{w}_X)$, so sector-specific unemployment (L_u) emerges.[7] Defining the unemployment ratio in manufacturing by $\lambda = L_u/L_X$, the well-known Harris–Todaro migration equilibrium is:

$$w_Y = \frac{\bar{w}_X}{(1 + \lambda)}. \tag{14.6}$$

That is, in equilibrium, the agricultural wage rate is equal to the expected wage rate in manufacturing, which is the actual wage rate $(\bar{w}_X)$ times the probability of finding a job in sector X, denoted by $1/(1 + \lambda)$. Furthermore, denoting the economy's labor endowment by $\bar{L}$, the market equilibrium condition for labor requires $L_X + L_u + L_Y = \bar{L}$. Thus, recalling the definition of λ, the condition can be written as:

$$(1 + \lambda)[m_w(\bar{w}_X, r_X)X + nF_w(\bar{w}_X, r_X)] + \alpha_w(w_Y, r_Y)Y = \bar{L}. \tag{14.7}$$

We turn next to the capital markets. To capture one of the salient features of a typical developing economy, we will distinguish the short-run equilibrium from the long-run equilibrium in the capital markets. The commonly observed weakness of home capital markets in developing countries causes sluggish movement of capital among sectors, and capital is virtually sector-specific in the short run. Denoting the endowment of home capital

---

[7]The Harris–Todaro unemployment model and its extended versions have been utilized for analyzing a variety of trade and developmental issues. For recent studies, see: Khan (1982a and 1982b), Batra and Naqvi (1987), Beladi (1988), Grinols (1991), and Choi and Yu (2006). The empirical validity of the Harris–Todaro model can be found in Feltenstein (1992) and Hatton and Williamson (1992).

stock for sector i by $\bar{K}_i$, the short-run equilibrium conditions for capital markets require:

$$m_r(\bar{w}_X, r_X)X + nF_r(\bar{w}_X, r_X) = \bar{K}_X + K^* , \qquad (14.8)$$

$$\alpha_r(w_r, r_Y)Y = \bar{K}_Y, \qquad (14.9)$$

where K^* is the exogenous inflows of foreign capital to sector X. The assumption of short-run capital specificity implies the unequal returns to capital, i.e., $r_X \neq r_Y$.

For the long run, however, capital is assumed to be intersectorally mobile until the returns are equalized, $r_X = r_Y$. Thus, the long-run equilibrium condition for capital markets requires:

$$m_r(\bar{w}_X, r_X)X + nF_r(\bar{w}_X, r_X) + \alpha_r(w_Y, r_Y)Y$$
$$= \bar{K}_X + \bar{K}_Y + K^* = \bar{K} + K^*, \qquad (14.10)$$

where $\bar{K} = \bar{K}_X + \bar{K}_Y$.

Equations (14.1) through (14.10) complete our specification of both the demand side and the production side of the model. In what follows, we will utilize this model to examine the resource allocation and welfare effects of foreign capital inflows in the presence of quantitative restrictions for developing economies.

14.3   Foreign Capital Inflows and Resource Allocation

In this section we examine the effects of exogenous foreign capital inflows on factor returns, sectoral outputs, and regional unemployment for the case of short-run capital specificity and long-run capital mobility. An exogenous inflow of foreign capital implies a relaxation of an existing quota on capital inflows (in addition to the quota on imports of goods) by the home country.[8]

The resource allocation effects of foreign capital due to "small" changes in K^* can be obtained from the equations of change. We begin with considering the effects of foreign capital inflows on the manufacturing

---

[8]We are indebted to Ronald Jones for pointing out this implication. This chapter considers only exogenous capital inflows. It seems worthwhile to explore the issue of the effects of endogenous policy-induced inflows of foreign capital in our future research.

output and capital-rental rates. Letting ' ^ ' be the percentage change, the output effect can be derived from the profit-maximization condition for the oligopolistic firms in sector X in (14.5) as:[9]

$$-s\left(\frac{1+\gamma}{n} - \frac{\gamma se}{n}\right)\hat{x} - \epsilon b\theta_{KX}^m \hat{r}_X = 0, \tag{14.11}$$

where $s = X/D_X$ denotes the domestic production/demand ratio for good X, which is less than 1 due to the existence of import quotas; $b = m/p_x$ is the ratio of the marginal cost to the price of good X; $\theta_{KX}^m = r_X m_r/m$ represents the marginal cost share of capital in sector X; $\epsilon = -\phi/D_X\phi'$ is the price elasticity of demand for good X; and $e = -D_X\phi''/\phi'$ is the elasticity of the slope of the demand for good X.[10] As shown in Appendix A.2, a sufficient condition of stability for the system is the coefficient of $\hat{x}$ in (14.11) to be negative, i.e., $\gamma se/n \leq 1 + \gamma/n$.

Since the manufacturing wage rate $\bar{w}_X$ is assumed fixed, changes in factor prices simply refer to changes in the rental rate in sector X. As can be seen in (14.11), a rise in the capital rental raises the marginal cost for firms in sector X, and hence output per firm x falls. Moreover, the change in the capital-rental rate is obtainable from the equilibrium conditions of the capital markets. Two cases regarding short-run capital specificity and long-run capital mobility can be analyzed and compared.

14.3.1   *Capital specificity*

Consider first the case of the short run in which capital is sector-specific. Assume that foreign capital flows only into the manufacturing sector. The capital-rental rate can be determined by totally differentiating (14.8):

$$\lambda_{KX}^m \hat{x} - s_{KX}\hat{r}_X = \delta\hat{K}^*, \tag{14.12}$$

where $\lambda_{KX}^m = m_r X/K_X$ denotes the share of domestic capital used as a variable input in sector X; $\delta = K^*/K_X$ is the share of foreign capital in sector X; and $s_{KX} \equiv (X m_{rw} w_X + n F_{rw} w_X)/K_X$.

---

[9]Recall that $\hat{n} = 0$ for the assumption of restricted entry in sector X. The derivations of (14.11) are provided in the Appendix.
[10]See Seade (1980) for a detailed discussion of the slope of the demand curve.

The manufacturing output and rental rate in sector X can be jointly determined. Solving (14.11) and (14.12) yields:

$$\frac{\hat{x}}{\hat{K}^*} = \frac{\delta \epsilon b \theta^m_{KX}}{D}, \tag{14.13}$$

$$\frac{\hat{r}_X}{\hat{K}^*} = -\delta s \frac{\left(\frac{1+\gamma}{n} - \frac{\gamma se}{n}\right)}{D}, \tag{14.14}$$

where $D = [\epsilon b \lambda^m_{KX} \theta^m_{KX} + ss_{KX}(1 + \gamma/n - \gamma se/n)] > 0$ by invoking the stability condition (see the Appendix). Thus, $\hat{x}/\hat{K}^* > 0$ and $\hat{r}_X/\hat{K}^* < 0$. An additional inflow of foreign capital leads to an expansion of the manufacturing firm's output and a decline in the capital-rental rate in sector X.

One of the salient features of developing economies is the existence of regional unemployment. To ascertain the effects of foreign capital inflows on the unemployment ratio in manufacturing, we differentiate the labor-migration equilibrium (14.6) and the labor market condition (14.7), and then utilize the result of the differentiation of (14.2), $\hat{w}_Y = -(\theta_{KY}/\theta_{LY})\hat{r}_Y$, to obtain:

$$A\hat{\lambda} = -(1+\lambda)\lambda^m_{LX}\hat{x} - (1+\lambda)s_{LX}\hat{r}_X \gtrless 0, \tag{14.15}$$

where $\theta_{LY} = w_Y \alpha_w/p_Y$ and $\theta_{KY} = r\alpha_r/p_Y$ represent the cost share of labor and capital in sector Y, and $\lambda^m_{LX} = m_w X/L$ denotes the share of labor used as a variable input in sector X. Here we define: $A = [\lambda/(1+\lambda)][(1+\lambda)\lambda_{LX} + (s_{LY} + \lambda_{LY}s_{KY})/\theta_{KY}]$, $s_{LX} = r_X(Xm_{wr} + nF_{wr})/\bar{L}$, $s_{LY} = q_{wr}r_Y Y/\bar{L}$ and $s_{KY} = a_{rw}w_Y Y/K_Y$, with $\lambda_{LX} = L_X/\bar{L}$ and $\lambda_{LX} = L_X/\bar{L}$ denoting the share of labor used in sectors X and Y, respectively.

Clearly, additional inflows of foreign capital generate two contrasting effects on the unemployment ratio in sector X: the output effect and the factor-substitution effect. Given that capital is sector-specific in the short run, inflows of foreign capital into manufacturing results in an increased production of manufacturing goods and, hence, an increased demand for labor by sector X. The new hires are drawn in part from the pool of unemployed labor, thereby causing a fall in the unemployment ratio. Concomitantly, the fall in the capital-rental cost induced by foreign capital inflows in manufacturing leads to a substitution of capital for labor and hence a decreased demand for workers in manufacturing. This factor-substitution effect causes λ to rise. The effect of foreign capital inflows on the regional unemployment ratio is thus indeterminate *a priori*. The sign of $\hat{\lambda}$ in (14.15) is dependent on the relative magnitudes of the two aforementioned effects.

14.3.2   *Capital mobility*

As noted earlier, in the long run, capital is mobile intersectorally, and so the rentals are equalized, $r_X = r_Y = r$. The equilibrium condition for capital markets is represented by (14.10). Differentiating (14.10) yields:

$$\lambda_{KX}^m \hat{x} + \lambda_{KY} \hat{Y} - B\hat{r} = \delta \hat{K}^*, \qquad (14.16)$$

where $\lambda_{KX} = K_Y/(\bar{K} + K^*)$ denotes the share of capital used in sector Y, and $\lambda_{KX}^m = m_r X/(\bar{K} + K^*)$ represents the share of capital used as a variable input in sector X. Here we define $\delta = K^*/(\bar{K} + K^*)$ and $B = (s_{KX} + s_{KY}/\theta_{LY})$, with $s_{KX} = (X m_{rw} w_X + n F_{rw} w_X)/(\bar{K} + K^*)$ and $s_{KY} = Y\alpha_{rw} w_Y/(\bar{K} + K^*)$. Note that $\delta, B, s_{KX}, s_{KY} > 0$.

Equation (14.16) states that an inflow of foreign capital affects the capital-rental rate, as well as the outputs of both good X and Y. The linkage between good X and Y can be derived from the labor market condition in (14.7) and by utilizing the changes in (14.2) and (14.6) as:

$$(1 + \lambda)\lambda_{LX}^m \hat{x} + \lambda_{LY} \hat{Y} + G\hat{r} = 0, \qquad (14.17)$$

where $G = (1 + \lambda)s_{LX} + [s_{LY} + \lambda_{LX}\theta_{KY}(1 + \lambda)/\theta_{LY}] > 0$.

By eliminating Y from (14.16) and (14.17) and then using (14.11) we can solve for the effects of foreign capital inflows on x and r as:

$$\frac{\hat{x}}{\hat{K}^*} = \frac{\delta \epsilon b \theta_{KX}^m}{\Delta}, \qquad (14.18)$$

$$\frac{\hat{r}}{\hat{K}^*} = -\delta s \frac{\left(\frac{1+\gamma}{n} - \frac{\gamma se}{n}\right)}{\Delta}, \qquad (14.19)$$

where $\Delta = s(1 + \gamma/n - \gamma se/n)(B + G\lambda_{KY}/\lambda_{LY}) + \epsilon b \theta_{KX}^m \lambda_{LX}^m M$. Note that $M = [\lambda_{KX}^m/\lambda_{LX}^m - (1 + \lambda)(\lambda_{KY}/\lambda_{LY})]$, representing the *marginal* capital intensity of sector X relative to sector Y for the mobile-capital Harris–Todaro economy.[11] A sufficient condition of stability for the extended mobile-capital Harris–Todaro economy is $M > 0$ and $e\gamma s/n < 1 + \gamma/n$ (see the Appendix). It follows that $\Delta > 0$, and, hence, $\hat{x}/\hat{K}^* > 0$ and $\hat{r}/\hat{K}^* < 0$. Hence, under stability conditions, additional inflows of foreign capital in the long run, similar to the case of the short run, generate the

---

[11]This is a generalization of the Khan (1980) and Neary (1981) stability condition for the mobile-capital Harris–Todaro economy. The concept of marginal-factor intensity originates with Jones (1968) and is utilized by Choi and Yu (1987) and Chao and Takayama (1990).

positive output effect for good X, as well as the factor-substitution effect as a result of the reduction in the rental cost of capital.

The output effect of foreign capital inflows raises the demand for manufacturing workers, whereas the factor-substitution effect reduces the demand for labor. However, contrasting to the case of short-run capital specificity, the output effect here always dominates the factor-substitution effect so that increases in foreign capital inflows unambiguously lower the unemployment ratio in manufacturing. This can be confirmed by differentiating (14.2) and (14.6) to obtain:

$$\frac{\hat{\lambda}}{\hat{K}^*} = \left[\frac{(1+\lambda)}{\lambda}\right]\left(\frac{\theta_{KY}}{\theta_{LY}}\right)\frac{\hat{r}}{\hat{K}^*} < 0. \tag{14.20}$$

We now summarize the effects of foreign capital inflows as follows.

Proposition 14.1 *For the developing economy with oligopolistic competition, restricted entry, and unemployment in the manufacturing sector, additional inflows of foreign capital raise manufacturing output and lower capital-rental costs, regardless of the degree of sectoral capital mobility. Moreover, an increase in foreign capital inflows may increase the unemployment ratio in manufacturing when capital is sector-specific in the short run, whereas the unemployment ratio always drops in the long run with perfect intersectoral capital mobility.*

14.4 Foreign Capital Inflows and National Welfare

The aim of this chapter is to ascertain the welfare for an economy with oligopolistic competition and restricted entry. The domestic welfare is represented by the consumers' indirect utility function, obtainable from utility maximization, as $V(p_X, p_Y, I)$ where, from (14.1), $p_X = \phi(X+Q)$, because good Y is chosen as the numeraire, so that $p_Y = 1$, and I denotes national income.

National income in the present framework is the sum of factor income, profits in sector X, and quota rents: $I = \bar{w}_X L_X + w_Y L_Y + r_X \bar{K}_X + r_Y \bar{K}_Y + n\pi + (p_X - p_X^*)Q$, where p_X^* denotes the foreign price of good X.[12] By using

---

[12] A crucial assumption here is that all quota rents are retained at home. Relaxing this assumption can make a big difference in the results. See Neary (1988) for elucidation.

(14.6) and (14.7), we can simplify the national income as:

$$I = w_Y \bar{L} + r_X \bar{K}_X + r_Y \bar{K}_Y + n\pi + (p_X - p_X^*)Q. \tag{14.21}$$

Totally differentiating the indirect utility function and using Roy's identity yields the change in national welfare as:

$$\frac{dV}{V_I} = -D_X \phi' dX + dI, \tag{14.22}$$

where $V_I = \partial V / \partial I$ represents the marginal utility of income. Note that the change in national income, dI, for both cases of short-run capital specificity and long-run capital mobility can be obtained by differentiating (14.21) as:[13]

$$dI = D_X \phi' dX + n(p_X - m)dx - K^* dr_X - w_Y L_X d\lambda. \tag{14.23}$$

Substituting (14.23) into (14.22) yields:

$$\frac{dV}{V_I} = -K^* dr_X + n(p_X - m)dx - w_Y L_X d\lambda$$

$$= -K^* dr_X + n\left(p_X - \frac{C}{x}\right) dx + n\left(\frac{F}{x}\right) dx - w_Y L_X d\lambda. \tag{14.24}$$

Equation (14.24) is instrumental in evaluating the welfare impact of foreign capital inflows. The first term on the right-hand side of (14.24) corresponds to the usual welfare effect of foreign capital inflows under perfect competition and constant returns to scale technology. Dei's (1985a) result that foreign capital inflows improve domestic welfare as a result of a fall in the rental payments to foreign capital is easily verified here.

For economies characterized by imperfect competition, scale economies as well as regional unemployment, the welfare impact is bit more complex. There are three additional effects as shown by the remaining terms in (14.24). Specifically, the second term captures the profit effect caused by imperfect competition. Restricted entry into manufacturing gives rise to positive profits for the incumbent firms, i.e., $p_X - C/x > 0$. An increase in foreign capital inflow leads to an expansion in the production of good X and hence generates "excess profits" for firms in sector X. In addition, the larger production of good X yields scale economies via a reduction in the

---

[13] The differential of (14.2), $\alpha_w dw_Y + \alpha_r dr_Y = 0$, is used to obtain (14.23).

sectoral average fixed costs, as shown in the third term of (14.24). Lastly, the fourth term captures the welfare effect of changes in the unemployment ratio in the manufacturing sector.

The earlier analysis of resource allocation effects of foreign capital inflows in Section 14.3 can now be utilized to ascertain the various welfare impacts. In the case of the short run with capital specificity, we can identify the component effects in (14.24) by using (14.13)–(14.15). Note that while the rental-payment effect, the excess-profit effect, and the scale-economy effect are all conducive to welfare, the unemployment effect is indeterminate, thereby leading to an ambiguous welfare effect of foreign capital inflows. However, if the unemployment effect is sufficiently small, or the economy is at full employment (a subset of the present model) foreign capital inflows in the presence of quotas are welfare improving.

On the other hand, in the long run, with intersectoral capital mobility, additional inflows of foreign capital always lower the unemployment ratio, as shown in (14.20). This favorable effect of the reduction in the unemployment ratio, in addition to the other beneficial effects of foreign capital inflows described in (14.24), will further improve national welfare in the long run.

The foregoing analysis of the welfare effects of foreign capital inflows can be summarized in the following proposition.

Proposition 14.2 *In the short run with sector-specific capital, additional inflows of foreign capital improve the welfare of an economy characterized by oligopoly, scale economics, and regional unemployment, provided that the unemployment effect is relatively insignificant. In the long run with mobile capital, additional inflows of foreign capital, however, always improve the welfare of such economies.*

For ease of comparison, the various components of the welfare impacts for the short run versus the long run are summarized as Table 14.1.

Table 14.1 Welfare effects of changes in foreign capital inflows.

	Payment to foreign capital	Excess profits	Scale economics	Unemployment	Total welfare
Short run	−	+	+	?	?
Long run	−	+	+	−	+

14.5 Concluding Remarks

This chapter has examined the effects of inflows of foreign capital on home resource allocation and welfare in a general equilibrium framework. The home country is characterized by oligopolistic competition, scale economies, and regional unemployment. Although the welfare effect of foreign capital for the short run is somewhat indeterminate and is dependent on the magnitude of the effects of excess profits and scale economies (relative to the unemployment effect in manufacturing), the inflows of foreign capital always improve welfare for such economies in the long run with capital mobility.

Our results, which stand in sharp contrast to those derived in the presence of tariffs (Brecher and Diaz Alejandro, 1977), lend support to the finding of Dei (1985a). Dei's key result is generalized to economies with imperfect competition in the short run and imperfect competition, along with regional unemployment, in the long run.

The use of quasi-linear preferences serves to focus on the price effect by suppressing the income effects on the demand for goods. It may be noted that when the income effects are presented in the model via more general preferences, the demand for goods would be further raised in the case of intersectoral mobility of capital. Hence, foreign capital inflows would be more welfare improving in the long run.

Appendix

A.1 *Derivations of* (14.11)

Total differentiation of (14.5), $\phi(X+Q) + \gamma x \phi'(X+Q) = m(w_X, r_X)$ yields:

$$\phi' dX + \gamma \phi' dx + \gamma x \phi'' dX = m_r dr_X,$$

by recalling that w_X is fixed and γ is exogenously given. By rearranging the terms in this equation, we have:

$$\phi' \left(\frac{1 + \gamma x \phi''}{\phi'} \right) dX + \gamma \phi' dx = m_r dr_X,$$

which is:

$$\phi' \left[1 + \left(\frac{\gamma}{n} \right) \left(\frac{X}{D_X} \right) \left(\frac{D_X \phi''}{\phi'} \right) \right] dX + \gamma \phi' dx = m_r dr_X,$$

then, using $s = X/D_X$ and $e = -D_X\phi''/\phi'$ yields:

$$\phi'\left(\frac{1-\gamma se}{n}\right)dX + \gamma\phi'dx = m_r dr_X.$$

By imposing the symmetric condition, $X = nx$, and due to restricted entry, $dn = 0$, the above equation can be written as:

$$\phi'\left(\frac{1-\gamma se}{n}\right)ndx + \gamma\phi'dx = m_r dr_X$$

which is:

$$\left(\frac{D_X\phi'}{\phi}\right)\left(\frac{X}{D_X}\right)\left(\frac{1}{n}\right)(n-\gamma se+\gamma)\hat{x} = \left(\frac{m}{\phi}\right)\left(\frac{m_r r_X}{m}\right)\hat{r}_X,$$

that is:

$$-\left(\frac{s}{\epsilon}\right)\left(\frac{1+\gamma}{n} - \frac{\gamma se}{n}\right)\hat{x} - b\theta^m_{KX}\hat{r}_X = 0,$$

where $\epsilon = -\phi/D_X\phi'$, $b = m/\phi$, and $\theta^m_{KX} = m_r r_X/m$. Multiplying ϵ on the both sides of the above equation, we obtain (14.11) in the text.

A.2   *Stability conditions*

To focus on the features of imperfect competition and scale economies, we follow Konishi *et al.* (1990) by assuming that while the factor markets and the agricultural market adjust instantly, the output of the manufacturing sector adjusts slowly. The adjustment process for x is defined by:

$$\dot{x} = \zeta\{\phi(X+Q) + \gamma x\phi'(X+Q) - m(w_X, r)\},$$

where the dot represents the time derivative and ζ is the positive adjustment coefficient. Note that due to restricted entry in manufacturing, it is assumed that the number of firms in that sector never adjusts.

Taking a linear approximation for the adjustment process around the equilibrium point x^*, and then, for the short run, utilizing (14.11) and (14.12) yields:

$$\dot{x} = -\zeta\left\{s\left(\frac{1+\gamma}{n} - \frac{\gamma se}{n}\right) + \frac{\epsilon b\lambda^m_{KX}\theta^m_{KX}}{s_{KX}}\right\}\hat{q},$$

and, for the long run, utilizing (14.11), (14.16), and (14.19) yields:

$$\dot{x} = -\zeta\left\{s\left(\frac{1+\gamma}{n} - \frac{\gamma se}{n}\right) + \frac{\epsilon bM\theta_{LY}\theta^m_{KX}}{\left(\frac{B+G\lambda_{KY}}{\lambda_{LY}}\right)}\right\}\hat{q}.$$

Thus, a sufficient condition for stability in the short run is that $\gamma se/n < 1 + \gamma/n$ and for the long run is $\gamma se/n < 1 + \gamma/n$ and $M > 0$.

Chapter 15

Profit-Sharing and International Capital Mobility

15.1 Introduction

Profit-sharing has been used in varying degrees for many centuries. In pre-industrial societies, sharecropping was the dominant system for paying hired labor within agriculture. Profit-sharing arrangements have persisted since the industrial revolution. As documented by Weitzman (1984), profit-sharing in terms of a "sliding scale" linking wages to firm output value was used by the coal and steel industries in Britain in the nineteenth century. A related system was also in place in textiles and other early industries in the United States. In recent years, profit-sharing plans have been in vogue in several prominent US corporations. In addition, many self-employed workers and professionals, salespersons for real estate and financial institutions, and workers in the service sectors are all paid a share of the output value.[1] Profit-sharing is also typical in the Japanese economy. A majority of industrial workers are paid profit-sharing bonuses twice a year. The success of the Japanese economy after World War II is attributed by Weitzman to the extensive adoption of the share system to supplement the wage system. In addition to industrialized advanced economies, share schemes and related systems have been commonly adopted by several newly industrialized economies (NIEs) as well as many developing nations. Among the NIEs, Taiwan and South Korea stand out in the group characterized by profit-sharing (Aoki, 1988, p. 151). In terms of the developing nations, China, the world's largest socialist country, has adopted extensive, multilayer

---

[1]US companies that have used "profit-sharing" or "employee stock ownership plans" include Eastman–Kodak, Proctor & Gamble, Xerox, Sears Roebuck, Texas Instruments, Kellogg, Chase Manhattan, and J. C. Penny. The list can go on. For details, see Weitzman (1984, Chapter 7).

bonuses and subsidy schemes to supplement workers' basic wages and salaries.[2]

There have been a limited number of studies on the ramifications of the share system subsequent to the publication of *The Share Economy* (Weitzman, 1984). The studies, such as Fung (1989), have focused on the cases of advanced economies, most notably Japan. The resource allocation effect of profit-sharing in the case of NIEs and developing nations, however, remains to be explored. The purpose of this chapter is to examine such effects of profit-sharing in a general equilibrium framework that captures several salient features of NIEs, notably somewhat uneven development between sectors (fast-growing urban manufacturing coexists with sluggish rural agriculture). Specifically, we study the effects of profit-sharing on rural–urban migration, the degree of competition among urban firms, and international mobility of capital. The key parameters in the economy are time dependent; we will thus conduct the analysis in two time horizons of a short run versus a longer run. The short run in the present analysis is identified with the presence of restrictions on both entry/exit of firms and inflows of foreign capital, whereas the long run is defined in terms of both free entry/exit of firms and perfect international mobility of capital.[3]

We find that although profit-sharing in the short run leads to a higher urban unemployment ratio, the share scheme can raise manufacturing employment. Nevertheless, profit-sharing in the long run results in substantial urban unemployment. Firms then exit from manufacturing, causing a contraction of the urban sector and a fall in the inflow of foreign capital.

15.2   The Model

Consider an NIE consisting of two sectors: urban manufacturing (X) and rural agriculture (Y). Goods are produced in both sectors by utilizing capital (K) and labor (L), and good X is capital-intensive relative to good Y. We assume that the country exports agricultural good Y and

---

[2]The basic monthly salaries of workers in China constitute about only a quarter of the pay package which includes all sorts of bonuses and subsidies.

[3]Khan (1982a) and Neary (1988) utilize the degree of international mobility of capital as a main measure for defining time horizons of long run versus short run. Both international capital mobility and entry/exit of firms are used in identifying short run versus long run.

imports foreign capital K^*, while good X is nontradable. Balance of trade is maintained.

The production of good Y exhibits constant returns to scale, and the market is perfectly competitive, so that its factor and goods prices are linked by the zero-profit condition:

$$\alpha(w, r) = p_Y, \qquad (15.1)$$

where p_Y is the price of good Y; w and r are the wage rate of labor and rental rate on capital; and $\alpha(\cdot)$ is the unit-cost function for good Y. Choosing Y as the numeraire, p_Y is normalized to one. The factors in sector Y are paid according to their marginal revenue products.

Concurrently, there are n-like oligopolists in urban manufacturing, each of which produces good x and the industry output is $X = nx$. Increasing returns to scale prevail in production owing to the presence of fixed costs, F. Following Sen (1997), only capital is used as a fixed input; so fixed cost solely depends on r. The marginal-cost component of good x, involving both labor and capital, is denoted by $m(z, r)$, where z is the urban wage rate paid according to the value of worker's marginal products. The variable cost of producing good x is $m(z, r)x$, being homogenous of degree one in z and r. Since the fixed cost is sunk, profit over marginal cost is $(p - m)x$, where p is the relative price of good X. Under profit-sharing, g portion of the profit will be returned to workers. Thus, each worker in urban manufacturing receives not only the wage rate, z, which is institutionally determined,[4] but also obtains a profit-sharing bonus, $g(p - m)/m_z$, where $m_z = \partial m/\partial z$ is the unit-output labor employment in each firm.

The introduction or upgrading of a profit-sharing scheme induces rural workers to move to urban areas in search of better opportunities; but not every migrant worker's search is rewarded. The expected income for each urban worker equals the realized income weighted by the probability of being employed, $1/(1 + \mu)$, where $\mu = U/nm_z$ is the urban unemployment ratio and U is the number of unemployed workers in the urban areas.[5] It is assumed that labor is perfectly mobile between sectors; labor market

---

[4]We follow Harris and Todaro (1970) in the formulation of urban wage.

[5]The urban unemployment rate is $\bar{\mu} = U/(nm_z + U) = \mu/(1 + \mu)$. Hence $d\bar{\mu}/d\mu = 1/(1 + \mu) > 0$.

equilibrium requires equality of rural wage and expected urban wage plus shared profits:[6]

$$w = \frac{\left\{ \frac{z+g[p-m(z,r)]}{m_z(z,r)} \right\}}{(1+\mu)}. \tag{15.2}$$

It has been observed that a shortage of labor in rural areas is quite common among NIEs; the rural wage (w) may exceed the government-regulated urban wage (z).[7] Profit-sharing in the urban manufacturing sector may, however, push up urban labor income to a level higher than the rural wage. Such a profit-sharing scheme provides an incentive for rural workers to migrate to the urban area.

To complete the model, we need to introduce the demand side. Social preferences are represented by a quasi-linear utility function, $U(X,Y) = u(X) + Y$, with $u' > 0$.[8] Maximization of utility subject to a budget constraint yields a demand function for good $X : p = p(X)$ with $p' < 0$. We further assume that the demand function for good X is linear, or $p'' = 0$.

Since the fixed cost is sunk, a representative firm in sector X maximizes profits over marginal cost (net workers' shares), $(1-g)(p-m)x$, with respect to x. The first-order condition implies:

$$p(X) + \gamma x p'(X) = m(z,r), \tag{15.3}$$

where $\gamma = \partial X/\partial x = 1 + \sum \partial x_{-i}/\partial x$ captures the firm's conjecture on the market-supply response to a change in its own output. The value of γ indicates the market structure: when $\gamma = 0$, then $p = c$ implying perfect competition; $\gamma = 1$ indicates Cournot competition; $\gamma = n$ signifies a cartel; and $\gamma = n = 1$ represents a monopoly. We assume that $\gamma \leq n$.

Turn to the factor markets. Denoting the economy's labor endowment by $\bar{L}$, employment of labor is subject to the following constraint:

$$(1+\mu)L_X + L_Y = \bar{L}, \tag{15.4}$$

where $L_X = m_z(z,r)X$ and $L_Y = \alpha_w(w,r)Y$, denoting labor employment in sectors X and Y, respectively.

---

[6]The results we will obtain in this chapter hold for the full-employment case in which workers either find jobs in the urban areas or are fully absorbed by the rural sector (i.e., $\mu = 0$).

[7]In the original Harris and Todaro (1970) model, actual urban wages always exceed rural wages.

[8]See Konishi *et al.* (1990) for applications of this type of utility functions in general equilibrium models.

However, the use of capital is constrained by its domestic endowment, $\bar{K}$, and the inflow of foreign capital, K^*. Letting $K = \bar{K} + K^*$, equilibrium in the capital market requires:

$$K_X + K_Y = K, \qquad (15.5)$$

where $K_X = m_z(z,r)X + F_r(r)$ and $K_Y = \alpha_r(w,r)Y$, denoting capital used in sectors X and Y, respectively.

We can identify two time-dependent equilibria. In the short run, the stock of foreign capital (K^*) is fixed but its domestic return (r) is flexible. However, in the long run, capital is perfectly mobile internationally. If the domestic rate of return exceeds the foreign rate (r^*), the available capital stock is augmented by inflows of foreign capital:

$$\dot{K} = \rho(r - r^*), \qquad (15.6)$$

where a dot denotes the time derivative, and $\rho' > 0$.

Furthermore, in the long run, firms enter or exit sector X, depending on whether or not the profits net of workers' shares can cover the fixed cost:

$$\dot{n} = \varphi[(1-g)(p-m)x - F(r)], \qquad (15.7)$$

where $\varphi' > 0$.

The dynamics of the two equations of motion (15.6) and (15.7) yield a steady-state equilibrium that is characterized by $\dot{K} = 0$ and $\dot{n} = 0$. The steady state defines a long-run equilibrium (K^e, n^e) such that:

$$r(K^e, n^e, g) = r^*, \qquad (15.8)$$

$$\pi(K^e, n^e, g) = 0, \qquad (15.9)$$

where $\pi \equiv (1-g)(p-m)x - F(r)$. The state variables are K and n. In the steady state, the world rate of return on capital prevails domestically, and each firm in sector X covers its fixed cost.[9]

15.3 The Short-Run Impacts of Profit-Sharing

We begin with the analysis of a short-run equilibrium in which both n and K are fixed. The short-run equilibrium is captured by (15.1)–(15.5) with endogenous variables, w, r, μ, x, and Y.

---

[9] An intermediate case involving restricted inflows of foreign capital and free entry of firms is conceivable. In this case both are endogenous, and hence the results are much more complicated.

Let a circumflex denote the percentage change in a variable. The output effect of a change in the profit share can be derived by totally differentiating (15.3), and rearranging the terms to yield:

$$\left(\frac{1+\gamma}{n}\right)\hat{x} + \varepsilon\delta\theta_{KX}^m\hat{r} = 0, \tag{15.10}$$

where $\varepsilon = -p/Xp'$ is the price elasticity of demand for good X, $\delta = m/p$ denotes the marginal cost-price ratio, and $\theta_{KX}^m = rm_r/m$ is the marginal cost share of capital in sector X. Equation (15.10) states that, in the case of short-run restricted entry, cost saving through a reduction in capital rental raises firm's output.[10]

The change in manufacturing output affects the urban unemployment ratio. Totally differentiating the labor market equilibrium condition in (15.2), and noting that $\hat{n} = 0$, yields:

$$\left[\frac{\mu}{(1+\mu)}\right]\hat{\mu} + \left(\frac{\beta}{\varepsilon}\right)\hat{x} - \phi\hat{r} = (\beta - b)\hat{\alpha}, \tag{15.11}$$

where $\beta = g(p/m_z)/w(1+\mu)$ and $b = g(m/m_z)/w(1+\mu)$. The values of β and b capture the relative impacts of p and c on profit-sharing with $\beta > b$, because $p > m$. By the stability conditions shown in Appendix A.2, $\phi = (\theta_{KY}/\theta_{LY}) - \theta_{KX}^m[b + \sigma_x^m(\beta - b)] > 0$ in (15.11), where $\sigma_x^m = mm_{zr}/m_zm_r$ is factor substitution in sector X. Equation (15.11) states that saving in capital cost results in greater urban production of good X, thereby lowering the urban unemployment ratio. An increase in profit-sharing, however, causes rural workers to migrate to urban areas, aggravating urban unemployment.

The exact relations between x, r, and μ can be obtained through the factor-market equilibrium conditions. By totally differentiating (15.4) and (15.5), we obtain:

$$(1+\mu)\lambda_{LX}\hat{x} + \lambda_{LY}\hat{Y} + \mu\lambda_{LX}\hat{\mu} + k\hat{r} = 0, \tag{15.12}$$

$$\lambda_{KX}^m\hat{x} + \lambda_{KY}\hat{Y} - h\hat{r} = 0, \tag{15.13}$$

where $h > 0$ and $k > 0$, and λ_{ij} denotes the ith factor's share in the jth sector (see the Appendix).

---

[10] Although the effects of profit-sharing and a higher urban minimum wage on workers are qualitatively the same, they are quite different to urban firms because a higher minimum wage may lower firm output.

Solving the system of (15.10)–(15.13), we have $\hat{x}/\hat{g} > 0$, $\hat{Y}/\hat{g} < 0$, $\hat{r}/\hat{g} < 0$, and $\hat{\mu}/\hat{g} > 0$ under the stability conditions. That is, profit-sharing in urban manufacturing causes rural–urban migration. Consequently, urban manufacturing expands but rural agriculture shrinks. Underlying the transformation is the release of capital from the rural sector for the urban sector and a resulting fall in the capital-rental rate. Insofar as not every migrating worker can find a job in the urban area, the urban unemployment ratio goes up.

Since $L_X = nxm_z(z, r)$, the effect of profit-sharing on urban employment can be expressed as:[11]

$$\frac{\hat{L}_x}{\hat{g}} = \frac{\hat{x}}{\hat{g}} + g_x^m \theta_{KX}^m \left(\frac{\hat{r}}{\hat{g}} \right), \tag{15.14}$$

where $\hat{x}/\hat{g} > 0$ and $\hat{r}/\hat{g} < 0$, the employment effect is ambiguous in general; profit-sharing raises urban employment only if the output effect dominates the factor-substitution effect in a general equilibrium setting. Weitzman (1984) proposes that profit-sharing yields greater stability of employment. In the presence of rural–urban migration, his proposition holds only under certain conditions.

15.4 The Long-Run Equilibrium and Dynamics

In contrast to the short-run case, in the long run capital is perfectly mobile internationally and firms can enter or exit from urban manufacturing as expressed by (15.6) and (15.7). We first examine the dynamics of capital movement and entry/exit of firms. Linearly approximating (15.6) and (15.7) around the steady state yields:

$$\dot{K} = \rho' \left(\frac{\partial r}{\partial K} \right) (K - K^e) + \rho' \left(\frac{\partial r}{\partial n} \right) (n - n^e), \tag{15.15}$$

$$\dot{n} = \varphi' \left(\frac{\partial \pi}{\partial K} \right) (K - K^e) + \varphi' \left(\frac{\partial \pi}{\partial n} \right) (n - n^e), \tag{15.16}$$

---

[11]Grinols (1991) shows that the elasticities of labor demand affect unemployment in a capital-specific Harris–Todaro model. However, for the mobile capital case here, the shifts in the labor demand curves render the relationship between the urban and rural labor-demand elasticities indeterminate.

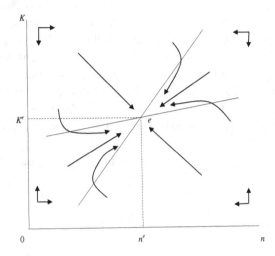

Figure 15.1   A stable node.

where $\partial r/\partial K < 0$, $\partial r/\partial n > 0$, $\partial \pi/\partial K > 0$, and $\partial \pi/\partial n < 0$ when sector X is capital-intensive relative to sector Y (see the Appendix). Since the trace is negative and the determinant is positive, the system of (15.15) and (15.16) provides a stable node. In Figure 15.1, the $\dot{K} = 0$ and $\dot{n} = 0$ loci represent the combinations of K and n that satisfy (15.15) and (15.16), respectively. The slopes of these two schedules are:

$$\frac{dK}{dn}\Big|_K = -\frac{\left(\frac{\partial r}{\partial n}\right)}{\left(\frac{\partial r}{\partial K}\right)} > 0, \tag{15.17}$$

$$\frac{dK}{dn}\Big|_n = -\frac{\left(\frac{\partial \pi}{\partial n}\right)}{\left(\frac{\partial \pi}{\partial K}\right)} > 0. \tag{15.18}$$

Thus, both schedules are upward sloping. By utilizing the stability conditions, the schedule of $\dot{n} = 0$ is steeper than that of $\dot{K} = 0$. A rightward (leftward) movement of (K, n) away from the $\dot{n} = 0$ schedule implies that the number of firms is declining (increasing), while a rightward (leftward) movement away from the $\dot{K} = 0$ schedule implies that capital is increasing (decreasing). Hence, the long-run equilibrium at point "e" in Figure 15.1 is a stable node, such that any mix of n and K off the equilibrium will converge to that point.

The long-run equilibrium can be expressed by (15.1)–(15.5), and (15.8) and (15.9). From (15.9), an increase in the workers' share immediately lowers the firm-owners' profits. To compensate for this loss, each firm increases output. As a result, price falls and some firms are driven out of business. It follows that total output of urban manufacturing falls and the urban unemployment ratio rises. These long-run results can be obtained by totally differentiating (15.1)–(15.5), (15.8), and (15.9) to yield:

$$\frac{\hat{x}}{\hat{g}} = \frac{g\varepsilon(1-\delta)}{2\left(\frac{\gamma}{n}\right)(1-g)} > 0, \tag{15.19}$$

$$\frac{\hat{n}}{\hat{g}} = -\left(\frac{1+\gamma}{n}\right)\left(\frac{\hat{x}}{\hat{g}}\right) < 0, \tag{15.20}$$

$$\frac{\hat{X}}{\hat{g}} = \frac{\hat{x}}{\hat{g}} + \frac{\hat{n}}{\hat{g}} = -\left(\frac{\gamma}{n}\right)\left(\frac{\hat{x}}{\hat{g}}\right) < 0, \tag{15.21}$$

$$\frac{\hat{\mu}}{\hat{g}} = \left[\frac{(1+\mu)}{\mu}\right]\left[(\beta - b) - \left(\frac{\beta}{\varepsilon}\right)\left(\frac{\hat{X}}{\hat{g}}\right)\right] > 0. \tag{15.22}$$

As capital is used in both urban manufacturing and rural agriculture, the effect of profit-sharing on capital works through the changes in the production of goods X and Y. Given good X is capital-intensive relative to good Y by the stability condition, the increase in profit-sharing leads to a reduction in the total production of good X and hence unambiguously a fall in capital available at home:[12]

$$\frac{\hat{K}}{\hat{g}} = \lambda_{KX}\left(\frac{\hat{X}}{\hat{g}}\right) + (\lambda_{KX}^m - \lambda_{KX})\left(\frac{\hat{x}}{\hat{g}}\right) + \lambda_{KT}\left(\frac{\hat{Y}}{\hat{g}}\right) < 0. \tag{15.23}$$

We can use Figures 15.2 and 15.3 to depict the above long-run effects of profit-sharing. Using (15.8) and (15.9), the vertical shifts of schedules of $\dot{K} = 0$ and $\dot{n} = 0$ caused by changes in profit-sharing are:

$$\frac{\partial K}{\partial g|_K} = -\frac{\left(\frac{\partial r}{\partial g}\right)}{\left(\frac{\partial r}{\partial K}\right)} < 0, \tag{15.24}$$

$$\frac{\partial K}{\partial g|_n} = -\frac{\left(\frac{\partial \pi}{\partial g}\right)}{\left(\frac{\partial \pi}{\partial K}\right)} \gtrless 0, \tag{15.25}$$

---

[12]$\hat{K}/\hat{g} = (A/\lambda_{LY})(\hat{X}/\hat{g}) - (\lambda_{KX} - \lambda_{KX}^m)(\hat{x}/\hat{g}) - \mu\lambda_{LX}(\lambda_{KY}/\lambda_{LY})(\hat{\mu}/\hat{g}) < 0$, where $A > 0$ (see the Appendix).

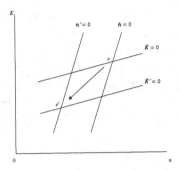

Figure 15.2   The case $\pi > (1-g)(\partial\pi/\partial g)$.

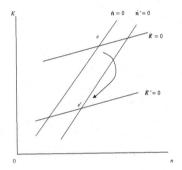

Figure 15.3   The case $\pi < (1-g)(\partial\pi/\partial g)$.

where $\partial r/\partial g < 0$, $\partial r/\partial K < 0$, $\partial\pi/\partial g \gtrless 0$, and $\partial\pi/\partial K > 0$ (see the Appendix). This implies that while an increase in profit-sharing causes a downward shift on the schedule of $\dot{K} = 0$, the $\dot{n} = 0$ schedule may shift upward or downward as depicted in Figure 15.2 or 15.3. Nevertheless, the aggregate capital stock and the number of firms in manufacturing unambiguously falls subsequently, regardless of the direction of the shift of the $\dot{n} = 0$ schedule.

In addition, since $L_X = Xm_z(z,r)$, and the home country is small in international capital markets (i.e., $r = r^*$ in the long run), the effect of profit-sharing on urban employment is:

$$\frac{\hat{L}_X}{\hat{g}} = \frac{\hat{X}}{\hat{g}} < 0, \tag{15.26}$$

which is always negative. That is, in the long run with free entry of firms and perfectly international mobility of capital, profit-sharing results in less stability of employment in the urban sector. This result is contrary to Weitzman's (1984) prescription.

15.5 Concluding Remarks

Weitzman (1984, Chapter 8) argues that, although a wage system and a share system yield basically the same equilibrium in a steady state, the share system is superior to a wage system in that the former has a stronger built-in mechanism for the economy to gravitate toward full employment. In the present chapter, we have analyzed a real-world relevant case, in which full employment is not attainable even in the long run (with international capital mobility and free entry/exit of firms) because of the existence of wage rigidity in the urban area.[13] In such an environment, profit-sharing results in falls in urban employment and inflow of foreign capital over the long run. The desirability of a share system relative to a wage system apparently hinges upon the institutional characteristics, such as wage rigidity, of an economy.

The present chapter focuses on rural versus urban wages. The welfare implications of profit-sharing can be readily derived and the results are available upon request. While we have analyzed two cases involving restrictions on both the inflow of foreign capital and entry of firms in the short run and no restrictions on capital inflows and firm entry in the long run, there are two intermediate-run cases, namely: perfect mobility of foreign capital with entry barriers and restricted foreign capital inflows with free entry of firms. It turns out that, in the former case, profit-sharing has no effect on urban output. This case is of little interest. In the latter situation, both the domestic rate of return on capital and the number of urban firms are endogenous. This makes the analysis complicated and the results are not cut and dried.

Appendix

A.1 *Comparative statics*

At the outset, we define the following notations. Let $h = (s_{KX} + s_{KY})/\theta_{LY}$ and $k = (1 + \mu)s_{LX} + s_{LY}/\theta_{LY}$, where $s_{LY} = \lambda_{LY}\sigma_Y\theta_{KY}$, $s_{KY} = \lambda_{KY}$

---

[13]Government wage policy can lead to long-run wage rigidity. See Upadhyay (1994).

$\sigma_Y \theta_{LY}$, $s_{LX} = \lambda_{LX}^m \sigma_X^m \theta_{KX}^m$ and $s_{KX} = \lambda_{KX}^m \sigma_X^m \theta_{LX}^m + \lambda_{KX}^F \sigma_X^F$. Note that the elasticities of factor substitution in sectors X and Y are defined by $\sigma_X^m = mm_{zr}/m_z m_r$ and $\sigma_Y = gg_{wr}/g_w g_r$. We also let $\sigma_X^F = -FF_{rr}/F_r F_r$. Factor shares are $\lambda_{KY} = g_r Y/K$, $\lambda_{KX}^m = m_r X/K$, etc. See Jones (1965) for details.

Solving (15.10)–(15.13) yields the comparative statics results as follows:

$$\frac{\hat{x}}{\hat{g}} = -\frac{(\beta - b)\varepsilon\delta\mu\lambda_{KY}\lambda_{LX}\theta_{KX}^m}{\Delta} > 0,$$

$$\frac{\hat{r}}{\hat{g}} = \frac{(\beta - b)\mu\lambda_{KY}\lambda_{LX}\left(\frac{1+\gamma}{n}\right)}{\Delta} < 0,$$

$$\frac{\hat{Y}}{\hat{g}} = \frac{(\beta - b)[\varepsilon\delta\mu\lambda_{KX}\lambda_{LX}\theta_{KX}^m + h\mu\lambda_{LX}\left(\frac{1+\gamma}{n}\right)}{\Delta} < 0,$$

$$\frac{\hat{\mu}}{\hat{g}} = -\frac{(\beta - b)[\varepsilon\delta\theta_{KX}^m M + (k\lambda_{KY} + h\lambda_{LY})\left(\frac{1+\gamma}{n}\right)}{\Delta} > 0,$$

where $M = \lambda_{KX}^m \lambda_{LY} - (1+\mu)\lambda_{KY}\lambda_{LX}$, being the *marginal* factor intensity condition. Note that $\Delta = -\{[\mu/(1+\mu)][\varepsilon\delta\theta_{KX}^m M + (k\lambda_{KY} + h\lambda_{LY})(1 + \gamma/n) + \mu\lambda_{LX}\lambda_{KY}[\phi(1+\gamma/n) + \beta\delta\theta_{KX}^m] < 0$. As shown below, the stability conditions of the system require that $M > 0$ and $\phi > 0$.

A.2   *Dynamics and stability*

By taking into consideration changes in n and K in the long run, we totally differentiate (15.3), (15.4), and (15.6), and combine the results to obtain:

$$-\left(\frac{1+\gamma}{n}\right)\hat{x} - \varepsilon\delta\theta_{KX}^m\hat{r} = \hat{n},$$

$$\left[\frac{\mu}{(1+\mu)}\right]\hat{\mu} + (\beta + \varepsilon)\hat{x} - \phi\hat{r} = (\beta - b)\hat{g} - \left(\frac{\beta}{\varepsilon}\right)\hat{n},$$

$$(1+\mu)\lambda_{LX}\hat{x} + \lambda_{LY}\hat{Y} + \mu\lambda_{LX}\hat{\mu} + k\hat{r} = -(1+\mu)\lambda_{LX}\hat{n},$$

$$\lambda_{KX}^m\hat{x} + \lambda_{KY}\hat{Y} - h\hat{r} = \hat{K} - \lambda_{KX}\hat{n}.$$

Solving the above equations, we obtain:

$$\frac{\hat{r}}{\hat{K}} = \frac{\lambda_{LY}\left(\frac{1+\gamma}{n}\right)\left[\frac{\mu}{(1+\mu)}\right]}{\Delta} < 0,$$

$$\frac{\hat{r}}{\hat{n}} = -\frac{\left\{\mu\lambda_{KX}\lambda_{LY}\left(\frac{\gamma}{n}\right)\left(\frac{\beta}{\varepsilon}\right) + \left[\frac{\mu}{(1+\mu)}\right]\left[A\left(\frac{\gamma}{n}\right) + \lambda_{LY}(\lambda_{KX} - \lambda_{KX}^m)\right]\right\}}{\Delta} > 0,$$

where $A = \lambda_{KX}\lambda_{LY} - (1+\mu)\lambda_{KY}\lambda_{LX}$, representing the *average* factor intensity condition.

The stability conditions of the system in (15.15) and (15.16) require:

$$\text{trace} = \rho'\left(\frac{\partial r}{\partial K}\right) + \varphi'\left(\frac{\partial \pi}{\partial n}\right) < 0,$$

$$\text{determinant} = \rho'\varphi'\left[\left(\frac{\partial r}{\partial K}\right)\left(\frac{\partial \pi}{\partial n}\right) - \left(\frac{\partial r}{\partial n}\right)\left(\frac{\partial \pi}{\partial K}\right)\right] > 0,$$

where the partial derivatives of π with respect to K and n are:

$$\frac{\partial \pi}{\partial K} = -\frac{2px\delta\lambda_{LY}\theta_{KX}\left(\frac{\gamma}{n}\right)\left[\frac{\mu}{(1+\mu)}\right]}{K\Delta - \left(\frac{F_r r}{K}\right)\left(\frac{\hat{r}}{K}\right)} > 0,$$

$\partial\pi/\partial n = -(1 - g)(px/\varepsilon n)[(1 - \gamma/n)(\hat{x}/\hat{n}) + 1 + \varepsilon\delta\theta_{KX}^m(\hat{r}/\hat{n})] - (F_r r/n)(\hat{r}/\hat{n}) < 0$. Thus, a sufficient condition for $\partial r/\partial K < 0$, $\partial r/\partial n > 0$, $\partial\pi/\partial K > 0$, and $\partial\pi/\partial n < 0$ is that $\phi > 0$, $M > 0$, and $A > 0$.

Note that the partial derivative of π with respect to α in (15.25) is $\partial\pi/\partial g = -(p-m)x - 2(\beta-b)px\delta\mu\lambda_{LX}\lambda_{KY}\theta_{KX}^m(\gamma/n)/g\Delta - (F_r r/g)(\hat{r}/\hat{g})\gtrless 0$ by the stability conditions.

Chapter 16

Privatization and
Foreign Competition
in Developing Economies

16.1 Introduction

The late "Iron Lady," Baroness Margaret Thatcher, is regarded as the "mother" of moves toward privatization across the world. In many countries even supposedly left-wing governments have sold public assets to private sectors. The Labor Party-run government in Australia privatized banks and airlines. The Marxist government in Bengal India also privatized many public assets. In addition to privatization, the world has also witnessed the delivery of a more market-oriented agenda in many former Communist countries. The rise of globalization and liberal reforms has been closely connected with trade reforms. In spite of such movements toward privatization and trade reforms, very few studies have been undertaken to assess their impact on wage inequalities. It should be noted that while privatization alters the rules by which firms are managed and governed, trade reforms change the nature of markets in which the firms operate.

Wage inequality between skilled and unskilled labor has been the focus of attention of many studies. In the literature, the skill premium can be primarily attributed to trade and technology:[1] The increased wage of the skilled comes from skilled-biased technological progress, while the falling wage of the unskilled is due to imports of cheaper unskilled-labor-intensive goods or outsourcing of unskilled-labor-intensive stages abroad.[2] The analyses on the skill premium mainly focus on the product restructuring toward

---

[1]The trade argument for rising wage inequality can be found in Wood (1995) and Leamer (1998), while the technology reason is provided in Francois and Nelson (1998).

[2]See Feenstra and Hanson (1996).

skill-biased technologies, often occurring in advanced economies. Nonetheless, for developing economies, rising wage inequality may be led by different sources, such as distortions, policies, and reforms. Studies have emerged on skill formation and wage inequality for developing economies. For example, Davis (1998) attributes the cause to unemployment, Kar and Beladi (2004) to migration, and Feenstra and Hanson (1997) and Marjit *et al.* (2003) to foreign direct investment (FDI). These studies are primarily on market distortions and the associated factor immobility. However, the impacts of economic policies and reforms on relative wages of the skilled and unskilled workers in developing countries have by and large not been examined. In this chapter we address these issues by analyzing the effects of policies and reforms on wage inequality. Specifically, we consider the following questions: Does privatization cause rising wage inequality in developing countries? And does increased foreign competition increase relative wage dispersion?[3]

Section 16.2 provides a dual structure for a developing economy, in which a state-owned monopolistic firm is in the urban sector while competitive and privately owned firms are located in the rural sector. Using this model, the effects of privatization and competition on the wages of the skilled and unskilled are examined in Section 16.3. In addition, the welfare implications of this policy and reform are discussed in Section 16.4. Section 16.5 offers concluding remarks.

16.2   The Model

We consider a developing economy that consists of two sectors: urban manufacture and rural agriculture. A partially state-owned firm in the urban area produces manufacturing good X, while competitive firms in the rural area produce agricultural good Y. The country exports good Y and imports good X. There are no impediments for the exports of good Y, but to protect the state-owned firm the government imposes a quota Q of good X on foreign exporters. Choosing good Y as the numeraire, the domestic relative price of good X is denoted by p.

Consumers' demand for these two goods, D_X and D_Y, and the utility function is quasi-linear: $U(D_X, D_Y) = u(D_X) + D_Y$, where $u'(D_X) > 0$. Letting I denote income, utility maximization subject to the budget

---

[3] Neary (2002) examines the effect of increased foreign competition on wage inequality for advanced economies, in which firms are privately owned.

constraint, $I = pD_X + D_Y$, gives the inverse demand function for good X: $p = p(D_X)$, with $p' < 0$, and the indirect utility function is: $V = V(p, I)$, with $V_p = -D_X$ and $V_I = 1$. In equilibrium, demand for good X meets its supply from domestic production and imports, i.e., $D_X = X + Q$.

Turn to the production side of the economy. In the urban sector, the state-owned monopolistic firm produces good X under increasing returns to scale: skilled labor along with capital is needed for producing fixed inputs, used along with unskilled labor and capital in production. Letting $F(\cdot)$ and $m(\cdot)$ be the fixed and marginal costs, total cost for producing good X is: $C(w_U, w_S, r, X) = F(w_S, r) + m(w_U, r)X$, where w_U and w_S are respectively the urban unskilled and skilled wages, and r is the capital-rental rate.

By the envelope property, the employments of skilled labor, unskilled labor, and capital in sector X are: $S = F_w(w_S, r)$, $L_X = m_w(w_U, r)X$, and $K_X = F_r(w_S, r) + m_r(w_U, r)X$, where the subscript represents the partial derivative. Since the firm in sector X is state owned, it cares not only about profits but is also welfare generated. The profit of firm X is: $\pi = p(X + Q)X - C(w_U, w_S, r, X)$, and welfare is the sum of the profit and consumer surplus: $W = \pi + CS$, where $CS = u(X + Q) - p(X + Q)X$. Therefore, the objective of the firm is to maximize a weighted average of profits and welfare, $k\pi + (1 - k)W$, where $k \in [0, 1]$.[4] Note that the weight k represents the degree of private ownership: the firm is fully state-owned when $k = 0$, whereas it is completely privately owned when $k = 1$. Hence, the larger the value of k, the greater the private ownership.[5] The firm chooses the output X to maximize the objective, and the consequent first-order condition is:

$$p(X + Q) + kp'(X + Q)X = m(w_U, r), \qquad (16.1)$$

where the left two terms express the marginal revenue (MR) of producing good X. For the fully state-owned firm ($k = 0$), marginal cost pricing is used

---

[4]This objective function of profits and welfare for the partially privatized firm is adapted from Matsumura (1998), and it utilized by Chao and Yu (2006) to examine the effect of privatization on optimum tariff.

[5]For generating some sort of consumer surplus, profit of the public enterprise may be negative. However, public firms can be profit making. Telstra in Australia is a good example of partial privatization: it does not charge monopoly prices and follows the strategy of privatization. This is because the Australian government is very concerned with ensuring services to the rural region and consumers do not pay for telephone services at the true cost of providing them.

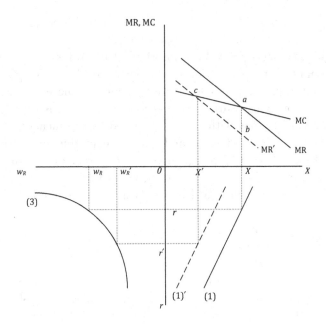

Figure 16.1   Privatization or competition on wage inequality.

in (16.1). When partial privatization takes place ($k > 0$) and because $p'(\cdot)$
< 0, the MR curve in (16.1) shifts downward in Figure 16.1. In addition,
the direct effect of a rise in Q on MR is: $\partial MR/\partial Q = (1 + kes)p'$, where
$s = X/(X + Q) < 1$ and $e = (X + Q)p''/p' = 0$. By the stability condition,
$1 + es > 0$, as shown in the Appendix, we have $\partial MR/\partial Q < 0$ and hence
increased foreign competition also causes the MR curve of the domestic
firm to shift downward as shown in Figure 16.1.[6]

Besides the welfare consideration, the state-owned urban firm also sets
a minimum wage for unskilled labor, which exceeds the unskilled wage in
the rural sector. The higher urban wage leads to rural–urban migration of
unskilled workers, thereby resulting in urban unemployment, L_u. Defining
the unemployment ratio of unskilled workers in the urban sector by $\mu = L_u/L_X$, the Harris–Todaro (1970) migration equilibrium is:

$$\frac{w_U}{(1 + \mu)} = w_R, \tag{16.2}$$

---

[6]See Chao and Yu (1997a) for a related study.

where w_R is the rural unskilled wage and $1/(1+\mu)$ expresses the probability to find a job for unskilled workers in the urban area. Thus, (16.2) states, in equilibrium, that the expected urban unskilled wage equals the rural unskilled wage.

As for the production of good Y, it requires unskilled labor and capital under constant returns to scale. The corresponding unit-cost function is denoted by $\beta(w_R, r)$, and the demands for unskilled labor and capital are: $L_Y = \beta_w(w_R, r)Y$ and $K_Y = \beta_r(w_R, r)Y$. Under perfect competition, unit cost equals the price of good Y:

$$\beta(w_R, r) = 1, \qquad (16.3)$$

where the price of good Y is normalized to unity.

Consider next the factor markets. The equilibrium conditions for skilled labor, unskilled labor, and capital are:

$$F_w(w_S, r) = S, \qquad (16.4)$$

$$(1 + \mu)m_w(w_U, r)X + \beta_w(w_R, r)Y = L, \qquad (16.5)$$

$$F_r(w_S, r) + m_r(w_U, r)X + \beta_r(w_R, r)Y = K, \qquad (16.6)$$

where S, L, and K denote the amounts of skilled labor, unskilled labor, and capital available in the economy.

Equations (16.1)–(16.6) describe the dual developing economy, which consists of six unknowns — w_R, w_S, r, μ, X, and Y. We will use this model to study the effects of partial privatization and foreign competition on the wages of skilled and unskilled labor. In addition, the implications on social welfare will be examined.

16.3 Wage Inequality

In this chapter, partial privatization is represented by a rise in the weight k toward profit maximization while foreign competition is reflected by an increase in the quota on foreign exports Q. Due to monopoly in sector X, changes in k or Q affect the marginal revenue of producing good X and hence the return to capital by (16.1). Letting a circumflex represent a percentage change, these effects can be obtained by totally differentiating (16.1):

$$\varepsilon b\theta^m_{KX}\hat{r} = -ks\hat{k} - (1-s)(1+kes)\hat{Q} - s[1 + k(1+es)]\hat{X}, \qquad (16.7)$$

where $\varepsilon = -p/(X + Q)p' > 0$, being the price elasticity of demand for good X. Note that $b = m/p < 1$ and θ_{jX}^m represents the distributive share of the jth factor in the X's variable cost.

As indicated by changes in k or Q and X on the right-hand side of (16.7), the policy of partial privatization or foreign competition not only directly but also indirectly influences the marginal revenue of producing good X. The former causes the MR curve to shift downward, while the latter leads to a movement along the curve via the change in X. Consequently, given the urban unskilled wage, the change in the capital return in (16.7) reflects the change in MR. This then affects the wages of unskilled and skilled labor according to (16.3) and (16.4), as follows:

$$\hat{w}_R = -\left(\frac{\theta_{KY}}{\theta_{LY}}\right)\hat{r}, \tag{16.8}$$

$$\hat{w}_s = \hat{r} - \frac{\hat{S}}{S_{SX}^F}, \tag{16.9}$$

where θ_{jY} represents the distributive share of the jth factor in industry Y and S_{SX}^F expresses the substitution effect in the demand for skilled labor in sector X.[7] In addition, the change in the rural unskilled wage causes rural–urban migration, thereby affecting the urban unemployment ratio by (16.2):

$$\hat{\mu} = -\left[\frac{(1+\mu)}{\mu}\right]\hat{w}_R. \tag{16.10}$$

To get the overall changes in the skilled and unskilled wages, we need to obtain the effects of partial privatization or foreign competition on the output of good X. Totally differentiating the resource constraints in (16.4) and (16.5), we have:

$$(1 + \mu)\delta_{LX}^m\hat{X} + \delta_{LY}\hat{Y}$$
$$= \hat{L} - [(1+\mu)S_{LX}^m + S_{LY}]\hat{r} + S_{LY}\hat{W}_R - \mu\delta_{LX}^m\hat{\mu}, \tag{16.11}$$

$$\delta_{KX}^m\hat{X} + \delta_{KY}\hat{Y}$$
$$= \hat{K} + (S_{KX}^m + S_{KY})\hat{r} - S_{KY}\hat{W}_R - S_{KX}^F(\hat{W}_S - \hat{r}), \tag{16.12}$$

---

[7]Since the fixed cost of sector X is $F(w_S, r)$, the elasticity of factor substitution between skilled labor and capital is $\sigma_X^F = FF_{wr}/F_wF_r$. Following Jones (1965), the substitution effect in skilled labor demand is: $S_{SX}^F = \sigma_X^F\theta_{KX}^F$ where $\theta_{KX}^F(= rF_r/F)$ is the distributive share of capital in the fixed cost of sector X.

where δ_{jX}^m and δ_{jY} are respectively the employment shares of factor j in industry X's and Y's variable inputs. Also, s_{ji} captures the effect of a change in the factor prices on the demand for factor j in sector i.[8] Substituting (16.7)–(16.10) into (16.11) and (16.12), we can solve for the effects of partial privatization or foreign competition on the output of good X:

$$\frac{\hat{X}}{\hat{k}} = -\frac{ksT}{\Delta} < 0, \tag{16.13}$$

$$\frac{\hat{X}}{\hat{Q}} = -\frac{(1-s)(1+kes)T}{\Delta} < 0, \tag{16.14}$$

where $\Delta = s[1+k(1+es)]T - \varepsilon b\theta_{LY}\theta_{KX}^m\delta > 0$ by stability and $T > 0$.[9] Note that $\delta[= (1+\mu)\delta_{LX}^m\delta_{KY} - \delta_{KX}^m\delta_{LY}]$ is positive (negative) if industry X is relatively labor-intensive to industry Y in variable inputs. Hence, regardless of the factor intensity, partial privatization or foreign competition puts a pressure on the output of good X and the consequent impact on its price can be obtained by differentiating the inverse demand function of good X, $p = p(X + Q)$:

$$\frac{\hat{p}}{\hat{k}} = -\left(\frac{s}{\varepsilon}\right)\left(\frac{\hat{X}}{\hat{k}}\right) > 0, \tag{16.15}$$

$$\frac{\hat{p}}{\hat{Q}} = -\left(\frac{1}{\varepsilon}\right)\left[1 - s + s\left(\frac{\hat{X}}{\hat{Q}}\right)\right] \gtrless 0. \tag{16.16}$$

Equation (16.15) states that partial privatization reduces domestic production of good X, thereby raising its price. However, in (16.16), depending on the relative increase in foreign exports and the fall in domestic production, the price effect of foreign competition is ambiguous. Furthermore, increased foreign competition can raise the domestic price of good X, if its domestic supply falls (i.e., $-dX/dQ > 1$).[10]

We are now ready to examine the effect of partial privatization or foreign competition on the wages of skilled and unskilled labor. From (16.7), partial privatization or foreign competition in sector X immediately causes

---

[8]For instance, $s_{LY} = \sigma_Y\theta_{KY}\lambda_{LY}$, where $\sigma_Y = gg_{wr}/g_wg_r$.

[9]We define A as: $A = \lambda_{LY}s_{KY} + \lambda_{KY}s_{LY} + \theta_{LY}\lambda_{LY}S_{KX}^m + (1+\mu)\lambda_{KY}\lambda_{LX}^m$.

[10]From (16.14), we can write: $-dX/dQ = (1+kes)/[1+kes+(k-\varepsilon b\theta_{LY}\theta_{KX}^m\delta/sT)] \gtrless 1$ if $ks \gtrless \varepsilon b\theta_{LY}\theta_{KX}^m\delta/T$. Here, the positive δ (i.e., the urban sector is relatively unskilled-intensive in variable inputs) is a necessary condition for $-dX/dQ > 1$.

a downward shift of its MR curve, and then the induced fall in the production of good X raises the marginal revenue along the MR curve. The changes in MR are depicted in Figure 16.1 from point a to b and then to point c. The higher MR at point c yields a higher return to capital, which leads to a higher wage for skilled labor but a lower wage for rural unskilled labor. These results on the wages can be obtained by substituting (16.13) and (16.14) into (16.7)–(16.9):

$$\frac{\hat{W}_R}{\hat{k}} = -\frac{ks\theta_{KY}\delta}{\Delta}, \tag{16.17}$$

$$\frac{\hat{W}_S}{\hat{k}} = -\left(\frac{\theta_{LY}}{\theta_{KY}}\right)\left(\frac{\hat{W}_R}{\hat{K}}\right), \tag{16.18}$$

$$\frac{\hat{W}_R}{\hat{Q}} = -\frac{(1-s)(1+kes)\theta_{KY}\delta}{\Delta}, \tag{16.19}$$

$$\frac{\hat{W}_S}{\hat{Q}} = -\left(\frac{\theta_{LY}}{\theta_{KY}}\right)\left(\frac{\hat{W}_R}{\hat{Q}}\right). \tag{16.20}$$

Therefore, partial privatization or foreign competition can lead to a rise in the skilled wage but cause a fall in the rural unskilled wage, if the urban sector is relatively unskilled-intensive to the rural sector in variable inputs. In addition, by (16.10), the fall in the rural unskilled wage results in rural–urban migration, giving rise to a higher urban unemployment ratio:

$$\frac{\hat{\mu}}{\hat{k}} = -\left[\frac{(1+\mu)}{\mu}\right]\left(\frac{\hat{W}_R}{\hat{k}}\right), \tag{16.21}$$

$$\frac{\hat{\mu}}{\hat{Q}} = -\left[\frac{(1+\mu)}{\mu}\right]\left(\frac{\hat{W}_R}{\hat{Q}}\right). \tag{16.22}$$

Note that rising wage inequality for the developing economy also can be attributed to the changes in factor endowments. From (16.7)–(16.12), we have:

$$\frac{\hat{W}_R}{\hat{L}} = -\frac{s[1+k(1+es)]\delta_{KY}\theta_{KY}}{\Delta} < 0, \tag{16.23}$$

$$\frac{\hat{W}_S}{\hat{L}} = -\left(\frac{\theta_{LY}}{\theta_{KY}}\right)\left(\frac{\hat{W}_R}{\hat{L}}\right) > 0. \tag{16.24}$$

$$\frac{\hat{W}_R}{\hat{S}} = -\frac{s[1 + k(1 + es)]\delta_{LY}\theta_{KY}\left(\frac{S_{KX}^F}{S_{SX}^F}\right)}{\Delta} > 0, \tag{16.25}$$

$$\frac{\hat{W}_S}{\hat{S}} = -\left(\frac{\theta_{LY}}{\theta_{KY}}\right)\left(\frac{\hat{W}_R}{\hat{S}}\right) < 0. \tag{16.26}$$

$$\frac{\hat{W}_R}{\hat{K}} = \frac{s[1 + k(1 + es)]\delta_{LY}\theta_{KY}}{\Delta} > 0, \tag{16.27}$$

$$\frac{\hat{W}_S}{\hat{K}} = -\left(\frac{\theta_{LY}}{\theta_{KY}}\right)\left(\frac{\hat{W}_R}{\hat{K}}\right) < 0. \tag{16.28}$$

Therefore, either inflows of unskilled labor or outflows of skilled labor and capital aggravate wage inequality for the economy. In summary, we have the following results.

Proposition 16.1 *For a developing economy with a state-owned firm in the urban sector, partial privatization or increased foreign competition can lead to rising wage inequality between the skilled and unskilled labor. In addition, changes in the endowments, such as inflows of unskilled labor or outflows of skilled labor and capital, can also give rise to the wage premium for skilled labor.*

16.4 Social Welfare

We turn next to examine the welfare implications of partial privatization and foreign competition for the developing economy, in which social welfare can be represented by the indirect utility function, $V = V(p, I)$, where I is national income. Note that national income comes from factor income plus profits of the state-owned firm in the urban sector: $I = w_U L_X + w_R L_Y + w_S S + rK + \pi$. Totally differentiating the indirect utility function and then using (16.1)–(16.6), we obtain the change in welfare:

$$dV = (p - m)dX - Qdp - w_R L_X d\mu. \tag{16.29}$$

Equation (16.29) captures three distortions in the economy: monopoly power of the state-owned firm, export restriction on foreign firms, and unemployment in the urban sector. Hence, lowering the distortions can improve social welfare in (16.29).

Firstly, the welfare effect of partial privatization can be obtained as follows:

$$\frac{dV}{dk} = (p - m)\left(\frac{dX}{dk}\right) - Q\left(\frac{dp}{dk}\right) - w_R L_X\left(\frac{d\mu}{dk}\right). \qquad (16.30)$$

Since $dX/dk < 0$, $dp/dk > 0$ and $d\mu/dk > 0$ by (16.13), (16.15), and (16.21), we have $dV/dk < 0$ in (16.30). Partial privatization unambiguously reduces social welfare because it worsens the monopoly power of the state-owned firm, increases the price of good X, and raises the unemployment ratio in the urban sector.

Secondly, from (16.29), the welfare effect of increased foreign competition is:

$$\frac{dV}{dQ} = (p - m)\left(\frac{dX}{dQ}\right) - Q\left(\frac{dp}{dQ}\right) - w_R L_X\left(\frac{d\mu}{dQ}\right). \qquad (16.31)$$

Although foreign competition reduces domestic output ($dX/dQ < 0$ in [16.14]) and raises urban unemployment ratio ($d\mu/dQ > 0$ in [16.22]), the welfare effect of foreign competition is in general ambiguous because $dp/dQ \gtrless 0$ in (16.16). However, if the increased foreign exports crowd out more domestic production of good X (i.e., $-dX/dQ > 1$), we have $dp/dQ > 0$ in (16.16) and hence $dV/dQ < 0$ in (16.31). The following proposition is immediate.

Proposition 16.2 *For the developing economy with a state-owned monopolistic firm in the urban sector, increasing partial privatization or foreign competition lowers the urban output. The output reduction can lead to rises in the urban goods price and unemployment ratio. These factors together yield negative impacts on the social welfare of the economy.*

16.5   Concluding Remarks

Using a dual structure depicting a developing economy, this chapter has examined the issues of partial privatization and foreign competition on wage inequality and social welfare. Increasing partial privatization or foreign competition can lead to wage inequality between the skilled and unskilled labor. In addition, rising wage inequality can be explained by the traditional reasons such as inflows of unskilled labor or outflows of skilled labor and capital. Further, partial privatization or foreign competition reduces the urban output, thereby raising the good price and unemployment ratio in the urban area. These factors lower the social welfare of the economy.

In this chapter, the efficiency issue of privatization has been ignored. Although empirical studies find mixed results of privatization on production efficiency and profits,[11] it should be of interest for future research to consider the efficiency issue in the general equilibrium analysis of privatization.[12]

Appendix: Stability

Let a dot over a variable be the time derivative, and the adjustments of the system can be expressed as:

$$
\begin{pmatrix} \dot{X} \\ \dot{Y} \\ \dot{W}_R \\ \dot{r} \end{pmatrix} = \begin{pmatrix} -S[1+k(1+es)] & 0 & 0 & -\varepsilon b\theta_{KX}^m \\ 0 & 0 & -\theta_{LY} & -\theta_{KY} \\ (1+\mu)\delta_{LX}^m & \delta_{LY} & -[(1+\mu)\delta_{LX}^m + S_{LY}] & (1+\mu)S_{LX}^m + S_{LY} \\ \delta_{KX}^m & \delta_{KY} & S_{KY} & -(S_{KX}^m + S_{KY}) \end{pmatrix} \begin{pmatrix} \hat{X} \\ \hat{Y} \\ \hat{W}_R \\ \hat{r} \end{pmatrix}.
$$

The principal minors of the above coefficient matrixes are:

$$\Delta_1 = -s[1+k(1+es)],$$
$$\Delta_2 = 0,$$
$$\Delta_3 = -s[1+k(1+es)]\delta_{LY}\theta_{LY},$$
$$\Delta_4 = \Delta.$$

The stability condition requires that the odd principal minors are non-positive and the even principal minors are non-negative. Hence, we need (a) $1 + es > 0$ and (b) $\Delta > 0$ for stability.

---

[11] For example, Oum *et al.* (2000) show weak evidence of privatization on efficiency for the airline industry. Dewenter and Malatesta (2001) also report poor long-run performance of corporations after privatization for a large cross-sectional sample.

[12] We thank the referee for pointing out that employment, rather than profits, may be another consideration for the public firm.

Chapter 17

Domestic Equity Control, Capital Accumulation, and Welfare: Theory and China's Evidence

17.1 Introduction

China has experienced remarkable economic growth since 1978 when its open-door policy and economic reform began. One important characteristic of the fast-growing Chinese economy is its increasing outward orientation. There has been a rapid inflow of foreign direct investment (FDI) into China.[1] Since the early 1990s, China has been one of the largest FDI recipients in the world. The World Bank has credited FDI as a main driver of China's economic success. An increasing amount of literature has indicated the positive role played by FDI in the economic development of China (see, for example, Kueh, 1992; Sun, 1998). However, the sectoral distribution of FDI in China is highly skewed. By 2000, more than 55% of the FDI has been concentrated in manufacturing industries such as garments, leather, and plastic products. Within the services sector, an overwhelming proportion of FDI has been in real estate (18.3%), while the FDI in high value-added services such as finance and insurance (0.2%), wholesale and retail trade (3.1%), and transport, storage, post, and telecommunications services (4.0%) has been low. Like many countries in this region,[2] China has sectoral

---

[1]Since the early 1990s, various incentives, like preferential tax rates, export duty rebates, etc., have been given to foreign firms. Nevertheless, as pointed out in Huang (1998, p. 11), one of the most important characteristics of the Chinese FDI regulatory schemes is its informal and discretionary aspects, offered by local governments to foreign investors from particular regions, such as Hong Kong and Taiwan. Also see Ng and Tuan (2001) for reference.

[2]For example, in 1984 India, Morocco, the Philippines, and South Korea restricted foreign ownership to 40, 50, 60 and 49%, respectively, and such ownership restrictions are still a common practice today especially in developing nations. A survey conducted by

and ownership restrictions regarding FDI. For example, foreign firms have been banned from entering the telecommunications industry. Their activity has been limited to technology licensing and the manufacturing of digital switching equipment. There are many reasons for imposing restrictions on ownership.[3] In the case of China, the most notable ones are probably to protect domestic firms and to tap into economic rents. Ownership restrictions play an important role in explaining the skewed sectoral pattern of China's FDI.

The market access issue was the central theme in the bilateral negotiations between China and the United States in China's bid to join the World Trade Organization (WTO) in 2001. China's offer for WTO entry involves quite substantial reductions in tariffs and NTBs. For example, China's accession into the WTO permits foreign telecommunications service suppliers to establish joint-venture enterprises in several cities inside China with no more than 25% ownership, and China has committed to further liberalize its practices on foreign investment. Within one year of accession, the services are expanded to other cities with foreign ownership no more than 35%. Within three years of accession, 49% ownership is allowed for foreign investment in all telecommunications services. China also lifts the geographical restrictions on foreign insurance companies and permits a 50% foreign ownership in life insurance and 51% in non-life insurance firms. These ratios have been increased to 100% wholly foreign-owned subsidiaries. In short, China's concessions over foreign ownership vary from industry to industry within the services sector. For some other products, such as cereals, tobacco, fuels, and minerals, China reserves the 100% right of state trading inside the country. Nevertheless, many of the restrictions imposed on foreign companies in China have been eliminated or considerably eased after a three-year phase-out period.[4]

A review of the literature reveals that the study on the impact of permitting foreign ownership in the form of joint ventures or wholly-owned has been largely confined to the firm-level variables, i.e., firm output, price, revenue, and profits.[5] Nonetheless, the full ramifications of foreign

---

Ching *et al.* (2001) also indicated that the most frequently encountered non-tariff barrier (NTB) to inward FDI in the Asia-Pacific region is the restriction on foreign ownership.

[3] Conklin and Lecraw (1997) provide detailed discussion on the reasons and consequences of restricting foreign ownership for these economies.

[4] See the WTO News dated September 17, 2001 (http://www.wto.org/english/news_e/news01_e/news01_e.htm).

[5] See, for example, Das and Katayama (2000).

ownership on macro, country-level variables, e.g., capital accumulation and economic welfare, remain by and large unexplored. This chapter is, therefore, to fill this lacuna by developing a simple framework to examine how equity controls affect accumulation of domestic assets and how the resulting asset accumulation affects output and national welfare. The implications of domestic equity controls on sectoral output and national welfare deduced will be tested using cross-section data for the Chinese economy.

To accomplish the above objectives, we organize this chapter, drawing on Chao *et al.* (2002), as follows. Section 17.2 presents a dynamic, open economy with both domestic-owned and foreign-funded enterprises. A domestic equity requirement is imposed on foreign firms, and its impacts on the accumulation of domestic assets and welfare will then be examined. Section 17.3 provides an empirical study of changes in domestic assets on China's industry outputs. Section 17.4 offers some concluding remarks.

17.2   The Model

In this section, we use a general equilibrium model to highlight the influence of domestic equity controls on capital accumulation and hence economic welfare in a dynamic, open economy. Consider that the host country consists of two types of firms: domestic owned and foreign funded. Domestic firms produce two kinds of goods, agriculture and manufacturing, and their production functions are: $Y = Y(L_Y, T)$ and $X_l = X^l(L_l, K_l)$, where labor $(L_i, i = Y, l)$ is perfectly mobile between sectors, but land (T) and domestic assets (K_l) in the form of physical and financial capital are assumed specific to sector Y and X, respectively. Concomitantly, foreign-funded firms in the economy produce manufacturing good X only, and the production function is: $X_m = X^m(L_m, K_m)$, where L_m and K_m are labor and capital assets used. The production structure of the economy displays a mixture of the Ricardo–Viner specific factors and Heckscher–Ohlin mobile capital models. This framework is amenable for the purpose of studying the implications of domestic equity controls on the economy.

Following Hill and Mendez (1992) and Chao and Yu (1996a, 2000), the host country imposes a domestic equity requirement on foreign-funded firms; say, $\beta\%$ of capital assets in foreign firms must be held by domestic residents, i.e., $K_m^d = \beta K_m$, where K_m^d denotes the domestic capital assets used in the foreign firms. Thus, total domestic capital assets of the host economy, K^d, consist of capital in the domestic firms plus $\beta\%$ capital in the foreign-funded firms, $K^d = K_l + K_m^d$. Note that foreign capital assets in foreign-funded firms are $K_m^f = (1 - \beta)K_m$, and total capital assets in the host economy are $K = K_l + K_m$.

We assume that domestic labor $(\bar{L})$ and land $(\bar{T})$ are fully employed: $L_Y + L_l + L_m = \bar{L}$ and $T = \bar{T}$. We use $L = L_Y + L_l$ to denote the workers employed in domestic firms, and $\bar{L} - L$ for the workers in foreign firms. The production side of the economy can be respectively summarized by the revenue functions of domestic and foreign firms, $R(L, K^d - \beta K_m)$ and $R^m(\bar{L} - L, K_m)$,[6] in which goods prices are given and normalized to unity.[7] By Shephard's lemma, the first-order partial derivatives of the revenue functions represent the rates of factor returns. Note that in the presence of a local equity requirement, the *effective* rate of assets return for foreign firms is the weighted average of the domestic and foreign rates:

$$R_K^m(\bar{L} - L, K_m) = \beta R_K(L, K^d - \beta K_m) + (1 - \beta)r^*, \qquad (17.1)$$

where r^* is the given cost for acquiring foreign capital assets in the world market. It is reasonable for us to assume that the domestic capital-rental rate is higher than the foreign rate, $R_K > r^*$, so that inflows of foreign assets take place. Equation (17.1) thus determines K_m.

Turn to the demand side of the economy. The agents choose the levels of consumption of both goods, C_i, and labor allocation, L, to maximize the intertemporal utility function:

$$\text{Max } W = \int_0^\infty U(C_X, C_Y)e^{-\rho t}dt, \qquad (17.2)$$

subject to the saving behavior in terms of the accumulation of domestic capital assets given by:

$$\dot{K}^d = R(L, K^d - \beta K_m) + R^m(\bar{L} - L, K_m) - C_X - C_Y - r^*(1 - \beta)K_m,$$

---

[6]The definitions of the revenue functions are: $R(L, K^d - \beta K_m) = \max\{Y(L_Y, T) + X(L_l, K_l) : L = L_Y + L_l, K_l = K^d - \beta K_m\}$ with respect to L_Y, L_l and K_l, and $R^m(\bar{L} - L, K_m) = X^m(L_m, K_m)$, where $L_m = \bar{L} - L$.

[7]Since the goods prices are fixed to the world prices, the terms-of-trade effect is not considered. We adopt this small-country assumption by focusing on the capital accumulation effect in the long run. Another justification for the small-country assumption is that China's exports only account for a small share (4% in 2000) in the world market, despite the fact that China is currently the largest FDI recipient among developing countries.

and the initial stock of domestic assets $K^d(0) = K_0^d$. Note that in (17.2), $U(\cdot)$ is the instantaneous utility function and ρ denotes the discount rate. As usual, the two goods are assumed to be normal in consumption and the instantaneous utility function is concave.

17.2.1   *Temporary resource allocation*

From the solution to the optimization problem in (17.2), we obtain the allocation of labor between domestic and foreign firms:

$$R_L(L, K^d - \beta K_m) = R_L^m(\bar{L} - L, K_m), \tag{17.3}$$

where R_L and R_L^m are, respectively, the wage rates in domestic and foreign firms. Equation (17.3) states that, in equilibrium, the wage rates will be equalized between domestic and foreign firms.

Temporary equilibrium is characterized by a given stock of domestic capital in the host economy. In equilibrium, the inflow of foreign capital is affected by its effective rate of return in (17.1) and the employment of labor is dependent on the wage rate in (17.3). Based on these two equations, we can then determine the amount of labor allocated in domestic firms and the amount of capital assets used in foreign firms. Both variables are functions of the domestic capital stock, K^d, and the policy instrument of domestic equity control, β. Since domestic and foreign firms in sector X form a Heckscher–Ohlin system, the factor-intensity condition plays a crucial role in the following comparative static analysis.

Consider the change of the domestic capital stock. If foreign firms are capital(labor)-intensive relative to domestic firms, a rise in the domestic capital stock increases (reduces) the output of foreign firms at the expanse of the domestic output. This lowers (raises) the demand for labor in domestic firms $[\partial L/\partial K^d < (>)0]$ but raises (lowers) the demand for capital assets in foreign firms $[\partial K_m/\partial K^d > (<)0]$.[8]

Turn next to the effects of tightening equity controls on foreign firms. An increase in domestic equity requirements directly raises the foreign demand for domestic capital. However, the higher rental cost of domestic capital hampers the production of foreign firms, which indirectly reduces their demand for capital assets. These positive direct and negative indirect effects render an indeterminate shift in the demand for capital assets by foreign

---

[8]The mathematic derivations are given in Appendix A.1.

firms $[\partial K_m/\partial \beta < (>)0]$. In addition, the changes in the foreign demand for capital affect the availability of capital assets to domestic firms, thereby altering their production via the Rybczynski effect. Specifically, the output of domestic firms increases (decreases) if domestic firms are relatively labor(capital)-intensive. Consequently, the labor demand in domestic firms rises (falls) $[\partial L/\partial \beta > (<)0]$.

17.2.2   Changes in the domestic capital stock

In the long run, domestic capital becomes a variable and it can be affected by the policy of equity restrictions. Using the comparative statics results obtained under the temporary equilibrium, we can examine the change in the domestic capital stock in the long run. The steady-state equilibrium of the economy can be characterized by no capital gains (losses) in domestic assets and no changes in its level of the stock. From these two conditions, we can obtain:

$$\frac{dK^d}{d\beta} = -\left(\frac{DR_{KK}}{\lambda B}\right)\left[K_m + \beta\left(\frac{dK_m}{d\beta}\right) - \left(\frac{R_{KL}}{R_{KK}}\right)\left(\frac{dL}{d\beta}\right)\right], \quad (17.4)$$

where, as defined in the Appendix, $D > 0$ and $B > 0$, and λ denotes the shadow price of domestic capital assets. The first term on the right-hand side of (17.4) expresses that tightening domestic equity requirements directly increases the demand for domestic capital by foreign firms. However, the induced higher rental cost lowers the demand for domestic capital, and even worse that foreign firms will hire additional labor to substitute for capital. These indirect effects are represented in the last two terms on (17.4).

The results in (17.4) can be depicted in Figure 17.1, in which the stable arm is represented by the SS schedule. The initial situation is at point E, which is the intersection of the equilibrium shadow price, λ, and the stock, K^d, of domestic capital assets. A rise in the domestic capital requirement on foreign firms can cause accumulation (reduction) of domestic capital, if the direct capital increase is larger (smaller) than the induced reduction via the higher rental cost. This consequently results in a jump of the shadow price of domestic capital from point E to point $U(D)$, thereby leading to accumulation (reduction) of domestic capital to point $E_1(E_2)$.

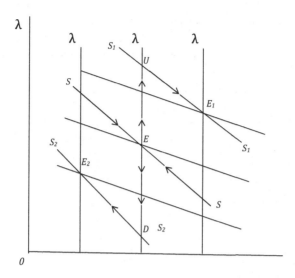

Figure 17.1   Changes in the domestic capital stock.

17.2.3   *Domestic welfare*

We are now ready to deduce the welfare implications of domestic equity controls in the long run. Since the goods prices are fixed to the world levels, the impact of domestic equity control on domestic welfare depends solely on the income effect, which can be expressed by:

$$\frac{dW}{d\beta} = -\left(\frac{\lambda}{\rho}\right)\left[(R_K - r^*)K_m - R_K\left(\frac{dK^d}{d\beta}\right)\right]. \qquad (17.5)$$

Apparently, the capital cost and capital accumulation effects determine the welfare effect of equity regulations in (17.5).[9] As domestic assets are more expensive than foreign assets, an increase in the domestic equity requirement raises the rental cost to foreign firms. This lowers welfare, as indicated by the first term on the right-hand side of (17.5). On the other hand, the domestic equity policy may yield a beneficial effect via

---

[9] In the short-run model with a given capital stock, the welfare effect of domestic equity controls depends only on the capital cost effect, as shown in Hill and Mendez (1992). However, in the long run, the adjustment of capital also contributes to the welfare change.

accumulation of the domestic capital stock, shown by the second term of (17.5). If the gain in capital accumulation outweighs the loss from the higher rental cost, the policy of domestic equity requirements can be welfare enhancing.

By way of summarizing the above discussions, we propose the following.

Proposition 17.1 *For an open economy with both domestic-owned and foreign-funded firms, domestic equity requirements for foreign firms may lead to accumulation of domestic capital assets and subsequently an improvement in welfare via the increases in outputs.*

We will use China's industry data to verify this proposition in the next section.

17.3   Empirical Results of Equity Control on China's Output

As mentioned in Section 17.1, the ownership restrictions have skewed the sectoral composition of FDI in China. In 2000, the manufacturing sector absorbed more than half of China's FDI. Foreign-funded firms supply a large portion of industrial output in garments, plastic products, electronic equipment, and office machinery,[10] while domestic firms produce a lion's share of the output in the services sector. To investigate the impacts of domestic equity ratio on the outputs across domestic firms, foreign firms, and industry as a whole, we specify the following reduced form equation:

$$X_i^j = \alpha_1^j + \alpha_2^j \left(\frac{K_i^d}{K_i} \right) + \varepsilon_i, \quad j = s, m, c, \qquad (17.6)$$

where X_i^s denotes the output produced by the state-owned firms in industry i, X_i^m is the output of the foreign-funded firms in industry i, and X_i^c is the combined output of the state and foreign firms in industry i. The ratio of K_i^d to K_i is a proxy for the domestic equity ratio in industry i, where K_i^d is the amount of domestic capital used by firms in industry i, and K_i is the total capital employed in industry i. Noted that ε_i is an error term.

Equation (17.6) is estimated by employing cross-section data on China's industrial enterprises for the calendar year 2000. The data cover state-owned enterprises and state holding majority shares enterprises,

---

[10]Detailed data are provided in Appendix A.2.

and foreign-funded enterprises in 28 manufacturing industries.[11] The data source is *China's Statistical Yearbook 2001*. For each manufacturing industry, data on industrial value added at market prices and total assets are collected. The dependent variable X_i^j is measured by the value added of the jth type enterprise, adjusted by the number of enterprises, at 1990 constant prices. The variables K_i^d and K_i are measured, respectively, by the fixed assets in state-owned enterprises and the sum of total assets in state-owned and foreign-owned enterprises. The ratio of K_i^d to K_i is a proxy for the domestic equity ratio in industry i.

Before presenting the empirical results, two technical notes regarding the industrial value added are in order. First, the data on industrial value added, originally measured at market prices, are adjusted to factor cost by subtracting an estimate of indirect taxes. These indirect taxes are calculated by multiplying the ratio of sales taxes and extra charges to total sales by the value added at market prices. Second, a price deflator, calculated by dividing the nominal total gross industrial output by industrial output at constant 1990 prices, is used to derive the value added at constant 1990 prices. The shares of value added at factor cost taken by state-owned and foreign-funded enterprises in the 28 manufacturing industries are presented in Appendix A.2. Descriptions of the variables used in the estimation and the data sources are presented in Appendix A.3.

Equation (17.6) is estimated using cross-section data for 2000. In each equation, the dependent variable is expressed in logarithmic form, while the variable on the right-hand side is in percentage. The results of the estimation are presented in Table 17.1. The fit is satisfactory in all three equations. The equity ratios (K_i^d/K_i) are significant at the 1% level, and the adjusted R^2 values are satisfactory, considering that the cross-section data were used. A chi-squared test based on the regression of squared residuals on squared fitted values suggests that there is no heteroscedasticity problem in the error term.

In Table 17.1, the elasticity of the domestic equity ratio for industry output is 0.026, suggesting that a 1% increase in the domestic capital ratio will result in an average increase of the industry output by 0.026%. That is, a rise in domestic equity ratios improves national welfare through the increase in industry output. This result is consistent with the implications deduced in Section 17.2.3. In short, a rise in domestic equity increases

---

[11] Cross-section data are not available for the services industries in China.

Table 17.1   Estimation of industrial output in China.

Dependent variable Explanatory variables:	$\text{Log}X_i^s$	$\text{Log}X_i^m$	$\text{Log}X_i^c$
(K_i^d/K_i)	0.039 (5.498)**	0.015 (3.741)**	0.026 (5.021)**
Constant	−4.458 (9.720)**	−2.533 (−9.467)**	−2.664 (−7.790)**
R^2	0.538	0.350	0.492
F-statistic	30.229**	13.991**	25.212**
Estimated σ	0.840	0.490	0.627
χ^2 for heteroscedasticity	2.303	0.634	2.345

Notes: The sample size is 28. *t*-statistics are in parentheses. σ is the standard error of the regression. ** denotes significant at the 1% level.

the rental cost of capital, thereby reducing welfare. On the other hand, the domestic equity policy leads to the accumulation of domestic assets, as implied in the regression results of the output of state-owned firms: the elasticity of the domestic equity ratio is 0.039. This beneficial accumulation of domestic assets appears to be a dominant force in boosting China's industrial output.

For foreign-funded firms, the domestic equity ratio for foreign firms is 0.015, suggesting the gain from increased domestic capital may be larger than the loss of the higher rental cost, rendering a positive welfare effect. Hence, our evidence supports the hypothesis that an increase in the domestic equity ratio for foreign firms has a positive effect on outputs and welfare.

17.4   Concluding Remarks

Facing intensifying competition, the use of domestic equity requirements has been a common practice in regulating foreign-funded firms in the host country. Using a dynamic framework, we have shown that an increase in domestic equity requirements can affect welfare via two channels: a detrimental higher rental cost effect and a favorable capital accumulation effect. Although an increase in domestic equity requirements raises the rental cost of capital to foreign firms, it may generate a beneficial effect through the accumulation of domestic capital assets. If the latter gain outweighs the former loss, the policy of domestic equity requirements can be welfare enhancing.

In the literature, the issues of domestic equity requirements have been studied mainly using static models.[12] In such models barring capital accumulation, it is not surprising to find that the policy of domestic equity requirements is unambiguously welfare reducing. The implication of this straightforward result apparently is at odds with the fact that such policies have been adopted by many nations, China in particular. The framework developed in this chapter allowing capital accumulation is useful for offering an economic explanation for this phenomenon. The foregoing empirical findings lend support to the implications deduced in the framework by showing that the accumulation of domestic assets resulting from higher domestic equity ratios plays a significant role in boosting China's industrial outputs.

Appendix

A.1 *Stability*

Solving (17.1) and (17.3), we have the effects of resource allocation in the short run: $\partial L/\partial K^d = -AR_{KK}R_{KK}^m/D \lesseqgtr 0$, $\partial K_m/\partial K^d = (\beta H - AR_{KK}R_{KL}^m)/D \lesseqgtr 0$, $\partial L/\partial \beta = [(R_K - r^*)(\beta R_{LK} + R_{LK}^m) + AK_m R_{KK}R_{KK}^m]/D \lesseqgtr 0$, $\partial K_m/\partial \beta = [(R_K - r^*)(R_{LL} + R_{LL}^m) + AK_m R_{KK}R_{LK}^m - \beta K_m H]/D \lesseqgtr 0$, where $A = \beta(K_m/L_m) - \sigma(K_l/L_l) \lesseqgtr 0$, capturing the factor-intensity condition, $D = \beta^2 H + R_{KK}R_{KK}^m A^2 + (\sigma - 1)R_{LK}R_{KK}^m k_X > 0$, and $H = R_{LL}R_{KK} - R_{LK}^2 > 0$. Here, $\sigma = Y_{LL}/(Y_{LL} + X_{LL})$. Note that $H = \sigma[X_{LL}^l X_{KK}^l - \sigma(X_{LK}^l)^2] > 0$ since $R_{LL} = \sigma X_{LL}^l$, $R_{LK} = \sigma X_{LK}^l$ and $R_{KK} = X_{KK}^l$. Also, we use $R_{LL}^m R_{KK}^m - (R_{LK}^m)^2 = 0$ to obtain D.

Letting λ be the shadow value of domestic assets, the optimum conditions with respect to C_X and C_Y in (17.2) are: $U_X(C_X, C_Y) = \lambda$ and $U_Y(C_X, C_Y) = \lambda$. These give: $dC_X/d\lambda = (U_{YY} - U_{XY})/J < 0$ and $dC_Y/d\lambda = (U_{XX} - U_{XY})/J < 0$, where $J = U_{XX}U_{YY} - (U_{XY})^2 > 0$. Note that the movement of λ is: $\dot{\lambda} = \lambda\rho - \lambda R_K(L, K^d - \beta K_m)$. Linearizing $\dot{K}^d$ and $\dot{\lambda}$ around steady states, $\tilde{K}^d$ and $\tilde{\lambda}$, yields:

$$
\begin{bmatrix} \dot{K}^d \\ \dot{\lambda} \end{bmatrix} = \begin{bmatrix} R_K & -\left(\frac{dC_X}{d\lambda} + \frac{dC_Y}{d\lambda}\right) \\ \frac{\lambda B}{D} & 0 \end{bmatrix} \begin{bmatrix} K^d - \tilde{K}^d \\ \lambda - \tilde{\lambda} \end{bmatrix},
$$

---

[12]See, for example, Chao and Yu (2000).

where $B = (1 - \sigma)(K_l/L_l)R_{KL}R_{KK}R^m_{KK} > 0$. The equilibrium is a saddle-point stability because the determinant of the matrix, $\lambda B(dC_X/d\lambda + dC_Y/d\lambda)/D$, is negative. The solutions are: $K^d(s) = \check{K}^d + (K_0^d - \check{K}^d)e^{\mu s}$ and $\lambda(s) = \tilde{\lambda} + \theta(K_0^d - \check{K}^d)e^{\mu s}$, where μ is the negative eigenvalue and $\theta = (R_K - \mu)/(dC_X/d\lambda + dC_Y/d\lambda) < 0$. The stable arm in Figure 17.1 is solved as: $\lambda - \tilde{\lambda} = \theta(K^d - \check{K}^d)$.

The steady-state equilibrium of the economy is: $\dot{\lambda} = 0$ and $\dot{K}^d = 0$; i.e., $R_K(L, K^d - \beta K_m) = \rho$ and $R(L, K^d - \beta K_m) + R^m(\bar{L} - L, K_m) - C_X - C_Y - r^*(1 - \beta)K_m = 0$. From these two equations, we obtain the change in domestic capital in (17.4). In addition, differentiating (17.2), we have: $dW/d\beta = (\lambda/\rho)(dC_X/d\lambda + dC_Y/d\lambda)(d\lambda/d\beta)$. Using the change of $\dot{K}^d = 0$ yields the welfare effect in (17.5).

A.2 Value added shares

Share of value added at factor cost in state-owned [a] and foreign-funded enterprises in manufacturing sector in 2000 (%).

	State-owned enterprises	Foreign-funded enterprises
Food Processing	62.50	37.50
Food Production	46.33	53.67
Beverage Production	68.48	31.52
Tobacco Processing	99.18	0.82
Textile Industry	64.01	35.99
Garments and Other Fiber Products	14.13	85.87
Leather, Furs, Down, and Related Products	10.66	89.34
Timber Processing, Bamboo, Cane, Palm Fiber, and Straw Products	39.53	60.47
Furniture Manufacturing	20.84	79.16
Papermaking and Paper Products	53.27	46.73
Printing and Record Medium Reproduction	62.36	37.64
Cultural, Educational, and Sports Goods	12.74	87.26
Petroleum Processing and Coking	94.71	5.29
Raw Chemical Materials and Chemical Products	73.43	26.57
Medical and Pharmaceutical Products	69.57	30.43
Chemical Fiber	60.88	39.12
Rubber Products	52.26	47.74

(*Continued*)

(*Continued*)

	State-owned enterprises	Foreign-funded enterprises
Plastic Products	21.47	78.53
Nonmetal Mineral Products	70.34	29.66
Smelting and Pressing of Ferrous Metals	94.81	5.19
Smelting and Pressing of Nonferrous Metals	83.86	16.14
Metal Products	33.08	66.92
Ordinary Machinery Manufacturing	67.74	32.26
For Special Purposes Equipment Manufacturing	77.33	22.67
Transport Equipment Manufacturing	69.53	30.47
Electric Equipment and Machinery	45.85	54.15
Electronic and Telecommunications Equipment	38.57	61.43
Instruments, Meters, Cultural, and Office Machinery	38.04	61.96

Note: Shares are calculated based on constructed data on value added at factor cost. See Appendix A.3 for the method of data construction.
[a] Includes state holding majority shares enterprises.

A.3 *Variable definitions*

Variable definitions and data sources

Variable	Description	Source and construction
X_i^s	Value added at factor cost of state-owned enterprises in 28 manufacturing industries in China, adjusted by the number of enterprises, in 1990 constant prices, 100 million Renminbi (RMB) yuan, where i = 1, 2, ..., 28.	Nominal value added at factor prices are derived by deducting sales taxes and extra charges from value added at market prices. Price deflator is calculated by dividing nominal gross output by gross output at 1990 constant prices. All data come from *China Statistical Yearbook*, 2001

(*Continued*)

(*Continued*)

Variable	Description	Source and construction
X_i^m	Value added at factor cost of foreign-funded enterprises in 28 manufacturing industries in China, adjusted by the number of enterprises, in 1990 constant prices, 100 million Renminbi (RMB) yuan, where i = 1, 2, ..., 28.	Nominal value added at factor prices are derived by deducting sales taxes and extra charges from value added at market prices. Price deflator is calculated by dividing nominal gross output by gross output at 1990 constant prices. All data come from *China Statistical Yearbook*, 2001
X_i^c	Total value added at factor cost of state-owned and foreign-funded enterprises, in 1990 constant prices, that is, $X_i^s + X_i^m$.	
K_i^d	Total assets of state-owned and state holding majority shares enterprises in 28 manufacturing industries in China	*China Statistical Yearbook*, 2001
K_i	The sum of total assets of state- owned enterprises and state holding majority shares enterprises, and foreign-funded enterprises in 28 manufacturing industries in China	*China Statistical Yearbook*, 2001

PART IV

Issues of Export Duty Rebates

Chapter 18

Export Duty Rebates and Export Performance: Theory and China's Experience

18.1 Introduction

The financial turmoil that broke out in July 1997 ravaged the Asian economies for a period of 18 months. Most of their currency values have consequently suffered dramatic falls. By the end of 1998, Indonesia's currency value fell by 70%, while currencies dropped by more than 30% in Thailand, Malaysia, the Philippines, and South Korea. China and Hong Kong are the notable exceptions, as they have hitherto resisted the temptation to devaluate their currencies.

As one country after another in a region undergoes currency depreciation, the countries that do not follow suit experience a deterioration in competitiveness, thereby precipitating a fall in their exports. In this regard, China's experience serves as a vivid case. Compared to the period of January through June 1998, China's exports declined by 4% in the first six months of 1999. As exports contribute about 21% of China's gross domestic profit (GDP), such a drop in exports precipitated a drop of 0.4% in China's GDP growth rate in 1999. China has been compelled by this slowdown in economic growth to consider either devaluing its currency or instituting other export-promoting policy measures.

It is notable that the production of final goods and services in China depends heavily on the use of foreign intermediate goods. According to the estimates provided by the People's Bank of China, every dollar of exports includes 50 cents of imported intermediate inputs. Instead of following in the footsteps of neighboring Asian countries and devaluing its currency,

China decided to implement a policy of input duty drawback, namely, giving tax rebates on the imported inputs and materials used in the production of exportable goods. This policy not only stimulates exports but also helps China's products to retain their competitive edge on world markets. The State Treasury of China implements this policy by first collecting taxes on imported intermediate goods and then rebating the tax revenue to exporters using the intermediate goods.

China's export tax rebate system was introduced in 1985, and the rates ranged from 7 to 11% before 1993; these were raised to 17% in 1994. The Chinese government later lowered the rebate rates to: 3% for primary products, including farm products and coal; 6% for processed products; and 9% for other products, including machinery and electrical appliances. However, facing the pressure resulting from the 1997 financial turmoil in neighboring countries, China raised export tax rebates for several product categories. Starting on June 1, 1998, the tax rebate rate for ship exports was raised from 9 to 14%; that for steel and cement exports was increased from 2 to 11%; and that for the coal industry was tripled to 9%. In fact, the tax rebate rates for several types of exports were also increased somewhat at the beginning of 2001. For example, the export tax rebate rate for textile products was raised from 9 to 11%. Export rebate rates for cotton and steel products were raised from 9 to 17%, which is effectively a zero net rate.

Increasing tax rebate rates in China is a policy move in line with World Trade Organization (WTO) practices for trade liberalization. In many countries, zero export taxation has been granted to all exports to eliminate preferential policies that favor certain industries over others.

These tax abatements help China to keep its export prices relatively low in order to maintain its export competitiveness in a world market that has been buffeted by several bouts of competitive devaluations in the East Asia and Southeast Asia regions in recent history.

This chapter examines the effectiveness of export tax rebates to boost exports theoretically and empirically. The chapter is organized as follows. Section 18.2 presents a simple three-sector, general equilibrium model to capture the effects of export tax rebates on the development of the down- and upstream industries. Empirical estimation of export tax rebates on China's export performance is provided in Section 18.3. The last section contains some concluding remarks.

18.2   A Theoretical Model

Consider a simplified economy that consists of three sectors: an exportable X, an importable Y, and an intermediate good M. Choosing good Y as the numeraire, the world prices of goods X and Y are p^* and 1, respectively. Let q denote the price of the domestically produced intermediate M, which is used only in the home country.

The production of good X requires the use of labor (L_x) and a composite intermediate good (I). For simplicity, we assume that there is a fixed one-to-one coefficient between L_x and I so that:[1]

$$X = X(L_X, I) = \min(L_X, I), \qquad (18.1)$$

where I is made up by the domestic and foreign intermediate goods in the Cobb–Douglas form:

$$I = M^\mu M_f^{1-\mu}, \qquad (18.2)$$

where M_f denotes the imported foreign intermediate input. Let q_f be the domestic, tax-inclusive price of good M_f. It is assumed that the home country imposes a tax, t_M, on the imports of M_f; that is, $q_f = q_f^* + t_M$, where q_f^* is the corresponding foreign price. Furthermore, the price index of the composite intermediate good is $q_I = cq^\mu q_f^{1-\mu}$, where $c = \mu^{-\mu}(1-\mu)^{\mu-1}$. The Cobb–Douglas specification, commonly adopted in the literature, sharpens the ensuing analysis.

Good X can be sold at home and abroad. To promote its export, the home country introduces a rebate of tax on M_f. Let the rebate be ρ, a portion of t_M; the effective price of selling good X abroad is $p^* + \rho t_M a$, where $a = M_f/X = c(1-\mu)(q/q_f)^\mu$, which is not fixed.[2] Since the tax

---

[1]This fixed input coefficient production function is used, for example, by Jones and Spencer (1989) in their study of raw-material export policy in a general-equilibrium framework. Chao and Yu (1993) and Chao *et al.* (2000) adopt this production structure to study the issues of content protection and environmental preservation, respectively.

[2]By (18.1), we have $a = M_f/X = M_f/I$ due to the one-to-one production of good X. In addition, from (18.2), we obtain $M_f = (1-\mu)q_I I/q_f$. This in turn yields $a = c(1-\mu)(q/q_f)^\mu$, which is not fixed.

rebate applies only to the export portion of good X, the rebate creates an incentive to sell abroad rather than at home. The subsequent fall in domestic sales generates an upward pressure on the price of good X at home. In equilibrium, the domestic price of $X(p)$ is equal to its effective foreign price; that is, $p = p^* + \rho t_M a$.[3]

Goods Y and M are produced by using only primary factors, labor and capital, under constant returns to scale. We specify:

$$Y = Y(L_Y, K_Y), \qquad (18.3)$$

$$M = M(L_M, K_M), \qquad (18.4)$$

where L_i and K_i are, respectively, the labor and capital employment in sector i, $i = Y, M$.

As for factor markets, the economy suffers from sector-specific unemployment. While capital is fully employed, labor is not. We assume that the wage rate in the exportable sector (w_X) is fixed and higher than that in the other sectors.[4] Due to wage rigidity, unemployment of labor (L_X) occurs in sector X. Rather than migrating to sectors Y and M, which are located quite apart from sector X, some of the unemployed workers prefer to wait and look for jobs in sector X. The probability of getting a job in sector X is $L_X/(L_X + L_u)$, which can be written as $1/(1 + \lambda)$. Note that $\lambda(= L_u/L_X)$ denotes the unemployment ratio in sector X. In equilibrium, the expected wage rate in sector X is equal to the wage rate in sectors Y and M:[5]

$$\frac{w_X}{(1 + \lambda)} = w, \qquad (18.5)$$

where w is the wage rate in sectors Y and M.

The above production structure of the economy can be represented by its dual, expressed in terms of costs. Let $\alpha(\cdot), \beta(\cdot)$, and $\gamma(\cdot)$ be, respectively, the unit cost of producing goods X, Y, and M. In competitive equilibrium,

---

[3] See Panagariya (1992) for a detailed explanation.

[4] Similar modeling on sector-specific unemployment can be found, for example, in Chao and Yu (1993), which deals with content protection.

[5] This is the basic Harris–Todaro (1970) migration equilibrium, which has been extensively utilized in the domestic migration literature.

unit price equals unit cost, so that:

$$p = \alpha(w_X, q_I) = w_X + cq^\mu q_f^{1-\mu}, \tag{18.6}$$

$$1 = \beta(w, r), \tag{18.7}$$

$$q = \gamma(w, r), \tag{18.8}$$

where r denotes the rate of return on capital, recalling that $p = p^* + \rho t_M a$.

Let L and K be the domestic endowment of labor and capital, respectively. The equilibrium conditions for factor markets are:

$$(1 + \lambda)X + \beta_w(w, r)Y + \gamma_w(w, r)M = L, \tag{18.9}$$

$$\beta_r(w, r)Y + \gamma_r(w, r)M = K, \tag{18.10}$$

where, by Shephard's lemma, the partial derivative of the unit-cost function, e.g., β_w, γ_w, represents the factor demand per unit of each good produced.

Furthermore, according to (18.2), the demands for the domestic and the foreign intermediate goods are, respectively:

$$M = \frac{\mu q_I X}{q}, \tag{18.11}$$

$$M_f = \frac{(1 - \mu)q_I X}{q}, \tag{18.12}$$

where $q_I = cq^\mu q_f^{1-\mu}$.

Equations (18.6)–(18.12) form the dual structure of the economy. Together with (18.5), there are eight equations with eight unknowns — $w, r, \lambda, q, X, Y, M$, and M_f — and a tax rebate instrument, ρ. We will examine the effects of changing the tax rebate rate on unemployment, sectoral output, exports, and welfare.

18.2.1 *Effects of tax rebates on unemployment and outputs*

The instrument to promote exports via a tax rebate, ρ, appears only in (18.6), and the unknown variable in (18.6) is q. Therefore, the effects of a tax rebate on unemployment and sectoral outputs work through q. For a given wage rate in sector X, we can derive the key result in this chapter, $dq = d\rho > 0$, from (18.6) (see Appendix A.1). That is, a tax rebate on the foreign intermediate goods used for exports raises the price of the domestic intermediate good and hence increases the effective price of the downstream good X. This leads to increases in the demand for the domestic intermediate input, thereby putting an upward pressure on its price.

Note that (18.7) and (18.8) form a Heckscher–Ohlin subsystem of sectors Y and M with both unknowns, w and r, as functions of q. In the Appendix, we derive comparative statics results. In particular, consistent with the Stolper–Samuelson theorem, we have $dw = dq < 0$ and $dr = dq > 0$ by assuming that sector M is relatively more capital-intensive than sector Y.[6] As the wage rate drops, some workers leave sectors Y and M for sector X. This implies that $dX = dq > 0$. In addition, the normal output-price response prevails, namely, $dM = dq < 0$ and $dY = dq < 0$. Furthermore, the increase in the production of good X raises the demand for the foreign intermediate $(dM_f = dq > 0)$. Thus, we can state the following proposition.

Proposition 18.1 *Export tax rebates have the effect of expanding the exportable and the intermediate-goods sector at the expense of the importable sector; assuming that the intermediate-goods sector is relatively more capital-intensive than the importable sector.*

Due to the movement of labor into the X sector, the unemployment ratio in sector X rises $(d\lambda = dq > 0)$, as can be seen from (18.5).

18.2.2   *Effects of tax rebates on welfare and exports*

Consider the welfare effect of export tax rebates on the use of the imported intermediate good. The demand side of the economy can be represented by

---

[6]To the best of our knowledge, detailed sectoral capital–labor ratios are not available for China. Nevertheless, McGuckin *et al.* (1992) may provide some crude indication of China's factor intensity rankings. According to McGuckin *et al.*, average output growth rates of manufacturing and non-manufacturing are 5.71 and 0.98% for the period 1980 to 1984. The contributions to output growth by capital and labor are, respectively, 2.31 and 0.22% in manufacturing and 0.94 and 0.08% in non-manufacturing. This suggests that the manufacturing sector, which may be primarily producing intermediate goods, tends to be relatively more capital-intensive than the non-manufacturing sector. In addition, the GTAP 4 database, compiled by the Center for Global Trade Analysis at Purdue University, provides data on China's factor demand by sector in value flow terms, which may be used to infer the capital–labor ratios for some sectors. However, the database does not define specifically what intermediate input sectors and importable sectors are. Furthermore, all sectors have exports and imports, and all sectors produce some inputs. To determine the factor intensity ranking between the importable and the intermediate-goods sectors, further research is required.

the expenditure function, which is $E(p, 1, u) = \min(pC_X + C_Y)$ subject to a utility constraint, $u(C_X, C_Y) \geq u$.

The budget constraint is given by:

$$E(p, 1, u) = (pX + Y) + t_M M_f - \rho t_M aH - (q_f^* + t_M)M_f, \qquad (18.13)$$

which states that total expenditure equals revenues from the production of the two final goods and import taxes on foreign material minus tax rebates of exports and payments for foreign material. Note that H is exports of good X and is defined as:[7]

$$H = X - E_p(p, 1, u), \qquad (18.14)$$

where $E_p(= E/\partial p) = C_X$ is the domestic demand for good X.

Totally differentiating (18.13) and (18.14) yields the change in welfare as:

$$E_u(1 - \rho t_M am/p)(du/dp)$$
$$= t_M(dM_f/d\rho) - \rho t_M a(dX/d\rho) - wL_X(d\lambda/d\rho) + \rho t_M aE_{pp}(dp/d\rho), \qquad (18.15)$$

where $E_u(= \partial E/\partial u)$ is the inverse of the marginal utility of income, and $m = pE_{pu}/E_u < 1$ denotes the marginal propensity to consume good X. The first term on the right-hand side of (18.15) expresses the effect of tax revenue collected from the imported intermediate. This effect is beneficial to the home economy and arises because the tax rebates promote exports and the production of good X via a higher effective price. This leads to a higher demand for the foreign intermediate good, and hence more tax revenue is generated. However, the enhanced tax revenue is mitigated by the cost of tax rebates, as shown in the second term. Although the expansion of good X attracts more workers from other sectors, some of them may not be able to find jobs. This causes a higher unemployment ratio in sector X, as indicated by the third term, which is detrimental to welfare. The last term in (18.15) captures the loss of consumer surplus because the tax rebate triggers a higher price of good X. Note that the change of the price

---

[7]In (18.13), $aH = a(X - E_p) = M_f[(X - E_p)/X]$ indicates the share of the imported foreign intermediate goods used in producing the export of good X.

of good X is given by

$$\frac{dp}{d\rho} = at_M \left[\frac{d\lambda}{d\rho} + \left(\frac{\rho\mu}{q} \right) \left(\frac{dq}{d\rho} \right) \right] > 0.$$

With regard to the effect of tax rebates on exports, we differentiate (18.14) and utilize (18.15) to obtain:

$$\frac{dH}{d\rho} = \frac{dX}{d\rho} - E_{pp} \left(\frac{dp}{d\rho} \right) - E_{pu} \left(\frac{du}{d\rho} \right). \tag{18.16}$$

Tax rebates can promote exports of good X if the income effect on consumption $E_{pu}(du/d\rho)$ is not too large.

In view of the welfare effect in (18.15) and the export effect in (18.16), we can state the following proposition.

Proposition 18.2 *Export tax rebates on the imported intermediates can promote exports because the rebates expand the related down- and upstream industries. However, the tax rebates may lower welfare due to a higher unemployment ratio, a reduction in tax revenue, and a fall in consumer surplus.*

18.3   Export Tax Rebates and China's Exports

To examine the effect of export tax rebates on China's exports of goods, we follow Arize *et al.* (2000) and Chowdhury (1993) to specify the long-run equilibrium export demand equation:

$$H_t = \beta_1 + \beta_2 I_t^* + \beta_3 P_t + \beta_4 v_t + \beta_5 TR_t + \epsilon_t, \tag{18.17}$$

where H_t denotes the real exports of goods, I_1^* is real foreign income, P_t is the relative goods price, v_t is the exchange rate volatility, TR_t, is the amount of export tax rebates, and ϵ_t is an error term.

Before presenting the empirical results, three technical notes regarding the use of variables are in order. First, the exchange rate volatility v_t in (18.17) is not observable and is estimated by the conditional variance of the real effective exchange rate index from an autoregressive conditional heteroscedastic (ARCH) process. Second, foreign income (I_t^*) is constructed by a weighted GDP index of six major trading partners of China, namely, Germany, Hong Kong, Japan, Singapore, the United Kingdom, and the United States. The relative price (P_t) is measured by the ratio of China's export price index to the world export price index. Descriptions of the variables used in the estimation and the data sources are presented in Appendix A.2. Equation (18.17) is estimated using annual data over the period 1985 to 1998. All variables are expressed in logarithmic form. Finally, to investigate whether a long-run relationship among the variables in (18.17) holds, we employ the cointegration test developed by Johansen and Juselius (1990, JJ hereafter). The JJ procedure uses two likelihood ratio (LR) test statistics, that is, the trace and the maximal-eigenvalue or λ-max statistics to test for the number of cointegrating vectors in non-stationary time series.

Prior to testing for cointegration, the stationarity property of the individual variables in (18.17) is examined by applying the augmented Dickey–Fuller (ADF) unit root tests to each individual time series.[8] According to the test results, the null of a unit root cannot be rejected at the 10% level for all series except for the log of exchange rate volatility. The ADF tests are also applied to the first-differenced series, and the null of a unit root can be rejected for all series. Despite its wide use in testing the stationarity of time series in the literature, the power of the ADF test is very low. Pantula *et al.* (1994) have shown that unit root tests on the ordinary least square (OLS) estimator are the least powerful among the statistics they studied. They found that a modified Dickey–Fuller test proposed by Elliot *et al.* (1996) (hereafter ERS) has superior power performance. We also apply ERS's Dickey–Fuller-generalized-least-squares (DF-GLS) test to each time series in (18.17),[9] and the results are reported in Table 18.1. The results indicate that all the variables in (18.17) are integrated of order 1, or $I(1)$, except for the exchange rate volatility and relative prices.

For those $I(1)$ series, we can test the cointegration relation in (18.17) using the JJ procedure. In applying the JJ procedure we allow for a structural break dummy variable (DUM) and an $I(0)$ variable such as the exchange rate volatility. The calculated trace statistic (52.205) and λ-max statistic (30.531) enable us to reject the null hypothesis of no cointegration at the 5% level[10] and establish the presence of one cointegrating vector. These results suggest that there is a long-run equilibrium relationship among real exports, foreign income, and export tax rebates in China.

---

[8]The regression equation used in the ADF tests does not allow for a linear trend. We follow the procedure of Campbell and Perron (1991) to select the autoregressive lag order.

[9]The finite sample critical values of the DF-GLS test are estimated based on Cheung and Lai (1995).

[10]Finite-sample corrections are made for the critical values as suggested by Cheung and Lai (1993).

Table 18.1   Unit root tests of individual variables.

Series		ADF statistic	Lag	C.V.[a] 5%	10%	DF-GLS statistic	Lag	C.V.[b] 5%	10%
$\log H$	Level	−0.888	0	−3.020	−2.650	−0.360	0	−2.528	−2.183
	Δ	−4.762**	0	−3.029	−2.655	−4.856**	0	−2.599	−2.241
$\log I^*$	Level	−1.453	0	−3.020	−2.650	−1.553	0	−2.580	−2.230
	Δ	−2.808*	0	−3.029	−2.655	−2.991*	0	−2.599	−2.241
$\log P$	Level	0.002	0	−3.020	−2.650	−2.879**		−2.580	−2.230
	Δ	−4.007**	0	−3.029	−2.665	−5.021**	0	−2.599	−2.241
$\log v$	Level	−3.837**	0	−3.040	−2.661	−3.935**	0	−2.618	−2.250
$\log TR$	Level	−2.269	0	−3.122	−2.704	−2.134	0	−2.704	−2.235
	Δ	−5.487**	0	−3.149	−2.718	−5.700**	0	−2.712	−2.203

Notes. The symbol Δ represents first-differenced series. Both tests do not allow for a linear trend. H is total real exports, I^* is real foreign income, P is relative prices, v is exchange rate volatility, and TR is export tax rebates. Sample period is 1978–1998 for H, I^*, and P, 1980–1998 for v, and 1985–1998 for TR. Double and single asterisks indicate significant at the 5 and 10% levels, respectively.
[a]Critical values are calculated based on Mackinnon (1991).
[b]Critical values are calculated based on Cheung and Lai (1995).

This finding implies that an error-correction representation in the following form exists:

$$\Delta \log H_t = \beta_1 + \beta_2 ECM_{t-1} + \gamma \Delta w_t + \delta z_t$$

$$+ \sum_{j=1}^{n} \theta_j \Delta w_{t-j} + \sum_{i=1}^{k} \delta_i \Delta \log H_{t-1} + \epsilon_t,$$

where Δ denotes the first difference operator, ECM is the error correction term, the vector w contains the explanatory variables $\log I^*$ and $\log TR$, and the vector z contains the variables DUM and $\log v$. The results of the estimation are presented in Table 18.2, in which the ECM term is generated from the JJ procedure. As can be seen from Table 18.2, the fit is satisfactory. The error correction term is significant at the 1% level and the adjusted R^2 is satisfactory, considering that the dependent variable is in first difference form. The Durbin–Watson (DW) test statistic indicates that no serial correlation exists in the error term.

The error correction term given in Table 18.2, which underlies the long-run elasticities, is highly significant, supporting the validity of an equilibrium relationship among total exports, foreign income, and export tax rebates. The long-run elasticities for export tax rebates and foreign income on China's exports are 0.344 and 2.102, respectively. The exchange

Table 18.2 Estimated error correction model for China's total exports (dependent variable: $\Delta \log$).

Explanatory variables	Estimated coefficients
ECM_{t-1}^{a}	-0.902
	$(-5.844)^{***}$
$\Delta \log$ TR	0.140
	$(3.710)^{***}$
$\log v$	-0.391
	$(-2.312)^{**}$
DUM^{b}	-1.081
	$(-2.739)^{**}$
Intercept	-0.167
	(-0.786)
Adjusted R^2	0.728
Estimated σ	0.088
DW statistic	1.876

Notes. The t-statistics are in parentheses, and 3/4 is the standard error of the regression. DW is the Durbin–Watson test statistic for first-order serial correlation. Triple and double asterisks denote significant at the 1 and 5% levels, respectively.
[a]Here,

$$\mathrm{ECM} = \log H - 0.344 \log \mathrm{TR} - 2.102 \log I^* - 15.531,$$
$$\qquad\quad (0.099) \qquad\quad (0.878) \qquad\quad (0.629)$$

where the numbers in parentheses beneath the estimated coefficients are standard errors.
[b]DUM is a dummy variable, with one assigned to 1989–1998.

rate volatility is found to have a negative (-0.391) and significant long-run effect on total exports. Regarding the dynamics of the export equation, only the export tax rebate has a significant short-run effect (0.140) on China's total exports. Finally, the export tax rebate has a larger effect on total exports in the long run compared to the case in the short run.

18.4 Concluding Remarks

This chapter presents a simple, three-sector general equilibrium model to capture the effects of export tax rebates on the development of down- and upstream industries. Specifically, we find that for an economy suffering from sector-specific unemployment, an increase in export tax rebates based on imported foreign intermediates expands its related down- and upstream industries. Therefore, export tax rebates can promote exports, although the tax rebates may lower welfare due to a higher unemployment ratio, a reduction in tax revenue, and a fall in consumer surplus.

Using an error-correction model, we have been able to investigate the short- and long-run factors that affect China's total exports. We find that the export tax rebate, foreign income, and exchange rate volatility contribute significantly to China's exports in the long run, but in the short run only the export tax rebate has the impact of promoting exports. This may provide an explanation as to why China has adopted the policy of export tax rebates, in lieu of devaluing its currency, to boost exports since 1997, granted that the latter policy can lead to the politically undesirable consequence of competitive currency devaluations in East and Southeast Asia.

Appendix

A.1   *Comparative statics*

Totally differentiating (18.6) and utilizing $p = p_f + \rho t_M a$ and $a = M_f/X = c(1 - \mu)(q/q_f)^{\mu}$, we can solve dq/dp as:

$$\frac{dq}{dp} = \frac{(1 - \mu)t_M q}{\mu[q_f^* + (1 - \rho + \mu\rho)t_M]} > 0.$$

The Cobb–Douglas specification of the composite intermediate good (I), i.e., $0 < \mu < 1$, is sufficient to yield $dq/d\rho > 0$. Other specifications for the composite intermediate good will also yield a positive relation between ρ and q. Hence, the result that $dq/d\rho > 0$ is quite robust.

To obtain the effects of factor returns and sectoral outputs, we first follow Jones (1965) to define $\theta_{LY} = w\beta_w/\beta$ and $\theta_{KY} = r\beta_r/\beta$ as the distributive shares of labor and capital in sector Y and $\lambda_{LY} = \beta_w Y/L$ and $\lambda_{KY} = \beta_r Y/K$ as the fraction of labor and capital employed in sector Y. Then, letting a circumflex over variables indicate the percentage change, the comparative statics results are obtained from (18.5) and (18.7) to (18.12), as follows:

$$\frac{\hat{w}}{\hat{q}} = \frac{-\theta_{KY}}{|\theta|} < 0,$$

$$\frac{\hat{r}}{\hat{q}} = \frac{\theta_{LY}}{|\theta|} > 0,$$

$$\frac{\hat{\lambda}}{\hat{q}} = -\left[\frac{(1+\lambda)}{\lambda}\right]\left(\frac{\hat{w}}{\hat{q}}\right) > 0,$$

$$\frac{\hat{M}}{\hat{q}} = \frac{\left\{(1-\mu)(1+\lambda)\lambda_{LX}\lambda_{KY} + \frac{[\lambda_{LY}\Delta_K + \lambda_{KY}\Delta_L + (1+\lambda)\lambda_{LX}\lambda_{KY}\theta_{KY}]}{|\theta|}\right\}}{|\lambda|} > 0,$$

$$\frac{\hat{X}}{\hat{q}} = \frac{(1-\mu)(\lambda_{LY} - \lambda_{KY})}{|\lambda|} + \frac{\hat{M}}{\hat{q}} > 0.$$

$$\frac{\hat{Y}}{\hat{q}} = -\left\{\frac{\begin{aligned}&(1-\mu)(1+\lambda)\lambda_{LX}\lambda_{KM} + [(\lambda_{LM} + (1+\lambda)\lambda_{LX})\Delta_K\\ &+\lambda_{KM}\Delta_L + (1+\lambda)\lambda_{LX}\lambda_{KM}\theta_{KY}]\end{aligned}}{|\lambda|}\right\} < 0,$$

where

$$|\theta| = \theta_{KM} - \theta_{KY} > 0 \quad \text{and} \quad |\lambda| = \lambda_{LY} - \lambda_{KY} > 0$$

by assuming that sector M is relatively more capital-intensive than sector Y. Note that $\Delta_L = \sigma_Y\theta_{KY}\lambda_{LY} + \sigma_M\theta_{KM}\lambda_{LM}$ and $\Delta_K = \sigma_Y\theta_{LY}\lambda_{KY} + \sigma_M\theta_{LM}\lambda_{KM}$. Using the above results, we can also obtain:

$$\frac{dM_f}{d\rho} = a\left[\frac{dX}{d\rho} + \left(\frac{\mu X}{q}\right)\left(\frac{dq}{d\rho}\right)\right] > 0,$$

where $dX/d\rho = (dX/dq)(dq/d\rho) > 0$.

A.2 Data sources

Variable	Description	Source and construction
H	Real total exports of goods, in billions of Renminbi (RMB)	*China's Customs Statistics*, various issues. Export price indices (1990D100) are used to obtain exports in constant prices
I^*	Trade-weighted real GDP index (1990 = 100) of Germany, Hong Kong, Japan, Singapore, United Kingdom, and United States	CD-ROM edition of *International Financial Statistics* of the IMF

(Continued)

(Continued)

Variable	Description	Source and construction
P	Export price index $(1990 = 100)$ of China to world export price $(1990 = 100)$	CD-ROM edition of *International Financial Statistics* of the IMF
v	Exchange rate volatility	Annual average of conditional variance estimated from an ARCH(1) model, using a quarterly real effective exchange rate index. The autoregressive model has four lags, and the error term is assumed to follow a t-distribution (see Chou, 2000, for details)
TR	Export tax rebates, in 100 million RMB yuan and in constant (1990) prices	1985–1988 figures are taken from Lardy (1992, p. 50) 1992–1998 figures are from *Finance Yearbook of China*, 1993–1999 Figures for 1989–1991 are estimated by interpolation method
DUM	Dummy variable	A dummy variable with one assigned to 1989–1998 to account for a significant level shift in total exports since 1989. The Zivot–Andrews (1992) unit root test with one structural break was applied to log H, and a structural break corresponding to a level shift was found to be significant from 1989.

Chapter 19

Import Duty Drawback
and VAT Rebate Policies:
A CGE Analysis for China

19.1 Introduction

The policies of import duty drawbacks and value-added tax (VAT) rebates have played important roles in promoting China's exports in the last three decades. Duty drawbacks and VAT rebates are, respectively, the reductions in tariffs and domestic taxes on imported inputs used for export processing.[1] For example, in 1998, a 17% tariff was imposed on the imports of machinery and an additional 17% domestic tax was levied on its value added in production. Both taxes are rebated when the machinery is used for export processing.[2] As these two policies discriminate against imported inputs used in goods sold domestically, they certainly create incentives for firms to sell products abroad.

How effective are duty drawbacks and tax rebates in promoting exports? Using China's aggregate data, Chao *et al.* (2001) showed that duty drawbacks expand the exportable and the intermediate-goods sectors. However,

---

[1] For imported inputs, the VAT levy is in addition to the import duty. Finished final goods are also subject to VAT. However, previously paid VAT on its inputs is deducted from the VAT payment on its final goods. When the final goods are exported, the previously paid VAT on imported inputs is rebated to the export processor. See China's Ministry of Finance, www.mof.gov.cn, and Ministry of Commerce, www.mofcom.gov.cn.

[2] In February 1997, China lowered the rebate rates to 3% for agricultural products and coal, 6% for processed products using agricultural inputs and for other products with a 13% applicable value-added tax, and 9% for products with a 17% applicable value-added tax. These rates were raised in 1998 to: 17% for machinery, electronics, and transportation equipment; 13% for agricultural machinery, textiles, steels, and cements; 11% for chemical and plastic products; 9% for processed products using agricultural inputs; and 5% for agricultural products. In July 1999, the rebate rates were raised and many products enjoyed zero value-added tax rates.

their study does not provide detailed sectoral responses by products to duty drawbacks. To study this issue, this chapter generalizes the model of Chao *et al.*, also presented in Chapter 18 for theoretical considerations, and then modifies a standard computable general equilibrium (CGE) model for illustrating the quantitative effects of the policies. As duty drawbacks and tax rebates apply to China's processing exports, it is necessary to separate export processing from domestic sales. Utilizing this modified model, we conduct two sets of counterfactual simulations to illustrate the sectoral and economy-wide effects of these two policies for the Chinese economy.

Applications of CGE models on tax and trade issues can be found in Dixon *et al.* (1982), Shoven and Whalley (1984), Srinivasan and Whalley (1986), and Robinson (1988). Also, CGE models have been used in analyzing trade and other issues in China. For example, Wang and Zhai (1998) consider the distributional effects of trade liberalization and tax policies of China; Xu and Chang (2000) study the employment effect of tariff reductions in China; and Wang (2003) evaluates the impact of China's World Trade Organization (WTO) membership and a "Greater China" free trade area on the economic relationship across the Taiwan Strait.

The chapter is organized as follows. Section 19.2 considers theoretical aspects of the tax rebate policy. Section 19.3 presents a CGE model, while Section 19.4 carries out policy simulations. Section 19.5 offers conclusions to the chapter.

19.2   A Theoretical Model of Tax Rebates

Since duty drawbacks and tax rebates are applied to mitigate the effects of the tariffs and taxes on imported intermediates used only for export processing, we need to extend the simple export tax rebate model of Chao *et al.* (2001) by considering a dual production structure of domestic sales and export processing. We further generalize their model by removing the distortions of fixed wages and the small-country setting so that the model is more descriptive of the current large economy of China.

The home economy produces two final goods, an exportable Y and an importable X, and one intermediate good M_d. There are two types of firms in sector Y: type-1 firms focus on domestic sales while type-2 firms are primarily for export processing. Firms of both types employ the same technology and use labor and intermediates for production. To promote exports, tax rebates on using imported intermediates for export processing are granted. The production function for Y^i exhibits a fixed-coefficient technology:

$$Y^i = Y(L_y^i, M^i) = \min(L_y^i, M^i), \quad i = 1, 2, \tag{19.1}$$

where L_y^i and M^i are respectively the labor and intermediate inputs for type i firms.

The input M^i in (19.1) is composed of domestic and foreign intermediates, M_d^i and M_f^i, in the form: $M^i = (M_d^i)^\mu (M_f^i)^{1-\mu}$. Choosing X as the numeraire, the prices for domestic and foreign intermediates are denoted by v_d and v_f. Owing to the Cobb–Douglas function of M^i, the aggregate price of the composite intermediate is: $v = c v_d^\mu v_f^{1-\mu}$, where $c = \mu^{-\mu}(1-\mu)^{\mu-1}$. Note that v_f, the tariff-included price of imported intermediates, consists of its foreign price and the tariff, i.e., $v_f = v_f^* + t$. Thus, taxes on production of one unit Y^i are: ta, where $a(= M_f^i/Y^i)$ is the imported intermediates used per unit of Y^i. Because of the tax rebate for export processing, $\rho\%$ of the taxes on imported intermediates are rebated for type-2 firms and its *effective* price for selling Y abroad is: $p^* + \rho ta$, where p^* is the foreign price of Y. Note that type-2 firms can also sell Y domestically. Letting p be the domestic price of Y, by no-arbitrage condition in equilibrium, the domestic price must equal its effective foreign price, i.e., $p = p^* + \rho ta$. This suggests that the tax rebate is equivalent to an export subsidy in this context.[3]

Turn to the production functions for the importable X and domestic intermediates M_d. They are assumed to have constant returns to scale technologies with diminishing marginal productivities:

$$X = X(L_y, K_y), \tag{19.2}$$

$$M_d = M_d(L_m, K_m), \tag{19.3}$$

where L_i and K_i are labor and capital employed in sector i.

Labor and capital are mobile factors, and full employment requires:

$$L_x^1 + L_x^2 + L_y + L_m = L, \tag{19.4}$$

$$K_y + K_m = K, \tag{19.5}$$

where L and K are the endowments of labor and capital in the economy.

---

[3]See Krugman and Obstfeld (2003, p. 197) for the discussion of export subsidies.

The above production structure can be represented by its dual in terms of input and output prices. Letting $\alpha(\cdot)$, $\beta(\cdot)$, and $\gamma(\cdot)$ be the unit-cost functions for producing Y^i, X, and M_d, under competitive equilibrium unit price equals unit cost:

$$p = \alpha(w, v) = w + v, \tag{19.6}$$

$$1 = \beta(w, r), \tag{19.7}$$

$$v_d = \gamma(w, r), \tag{19.8}$$

where w and r are the wage and capital-rental rates, and recalling that $v = cv_d^{\mu} v_f^{1-\mu}$. By the envelope theorem, $\beta_w(\cdot)$ represents the labor demand for producing one unit of X, etc.

Using the unit-cost functions in (19.6)–(19.7), we can rewrite the market-clearing conditions for labor and capital in (19.4) and (19.5) as:

$$Y^1 + Y^2 + \beta_w(w, r)X + \gamma_w(w, r)M_d = L, \tag{19.9}$$

$$\beta_r(w, r)X + \gamma_r(w, r)M_d = K. \tag{19.10}$$

Moreover, the equilibrium condition for domestic intermediates requires that its demand meet supply:

$$\frac{\mu v \left(M^1 + M^2 \right)}{v_d} = M_d, \tag{19.11}$$

where $M^i = Y^i$ from (19.1). In addition, the demand for foreign intermediates is: $M_f^i = (1 - \mu)v M^i / v_f$.

By considering total output of $Y (= Y^1 + Y^2 = M^1 + M^2)$, the economy described in (19.6)–(19.11) has six unknowns — w, r, v_d, Y, X, and M_d — with a tax rebate instrument, ρ. Recall that $p = p^* + \rho ta$ in (19.6), where $a = M_f^i / M^i = c(1 - \mu)(v_d / v_f)^{\mu}$ in equilibrium. For a large-country case, the terms-of-trade effect exists because the exports of Y will affect the foreign price p^*. However, the change of p^* cannot be determined by this single home-country model.

The above theoretical model is used to illustrate the impacts of the tax rebate policy on factor prices, sectoral output, and welfare. First, consider the effects of the policy on factor returns by totally differentiating

(19.6)–(19.8), and then solving:

$$\frac{dw}{d\rho} = \frac{\beta_r \left(\frac{ta+dp^*}{d\rho} \right)}{\Delta}, \tag{19.12}$$

$$\frac{dr}{d\rho} = \frac{-\beta_w \left(\frac{ta+dp^*}{d\rho} \right)}{\Delta}, \tag{19.13}$$

$$\frac{dv_d}{d\rho} = \left(\frac{ta+dp^*}{d\rho} \right) \frac{(\beta_r\gamma_w - \beta_w\gamma_r)}{\Delta}, \tag{19.14}$$

where $\Delta = \beta_r + K(\beta_r\gamma_w - \beta_w\gamma_r) > 0$ and $K = [a\mu/v_d(1 - \mu)][v_f + t(1 - \rho + \mu\rho)] > 0$. Note that $\Delta > 0$ by the stability condition (shown in the Appendix) that $\beta_r\gamma_w > \beta_w\gamma_r$; i.e., the importable sector is capital-intensive relative to the intermediate-goods sector. Further, $ta + dp^*/d\rho$ in (19.12)–(19.14) measures the direct impact of a rise in the tax rebate on p and its sign is indeterminate.

The economic reasons for (19.12)–(19.14) are straightforward. A tax rebate of imported intermediates gives a direct rise (fall) in the effective price of good Y when $ta + dp^*/d\rho > (<) 0$, thereby raising (reducing) its production. This results in higher (lower) derived demands for labor and composite intermediates, which pushes up (down) the wage rate and the price of domestic intermediates in (19.12) and (19.14). On the contrary, the lowered (increased) supply of labor in the other sectors reduces (raises) the productivity of capital and hence its rate of return as expressed in (19.13).

By taking into account the change in the price of domestic intermediates in (19.14), the total effect of tax rebates on the price of good Y can be obtained by differentiating $p = p^* + \rho ta$ to yield:

$$\frac{dp}{d\rho} = \left(\frac{ta+dp^*}{d\rho} \right) \left[1 + \left(\frac{\rho}{v_d} \right) \left(\frac{dv_d}{d\rho} \right) \right]. \tag{19.15}$$

Hence, the tax rebate policy raises the domestic price of Y when $ta + dp^*/d\rho > 0$. However, the price effect in (19.15) is ambiguous when $ta + dp^*/d\rho < 0$.

Using the information on factor returns in (19.12)–(19.14), we can examine the effects of tax rebates on sectoral outputs. Solving (19.9)–(19.11) yields:

$$\frac{dY}{d\rho} = \frac{[B\beta_r + O\beta_w + G(\beta_r\gamma_w - \beta_w\gamma_r)]}{\Delta'}, \qquad (19.16)$$

where $B = -(\beta_{ww}X + \gamma_{ww}M_d)(dw/d\rho) - (\beta_{wr}X + \gamma_{wr}M_d)(dr/d\rho) >$ $(<) 0$, $O = (\beta_{rw}X + \gamma_{rw}M_d)(dw/d\rho) + (\beta_{rr}X + \gamma_{rr}M_d)(dr/d\rho) > (<) 0$ as $ta + dp^*/d\rho > (<) 0$. In addition, we have $G = \mu a v_f Y/v_d^2 > 0$ and $\Delta' = \beta_r + \mu c(v_d/v_f)^{\mu-1}(\beta_r\gamma_w - \beta_w\gamma_r) > 0$. Hence, tax rebates raise output of Y as its effective price increases when $ta + dp^*/d\rho > 0$. However, the change in Y is indeterminate when $ta + dp^*/d\rho < 0$.

Further, changes in Y yield repercussions throughout the economy. When $ta + dp^*/d\rho < 0$, the effects on the other sectors are ambiguous. Therefore, we focus on the case that $ta + dp^*/d\rho > 0$, and hence $dp/d\rho > 0$ in (19.15) and $dY/d\rho > 0$ in (19.16). This implies that the supply of labor in sectors X and M_d falls due to labor reallocation to sector Y. For given factor returns, similar to the Rybczynski effect, this lowers production of M_d but raises the output of X because the former is relatively labor-intensive to the latter. This output effect will be amplified by the changes in factor returns: the higher wage in (19.12) further lowers production of M_d but the lower capital rental in (19.13) causes greater production of X. However, the tax rebate raises the price of domestic intermediates, which in turn increases the output of M_d but reduces production of X. In sum, the above two conflicting forces make the changes in X and M_d ambiguous even when $ta + dp^*/d\rho > 0$. These can be confirmed by solving (19.9)–(19.11) to obtain:

$$\frac{dX}{d\rho} = \frac{-\left[D + \mu c\left(\frac{v_d}{v_f}\right)^{\mu-1}(B\gamma_r + D\gamma_w) - G\gamma_r\right]}{\Delta'} \gtrless 0, \qquad (19.17)$$

$$\frac{dM_d}{d\rho} = \frac{\left[\mu c\left(\frac{v_d}{v_f}\right)^{\mu-1}(B\beta_r + D\beta_w) - G\beta_r\right]}{\Delta'} \gtrless 0, \qquad (19.18)$$

Lastly, we examine the tax rebate policy on the imports of foreign intermediates by differentiating M_f with respect to ρ to yield:[4]

$$\frac{dM_f}{d\rho} = a \left[\left(\frac{\mu Y}{v_d} \right) \left(\frac{dv_d}{d\rho} \right) + \frac{dY}{d\rho} \right]. \tag{19.19}$$

Note that tax rebates lower the cost of using foreign intermediates, this renders favorable factor-substitution and output effects resulting in an increased demand for them, when $ta + dp^*/d\rho > 0$. Hence, the tax rebate policy promotes the exportable sector, but the policy may harm the domestic intermediate-goods sector. However, $dM_f/d\rho$ in (19.19) may take any sign when $ta + dp^*/d\rho < 0$.

Consider next the welfare effect of the tax rebate policy. The welfare of the economy is measured by the utility, $u = U(D_x, D_y)$, where $U(\cdot)$ denotes the utility function and D_i is the demand for good $i, i = x, y$. Given the utility level u, the expenditure function is defined as: $E(p, 1, u) = \min\{pD_y + D_x : u = u(D_x, D_y)\}$. By Shephard's lemma, we have: $E_p(= \partial E/\partial p) = D_y$, the compensated demand for good Y. The budget constraint of the economy is therefore:

$$E(p, 1, u) = pY + X + tM_f - \rho ta Y^2 - (v_f^* + t)M_f. \tag{19.20}$$

Total expenditure equals production revenue from the two final goods and import tariff revenue from foreign materials minus tax rebates and payments for imported foreign materials. Note that the exports of good Y are the difference between its total production and domestic consumption:

$$Y^2 = Y - E_p(p, 1, u). \tag{19.21}$$

Differentiating (19.20) and (19.21) yields the welfare effect of the tax rebate policy:

$$
(E_u - \rho ta E_{pu}) \left(\frac{du}{d\rho} \right)
$$
$$
= t \left(\frac{dM_f}{d\rho} \right) - \rho ta \left[\frac{dY}{d\rho} - E_{pp} \left(\frac{dp}{d\rho} \right) \right] + Y^2 \left(\frac{dp^*}{d\rho} \right), \tag{19.22}
$$

---

[4]This result is obtained by differentiating $M_f = (1 - \mu)v_d Y/v_f$ with respect to ρ.

where $E_u(= \partial E/\partial u)$ is the inverse of the marginal utility of income and $E_{pu}(= \partial E_p/\partial u) > 0$, assuming that D_y is a normal good. Note that $E_u - \rho t a E_{pu} > 0$,[5] and $E_{pp}(= \partial E_p/\partial p) < 0$. Equation (19.22) reveals that the welfare effect of tax rebates depends upon the effects of tariffs on imported materials and tax rebates on exports, plus the terms-of-trade effect. This overall welfare effect is ambiguous, even when $ta + dp^*/d\rho > 0$. Let us examine for this case the various effects on welfare. Tax rebates increase the use of foreign materials, which are restricted by tariffs, contributing positively to economic welfare as indicated in the first term on the right-hand side of (19.22). However, the gain in production is tempered by cost of tax rebates, as shown in the second term. In addition, tax rebates alter the terms of trade, thereby affecting welfare as indicated in the last term of (19.22). These conflicting forces render the welfare effect of tax rebates indeterminate. Therefore, a numerical method will be employed for evaluating the effects of tax rebates for the Chinese economy.

19.3   Modeling China's Duty Drawbacks and Tax Rebates in a CGE Framework

We now turn to the modeling of the duty drawback and tax rebate policies in a CGE framework. We start with the standard GTAP (Global Trade Analysis Project) model (Hertel, 1997). This model features nested constant elasticity of substitution (CES) production structure and a constant difference elasticity (CDE) demand system.[6] The final product of each single-output industry in a country/region are sold as exports, sales to the international transportation sector, government and private consumption at home, and intermediate inputs to domestic industries. On the production side, the final output in each industry is a Leontief composite of a value-added composite and n composite intermediates. The value-added composite is a CES mixture of primary factors, while the composite industry demand for individual intermediate input is a CES composite of an imported variety and a domestically produced variety of the same input. Last, each imported input is a CES composite consisting of imports from different sources.

---

[5]Since $E(\cdot)$ is homogenous of degree one in goods prices, we have $pE_{pu}/E_u < 1$ and $E_u - \rho t a E_{pu} = E_u[1 - (\rho t a/p)(pE_{pu}/E_u)] > 0$.

[6]The CDE functional form was first proposed by Hanoch (1975).

Due to the above-described single-output production structure in each industry, we need to modify the standard GTAP model to mimic the separation of the export-processing activity from the domestic production in each industry. Specifically, we build two nested Leontief–CES production "trees" in each industry (one for domestic production and the other for export processing), and separate imports used by export processors from those used by domestic users. To make matters simple, in the modification we assume that outputs from the export-processing activities are sold as exports exclusively, whereas outputs from the domestic activity serve all other demands. As we assume that outputs from export processing are all exports, domestic intermediate inputs used by both activities are all drawn from the outputs of domestic production. However, the two activities compete for primary factors on the same perfectly competitive factor markets.

The import demand structure in the standard GTAP model is also modified to allow for the separation of imported inputs used in export processing from all other uses and different tariffs and domestic taxes applied to the two types of imports. This separation is assumed to happen at the bilateral level. That is, each exporter supplies two distinct flows of exports to China, satisfying import demands by export processors and by all other domestic uses, respectively. The advantage of this treatment is that import tariff rates (hence duty drawbacks) may be different from one exporter to another. Once these imports enter China, they are aggregated separately into two CES composite goods, implying that users cannot identify the sources of these imports. As such, although these two types of imports share the same world market, their domestic market prices in China may be different, due to potentially different import tariffs and different shares by exporters.

Two sets of policy instruments can be built in the modified structure to represent the different tariff and VAT rates applied to imports. The first set of instruments consists of the bilateral import tariffs on import i from exporter s. The set captures the wedges between the world prices and the domestic pre-VAT prices of imports. We denote the tariffs on imports used in export processing as $tmsx_{is}$, which differ from the tariffs levied on imports used in domestic production (tms_{is}). To simulate an increase (decrease) in duty drawback rates, one needs to reduce (increase) $tmsx_{is}$ while keeping tms_{is} unchanged. The second set of instruments consists of the VATs. There are two types of VAT: one on the composite imports i used in producing export j ($tfmx_{ij}$), and the other on imports i used in domestic production of j (tfm_{ij}). To simulate an increase (decrease) in

VAT rebate rates, one needs to reduce (increase) the former while keeping
the latter constant.

19.4   Effects of Duty Drawbacks and Tax Rebates: Illustrative Experiments

In this section we present illustrative experiments based on the modified
CGE model. To use the GTAP database (Dimaranan and McDougall, 2002)
for our analysis, recalibration is necessary. Specifically, the model structure
of dual production and dual import demand needs to be substantiated
by a split of cost data and bilateral import data. But such data are not
available from the GTAP database. Without additional information, we
choose to use the value shares of domestic outputs and exports to determine
equi-proportionally an initial split of primary factors, domestic inputs, and
imported inputs used in the two activities for each industry. In the case
of imported inputs, the split applies at the bilateral level. This simplistic
approach is adopted as a crude solution to tackle the problem of lack of data
on the different input/output coefficients, especially the imported input
intensity, in the two activities.

The GTAP version 5 database, using 1997 as its base year, consists of
65 regions and 57 industries. To focus on the pertinent sectors for China,
we aggregate the economy into 10 regions/countries and 11 industries.[7] The
aggregation is guided by China's exporting industries, namely textiles and
clothing, chemical and plastic products, electronics, machinery, motor vehicles and other transportation equipment, other manufacturing, as well as
natural resources, agricultural and food, communications, financial services,
and other services.

Two series of experiments are conducted. In the first series (Exp1–4),
we explore the impact of increasing duty drawbacks by carrying out four
experiments in which the tariff rates on imported inputs used in the exporting activity ($tmsx_{is}$) are progressively reduced by 25, 50, 75, and 100%. In
the second series (Exp5–8), we increase the VAT rebate rates by progressively reducing tfm_{ij} by 25, 50, 75, and 100%. The respective tariff and
VAT rates in the experiments are shown in Table 19.1.

---

[7]They are mainland China, its main trading partners (Hong Kong, Taiwan, Japan,
Korea, The Association of Southeast Asian Nations [ASEAN], Australia and New
Zealand, North American Free Trade Agreement [NAFTA], and the European Union
[EU]), and a rest of the world region.

Table 19.1   Targeted tariff rates and VAT rates (%) on imported inputs used in export processing under Experiments 1–8.

	Tariff rates in Exp1–4 $(tmsx)^*$				VAT rates in Exp5–8 $(tfmx)^{**}$			
	Exp1	Exp2	Exp3	Exp4	Exp5	Exp6	Exp7	Exp8
Agrifood	29.5	19.67	9.83	0	−1.15	−2.3	−3.44	−4.59
Resources	1.56	1.04	0.52	0	−1.38	−2.76	−4.14	−5.52
Textiles	15.23	10.15	5.08	0	−1.17	−2.34	−3.51	−4.68
Chemicals	10.03	6.68	3.34	0	−1.54	−3.08	−4.62	−6.16
Motor vehicles	12.53	8.35	4.18	0	−1.23	−2.47	−3.7	−4.94
Electronics	8.8	5.87	2.93	0	−0.95	−1.91	−2.86	−3.81
Machinery	10.3	6.87	3.43	0	−1.15	−2.31	−3.46	−4.61
Manufacturing	8.85	5.9	2.95	0	−1.25	−2.5	−3.74	−4.99
Communication	0	0	0	0	−1	−2	−3	−4
Finance	0	0	0	0	−3.8	−7.59	−11.39	−15.18
Services	0	0	0	0	−1.09	−2.18	−3.27	−4.36

*:For simplicity, these tariff rates are the simple average of China's bilateral tariff rates.
**: These VAT rates apply to the industry's demand for all imported intermediates. Negative numbers signal positive subsidies.

Note that the effective import tariff rates for imported inputs should be zero for many products due to the drawbacks and exemptions provided. However, the GTAP database does not differentiate imports for export-processing purposes and ordinary imports. Thus, the same tariff rates are presented for imports for various purposes and they are likely the averages of the actual tariffs levied on ordinary imports and the virtually zero tariffs on imported components of exported goods. We start in the experiments with these "average" tariff rates. The tariffs imposed on export processors are reduced, while the ones faced by ordinary import users are kept constant. Clearly, here we simulate the effects of tariff drawbacks in a counterfactual sense.

As for the VAT rates, the GTAP database displays none for imported inputs. Instead, all the input-related domestic distortions are lumped together into the category of output tax. To have a somewhat meaningful starting point for the VAT rebate experiments, we choose to reduce the VAT rebate rate as if there were a VAT rate that is equal to the output tax rate.[8]

---

[8]Since the VAT rates in the database are zero, these shocks lead to subsidies for imported inputs.

19.4.1 *Results: Duty drawbacks*

We discuss the effects of duty drawbacks on final outputs of domestic sales and export processing, and then trace the driving forces of these changes by examining changes in domestic and export activities' demands for imported and domestic inputs, and primary factors. We also report the changes in welfare.

19.4.1.1 *Domestic outputs and exports*

First, we observe from Table 19.2 that reducing $tmsx_{ir}$ leads to an expansion of export processing and a slight contraction of domestic production in most industries. For example, under Exp1 (25% reduction), total exports of textile and clothing, motor vehicles, and electronics increase by 2.7, 1.7, 5.8%, respectively, whereas total domestic outputs of these products decrease slightly (< 1%). We also observe that exports of services (including communication, financial services, and other services) decrease slightly due to the fact that the initial *ad valorem* tariff rates for these sectors in the GTAP database (see Table 19.1) are zero.[9] Therefore, sectors with actual tariff reductions expand at the expense of the service sectors by drawing resources out of the latter. Exports of agricultural and food products also decrease, despite the significant tariff cut as shown in Table 19.1. This

Table 19.2   Domestic outputs and exports in China, % change from base data.

	Domestic production				Export processing			
	Exp1	Exp2	Exp3	Exp4	Exp1	Exp2	Exp3	Exp4
Agrifood	−0.09	−0.2	−0.35	−0.54	−0.87	−1.7	−2.42	−2.89
Resources	−0.2	−0.42	−0.69	−1.01	0.09	0.19	0.31	0.45
Textiles	−0.49	−1.05	−1.68	−2.4	2.7	6.08	10.35	15.84
Chemicals	−0.22	−0.46	−0.74	−1.05	0.96	1.95	2.99	4.07
Motor vehicles	−0.37	−0.83	−1.39	−2.1	1.72	5.04	11.05	21.57
Electronics	−0.05	−0.17	−0.37	−0.68	5.84	12.17	19.03	26.39
Machinery	−0.23	−0.49	−0.8	−1.15	0.82	1.61	2.36	3.02
Manufacturing	−0.18	−0.4	−0.65	−0.94	−0.59	−1.3	−2.15	−3.2
Communication	−0.03	−0.06	−0.1	−0.16	−1.55	−3.31	−5.31	−7.61
Finance	−0.04	−0.1	−0.17	−0.26	−1.52	−3.24	−5.19	−7.4
Services	0.04	0.09	0.13	0.17	−1.35	−2.83	−4.46	−6.28

Source: Simulation results from Experiments 1–4.

---

[9]The GTAP database does not take account of non-tariff protections imposed on services.

seemingly paradoxical result can be explained by the cost structure of these products, which is dominated by domestic inputs and primary factors. The incentive offered through the reduction of tariffs on imported inputs does little in boosting their outputs, as imported inputs are not used intensively (with a cost share of only about 4% as shown in the GTAP database). The expansion of other sectors also contributes to a decreased use of domestic inputs and primary factors in agriculture.

Second, for most products, the percentage changes in exports and domestic production increase in absolute terms as drawback rates increase from 25 to 100%, indicating that it is indeed effective to use duty drawback to boost exports, albeit this instrument may have a negative impact on domestic production. Taking electronics as an example, exports increase by 5.8% with a 25% drawback, jumping to 26.4% when the drawback rate rises to 100%, whereas domestic output decreases by 0.05 and 0.68% respectively under the two scenarios. Similar changes can be also observed for textiles and clothing, and motor vehicles. Again, agriculture and food products remain an exception. The effects on exports of agriculture and food are negative, intensifying from a 0.9% decrease (with a 25% drawback) to a reduction of 2.9% (with 100% drawback).

Lastly, the smaller relative changes in domestic outputs, as compared to export processing, suggest that the expansion of export activities does not come entirely at the expense of domestic production. Rather, it is the greater and cheaper access to foreign-produced inputs that are primarily responsible for these expansions.

19.4.1.2 *Imported and domestic inputs*

What drives the above changes in exports and domestic production in China? To answer this question, we need to look at how imported and domestically produced intermediates used in the two production activities are affected by the reductions of tariff rates (or increases in duty drawbacks). These results are reported in Tables 19.3 and 19.4. Starting with the lower panel of Table 19.3, we observe that imported inputs used by export processing increase at different rates. For instance, the last column of Table 19.3 shows that total imports of agriculture, textile, motor vehicles, and electronics used by exporting activities increase the most, whereas imports of natural resources change very little. Imported input demands by domestic activities (upper panel of Table 19.3) also increase, but at much smaller scales (almost all less than 1%). The reason that such demands also

Table 19.3 Imported intermediate inputs in China under Experiment 1, % changes from base data.

	Agri.	Resour.	Textile	Chemic.	Motor	Electr.	Machine	Manuf.	Comm.	Finance	Service	Total*
	Imported inputs used in domestic production											
Agrifood	0.64	0.55	0.17	0.47	0.16	0.54	0.54	0.56	0.54	0.69	0.78	0.67
Resource	0.33	0.21	-0.07	0.2	0.03	0.36	0.15	0.19	0.41	0.38	0.47	0.21
Textiles	0.61	0.62	0.28	0.54	0.41	0.67	0.55	0.59	0.83	0.77	0.85	0.49
Chemical	0.32	0.19	-0.12	0.18	0.06	0.33	0.18	0.22	0.41	0.37	0.5	0.22
Motor	1.24	1.13	0.83	1.11	0.98	1.27	1.02	1.15	1.33	1.29	1.28	1.25
Electronic	0.29	0.15	-0.13	0.15	-0.03	0.24	0.05	0.14	0.37	0.28	0.39	0.31
Machinery	0.61	0.37	0.06	0.36	0.25	0.61	0.39	0.4	0.64	0.48	0.68	0.58
Manuf.	0.52	0.43	0.12	0.39	0.24	0.54	0.37	0.44	0.59	0.57	0.69	0.51
Commun.	0.58	0.48	0.18	0.45	0.3	0.62	0.44	0.49	0.65	0.63	0.72	0.62
Finance	0.54	0.43	0.13	0.4	0.27	0.55	0.39	0.45	0.56	0.59	0.67	0.56
Services	0.54	0.43	0.14	0.42	0.27	0.59	0.4	0.45	0.61	0.55	0.65	0.64
	Imported inputs used in export processing											
Agrifood	19.76	21.32	21.93	20.56	16.53	23.15	22.92	20.41	13.79	18.92	19.22	21.02
Resource	-0.13	0.81	3.47	1.71	2.44	6.61	1.51	0.07	-0.79	-0.79	-0.61	0.21
Textiles	11.95	15.39	17.6	15.17	16.51	19.94	15.52	13.66	14.39	13.38	13.48	17.29
Chemicals	4.13	4.8	7.41	5.86	7.12	10.75	5.97	4.35	3.74	3.49	4.17	6.69
Motor	23.24	24.34	27.49	25.35	26.77	31.28	23.6	23.51	22.82	22.31	20.56	24.79
Electronic	4.25	4.76	7.85	6.04	6.37	9.97	4.61	3.8	3.79	2.71	3.32	9.36
Machine	7.6	6.85	9.57	7.94	9.28	14.3	8.37	6.46	6.36	4.65	6.17	8.77
Manuf.	5.48	6.7	9.33	7.41	8.2	12.36	7.12	5.86	4.75	4.75	5.34	7.1
Commun.	-0.2	0.77	3.39	1.64	2.41	6.55	1.5	0.08	-0.89	-0.86	-0.68	1.3
Finance	-0.25	0.71	3.34	1.58	2.37	6.47	1.44	0.04	-0.98	-0.9	-0.73	1.69
Services	-0.25	0.72	3.35	1.6	2.36	6.51	1.45	0.04	-0.94	-0.95	-0.76	0.39

Source: Simulation results from Experiment 1.

Note: Column headings refer to industries whereas row headings refer to intermediate inputs. Subsequent tables also share this convention. The last column of the upper panel refers to changes in imports for all domestic uses, not just for intermediate input use, whereas the last column of the lower panel refers to changes in imports used in export processing.

Table 19.4 Domestic inputs used in domestic production and export processing in China under Experiment 1, % changes from base data.

	Agri.	Resour.	Textile	Chemic.	Motor	Electr.	Machin.	Manuf.	Comm.	Finance	Service
	Domestic inputs used in domestic production										
Agrifood	-0.13	-0.22	-0.59	-0.3	-0.6	-0.23	-0.23	-0.21	-0.23	-0.08	0.01
Resource	-0.11	-0.23	-0.51	-0.24	-0.41	-0.08	-0.28	-0.25	-0.03	-0.06	0.03
Textiles	-0.34	-0.33	-0.67	-0.41	-0.54	-0.28	-0.4	-0.36	-0.12	-0.18	-0.1
Chemicals	-0.2	-0.33	-0.64	-0.34	-0.45	-0.19	-0.33	-0.3	-0.11	-0.14	-0.02
Motor	-0.27	-0.38	-0.68	-0.41	-0.54	-0.24	-0.49	-0.37	-0.19	-0.23	-0.23
Electronic	-0.32	-0.46	-0.73	-0.46	-0.64	-0.37	-0.56	-0.47	-0.24	-0.33	-0.22
Machinery	-0.18	-0.42	-0.73	-0.43	-0.54	-0.18	-0.4	-0.38	-0.15	-0.31	-0.12
Manuf.	-0.18	-0.26	-0.57	-0.3	-0.46	-0.16	-0.33	-0.26	-0.11	-0.13	-0.01
Communic.	-0.1	-0.21	-0.51	-0.23	-0.38	-0.07	-0.24	-0.2	-0.04	-0.06	0.03
Finance	-0.13	-0.24	-0.54	-0.27	-0.4	-0.12	-0.28	-0.22	-0.11	-0.07	0
Services	-0.1	-0.21	-0.5	-0.22	-0.38	-0.06	-0.24	-0.19	-0.04	-0.1	0
	Domestic inputs used in export processing										
Agrifood	-1.85	-0.57	-0.07	-1.19	-4.5	0.93	0.74	-1.31	-6.74	-2.53	-2.29
Resource	-0.9	0.04	2.67	0.93	1.65	5.79	0.73	-0.7	-1.55	-1.56	-1.37
Textiles	-5.27	-2.36	-0.49	-2.54	-1.41	1.49	-2.25	-3.82	-3.21	-4.06	-3.97
Chemicals	-2.14	-1.51	0.94	-0.52	0.68	4.08	-0.41	-1.93	-2.51	-2.74	-2.1
Motor	-4.05	-3.19	-0.74	-2.41	-1.3	2.21	-3.77	-3.84	-4.38	-4.77	-6.14
Electronic	-3.94	-3.47	-0.62	-2.29	-1.99	1.33	-3.6	-4.35	-4.36	-5.36	-4.8
Machinery	-1.91	-2.59	-0.11	-1.59	-0.37	4.2	-1.2	-2.94	-3.03	-4.59	-3.21
Manuf.	-1.74	-0.6	1.85	0.06	0.79	4.67	-0.21	-1.38	-2.42	-2.41	-1.86
Communic.	-0.88	0.08	2.68	0.94	1.71	5.82	0.81	-0.61	-1.57	-1.54	-1.36
Finance	-0.91	0.04	2.65	0.9	1.69	5.76	0.77	-0.63	-1.64	-1.56	-1.39
Services	-0.88	0.08	2.69	0.95	1.71	5.83	0.81	-0.6	-1.57	-1.58	-1.39

Source: Simulation results from Experiment 1.

increase is that as domestic outputs decline (due to resources moving out of the domestic activities), market prices for domestic products are pushed up by aggregated domestic demands (including consumer demands). These rises in domestic prices, coupled with little changes in import prices, make it natural for domestic firms to substitute domestic inputs with imported inputs. Nonetheless, the overall decline of domestic outputs makes this increase very limited.

To further illustrate the substitution between domestic and imported intermediate inputs in the two activities, we also present changes in domestic inputs used in the two activities in Table 19.4 (results from experiment 1). From Table 19.4, several observations can be made. First, uses of domestic inputs in all domestic production activities and many export-processing activities decrease. Second, for a few exporting products such as electronics, motor vehicles, and textiles, domestic input uses actually increase, due to strong output expansions in these products. Nevertheless, these increased uses of domestic inputs lag far behind their uses of imported inputs (as shown in Table 19.3). Third, for most sectors, the relative deceases of domestic inputs used by export processing, as compared to the increased uses of imported inputs, are much greater than that by their domestic counterparts. For instance, decreases in domestic inputs used by domestic production of electronics (column 7 in Table 19.4) are less than 0.4%, which are modest declines compared to the small increased uses of imported inputs (shown in column 7 of Table 19.3). In contrast, the gaps between the changes of imported and domestic inputs used by the production of electronics exports are much wider. Lastly, note that the actual degree of substitution in the export-processing activities might not be fully visible by only looking at Table 19.4 — one has to realize that these decreases happen at the same time as the actual final outputs of most export-processing activities increase. To illustrate these points, again take motor vehicles as an example. Uses of domestically produced motor vehicle parts and electronics by motor vehicles decrease by 1.3 and 2%, respectively, whereas uses of their imported counterparts rise by 26.8 and 6.4%, respectively. These ups and downs result in a 1.7% increase in the final output of motor vehicles. Considering the modest actual tariff reductions implied by the 25% cut (cuts of bilateral tariff rates ranging from 3% for electronics, to 4.2% for motor vehicles), these substitutions are quite dramatic.

Table 19.5   Primary factors used in domestic and export activities under Experiments 1–4, % changes from base data.

	Domestic production				Export processing			
	Exp1	Exp2	Exp3	Exp4	Exp1	Exp2	Exp3	Exp4
Land	0	−0.02	−0.05	−0.1	0.08	0.36	0.93	1.98
Unskilled labor	−0.1	−0.21	−0.36	−0.54	1.06	2.34	3.93	5.92
Skilled labor	−0.05	−0.11	−0.19	−0.29	0.74	1.62	2.7	4.04
Capital	−0.14	−0.3	−0.49	−0.72	1.29	2.8	4.6	6.78
Natural resources	0	−0.01	−0.02	−0.03	0.04	0.12	0.28	0.54

Source: Simulation results from Experiments 1–4.

19.4.1.3 *Primary factors*

Changes in aggregated factor uses by the two activities also deserve some comments. Table 19.5 illustrates that factor demands by domestic activities all decline, whereas those by export activities all increase. With fixed factor endowments in our static simulation, this implies a reallocation of factors from domestic activities to export activities. The most notable movement happens in labor and capital. Under Experiment 4, export processors' demands for skilled labor grow by over 4% whereas demands for capital grow by almost 7%. These results again illustrate the effects of duty drawbacks in promoting exports not only by attracting more resources from abroad, but also by reallocating resources within the national boundary. Indeed, China's export-processing industries, especially in its coastal areas, are increasingly becoming major employers of workers moved out of traditionally inward-looking state-owned enterprises and labor that has migrated from the rural areas.

19.4.1.4 *Welfare*

While our theoretical analysis points out that the efficiency and hence welfare effect of increasing duty drawbacks is ambiguous, our CGE model is able to evaluate such effects numerically. We present these results in Table 19.6. Total welfare changes in China as measured in equivalent variations are all positive in the four experiments, ranging from US$255 million (Exp1) to US$467 million (Exp4).

These welfare changes result mainly from two conflicting effects: the efficiency gain from lowering the distortions associated with import duties

Table 19.6   Welfare results for selected countries/regions under Experiments 1–4.

	Exp1	Exp2	Exp3	Exp4
Total welfare changes (equivalent variations in million US$)				
China	255.5	430.2	467	272.2
Hong Kong	45.5	103.7	179	276.9
Japan	146	325.2	546.4	822.3
Korea	16.3	36.5	62.1	95.4
NAFTA	123.6	268.8	442.2	653
EU	80.6	167.7	262.7	366.5
Terms of trade, % changes from base data				
China	−0.155	−0.334	−0.545	−0.796
Hong Kong	0.056	0.129	0.226	0.358
Japan	0.022	0.05	0.084	0.129
Korea	0.012	0.026	0.042	0.06
NAFTA	0.006	0.012	0.02	0.029
EU	0.001	0.003	0.004	0.006

Source: Simulation results from Experiments 1–4.

and the deterioration in terms of trade. The latter results are reported in Table 19.6. The percentage changes in the terms of trade for China range from −0.15% in Exp1 to about −0.8% in Exp4, thereby leading to losses in welfare. The terms-of-trade loss is so significant in Exp4 that it wipes out a big portion of the efficiency gain, leading to a smaller overall welfare change of US$272 million, as compared to that in Exp3 (where the drawback rate is smaller).[10]

Table 19.6 also provides welfare results for several trading partners of China. In general, these countries benefit from lower tariffs imposed by China on their exports. When import tariffs are completely removed, benefits accruing to Japan, NAFTA, and Hong Kong exceed the gains to China itself. These gains to China's trading partners can again be attributed to the terms-of-trade effects in the form of transfer of tariff revenues.

19.4.2   *Results: VAT rebates*

A reduction of VAT achieves the same qualitative effects as lowering tariff rates for imports used for the same purposes. It is noteworthy that due to declining use of duty drawbacks, VAT rebate has become a major policy instrument for promoting exports.

---

[10]The efficiency gains are implicit in the table. They are roughly the differences between the total welfare changes and the terms-of-trade effects.

Table 19.7   Final outputs in domestic and exporting activities in China under Experiments 5–8, % changes from base data.

	Domestic production				Export processing			
	Exp5	Exp6	Exp7	Exp8	Exp5	Exp6	Exp7	Exp8
Agrifood	−0.03	−0.06	−0.1	−0.13	−0.5	−0.99	−1.49	−1.98
Natures	−0.08	−0.16	−0.24	−0.32	0.26	0.53	0.8	1.07
Textiles	−0.21	−0.42	−0.63	−0.85	0.45	0.9	1.37	1.85
Chemicals	−0.08	−0.16	−0.24	−0.32	0.77	1.54	2.31	3.08
Motor vehicles	−0.11	−0.22	−0.33	−0.45	0.65	1.33	2.07	2.84
Electronic	−0.03	−0.06	−0.09	−0.13	2.06	4.15	6.27	8.42
Machinery	−0.08	−0.16	−0.23	−0.31	0.51	1.03	1.54	2.06
Manufacturing	−0.05	−0.11	−0.16	−0.22	0.1	0.21	0.32	0.42
Communication	−0.01	−0.01	−0.02	−0.03	−0.54	−1.08	−1.62	−2.16
Finance	−0.02	−0.04	−0.06	−0.08	1.31	2.62	3.94	5.27
Services	0.01	0.03	0.04	0.05	−0.37	−0.73	−1.1	−1.46

Source: Simulation results from Experiments 5–8.

We first look at changes in final output in the two activities (Table 19.7). Domestic outputs mostly decline slightly, even under Experiment 8 where the VAT is fully rebated. In contrast, exports increase in all but a few sectors. These increases are generally small with a 25% rebate, but become more visible when the VAT is fully rebated. Second, we turn to changes in input and factor uses. For simplicity we only discuss the results for motors and electronics from Experiment 5 (25% rebate). Table 19.8 shows small increases in the use of imported inputs and small declines of domestic inputs in domestic production. In contrast, in the export-processing activities, imported inputs increase quite dramatically, whereas domestic inputs either increase or decrease. For export processing of electronics, substitutions of imported inputs for domestic inputs does not push down the use of domestic inputs. In fact, uses of most domestic inputs increase by more than 1%. Still, these changes are much smaller than that for imported inputs, indicating that the imported input intensity rises in production of electronics. For the export processing of motor vehicles, as uses of many domestic inputs decline, it is quite obvious that imported inputs are used more intensively as a result of tax rebates. Lastly, reallocation of factors follows quite the same pattern in that factors move out of domestic production and into export processing. The sizes of the reallocation increase with increased tax rebate rates.[11]

---

[11]Detailed results from Experiments 5–8 are available from the authors upon request.

Table 19.8   Input uses in domestic production and export processing of motor vehicles and electronics in China, % changes from base data (Experiment 5).

	Domestic production				Export processing			
	Imported inputs		Domestic inputs		Imported inputs		Domestic inputs	
	Motors	Electr.	Motors	Electr.	Motors	Electr.	Motors	Electr.
Agrifood	0.07	0.18	−0.19	−0.09	3.01	4.14	−0.38	1.45
Resource	0.05	0.14	−0.13	−0.04	4.16	4.92	0.29	1.89
Textiles	0.16	0.22	−0.17	−0.11	4.46	4.84	−0.18	1.18
Chemicals	0.05	0.11	−0.14	−0.08	2.89	3.61	0.21	1.5
Motor	0.38	0.45	−0.17	−0.1	7.33	7.22	−0.17	1.31
Electronic	0.01	0.08	−0.21	−0.14	2.79	3.51	−1.08	0.47
Machinery	0.11	0.21	−0.17	−0.08	3.75	4.69	−0.22	1.55
Manuf.	0.11	0.19	−0.14	−0.07	3.7	4.4	0.21	1.64
Communic.	0.13	0.21	−0.11	−0.03	3.34	4.2	0.59	2.02
Finance	0.12	0.19	−0.12	−0.05	3.26	4	0.52	1.83
Services	0.12	0.2	−0.11	−0.03	3.42	4.26	0.62	2.04

Source: Simulation results from Experiment 5.

19.5   Concluding Remarks

We have used a general equilibrium model to illustrate the output and welfare effects of duty drawbacks and VAT rebates, respectively. The theoretical propositions are substantiated with simulations using a modified GTAP model, which is characterized by dual production (domestic production and export processing) and dual import structure (imports for domestic uses and for export processing) for the Chinese economy. We have obtained several results by conducting two sets of simulations. First, these policies are generally export promoting. Second, a small part of export expansion comes at the expense of a slight decline of domestic production through factor reallocation and input substitution, whereas a large part can be attributed to greater and cheaper access to foreign inputs. Third, substitution toward more imported inputs not only happens in export processing, but also in domestic activities although to a smaller degree. This is mainly due to competition for limited domestic products by consumers and industries. Fourth, sectoral results differ substantially. Electronics, motor vehicles and other transport equipment, chemical and plastic products, other manufacturing, textile and clothing benefit from the policy change, while agricultural and food products, as well as natural resources are sectors with little or even adverse impacts. These results are hardly surprising given the former are all major exports of China. Lastly, although our theoretical analysis of welfare is ambiguous, simulation results show that increasing the drawbacks and rebates does raise welfare. The negative terms-of-trade effect is also obtained from the simulations.

Some caveats regarding the data used in the simulations need to be pointed out. The first is the lack of data on the cost structure of domestic production and export processing. To deal with this problem, we choose to recalibrate their respective cost structures according to the value of their final output shares. It would be coincidental if this simplistic treatment reveals the actual cost shares of imported inputs in export-processing activities. As such, the results obtained from the experiments should be treated as illustrative only, and any serious attempt to accurately capture the effects of the policies obviously needs to build on a better representation of the actual cost shares. Our second limitation is related to the assumption that the same initial tariff rates are imposed on imports used as inputs in producing exports and those used elsewhere. These initial rates are probably a weighted average of the rates applied on the two types of imports. When both types of tariff rates are included in a future version of the GTAP database, we can re-run the duty drawback experiments by raising the tariff rates on imported inputs. We can then look at how the statutory tariff rates would have restricted trade and how exports from China would have reacted to the tariff reductions.[12]

Appendix: Stability

Following Chang (1981), the dynamic adjustment process for the model is specified as follows:

$$\dot{Y} = a_1\{p - \alpha(w,v)\} = a_1\left\{p^* + \rho tc(1-\mu)\left(\frac{v_d}{v_f}\right)^{\mu} - w - v_d^{\mu}v_f^{1-\mu}\right\},$$

$$\dot{X} = a_2\{1 - \beta(w,r)\},$$

$$\dot{M}_d = a_3\{v_d - \gamma(w,r)\},$$

$$\dot{w} = a_4\{Y + \beta_w(w,r)X + \gamma_w(w,r)M_d - L\},$$

---

[12]This "backcasting" application of CGE models was first used by Gehlhar (1997) and was utilized by Coyle *et al.* (1998).

$$\dot{r} = a_5\{\beta_r(w,r)X + \gamma_r(w,r)M_d - K\},$$

$$\dot{v}_d = a_6\left\{\frac{\mu v Y}{v_d} - M_d\right\},$$

where a dot over the variable denotes the time derivative, and a_i is the positive speed of the adjustment. Linearization of the above system around the equilibrium values gives:

$$
\begin{bmatrix} \dot{Y} \\ \dot{X} \\ \dot{M}_d \\ \dot{w} \\ \dot{r} \\ \dot{v}_d \end{bmatrix}
=
\begin{bmatrix}
0 & 0 & 0 & -1 & 0 & -K \\
0 & 0 & 0 & -\beta_w & -\beta_r & 0 \\
0 & 0 & 0 & -\gamma_w & -\gamma_r & 1 \\
1 & \beta_w & \gamma_w & -F & H & 0 \\
0 & \beta_r & \gamma_r & H & -S & 0 \\
\mu c \left(\dfrac{v_d}{v_f}\right)^{\mu-1} & 0 & -1 & 0 & 0 & -G
\end{bmatrix}
\begin{bmatrix} dY \\ dX \\ dM_d \\ dw \\ dr \\ dv_d \end{bmatrix},
$$

where $F = -\beta_{ww}X - \gamma_{ww}M_d$, $H = \beta_{wr}X + \gamma_{wr}M_d$ and $S = -\beta_{rr}X - \gamma_{rr}M_d$. The D-stability (for all speeds of adjustment) of the original non-linear system requires that every principle minor of odd order is non-positive. Denoting the principle minor by J_i, we have:

$$J_1 = J_2 = J_3 = J_4 = J_5 = 0,$$

$$J_6 = \beta_r^2 + \beta_r\left[K + \mu c\left(\frac{v_d}{v_f}\right)^{\mu-1}\right](\beta_r\gamma_w - \beta_w\gamma_r)$$

$$+ K\mu c\left(\frac{v_d}{v_f}\right)^{\mu-1}(\beta_r\gamma_w - \beta_w\gamma_r)^2.$$

The stability condition requires $J_6 > 0$ and hence a sufficient condition for stability is $\beta_r\gamma_w - \beta_w\gamma_r > 0$.

Chapter 20

Summary and Suggestions for Future Research

The main objective of this book is to study the complex relationships between inward foreign investment and international trade for an economy, especially a developing economy. As foreign firms attempt to penetrate and capture the domestic markets, and the host country strives to protect domestic producers, the interest of foreign firms appears in conflict with the national interest of the host country. To regulate foreign firms in the past, output-based trade-related investment measure (TRIMs), exemplified by export requirements and tax rebates, and input-based TRIMs, such as content protection and ownership controls, had been implemented.

It is notable that, due to the current trend of liberalization and globalization in trade and investment, most of the TRIMs on foreign firms have been phased out over the last decade. Nonetheless, the historical contributions made by TRIMs to enhance national income and trade balance cannot be overlooked. To provide a proper documentation with analysis of TRIMs is another purpose for writing this book. We start with a questionnaire survey in Chapter 2 regarding TRIMs used in China on foreign firms and then provide theoretical foundations for TRIMs in Chapters 3 to 15 by probing various conditions for which TRIMs lead to higher national welfare, while empirical testing and numerical simulations for the viability of TRIMs in China are provided in Chapters 16 to 19.

This book has examined the resource allocation and welfare effects of various TRIMs, with a focus on the optimal level of individual measure and jointly optimal policy mixes. We identify the second-best outcomes for the economy in which preexisting distortions of import tariffs and quotas are present. Although we have substantively investigated the TRIMs, there still remain many unexplored but interesting issues worthy of future research. A few such topics are suggested, as follows.

20.1   TRIMS and the Environment

The linkage and interaction between international trade and the environment have been extensively studied in the literature. Using a general equilibrium framework, Copeland (1994) begins with the study on the first- and second-best policy reforms on trade and pollution taxes, and finds that a uniform reduction of all policy distortions toward the first-best solution improves welfare of a small open economy. Neary (2006) diagrammatically illustrates the deviations between the first- and second-best rules and highlights the policy coordination and adjustments between trade and pollution taxes. Michael and Hatizipanayotou (2009) investigate the government revenue effect of these two taxes.

In light of the above studies, a topic for further study would be the effects on resource allocation, revenue, and welfare of TRIMs for a polluted economy. In general, the TRIMs, notably export requirements and content protection, raise production costs and hence restrict the production activities of foreign firms in the host country. Naturally, we would like to seek answers to the following questions: Can TRIMs alleviate pollution emissions and lead to a cleaner environment? Can TRIMs have any impacts on the designs of pollution and investment taxes on foreign firms? If yes, what are the conditions?

20.2   TRIMs and Firm Productivity

In the seminal paper by Melitz (2003), firm heterogeneity and efficiency play the central role in explaining the patterns of exports and outsourcing by the firm level. Following this line of research, the main issue is to identify firms' characteristics that facilitate exports and outsourcing. The general finding is that goods exports and production outsourcing can be undertaken only by more productive firms. In particular, trade costs and entry costs are among the key factors that drive the result on the so-called efficiency ranking of firms. Do input TRIMs, such as privatization and the structure of firm ownership, affect firm-level productivity that in turn induces the activities of goods exports and production outsourcing? This should be an interesting topic for future research.

20.3   TRIMs and Technological Progress

Technological innovation and progress have become crucial contributors to spur and sustain the growth of an economy. In addition, rapid advances in communication and information technology have resulted in switching of the attention from trade in outputs to trade in factors and/or technology, and the latter are regarded as the main sources of improving international competitiveness and welfare of a nation. Output TRIMs, e.g., export requirements, on foreign firms limit the quantities of domestic sales, while input TRIMs regarding equity controls restrict foreign ownership in firms. Do limited domestic sales cause foreign firms to gain more value-added by switching production from labor-intensive to capital- or skilled-intensive goods? Does equity control result in an obstacle for technological transfer from advanced countries to developing economies?

20.4   TRIMS and Social Conflict

Asset distribution toward the rich has become a worldwide phenomenon, not only in developed but also in developing economies. For example, in 2012, the top 10% of Americans have 80% of the financial asset in the US, while the equivalent group in China has 84.6% of the wealth. The trend of growing asset inequality has led to social conflict and resentment against the rich. In his recent book, *The Price of Inequality*, Stiglitz (2012) discusses adverse impacts of asset inequality on economic development and social harmony for the US economy.

By restricting foreign investments, TRIMs basically protect domestic production of importable sectors. How would the protection affect income inequality and asset distribution in the economy? This issue on income disparity is important in view of its strong social and economic implications. It is thus worthwhile to conduct further investigation.

20.5   Other Suggested Topics for Future Research

In several of the conclusion sections of the preceding chapters, topics related to various issues of TRIMs not yet fully explored but worthy of further studies, are indicated. Interested readers are referred to those sections for additional research topics.

References

Almansi, A.A., 1989, "Patterns of external adjustment in LDCS: do we understand them?" *International Economic Review*, 30, 77–84.

Anderson, J.E. and J.P. Neary, 1992, "Trade reform with quotas, partial rent retention and tariffs," *Econometrica*, 60, 57–76.

Antweiler, W., 1996, "The pollution terms of trade," *Economic Systems Research*, 8, 361–365.

Aoki, M., 1988, *Information, Incentives, and Bargaining in the Japanese Economy*, Cambridge: Cambridge University Press.

Arize, A.C., T. Osang, and D.J. Slottje, 2000, "Exchange-rate volatility and foreign trade: evidence from thirteen LDCs," *Journal of Business and Economic Statistics*, 18 (1), 10–17.

Armington, P.A., 1969, "A theory of demand for products distinguished by place of production," *IMF Staff Papers*, 16, 159–178.

Asakai, K., 1994, "An Integrated Perspective," in *The New World Trading System*, Paris: OECD.

Balasubramanyam, V.N., 1991, "Putting TRIMs to good use," *World Development*, 19, 1215–1224.

Batra, R.N., 1972, "Resource allocation in a general equilibrium model of production under uncertainty," *Journal of Economic Theory*, 8, 50–63.

Batra, R.N., 1973, "Nontraded goods, factor market distortions, and the gains from trade," *American Economic Review*, 63, 706–713.

Batra, R.N., 1975, *The Pure Theory of International Trade Under Uncertainty*, New York: Wiley.

Batra, R.N., 1986, "A general equilibrium model of multinational corporations in developing economies," *Oxford Economic Paper*, 38, 342–353.

Batra, R.N. and H. Beladi, 1990, "Pattern of trade between underemployed economies," *Economica*, 57, 485–493.

Batra, R.N. and F.R. Casas, 1976, "A synthesis of the Heckscher–Ohlin and the neoclassical models of international trade," *Journal of International Economics*, 6, 21–38.

Batra, R.N. and N. Naqvi, 1987, "Urban unemployment and gains from trade," *Economica*, 54, 381–395.

Batra, R.N. and R.V. Ramachandran, 1980, "Multinational firms and the theory of international trade and investment," *American Economic Review*, 70, 278–290.

Batra, R.N. and G.W. Scully, 1971, "The theory of wage differentials: welfare and immiserizing growth," *Journal of International Economics*, 241–247.

Beladi, H., 1988, "Variable returns to scale, urban unemployment and welfare," *Southern Economic Journal*, 55, 412–423.

Beladi, H., N.H. Chau, and M.A. Khan, 2000, "North–South investment flows and optimal environmental policies," *Journal of Environmental Economics and Management*, 40, 275–296.

Beladi, H. and S. Marjit, 1992, "Foreign capital and protectionism," *Canadian Journal of Economics*, 25, 233–238.

Beladi, H. and A.K. Parai, 1993, "Sluggish intersectoral factor movements and alternative trade policies," *Southern Economic Journal*, 59, 760–767.

Bhagwati, J.N., 1964, "The Pure Theory of International Trade: A Survey," *Economic Journal* 74, 1–78.

Bhagwati, J.N., 1971, "The generalized theory of distortions and welfare," in J.N. Bhagwati, R.W. Jones, R.A. Mundell, and J. Vanek (eds), *Trade, Balance of Payments, and Growth*, Amsterdam and London: North-Holland.

Bhagwati, J.N., 1973, "The theory of immiserizing growth: further applications," in B. Connolly and A.K. Swoboda (eds), *International Trade and Money*, London: Allen & Unwin.

Bhagwati, J.N., R.W. Jones, R.A. Mundell, and J. Vanek (eds), 1971, *Trade, Balance of Payments, and Growth*, Amsterdam and London: North-Holland.

Blackorby, C., D. Primont, and R. Russel, 1978, *Duality, Separability and Functional Structure: Theory and Applications*, Amsterdam: North-Holland.

Bond, E.W., 1991, "Optimal tax and tariff policies with tax credits," *Journal of International Economics*, 30, 317–329.

Bovenberg, A. Lans, and Rund A. de Mooij, 1994, "Environmental levies and distortionary taxation," *American Economic Review*, 84, 1085–1089.

Brander, J.A. and B.J. Spencer, 1985, "Export subsidies and international market share rivalry," *Journal of International Economics*, 18, 83–100.

Brecher, R.A. and C.F. Diaz Alejandro, 1977, "Tariffs, foreign capital and immiserizing growth," *Journal of International Economics*, 7, 317–322.

Buffie, E.F., 1985, "Quantitative restrictions and the welfare effects of capital inflow," *Journal of International Economics*, 19, 291–303.

Buffie, E.F., 2001, *Trade Policy in Developing Countries*, Cambridge: Cambridge University Press.

Campbell, J.Y. and P. Perron, 1991, "Pitfalls and opportunities: what macroeconomists should know about unit roots," in O.J. Blanchard and S. Fischer (eds), *NBER Macroeconomics Annual*, Cambridge, MA: MIT Press.

Casas, F.R., 1985, "Tariff protection and taxation of foreign capital: the welfare implication for a small country," *Journal of International Economics*, 19, 181–188.

Chang, W.W., 1981, "Production externalities, variable returns to scale and the theory of international trade," *International Economic Review*, 22, 511–525.

Chao, C.C., W.L. Chou, and E.S.H. Yu, 2001, "Export duty rebates and export performance: theory and China's experience," *Journal of Comparative Economics*, 29, 314–326.

Chao, C.C., W.L. Chou, and E.S.H. Yu 2002, "Domestic equity control, capital accumulation and welfare: theory and China's evidence," *The World Economy*, 25, 8.

Chao, C.C., B. Hazari, and E.S.H. Yu 2006, "Rising wage inequality in developing economies: privatization and competition," *Journal of International Trade and Economic Development*, 15, 375–385.

Chao, C.C., B. Hazari, J. Laffarguf and E.S.H. Yu, 2009, "A Dynamic Model of Tourism, Employment and Welfare: The Case of Hong Kong," *Pacific Economic Review*, 14, 2, 232–245.

Chao, C.C., C. Ingene, and E.S.H. Yu, 2004, "The impact of export-share requirements under production uncertainty," *International Review of Economics and Finance*, 13, 201–215.

Chao, C.C., J. Kerkvliet, and E.S.H. Yu, Eden, 2000, "Environmental preservation, sectoral unemployment, and trade in resources," *Review of Development Economics*, 4(1), 39–50.

Chao, C.C. and A. Takayama, 1990, "Monopolistic competition, nonhomotheticity, and the stability of the Chamberlinian tangency solution," *International Economic Review*, 31, 73–86.

Chao, C.C. and E.S.H. Yu, 1990, "Urban unemployment, terms of trade and welfare," *Southern Economic Journal*, 56, 743–751.

Chao, C.C. and E.S.H. Yu, 1993, "Content protection, urban unemployment and welfare," *Canadian Journal of Economics*, 26, 481–492.

Chao, C.C. and E.S.H. Yu, 1994a, "Export-share requirements and welfare in less developed countries: a three-sector general equilibrium analysis," *Journal of International Trade and Economic Development*, 3, 33–50.

Chao, C.C. and E.S.H. Yu, 1994b, "Foreign capital inflows and welfare in an economy with imperfect competition," *Journal of Development Economics*, 45, 141–154.

Chao, C.C. and E.S.H. Yu, 1994c, "Should export-share requirements be implemented under quota protection?" *Canadian Journal of Economics*, 27, 568–579.

Chao, C.C. and E.S.H. Yu, 1995, "The shadow price of foreign exchange in a dual economy," *Journal of Development Economics*, 46, 195–202.

Chao, C.C. and E.S.H. Yu, 1996a, "Are wholly foreign-owned enterprises better than joint ventures?" *Journal of International Economics*, 40, 225–237.

Chao, C.C. and E.S.H. Yu, 1996b, "Optimal policies of taxation on foreign investment and export performance requirements," *Public Finance*, 51, 201–216.

Chao, C.C. and E.S.H. Yu, 1997a, "Trade liberalization in oligopolistic competition with unemployment: a general equilibrium analysis," *Canadian Journal of Economics*, 30, 479–496.

Chao, C.C. and E.S.H. Yu, 1997b, "TRIMs, TREMs, and foreign investment." Mimeo.

Chao, C.C. and E.S.H. Yu, 1998a, "Export-share requirements, trade balances and welfare: a two-period analysis," *Journal of Development Economics*, 56, 217–228.

Chao, C.C. and E.S.H. Yu, 1998b, "Optimal pollution and foreign-investment taxes in a small open economy," *Journal of International Trade and Economic Development*, 7, 71–85.

Chao, C.C. and E.S.H. Yu, 1998c, "On investment measures and trade," *The World Economy*, 549–561.

Chao, C.C. and E.S.H. Yu, 1999, "Profit-sharing and international capital mobility in developing countries," *Review of International Economics*, 7, 755–752.

Chao, C.C. and E.S.H. Yu, 2000a, "Domestic equity controls of multinational enterprises," *The Manchester School*, 68, 321–330.

Chao, C.C. and E.S.H. Yu, 2000b, "TRIMs, environmental taxes, and foreign investment," *Canadian Journal of Economics*, 33, 799–817.

Chao, C.C. and E.S.H. Yu, 2003, "Export-performance requirements, foreign investment quotas, and welfare in a small dynamic economy," *Journal of Development Economics*, 72, 387–400.

Chao, C.C. and E.S.H. Yu, 2004, *Environmental Policy, International Trade, and Factor Markets*, Amsterdam: Elsevier.

Chao, C.C. and E.S.H. Yu, 2006, "Partial Privatization, Foreign Competition and Optimum Tariff," *Review of International Economics*, 14, 1, 97–102.

Chao, C.C. and E.S.H. Yu, 2007, "Trade liberalization, foreign ownership, and the environment in a small open economy," *International Review of Economics and Finance*, 16, 471–477.

Chao, C.C., E.S.H. Yu, and W. Yu, 2006, "China's import duty drawback and VAT rebate policies: a general equilibrium analysis," *China Economic Review*, 432–448.

Cheung, Y.-W. and K.S. Lai, 1993, "Finite-sample sizes of Johansen's likelihood ratio tests for cointegration," *Oxford Bulletin of Economics and Statistics*, 55, 313–328.

Cheung, Y.-W. and K.S. Lai, 1995, "Lag order and critical values of a modified Dickey–Fuller test," *Oxford Bulletin of Economics and Statistics*, 57, 411–419.

Ching, S., C.Y.P. Wong, and A. Zhang, 2004, "Non-tariff barriers to trade in the Pacific Rim," *Pacific Economic Review*, 9, 65–73.

Choi, E.K. and H. Beladi, 1993, "Optimal trade policies for a small open economy," *Economica*, 60, 475–486.

Choi, J.Y. and E.S.H. Yu, 1987, "Technical progress and output under variable returns to scale," *Economica*, 249–253.

Choi, J.Y. and E.S.H. Yu, 2006, "Industrial targeting and non-shiftable capital in the Harris–Todaro model," *Review of International Economics*, 14, 910–921.

Chou, W.L., 2000, "Exchange rate variability and China's exports," *Journal of Comparative Economics*, 28, 61–79.

Chowdhury, A.R., 1993, "Does exchange rate volatility depress trade flows? Evidence from Error-Correction model," *Review of Economics and Statistics*, 75, 700–706.

Conklin, D. and D. Lecraw, 1997, "Restrictions of foreign ownership during 1984–1994: developments and alternative policies," *Transnational Corporations*, 6, 1–30.

Copeland, B.R., 1994, "International trade and the environment: policy reform in a polluted small open economy," *Journal of Environmental Economics and Management*, 26, 44–65.

Copeland, B.R. and M.S. Taylor, 1994, "North–South trade and the environment," *Quarterly Journal of Economics*, 109, 755–787.

Copeland, B.R. and M.S. Taylor, 1997, "A simple model of trade, capital mobility, and the environment," NBER Working Paper Series, no. 5898.

Corden, W.M., 1971, *The Theory of Protection*, Oxford: Clarendon Press.

Coyle, W., M. Gehlhar, T. Hertel, Z. Wang, and W. Yu, 1998, "Understanding the determinants of structural change in world food markets," *American Journal of Agricultural Economics*, 80, 1051–1061.

Das, S.P., 1977, "Uncertainty and the Heckscher–Ohlin theorem: a comment," *Review of Economic Studies*, 44, 189–190.

Das, S.P. and S. Katayama, 2000, "International joint venture and host-country policies," Presented at the Conference of International Trade and Asia, City University of Hong Kong, July 19–21.

Davis, D.R., 1998, "Technology, unemployment and relative wages in a global economy," *European Economic Review*, 42, 1613–1633.

Dei, F., 1985a, "Welfare gains from capital inflows under import quota," *Economics Letters*, 18, 237–240.

Dei, F., 1985b, "Voluntary export restraints and foreign investment," *Journal of International Economics*, 19, 305–312.

Dewenter, K.L. and P.H. Malatesta, 2001, "State-owned and privately owned firms: an empirical analysis of profitability, leverage, and labor intensity," *American Economic Review*, 91, 320–334.

Diewert, W., 1978, "Duality Approaches to Microeconomic Theory," in K. Arrow and M. Intriligator (eds), *Handbook of Mathematical Economics*, Amsterdam: North-Holland.

Dimaranan, B.V. and R.A. McDougall, 2002, *Global Trade, Assistance, and Production: The GTAP 5 Data Base*, Purdue University, West Lafayette, IN: Center for Global Trade Analysis.

Dixit, A.K. and V. Norman, 1980, *Theory of International Trade*, Cambridge: Cambridge University Press.

Dixon, P.B., B.R. Parmenter, J. Sutton, and D.P. Vincent, 1982, *ORANI: A Multisectoral Model of the Australian Economy*, Amsterdam and London: North-Holland.

Elliott, G., T.J. Rothenberg, and J.H. Stock, 1996, "Efficient tests for an autoregressive unit root," *Econometrica*, 64, 813–836.

Epping, M.G., 1986, "Tradition in transition: the emergence of new categories in plant location," *Arkansas Business and Economic Review*, 19, 16–25.

Ethier, W.J., 1986, "The multinational firm," *Quarterly Journal of Economics*, 101, 805–833.

Feenstra, R.C., 2004, *Advanced International Trade: Theory and Evidence*, Princeton: Princeton University Press.

Feenstra, R.C. and G.H. Hanson, 1996, "Globalization, outsourcing, and wage inequality," *American Economic Review*, 86, 240–245.

Feenstra, R.C. and G.H. Hanson, 1997, "Foreign direct investment and relative wages: evidence from Mexico's maquiladoras," *Journal of International Economics*, 42, 371–393.

Feltenstein, A., 1992, "Oil prices and rural migration: the Dutch disease goes south," *Journal of International Money and Finance*, 11, 273–291.

Francois, J.F. and D. Nelson, 1998, "Trade, technology, and wages: general equilibrium mechanics," *Economic Journal*, 108, 1483–1499.

Fung, K.C., 1989, "Unemployment, profit-sharing and Japan's economic success," *European Economic Review*, 33, 783–796.

Fung, M.K.Y., 1994, "Content protection, resource allocation, and variable labor supply," *Canadian Journal of Economics*, 27, 175–182.

Gehlhar, M., 1997, "Historical analysis of growth and trade patterns in the pacific rim: an evaluation of the GTAP framework," in T.W. Hertel (ed.), *Global Trade Analysis: Modeling and Applications*, New York: Cambridge University Press.

Graham, E.M. and P. Sauve, 1998, "Toward a rules-based regime for investment: issues and challenges," in R. Howse (ed.), *The World Trading System*, London: Routledge.

Gray, W.B., 1997, "Manufacturing plant location: does state pollution regulation matter?" NBER Working Paper Series, no. 5880.

Greenaway, D., 1992, "Trade-related investment measures and development strategy," *Kyklos*, 45, 139–159.

Grinols, E.L., 1991, "Unemployment and foreign capital: the relative opportunity costs of domestic labor and welfare," *Economica*, 58, 107–121.

Grossman, G.M., 1981, "The theory of domestic content protection and content preferences," *Quarterly Journal of Economics*, 96, 583–603.

Grossman, G.M. and A.B. Krueger, 1993, "Environmental impacts of a North American Free Trade Agreement," in P. Garber (ed.), *The Mexico-U.S. Free Trade Agreement*, Cambridge, MA: MIT Press.

Gruen, F. and W.M. Corden, 1970, "A tariff that worsens the terms of trade," in R. Snape (ed.), *Studies in International Economics*, Amsterdam and London: North-Holland.

Gu, W. and S. Yabuuchi, 2003, "Local content requirements and urban unemployment," *International Review of Economics and Finance*, 12, 481–494.

Guisinger, S. and Associates, 1985, *Investment Incentives and Performance Requirements*, New York: Praeger.

Hamada, K., 1974, "An economic analysis of the duty-free zone," *Journal of International Economics*, 4, 225–241.

Hanoch, G., 1975, "Production and demand models in direct and indirect implicit additivity," *Econometrica*, 43, 395–419.

Harris, J.R. and M. Todaro, 1970, "Migration, unemployment and development: a two-sector analysis," *American Economic Review*, 60, 126–142.

Hatton, T.J. and J.G. Williamson, 1992, "What explains wage gaps between farm and city? Exploring the Todaro model with American evidence: 1890–1941," *Economic Development and Cultural Change*, 40, 267–294.

Hatzipanayotou, P. and M.S. Michael, 1993, "Import restrictions, capital taxes and welfare," *Canadian Journal of Economics*, 26, 727–738.

Hatzipanayotou, P. and M.S. Michael, 1995, "Tariffs, quotas, and voluntary export restraints with endogenous labor supply," *Journal of Economics*, 62, 185–201.

Hatzipanayotou, P. and M.S. Michael, 2001, "Public goods, tax policies, and unemployment in LDCs," *Southern Economic Journal*, 68, 107–119.

Hazari, B. and P. Sgro, 1992, *Models of Unemployment and Economic Development*, New York: Routledge.

Hazari, B. and P. Sgro, 2004, *Tourism, Trade and National Welfare*, Amsterdam: Elsevier.

Herander, M.G. and C.R. Thomas, 1986, "Export performance and export–import linkage requirements," *Quarterly Journal of Economics*, 101, 591–607.

Hertel, T.W., 1997, *Global Trade Analysis: Modeling and Applications*, New York: Cambridge University Press.

Hill, J.K. and J.A. Mendez, 1992, "Equity control of multinational firms by less developed countries: a general equilibrium analysis," *The Manchester School*, 60, 53–63.

Hollander, A., 1987, "Content protection and transnational monopoly," *Journal of International Economics*, 23, 283–297.

Hsieh, Y.N., W.Y. Chang, and C.C. Lai, 1998, "Endogenizing labor–leisure choice: investment and the relative price of non-traded goods", *Economics Letters*, 60, 105–111.

Huang, Y., 1998, *FDI in China*, Hong Kong: The Chinese University Press.

Jaffe, A.D., S.R. Peterson, P.R. Portney, and R.N. Stavins, 1993, "The effect of environmental regulation on international competitiveness: what the evidence tells us," *Journal of International Literature*, 33, 124–140.

Jaffe, A.D., S.R. Peterson, P.R. Portney, and R.N. Stavins, 1995, "Environmental regulation and the competitiveness of U.S. manufacturing: what does the evidence tell us?" *Journal of Economic Literature*, 33, 132–163.

Johansen, S. and K. Juselius, 1990, "Maximum likelihood estimation and inference on cointegration: with applications to demand for money," *Oxford Bulletin of Economics and Statistics*, 52, 169–210.

Johnson, H.G., 1963a, "The Bladen plan for increased protection of the Canadian automotived industry," *Canadian Journal of Economics and Political Science*, 29, 212–238.

Johnson, H.G., 1963b, "The theory of content protection," in H.G. Johnson (ed.), *Aspects of the Theory of Tariffs*, Cambridge, MA: Harvard University Press.

Jones, R.W., 1965, "The structure of simple general equilibrium models," *Journal of Political Economy*, 73, 557–572.

Jones, R.W., 1967, "International capital movements and the theory of tariffs and trade," *Quarterly Journal of Economics*, 81, 1–38.

Jones, R.W., 1968, "Variable returns to scale in general equilibrium theory," *International Economic Review*, 9, 261–272.

Jones, R.W., 1969, "Tariffs and trade in general equilibrium: comment," *American Economic Review*, 59, 418–424.

Jones, R.W., 1971, "A three-factor model in theory, trade and history," in J.N. Bhagwati, R.W. Jones, R.A. Mundell, and J. Vanek (eds), *Trade, Balance of Payments and Growth*, Amsterdam and London: North-Holland.

Jones, R.W., 1984, "Protection and the harmful effects of endogenous capital flows," *Economics Letters*, 15, 325–330.

Jones, R.W., 1987, "Tax wedges and mobile capital," *Scandinavian Journal of Economics*, 89, 335–346.

Jones, R.W. and S. Marjit, 1992, "International trade and endogenous protection structure," in W. Neufiend and R. Riezman (eds), *Economic Theory and International Trade: Essays in Honor of J. T. Rader*, Heidelberg, Germany: Springer-Verlag.

Jones, R.W. and B.J. Spencer, 1989, "Raw materials, processing activities, and protectionism," *Canadian Journal of Economics*, 22, 469–486.

Kar, S. and H. Beladi, 2004, "Skill formation and international migration: welfare perspective of developing countries," *Japan and the World Economy*, 16, 35–54.

Kemp, M.C., 1966, "The gains from international trade and investment: a neo-Heckscher–Ohlin approach," *American Economic Review*, 56, 788–809.

Khan, M.A., 1980, "Dynamic stability, wage subsidies and the generalized Harris–Todaro model," *Pakistan Development Review*, 19, 1–24.

Khan, M.A., 1982a, "Social opportunity costs and immiserizing growth: some observations on the long run versus the short," *Quarterly Journal of Economics*, 97, 353–362.

Khan, M.A., 1982b, "Tariffs, foreign capital and immiserizing growth with urban unemployment and specific factors of production," *Journal of Development Economics*, 10, 245–256.

Khan, M.A., 1996, "Free trade and the environment," *Journal of International Trade and Economic Development*, 5, 113–136.

Khan, M.A. and S.N.H. Naqvi, 1983, "Capital markets and urban unemployment," *Journal of International Economics*, 15, 367–385.

Kim, T.H., 1997, "Domestic content protection in a dynamic small open economy," *Canadian Journal of Economics*, 30, 429–441.

Komiya, R., 1967, "Non-traded goods and the pure theory of international trade," *International Economic Review*, 8, 132–152.

Konishi, H., M. Okuno-Fujiwara, and K. Suzumura, 1990, "Oligopolistic competition and economic welfare," *Journal of Public Economics*, 42, 67–88.

Krueger, A., 1984, "Trade policies in developing countries," in R.W. Jones and P.B. Kenen (eds), *Handbook of International Economics, Vol. 1*, Amsterdam and London: North-Holland.

Krugman, P.R. and M. Obstfeld, 2003, *International Economics: Theory and Policy*, 6th edition, Boston, MA: Addison-Wesley.

Krutilla, K., 1991, "Environmental regulation in an open economy," *Journal of Environmental Economics and Management*, 20, 127–142.

Kueh, Y.Y., 1992, "Foreign investment and economic change in China," *The China Quarterly*, 690–737.

Lahiri, S. and Y. Yano, 2003, "Export-oriented foreign direct investment and local content requirement," *Pacific Economic Review*, 8, 1–14.

Lardy, N.R., 1992, *Foreign Trade and Economic Reform in China: 1978–1990*, Cambridge: Cambridge University Press.

Leamer, E.E., 1998, "In Search of Stolper–Samuelson linkages between international trade and lower wages," in S. Collins (ed.), *Imports, Exports and the American Worker*, Washington, D.C.: Brookings Institution.

Levinson, A., 1996a, "Environmental regulations and manufacturer's location choices: evidence from the census of manufactures," *Journal of Public Economics*, 61, 5–29.

Levinson, A., 1996b, "Environmental regulations and industry location: international and domestic evidence," in J. Bhagwati and R.E. Hudec (eds), *Fair Trade and Harmonization*, Cambridge, MA: MIT Press.

López, R.E. and D. Rodrik, 1991, "Trade restrictions with imported intermediate inputs," *Journal of Development Economics*, 34, 329–338.

MacKinnon, J.G., 1991, "Critical values for cointegration tests," in R.F. Engle and C.W.J. Granger (eds), *Long-Run Economic Relationships*, Oxford: Oxford University Press.

Marjit, S., 1990, "A simple production model in trade and its applications," *Economic Letters*, 32, 257–260.

Marjit, S., 1991, "Agro-based industry and rural-urban migration: the case for an urban employment subsidy," *Journal of Development Economics*, 35, 393–398.

Marjit, S., H. Beladi, and A. Chakrabarty, 2003, "Trade and wage inequality in developing countries," *Economic Inquiry*, 42, 295–303.

Markusen, J.R., 1975, "International externalities and optimal tax structures," *Journal of International Economics*, 5, 15–29.

Markusen, J.R., 1983, "Factor movements and commodity trade as complements," *Journal of International Economics*, 14, 341–356.

Maskus, K.E. and D.R. Eby, 1990, "Developing new rules and disciplines on trade-related investment measures," *The World Economy*, 13, 523–540.

Matsumura T., 1998, "Partial Privatization in Mixed Oligopoly," *Journal of Public Economics*, 70, 473–483.

Mayer, W., 1974, "Variable returns to scale in general equilibrium theory: a comment," *International Economic Review*, 15, 225–235.

McFadden, D., 1978, "Cost, Revenue and Profit Functions," in M. Fuss and D. McFadden (eds), *Production Economics: A Dual Approach to Theory and Applications,* Vol. 1, Amsterdam: North-Holland.

McGuckin, R.H., S.V. Nguyen, J.R. Taylor, and C.A. Waite, 1992, "Post-reform productivity performance and sources of growth in Chinese industry: 1980–85," *Review of Income and Wealth*, 38, 249–266.

McGuire, M.C., 1982, "Regulation, factor rewards, and international trade," *Journal of Public Economics*, 17, 335–354.

Melitz, M.J., 2003, "The impact of trade on intra-industry reallocations and aggregate industry productivity," *Econometrica*, 71, 1695–1725.

Michael, M.S. and P. Hatizipanayotou, 2009, "Three-win strategies of trade and domestic tax reforms in the presence of pollution," Presented at CESifo Area Conference on Public Sector Economics, CESifo Conference Centre, Munich, April 24–26.

Minabe, N., 1974, "Capital and technology movements and economic welfare," *American Economic Review*, 64, 1088–1100.

Miyagiwa, K.F., 1986, "A reconsideration of the welfare economics of a free-trade zone," *Journal of International Economics*, 21, 337–350.

Mundell, R., 1957, "International trade and factor mobility," *American Economic Review*, 47, 321–335.

Munk, B., 1969, "The welfare cost of content protection: the automobile industry in Latin America," *Journal of Political Economy*, 77, 85–98.

Mussa, M., 1979, "The two-sector model in terms of its dual," *Journal of International Economics*, 9, 513–526.

Mussa, M., 1984, "The economics of content protection," NBER working paper no. 1457.

Neary, J.P., 1978, "Short-run capital specificity and the pure theory of international trade," *Economic Journal*, 88, 488–510.

Neary, J.P., 1981, "On the Harris–Todaro model with intersectoral capital mobility," *Economica*, 48, 219–234.

Neary, J.P., 1988, "Tariffs, quotas, and voluntary export restraints with and without internationally mobile capital," *Canadian Journal of Economics*, 21, 714–735.

Neary, J.P., 1993a, "Trade liberalization and shadow prices in the presence of tariffs and quotas," *International Economic Review*, 36, 531–554.

Neary, J.P., 1993b, "Welfare effects of tariffs and investment taxes," in W.J. Ethier, E. Helpman, and J.P. Neary, (eds), *Theory, Policy and Dynamics in International Trade: Essays in Honor of Ronald W. Jones*, Cambridge: Cambridge University Press.

Neary, J.P., 1995, "Factor mobility and international trade," *Canadian Journal of Economics*, 28, S4–S23.

Neary, J.P., 1999, "International trade and the environment: theoretical and policy linkages," Lecture to the European Association for Environmental and Resource Economics Conference, Oslo.

Neary, J.P., 2002, "Foreign competition and wage inequality," *Review of International Economics*, 10, 680–693.

Neary, J.P., 2006, "International trade and the environment: theoretical and policy linkage," *Environmental and Resource Economics*, 33, 95–118.

Neary, J.P. and F. Ruane, 1988, "International capital mobility, shadow prices, and the cost of protection," *International Economic Review*, 29, 571–585.

Ng, L.F.Y. and C. Tuan, 2001, "Building a favorable investment environment: an empirical investigation on the facilitation of FDI in China," Presented at the Symposium on the Chinese Economies after the WTO Accession, Hong Kong, December 7–8.

Oum, T.H., A. Zhang, and Y. Zhang, 2000, "Socially optimal capacity and capital structure in oligopoly: the case of the airline industry," *Journal of Transport Economics and Policy*, 34, 55–68.

Panagariya, A., 1992, "Input tariffs, duty drawbacks, and tariff reforms," *Journal of International Economics*, 32, 131–147.

Pantula, S.G., G. Gonzalez-Farias, and W.A. Fuller, 1994, "A comparison of unit-root test criteria," *Journal of Business and Economic Statistics*, 12, 449–459.

Parai, A.K. and R.N. Batra, 1987, "Customs unions and unemployment in LDCs," *Journal of Development Economics*, 27, 311–319.

Pethig, R., 1976, "Pollution, welfare, and environmental policy in theory of comparative advantage," *Journal of Environmental Economics and Management*, 2, 160–169.

Quirk, J. and R. Saposnik, 1968, *Introduction to General Equilibrium Theory and Welfare Economics*, New York: McGraw-Hill.

Ricardo, D., 1817, *The Principles of Political Economy and Taxation*, Reprinted 1977, London: J.M. Dent & Sons.

Richardson, M., 1989, "Content protection," Mimeo.

Richardson, M., 1993, "Content protection with foreign capital," *Oxford Economic Papers*, 45, 103–117.

Robinson, S., 1988, "Multisectoral models of developing countries: a survey," in H. Chenery and T.N. Srinivasan (eds), *Handbook of Development Economics*, Amsterdam and London: North-Holland.

Rodrik, D., 1987, "The economics of export-performance requirements," *Quarterly Journal of Economics*, 102, 633–650.

Rodrik, D., 1988, "Imperfect competition, scale economies, and trade policy in developing countries," in R.E. Baldwin (ed.), *Trade Policy Issues and Empirical Analysis*, Chicago, IL: The University of Chicago Press.

Rybczynski, T., 1955, "Factor endowments and relative commodity prices," *Economica*, 22, 336–341.

Samuelson, P.A., 1953, "Prices of Factors and Goods in General Equilibrium," *Review of Economic Studies,* 21, 1–20.

Samuelson, P.A., 1971, "Ohiln was right," *Swedish Journal of Economics*, 73, 365–384.

Seade, J., 1980, "On the effects of entry," *Econometrica*, 48, 479–489.

Sen, P., 1997, "Immiserizing growth in a monopolistic competition model," *Review of International Economics*, 5, 188–194.

Shoven, J.B. and J. Whalley, 1984, "Applied general equilibrium models of taxation and international trade: an introduction and survey," *Journal of Economic Literature*, 22, 1007–1051.

Siebert, H., 1977, "Environmental quality and the gains from trade," *Kyklos*, 30, 657–673.

Spinanger, D., 1984, "Objectives and impact of economic activity zones: some evidence from Asia," *Weltwirtschaftliches Archiv*, 120, 64–89.

Srinivasan, T.N. and J. Whalley, 1986, *General Equilibrium Trade Policy Modeling*, Cambridge, MA: MIT Press.

State Statistical Bureau, 2001, *China's Statistical Yearbook 2000*, Beijing: Statistical Publishing House.

Stiglitz, J.E., 2012, *The Price of Inequality: How Today's Divided Society Endangers Our Future*, New York: W.W. Norton and Company.

Sun, H., 1998, "Macroeconomic impact of direct foreign investment in China: 1979–96," The World Economy, 21, 675–694.

Svensson, L.E.O., 1984, "Factor trade and goods trade," Journal of International *Economics*, 16, 365–378.

Takayama, A., 1972, *International Trade*, New York: Holt, Rinehart, and Winston.

Tanigaki, K., 1988, "A note on nontraded goods and the welfare effect of foreign investment," *Journal of International Economics*, 25, 185–187.

Tisdell, C.A., 2013, *Handbook of Tourism Economics*, Singapore: World Scientific Publishing.

Tobey, J.A., 1990, "The effects of domestic environmental policies on patterns of world trade: an empirical test," *Kyklos*, 43, 191–209.

Turnovsky, S. J. and P. Sen, 1991, "Fiscal policy, capital accumulation, and debt in an open economy," *Oxford Economic Papers*, 43, 1–24.

Upadhyay, M.P., 1994, "Accumulation of human capital in LDCs in the presence of unemployment," *Economica*, 61, 355–378.

Viner, J., 1931, "Cost curves and supply curves," *Zeitschrift für Nationalökonomie*, 3, 23–46.

Vousden, N., 1987, "Content protection and tariffs under monopoly and competition," *Journal of International Economics*, 23, 263–282.

Vousden, N., 1990, *The Economics of Trade Protection*, Cambridge: Cambridge University Press.

Wang, Z., 2003, "WTO accession, the 'Greater China' free trade area, and economic integration across the Taiwan Strait," *China Economic Review*, 14(3), 316–349.

Wang. Z. and F. Zhai, 1998, "Tariff reduction, tax replacement, and implications for income distribution in China," *Journal of Comparative Economics*, 26(2), 358–387.

Weitzman, M.L., 1984, *The Share Economy*, Cambridge, MA: Harvard University Press.

Wong, C.M., 1992, "Export-share requirement on foreign direct investment in China," Unpublished MBA Project Report, The Chinese University of Hong Kong.

Wonnacott, R.J. and P. Wonnacott, 1976, *Free Trade between the United States and Canada*, Cambridge, MA: Harvard University Press.

Wood, A., 1995, "How trade hurt unskilled workers," *Journal of Economic Perspectives*, 9, 57–80.

Woodland, A.D., 1982, *International Trade and Resource Allocation*, Amsterdam: North-Holland.

Xu, D. and G.H. Chang, 2000, "Impact of tariff reduction on structural employment in China: a computable general equilibrium analysis," *Pacific Economic Review*, 5, 157–167.

Yabuuchi, S. and H. Beladi, 2001, "Urban unemployment, informal sector and development policies," *Journal of Economics*, 74, 301–314.

Yano, M. and J.B. Nugent, 1999, "Aid, nontraded goods, and the transfer paradox in small countries," *American Economic Review*, 893, 431–449.

Yohe, G.W., 1979, "The backward incidence of pollution control: some comparative statics in general equilibrium," *Journal of Environmental Economics and Management*, 6, 187–198.

Yu, E.S.H., 1980, "A note on air pollution and optimal interventions," *Atlantic Economic Journal*, 8, 72–76.

Yu, E.S.H. and C.C. Chao, 1998, "On investment measures and trade," *The World Economy*, 21, 549–560.

Yu, E.S.H. and C.A. Ingene, 1982, "The backward incidence of pollution control in a rigid-wage economy," *Journal of Environmental Economics and Management*, 9, 304–310.

Zivot, E. and D.W.K. Andrews, 1992, "Further evidence on the great crash, the oil-price shock, and the unit-root hypothesis," *Journal of Business and Economic Statistics*, 10(3), 251–271.

Index

Printed in the United States
By Bookmasters